CliffsNotes®

FTCE Professional Education Test

3RD EDITION

by
Sandra Luna McCune, Ph.D., and Vi Cain Alexander, Ph.D.

Houghton Mifflin Harcourt
Boston • New York

About the Authors

Sandra Luna McCune, Ph.D., is a former Regents professor in the Department of Elementary Education at Stephen F. Austin State University, where she received the Distinguished Professor Award. She now is a full-time author and consultant and resides in Austin, Texas.

Vi Cain Alexander, Ph.D., is a professor and Reading Education Coordinator in the Department of Elementary Education at Stephen F. Austin State University in Texas. She resides in Nacogdoches, Texas.

Authors' Acknowledgments

The authors wish to thank our parents, Joe and Cash Luna and Evan and Lee Cain, for their love, encouragement, and support throughout our lives.

Editorial

Executive Editor: Greg Tubach

Senior Developmental Editor: Christina Stambaugh

Copy Editor: Lynn Northrup

Technical Editor: Carolyn J. Stufft, Ed.D.

Proofreader: Donna Wright

CliffsNotes® FTCE Professional Education Test, 3rd Edition

Copyright © 2015 by Houghton Mifflin Harcourt Publishing Company

All rights reserved.

Cover image © Shutterstock / Mavrick

Library of Congress Control Number: 2014940266
ISBN: 978-0-544-23058-3 (pbk)

Printed in the United States of America
DOO 10 9 8 7 6 5 4   4500603932

For information about permission to reproduce selections from this book, write to trade.permissions@hmhco.com or to Permissions, Houghton Mifflin Harcourt Publishing Company, 3 Park Avenue, 19th Floor, New York, New York 10016.

www.hmhco.com

Table of Contents

Introduction

General Description

The Florida Teacher Certification Examination (FTCE) Professional Education (PEd) Test is a computer-based test designed to assess general knowledge about learning, teaching, and professional conduct. The test is composed of 120 multiple-choice items.

Each multiple-choice question has four response options. You record your answer by clicking the oval corresponding to your answer choice. No penalty is imposed for wrong answers (you merely score a zero for that test question). You are given 2½ hours to complete the test.

The PEd Test Competencies

The PEd Test is based on a set of eight broad competencies that are meant to ensure that entry-level teachers have the necessary professional knowledge to teach effectively in Florida public schools. Each competency is defined by a list of specific skills demonstrating application of the competency. As listed in the *Competencies and Skills Required for Teacher Certification in Florida*, 20th Edition (www.fldoe.org/asp/ftce/pdf/ftce20edition.pdf), the competencies/skills (and their percentages) of the FTCE PEd Test are as follows.

Competency 1: Instructional Design and Planning

Knowledge of instructional design and planning (18 percent of the test):

- Choose appropriate methods, strategies, and evaluation instruments (e.g., formative assessment, summative assessment) for assessing and monitoring student performance levels, needs, and learning.
- Select a variety of instructional practices, materials, and technologies that foster critical, creative, and reflective thinking aligned with state-adopted standards at the appropriate level of rigor.
- Determine and apply learning experiences and activities that require students to demonstrate a variety of applicable skills and competencies.
- Identify instructional resources based on measurable objectives, individual student learning needs, and performance levels.
- Apply learning theories to instructional design and planning.
- Determine long-term instructional goals and short-term objectives appropriate to student learning needs and performance levels aligned with state-adopted standards at the appropriate level of rigor.
- Select and use culturally (i.e., regional, socioeconomic, home language) responsive instructional materials and practices in planning.
- Select lessons and concepts that are sequenced to activate prior knowledge and ensure coherence among the lessons.
- Identify patterns of physical, social, and academic development to differentiate instructional design for student mastery.
- Determine and apply appropriate intervention strategies based on individual student needs and data.

Competency 2: Learning Environments

Knowledge of appropriate student-centered learning environments (15 percent of the test):

- Select and use appropriate techniques for organizing, allocating, and managing the resources of time, space, and attention in a variety of learning environments (e.g., face-to-face, virtual).
- Apply appropriate strategies and procedures to manage individual student behaviors and group dynamics.

- Use effective techniques for communicating high expectations to all students.
- Evaluate and adapt the learning environment to accommodate the needs and backgrounds (i.e., cultural, home language, family) of all students.
- Apply relevant techniques for modeling appropriate oral and written communication skills.
- Determine skills and practices that encourage innovation and foster a safe climate of openness, inquiry, equity, and support for all students.
- Apply information and communication technologies to maintain a student-centered learning environment.
- Identify assistive technologies that enable all students to effectively communicate and achieve their educational goals.

Competency 3: Instructional Delivery

Knowledge of instructional delivery and facilitation through a comprehensive understanding of subject matter (18 percent of the test):

- Use motivational strategies to engage and challenge all students.
- Apply appropriate instructional practices for developing content area literacy.
- Analyze gaps in students' subject matter knowledge in order to improve instructional delivery.
- Assess and adapt instruction to address preconceptions and misconceptions of subject matter.
- Relate subject matter to life experiences and across disciplines.
- Apply techniques for developing higher-order critical thinking skills.
- Select varied strategies, resources, and appropriate technology for relevant and comprehensible instruction.
- Identify differentiated instructional practices based on assessment of learning needs, individual differences, and continuous student feedback.
- Determine and apply techniques to provide feedback in order to promote student achievement.
- Apply appropriate subject area activities to accommodate learning needs, developmental levels, and experiential backgrounds of all students.

Competency 4: Assessment

Knowledge of various types of assessment strategies for determining impact on student learning (14 percent of the test):

- Analyze assessment data from multiple sources to guide instructional decisions.
- Select formative and summative assessments that match learning objectives leading to student mastery.
- Use a variety of assessment tools to monitor student progress, achievement, and learning gains.
- Determine appropriate assessments and testing conditions to accommodate learning styles and varying knowledge levels of students.
- Identify ways to share the importance and outcomes of student assessment data with students and stakeholders.
- Use technology to organize and integrate assessment data.

Competency 5: Continuous Improvement

Knowledge of relevant continuous professional improvement (12 percent of the test):

- Determine relevant and measurable professional development goals to strengthen the effectiveness of instruction based on educator and students' needs.
- Analyze and apply data-informed research to improve instruction and student achievement.
- Use a variety of data, independently and in collaboration with colleagues, to evaluate learning outcomes, adjust planning, and continuously improve and reflect upon the effectiveness of lessons and practices.

- Identify ways to collaborate with home, school, and other stakeholders to foster communication and obtain resources in order to support diverse student learning and continuous improvement.
- Select and determine appropriate professional growth opportunities and reflective practices to improve teacher performance and impact student learning.
- Analyze the implementation of professional development experiences and application to the teaching and learning process.
- Choose appropriate professional growth opportunities in technology for the design and delivery of instruction to impact student learning.

Competency 6: Professional Conduct

Knowledge of the Code of Ethics and Principles of Professional Conduct of the Education Profession in Florida (9 percent of the test):

- Apply the Code of Ethics and Principles of Professional Conduct to realistic professional and personal situations.
- Identify statutory grounds and procedures for disciplinary action, the penalties that can be imposed by the Educational Practices Commission against a certificate holder, and the appeals process available to the individual.
- Apply knowledge of rights, legal responsibilities, and procedures for reporting incidences of abuse, neglect, or other signs of distress.
- Identify and apply policies and procedures for the safe, appropriate, and ethical use of technologies.
- Determine and apply the appropriate use and maintenance of students' information and records.

Competency 7: Teaching English Language Learners (ELLs)

Knowledge of research-based practices appropriate for teaching English Language Learners (ELLs) (7 percent of the test):

- Relate the nature and role of culture, cultural groups, and individual cultural identities into learning experiences for all students.
- Analyze student developmental characteristics in relation to first- and second-language literacy acquisition stages to design instruction for students.
- Interpret the Consent Decree to integrate teaching approaches, methods, strategies, and communication with stakeholders in order to improve learning for ELLs.
- Evaluate and differentiate standards-based curriculum, materials, resources, and technology for ELLs based on multicultural, multilevel learning environments.
- Analyze assessment issues as they affect ELLs and determine appropriate accommodations according to ELLs' varying English proficiency levels and academic levels.

Competency 8: Literacy Strategies

Knowledge of effective literacy strategies that can be applied across the curriculum to impact student learning (7 percent of the test):

- Apply effective instructional practices to develop text reading skills in the appropriate content area.
- Select instructional practices for developing and using content area vocabulary.
- Determine instructional practices to facilitate students' reading comprehension through content areas.
- Apply appropriate literacy strategies for developing higher-order critical thinking skills.
- Select appropriate resources for the subject matter and students' literacy levels.
- Differentiate instructional practices based on literacy data for all students.

Don't panic! You will not be asked direct questions about the competencies on the FTCE PEd Test. Nevertheless, a strong understanding of the competencies is essential for successful performance on the test. The competencies are broad statements of skills, knowledge, and understanding that you need in order to be an effective classroom teacher in Florida. You should read them carefully to familiarize yourself with the specific knowledge you will need to demonstrate on the test. You should reflect on them, so that you understand their meanings and can apply the terms and concepts used in them to actual teaching situations. This book is designed to help you learn to do that.

The Role of the PEd Test in Teacher Certification

The FTCE PEd Test is one of the state-mandated teacher certification tests in Florida. Florida law (Section 1012.56, Florida Statutes; Rule 6A-4.0021, Florida Administrative Code [FAC]) requires that teachers demonstrate mastery of basic skills, professional knowledge, and content area of specialization. Thus, if you want to teach in a Florida public elementary, middle, or secondary school, you likely will have to take and pass at least three tests: the FTCE General Knowledge Test, the FTCE PEd Test, and a Subject Area Examination (SAE) in the field in which you want to be certified. The FTCE General Knowledge Test assesses your basic skills in reading, writing, and mathematics. For the FTCE PEd Test, you have to demonstrate your knowledge about learning, teaching, and professional conduct—which is what this book is designed to help you do. The SAE covers the content that you are required to teach. The purpose of the certification program in Florida is to ensure that certified teachers possess sufficient professional knowledge and skills to effectively perform their roles as teachers in Florida schools. Anyone who wants to teach in Florida must pass FTCE certification tests, so this is a challenge you will face before becoming a Florida teacher. It is the law, so you have no choice but to take the tests.

The content of the PEd Test was identified and validated by statewide committees of education specialists. The committee members consisted of public school teachers, district supervisors, and college faculty—with public school teachers composing the majority of the committees. Selection to committee membership was based on recommendations by professional organizations, subject area experts, and teachers' unions. The test development process involved an extensive literature review, interviews with selected public school teachers, a large-scale survey of teachers, and pilot testing.

Questions Commonly Asked About the FTCE PEd Test

Q. **What is the FTCE PEd Test?**

A. The FTCE PEd Test is the required pedagogy test adopted by the Florida Legislature for assessing general knowledge about learning, teaching, and professional conduct of applicants for the Florida Teacher Professional Certificate. It consists of 120 multiple-choice questions.

Q. **Who oversees administration of the FTCE PEd Test?**

A. The Florida Department of Education (FLDOE) oversees administration of the FTCE PEd Test. The Commissioner of Education designates the registration deadlines, administration sites, and examination dates (Rule 6A-4.0021, FAC).

Q. **When and where is the FTCE PEd Test given?**

A. Currently, the FTCE PEd Test is 100 percent computer-based. It is offered at flexible times throughout the year at locations throughout the State of Florida and in select cities nationwide. Check www.fl.nesinc.com/FL_TestDates.asp for an up-to-date list of test sites. Also, check the testing contractor's website for updated information regarding changes in tests and application procedures (www.fl.nesinc.com/index.asp).

Q. Where can I find registration information for the FTCE PEd Test?

A. The most recent registration information is available online at www.fldoe.org/asp/ftce/ftceTRI.asp. There are no deadlines for computer-based testing registrations. However, you should register as early as possible before your target test date because test sites accept registrations on a first-come, first-served basis and seating is limited. Be sure to review the testing contractor's testing policies on registration, testing, and score reporting available at www.fl.nesinc.com/FL_policies.asp.

Q. What are the fees for the test?

A. The registration fee in 2014 for first-attempt testing is $150. The registration fee for retake testing is $170. If you have additional questions about fees or need help calculating the total amount you need to pay to register, call Customer Service at 413-256-2893 or go to www.fl.nesinc.com/FL_testfees.asp to find information on the testing contractor's website.

Q. What should I bring to the test site?

A. You will receive your admission ticket by e-mail after your registration has been processed. Your admission ticket will include your name, the test(s) you are registered to take, the test date, the test site address, the reporting time, and a reminder of what to bring to the test site. Check the information on your admission ticket to make sure that it is correct. You will not be allowed to make changes at the test site.

The day of the test, you must bring your admission ticket and two valid, unexpired identification forms that are printed in English, including one that is government issued with a recent, clear photo and signature, such as a driver's license, state-issued ID card, U.S. military ID with signature, or passport. Your valid admission ticket and correct identification are required for entrance into the examination site.

Q. Can I bring my cellphone into the testing room?

A. Absolutely not! If a cellphone (regardless of whether it is turned on) or another prohibited personal item is found in your possession, you will not be allowed to continue testing. The test site will report this information to the FLDOE, and your score will be invalidated. So, to be safe, you should not bring a cellphone to the testing site. You will find a complete list of prohibited items under "Testing Policies" at www.fl.nesinc.com/FL_policies.asp. It is best to not have any such items in your possession when you arrive at the testing site. However, the testing sites do have secure storage in which you may store personal belongings, including prohibited items, during testing.

Q. Is the FTCE PEd Test divided into timed sections?

A. No, you have 2½ hours to complete the 120 multiple-choice questions. You may work through the questions at your own pace as long as you stay within the 2½-hour time frame.

Q. When will I get my score report?

A. You automatically receive an official score report through your account on the FTCE/FELE contractor website (www.fl.nesinc.com). Your passing scores are submitted electronically to the Bureau of Educator Certification. Official score reports are released within 4 weeks after your test date. Your score report will be available to you for 60 days.

Q. What is the passing score?

A. The passing score for the FTCE PEd Test is a scaled score of 200 or higher.

Q. How many questions must I answer correctly to pass the test?

A. Because the number of correct answers needed to pass the FTCE PEd Test might vary slightly from one form of the examination to another, the FLDOE provides only general guidelines about how many questions must be answered correctly in order to pass. Currently, the scaled passing score of 200 is equivalent to 85 (71 percent) correct items on the May 2013 test administration of the PEd Test (Rule 6A-4.0021, FAC); furthermore, you are required to answer no more than 85 questions (71 percent) correctly (www.fldoe.org/faq/default.asp?ALL=Y&Dept=179&Cat=83).

Q. How many times may I retake the PEd Test?

A. You may retake the test as many times as is necessary to pass, but you must wait at least 31 calendar days before retaking. Also, you must submit a new registration application form and pay the retake fee of $170 every time you retake the test. You will not be given extra testing time when you are retaking a test.

Q. What other tests must teacher candidates take?

A. Candidates applying for a Professional Teaching Certificate must take the FTCE PEd Test and the FTCE General Knowledge Test. In addition, candidates applying for a Professional Certificate and those adding a subject area to a Professional Certificate may need to pass an SAE in a field in which they are seeking certification.

Q. Can I take all my teacher tests on one day?

A. Not likely. You can register for one test per appointment. You might be able to register for multiple appointments on the same day at the same test site; however, there is no guarantee that multiple appointments can be scheduled on the same day.

Here is a word of advice: Even though you might be able to schedule another test on the same test date as the PEd Test, it is a better idea to take the tests on two separate dates to avoid mental fatigue. This strategy would also give you more time to prepare for each test.

Q. Should I guess on the test?

A. Yes! There is no penalty for guessing, so guess if you have to. First, try to eliminate some of the choices to increase your chances of choosing the right answer. But do not leave any question unanswered.

Q. What if I've never taken a computer-based test before?

A. After you are seated for your computer-based test, you will complete a tutorial before you take the actual test. The tutorial shows you how to move from question to question, how to mark and change answers, and how to go back and review previously answered or skipped questions.

Q. How should I prepare for the PEd Test?

A. Now that you're ready to begin taking your certification exams, using this test-prep book is your best preparation for the PEd Test. This study guide gives you insights, reviews, and strategies for the question types.

Q. How do I get more information about the Florida Teacher Certification Examination program?

A. Check the Florida Department of Education Office of Assessment FTCE website at www.fldoe.org/asp/ftce/ftceTRI.asp. As new information on the testing program becomes available, it is posted on this site.

How to Use This CliffsNotes Book

This book is organized around the eight competencies of the FTCE PEd Test. It includes a thorough review of the knowledge base related to each competency, study strategies for the test, and two full-length practice tests. The answers to the tests are keyed to the competencies, with explanations supported by educational theory of effective practice. Upon completion of this book, not only will you be better prepared to take the FTCE PEd Test, but you will be better prepared to teach in a Florida public school.

When you read through the list of competencies and skills covered on the FTCE PEd Test, you might feel overwhelmed by the task of preparing for the test. Here are some suggestions for developing an effective study program using this book:

- **To help you organize and budget your time, set up a specific schedule of study sessions.** Try to set aside approximately 2 hours for each session. If you complete one session per day (including weekends), it should take you about 5 to 6 weeks to work your way through the review and practice material provided in this book. If your target test date is coming up soon, you may need to increase your study time per day.

- **Choose a place for studying that is free of distractions and undue noise, so that you can concentrate.** Make sure you have adequate lighting and a room temperature that is comfortable—neither too warm nor too cold. Be sure you have an ample supply of water to keep your brain hydrated; you might also want to have some light snacks available. To improve mental alertness, choose snacks that are high in protein and low in carbohydrates. Try to have all the necessary study aids (paper, pen, note cards, and so on) within easy reach, so that you don't have to interrupt your studying to go get something you need. Ask friends not to call you during your study time.

- **Don't make excuses.** Studying for the PEd Test must be a priority. It will require a lot of time and a conscientious commitment on your part. Think of it as a job that you must do. In reality, studying for the PEd Test is one of the most important jobs you will ever do. The outcome of the test can determine your future career opportunities. Do not avoid studying for it by making excuses or procrastinating.

- **Read through the list of competencies/skills for the PEd Test to get a general picture of what the test covers; then take Practice Test 1 to help you discover your strengths and weaknesses.** Read the answer explanations for all the questions, not just the ones you missed, because you may have answered some questions correctly by guessing. Make a list of the competency areas with which you had problems.

- **Carefully study the review chapters, being sure to concentrate as you go through the material.** Don't let yourself be diverted by extraneous thoughts or outside distractions. Monitor yourself by making a check mark on a separate sheet of paper when your concentration wanders. Work on reducing the number of check marks you record each study session.

- **Take notes as you study, using your own words to express ideas.** Leave ample room in the left margin, so that you can revise or make comments when you review your notes. Extract key ideas and write them in the left margin to use as study cues later. Make flashcards to aid you in memorizing key ideas and keep them with you at all times. When you have spare time, take out the flashcards and go over the information you've recorded on them.

- **Take several brief 2- to 3-minute breaks during your study sessions to give your mind time to absorb the review material you just read.** According to brain research, you remember the first part and last part of something you've read more easily than you remember the middle part. Taking several breaks will allow you to create more beginnings and endings to maximize the amount of material you remember. The review material is organized to facilitate taking breaks. The Checkpoint exercises provide a natural way to have more beginnings and endings as you study. It is best not to leave your study area during a break. Try stretching or simply closing your eyes for a few minutes.

- **Set aside certain days to review material you have already studied.** This strategy will allow you to reinforce what you have learned and identify topics you may need to restudy.

- **Plan to master the competencies.** Developing a strong understanding of the PEd Test competencies is essential to successful performance on the test. The reason is that the test is based on these competencies and is designed to ensure that individuals who become teachers in Florida can recognize and apply these "best practices" of classroom instruction. Try to relate the competencies to your own experiences so that they will be more meaningful to you.

- **When you complete your review, take Practice Test 2.** Take this test under the same conditions you expect for the actual test, being sure to adhere to the 2½-hour time limit. When you finish taking the test, as you did for Practice Test 1, carefully study the answer explanations for *all* the questions. Analyze the results of the practice test and go back and review competency areas in which you are still weak.

- **Organize a study group, if possible.** A good way of learning and reinforcing the material is to discuss it with others. If possible, set up a regular time to study with one or more classmates or friends. Ask questions among yourselves to discover new insights. Seeing the material from others' perspectives will help you to better formulate your understanding of the content.

After completing your study program, you should find yourself prepared and confident to achieve a passing score on the FTCE PEd Test.

How to Prepare for the Day of the Test

You can do several things to prepare for the day of the test:

- Know where the test center is located and how to get there.

- Make dependable arrangements to get to the test center in plenty of time and know where to park if you plan to go by car.

- Keep all the materials you will need to bring to the test center—especially your admission ticket and two forms of identification—in a secure place, so that you can easily find them on the day of the test.

- Go to bed in time to get a good night's rest the night before your test. Avoid taking nonprescription drugs or drinking alcohol the day before the test, as the use of these products might impair your mental faculties on test day.

- On the day of the test, plan to get to the testing center early.

- Dress in comfortable clothing and wear comfortable shoes. Even if it is warm outside, wear a light jacket that can be removed or put on, depending on the temperature in the testing room.

- Eat a light meal. Select foods that you have found usually give you the most energy and stamina.

- Drink plenty of water to make sure your brain remains hydrated during the test for optimal thinking.

- Make a copy of this list and post it in a strategic location. Check it over before you leave for the testing center.

What to Do During the Test

Here are some general test-taking strategies to help maximize your score on the test:

- When you receive the test, take several deep, slow breaths, exhaling slowly while mentally visualizing your-self performing successfully on the test before you begin. Do not get upset if you feel nervous. Most of the people taking the test with you will be experiencing some measure of anxiety.

- During the test, follow all the directions, including the oral directions of the test proctor and the written directions on the computer screen. If you do not understand something in the directions, ask the test proctor for clarification. The test proctor will indicate how you are to ask for assistance.

- Move through the test at a steady pace. The test consists of 120 (scorable) multiple-choice questions. **Note**: Your test might have 6 to 10 extra questions on it. These questions are experimental (field test) items and are NOT used to calculate your score. As you begin the test, make a mental note that question 60 is about the halfway point. When you get to question 60, check the on-screen timer to see how much time you have left. If less than 1 hour and 15 minutes remains, you will need to pick up the pace. Otherwise, continue to work as rapidly as you can without being careless, *but do not rush.*

- Try to answer the questions in order. However, if a question is taking too much of your time, mark the question as one to come back to and move on.

- Read each question entirely. Skimming to save time can cause you to misread a question or miss important information. If the question is complex or wordy, restate it in your own words.

- Try to determine which competency is the primary focus of the question. The answer must relate to that competency.

- Note the students' age/grade level, so that you can assess whether the answer choices are developmentally appropriate.

- Read all the answer choices before you select an answer. You might find two answer choices that sound good, but one is a better answer to the question. For instance, it is better to select answer choices that indicate the benefit to students over those that indicate the benefit to the teacher. *Tip:* Always keep this suggestion in mind as you take the test: Pick the choice that is best for students!

- Try to eliminate at least two answer choices. Be especially watchful for answer choices that express ideas that you agree with but that are too off-topic (not relating to the focus of the question) to apply to the situation being described. Before you make your final choice, reread the question (don't skip doing this!) and select the response that best answers the question and is aligned with the competency that the question is assessing.

- Eliminate answer choices in which teachers appear to give up on students. For instance, if a student is struggling to answer a question, the teacher should *not* move on to a different student or switch to an easier question.

- Don't read too much into a question. You should not assume that something is going on or will happen unless it is clearly and plainly stated in the description of the classroom situation.

- Change an answer only if you have a good reason to do so.

- If you are trying to recall information during the test, close your eyes and try to visualize yourself in your study place. This may trigger your memory.

- Remain calm during the test. If you find yourself getting anxious, stop and take several deep, slow breaths and exhale slowly to help you relax. Do not be upset if the person next to you finishes, gets up, and leaves before you do. Keep your mind focused on the task at hand: completing your exam. Trust yourself. You should not expect to know the correct response to every question on the exam. Think only of doing your personal best.

- Before exiting the test, make sure you have marked an answer for every question. Even if you have no clue about the correct answer for a question, make a guess.

Practice these strategies. As you work through the practice tests, consciously use the strategies suggested in this section as preparation for the actual PEd Test. Try to reach the point that the strategies are automatic for you.

You will benefit greatly from this CliffsNotes book. By using the recommendations provided here as you complete your study program, you will be prepared to walk into the testing room with confidence. Good luck on the test and in your future career as a Florida teacher!

Chapter 1

Competency 1: Instructional Design and Planning

Competency Description and Key Indicators

According to the *Competencies and Skills Required for Teacher Certification in Florida,* 20th Edition (available at www.fldoe.org/asp/ftce/pdf/ftce20edition.pdf), **Competency 1** of the FTCE PEd Test addresses **Instructional Design and Planning** as follows:

> *Knowledge of instructional design and planning*

Key indicators:

- Choose appropriate methods, strategies, and evaluation instruments (e.g., formative assessment, summative assessment) for assessing and monitoring student performance levels, needs, and learning.
- Select a variety of instructional practices, materials, and technologies that foster critical, creative, and reflective thinking aligned with state-adopted standards at the appropriate level of rigor.
- Determine and apply learning experiences and activities that require students to demonstrate a variety of applicable skills and competencies.
- Identify instructional resources based on measurable objectives, individual student learning needs, and performance levels.
- Apply learning theories to instructional design and planning.
- Determine long-term instructional goals and short-term objectives appropriate to student learning needs and performance levels aligned with state-adopted standards at the appropriate level of rigor.
- Select and use culturally (i.e., regional, socioeconomic, home language) responsive instructional materials and practices in planning.
- Select lessons and concepts that are sequenced to activate prior knowledge and ensure coherence among the lessons.
- Identify patterns of physical, social, and academic development to differentiate instructional design for student mastery.
- Determine and apply appropriate intervention strategies based on individual student needs and data.

Overview

Instructional Design and Planning is the decision-making process teachers use to develop instructional plans. Effective teachers know that well-designed instructional plans are the key to improved student learning. Based upon student assessment data and with the guidance of the Next Generation Sunshine State Standards (NGSSS), they identify appropriate goals and objectives for their students and then design developmentally appropriate learning opportunities that will move students toward achievement of those goals and objectives. Lessons are carefully planned and differentiated according to Florida's Multi-Tiered System of Supports (MTSS) Problem-Solving/Response to Intervention (PS/RtI) process, using a mixture of instructional strategies and supports of varying intensity levels in varied learning settings: whole class, small group, or individual.

This chapter provides a general review of Instructional Design and Planning with sample questions and explanations at the end of the chapter. Checkpoint exercises are found throughout the review material. These exercises give you an opportunity to practice what you just learned. The answers to the Checkpoint exercises are found immediately following the set of exercises. When doing the Checkpoint exercises, you should cover up the answers. Then check your answers when you've finished the exercises. The sample questions at the end of this chapter are multiple-choice questions that are similar to what you might expect to see on the FTCE PEd Test. The answer explanations for the sample questions are provided immediately after the questions.

Effective Planning

Planning is the decision-making process in which a teacher decides what, why, when, and how to teach. Effective planning is an important component of effective instruction (Reinhartz & Beach, 1997). Furthermore, planning is critical to successful alignment of curriculum, instruction, and assessment. Effective teachers use student assessment data to inform their instructional planning so that instruction is matched to students' academic needs. In addition, they take into account the diverse ways students learn, their developmental levels, linguistic development, and the various backgrounds, cultural heritage, interests, and experiences they bring to the classroom. They work within the framework of the MTSS PS/RtI process with the goal of maximizing achievement for all students (see the section "MTSS PS/RtI" later in this chapter for a discussion of this topic).

Effective planners design their lessons around research- and/or evidence-based instruction that will promote student achievement. They proceed thoughtfully and deliberately. They write out what they are planning to do, how they are going to do it, and how they will determine that it worked. After developing a lesson plan, they **preplan.** That is, they go through the lesson mentally from a student's point of view and anticipate explanations, information, directions, additional instruction, and so on that they will need in order to carry out the lesson successfully.

Before planning a lesson, a teacher must first determine instructional long-term goals appropriate to students' grade level and individual needs. The goals must be aligned with the Next Generation Sunshine State Standards (NGSSS). (See the section "NGSSS" that follows for a discussion of these standards.)

A teacher's first step in planning a lesson is to identify, within the framework of the state-adopted standards, the instructional objective(s) for the lesson. To do this, the teacher must answer the following questions: What do I want students to learn and be able to do at the end of this lesson? Which specific benchmark(s) will this lesson address? (See the section "Instructional Objectives" later in this chapter for a discussion of instructional objectives.)

The next step in planning the lesson is deciding on the research- and/or evidence-based instructional methods that will best support the instructional objective and result in student achievement. (See the section "Instructional Methods" in Chapter 3 for descriptions of various instructional methods.) When designing instruction, the teacher should focus on the desired instructional objective while considering appropriate differentiated strategies and grouping arrangements. At the same time, the teacher should take into account input from students; students' learning preferences, backgrounds, interests, experiences, and prior knowledge; the content of instruction; available materials and resources; time and space constraints; and assessment issues. When planning what to do in the lesson to engage students in learning, teachers should do the following:

- Use developmentally appropriate activities and strategies.
- Apply knowledge of learning theories to classroom practices.
- Routinely involve students in choosing and planning their own learning activities.
- Activate students' prior knowledge related to the concepts to be learned.
- Provide challenging experiences that actively engage students.
- Incorporate Marzano's high yield strategies into lesson planning (see "Marzano's High Yield Instructional Strategies" in Chapter 3 for a discussion of this topic).
- Use a variety of materials and/or technologies.
- Provide meaningful experiences that reflect students' own interests and experiences.
- Routinely use hands-on, minds-on activities.
- Use activities that address students' individual needs and abilities.
- Provide opportunities for whole-group, small-group, and individual work.
- Allow opportunities for students to talk and discuss their learning among themselves and with the teacher.
- Make the learning student-centered, not teacher-focused.
- Avoid relying solely on the textbook when planning or providing limited options for students.

- Avoid using worksheets or workbooks; meaningless drills; or excessive, quiet seatwork.

- Make sure that students with special needs—for example, Exceptional Student Education (ESE) learners or English Language Learners (ELLs)— participate in the lesson to the fullest extent possible.

- Offer learning activities congruent with the cultural and individual learning preferences and strengths of students (see "Multiculturalism: Celebrating Diversity" in Chapter 7 for a discussion on this topic).

The teacher's final step in planning a lesson is to decide on the assessment method: how to determine that the students "got it." Good assessment reflects what is taught—it's aligned with the curriculum and how it is taught; that is, it matches the instructional objective and the method of instruction. For best results, the teacher should plan to use multiple assessment approaches and ensure that assessment is ongoing and an integral part of the lesson. There are many ways to find out how well students know, understand, and are able to apply the curriculum. One very effective way is to use informal observation and questioning—in other words, watching the students when they are working to see whether they are "getting it" and asking questions about what they are doing and what they are thinking as they work. This approach will give much insight into the effectiveness of a lesson. Other assessment strategies include formal interviews, collections of students' work over time (portfolios), self-assessment, peer assessment, formal performance assessments, and traditional tests. The teacher's assessment strategies will be most useful when they aim to help the students by identifying their unique strengths and needs so as to inform planning. (See Chapter 4 for a full discussion of assessment.)

Checkpoint

Fill in the blank.

1. Planning is critical to successful _____ of curriculum, instruction, and assessment.

2. When designing instruction, teachers should focus on the desired instructional _____.

3. Good assessment reflects what is _____.

Mark as true or false.

4. _____ (a) When planning lessons, teachers should rely solely on their textbooks.

    _____ (b) Worksheets and drills are the hallmarks of effective instruction.

Checkpoint Answers

1. alignment

2. objectives

3. taught

4. (a) false; (b) false

NGSSS

The **NGSSS** specify the core content knowledge and skills that K-12 public school students are expected to acquire for language arts, mathematics, science, social studies, visual and performing arts, physical education, health, and foreign languages. Florida law specifies that the standards must be relevant, rigorous, and logically sequential. "Content for all subjects must integrate critical-thinking, problem-solving, and workforce-literacy skills; communication, reading, and writing skills; mathematics skills; collaboration skills; contextual and applied-learning skills; technology-literacy skills; information and media-literacy skills; and civic-engagement skills" (1003.41.(1), F. S.).

In 2010, the State of Florida adopted the **Common Core State Standards (CCSS)** in English Language Arts and Mathematics. The CCSS, the result of an initiative by the National Governors Association and the Council of Chief State School Officers, have been adopted in over 40 states and Washington, D.C. In Florida, the state-adopted common core standards were revised in 2014 based on public input and are currently denoted as

Mathematics Florida Standards (MAFS) and **Language Arts Florida Standards (LAFS)**. Both of the finalized MAFS and LAFS are now incorporated into the NGSSS and were fully implemented across the grades in the 2014–15 school year.

By Florida Statute (1003.41), teachers are responsible for designing instruction that addresses the standards for their grade levels. The NGSSS establish the core content of the curricula to be taught in Florida. The standards include distinct grade-level expectations for the core content knowledge and skills that a student is expected to have acquired by each individual grade level from kindergarten through grade 8 for language arts, science, mathematics, and social studies and through grade 5 for visual and performing arts, physical education, health, and foreign languages. For higher grade levels, the standards might be organized by grade clusters of more than one grade level. The standards are divided into smaller units called **benchmarks,** which outline the specific content, knowledge, and skills that students are expected to learn in school.

CPALMS, an online source of information, expert-reviewed resources, and interactive tools, is the State of Florida's official website for standards information and course descriptions (available at www.cpalms.org/Public/). It provides free access to full lesson plans, units of instruction, assessments, videos, simulations, games, professional development apps, and many other materials to assist educators in effectively implementing the standards. CPALMS was built primarily for Florida's educators, but it is also available free to parents*, students, and anyone else with a need for or an interest in educational resources.

*Note: By Florida school law, a *parent* is either or both parents, a guardian, or any person in a parental relationship to a student or who has charge over a student in place of the parent.

Checkpoint

Fill in the blank.

1. The NGSSS establish the core _____ of the curricula to be taught in Florida.
2. Florida law specifies that the standards must be relevant, _____, and logically sequential.
3. The standards are divided into smaller units called _____.
4. _____ is the State of Florida's official source for standards information and course descriptions.

Checkpoint Answers

1. content
2. rigorous
3. benchmarks
4. CPALMS

Instructional Objectives

An **instructional objective** is a clearly written statement of what students are expected to know and be able to do as a result of an instructional learning experience. Well-written instructional objectives consist of three elements: **action,** what the student will do; **conditions,** the circumstances in which the action will take place; and **level of mastery,** the level of proficiency expected for the action (Houston & Beech, 2002). Additionally, although the grading criteria are not part of an instructional objective, the objective should be aligned with the assessment procedure. With this requirement in mind, teachers need to be sure that instructional objectives are written as measurable behaviors; that is, as behaviors that can be observed, recorded, and assessed. The best way to write measurable objectives is to use **action verbs** such as *analyze, arrange, assess, classify, compare, compose, contrast, create, define, discuss, identify, judge, list, predict, recite, show, solve,* and *summarize* to describe exactly what the student is expected to do to achieve the objective.

To determine whether a lesson objective is at an appropriate level of difficulty, a task analysis should be conducted for each instructional objective. **Task analysis** is the process of identifying the prerequisite skills and prior knowledge that students must have in order to achieve the instructional objective with a high degree of success.

Instructional objectives differ in both the types of learning involved and the level of learning involved. Teachers need to write objectives that result in the types and levels of learning desired for students. A classic and widely used guide in identifying and writing instructional objectives is the *Taxonomy of Education Objectives* by Benjamin Bloom and colleagues (1956), commonly known as **Bloom's Taxonomy.** The classification system was developed by psychologists, teachers, and test experts for use in curriculum development, teaching, and testing and consists of three general categories called **domains** that encompass the possibilities of learning outcomes that might be expected from instruction:

- The **cognitive domain** is the category for learning that involves thinking capabilities, from recalling simple facts to judging the quality of an argument. (See the section "Skillful Questioning" in Chapter 3 for additional discussion of the cognitive domain of Bloom's Taxonomy.)
- The **affective domain** is the category for learning that involves feeling, values, and dispositions.
- The **psychomotor domain** is the category for learning that involves manual, athletic, and other physical skills.

Each domain consists of a set of subcategories that have a hierarchical relationship going from the simplest outcomes to the most complex, as shown in the following chart.

Cognitive Domain	Affective Domain	Psychomotor Domain
Knowledge: Involves remembering, memorizing, recognizing, recalling, and so on.	Receiving: Involves the willingness to be open to stimuli and messages in the environment, willingness to receive a message or to acknowledge that a phenomenon is taking place.	Generic movement: Includes the perception of body positions and motor acts and the arrangement of movement to achieve a skill.
Comprehension: Involves interpreting and understanding meaning, stating or describing in one's own words.	Responding: Involves attending to and reacting to a stimulus or replying to a message.	Ordinate movement: Includes organizing, refining, and performing movement skillfully; achieving precision in motor performance.
Application: Involves applying information to produce results, transferring learning to a new context, or problem solving.	Valuing: Involves accepting an idea, phenomenon, or stimulus and internalizing it.	Creative movement: Includes the invention or creation of movement personally unique to the performer.
Analysis: Involves the subdividing or breaking down of a stimulus or concept to show how it's put together.	Organizing: Involves classifying and ordering values, ranking by priorities.	
Synthesis: Involves the creation of a unique product that might be verbal, abstract, or physical in form; putting together concepts to form a whole.	Internalizing: Involves committing totally to certain attitudes, beliefs, or dispositions; "buying in" to the point that values are reflected in one's behavior.	
Evaluation: Involves making value decisions about a phenomenon, an idea, or a stimulus.		

Examples of instructional objectives for each domain are shown in the following chart.

Domain	Sample Instructional Objective
Cognitive	Given a list of 10 animals, the student will classify the animals as herbivores, carnivores, or omnivores with 90 percent accuracy.
Affective	While participating in a whole-class discussion, the student will show respect for others by not interrupting when others are talking for 100 percent of the discussion time.
Psychomotor	Given a set of 10 functions, the student will graph the functions on a graphing calculator with 90 percent accuracy.

Checkpoint

Fill in the blank.

1. The circumstances in which the action of an instructional objective will take place are called the _____.

2. "The student will catch the ball" is an action that falls in the _____ domain of instructional objectives.

3. The process of identifying the prerequisite skills and prior knowledge that students must have in order to achieve an instructional objective is called _____ (two words).

Mark as true or false.

4. _____ (a) The cognitive domain is the category for learning that involves thinking capabilities.

   _____ (b) The action in an instructional objective must be observable.

Checkpoint Answers

1. conditions

2. psychomotor

3. task analysis

4. (a) true; (b) true

Levels of Content Complexity

Content complexity refers to the level of cognitive demand that standards and curriculum place on learners. Florida has adopted Webb's (2002) depth of knowledge (DOK) model of content complexity as a means of classifying the cognitive demand presented by standards and curriculum. The DOK model consists of four levels as shown in the following chart.

Level of Complexity	Student Expectations	Examples
Level 1: Recall	Recall, identify, locate, or recognize facts or information and demonstrate simple skills or abilities.	• In reading, locate details in a passage. • In writing, identify incorrect punctuation. • In math, identify a number as prime. • In science, retrieve information from a chart.
Level 2: Basic Application of Concepts & Skills	Demonstrate comprehension and processing of information.	• In reading, determine the main idea of a passage. • In writing, write a summary of a passage. • In math, solve a multiple-step but routine-type problem. • In science, give examples and nonexamples of a concept.

(*continued*)

Level of Complexity	Student Expectations	Examples
Level 3: Strategic Thinking & Complex Reasoning	Demonstrate the use of higher-order thinking skills, including abstract reasoning.	• In reading, identify cause-and-effect relationships. • In writing, develop a constructed response to a prompt. • In math, determine a formula for the general term of a sequenced numerical pattern. • In science, draw a conclusion based on data.
Level 4: Extended Thinking & Complex Reasoning	Demonstrate significant conceptual understanding and higher-order thinking extended over time and multiple resources.	• In reading, analyze and synthesize common themes in several authors' works. • In writing, write a research paper on a multifaceted topic. • In math, model the relationship between two variables by collecting and analyzing data. • In science, conduct a scientific investigation of a hypothesis.

Checkpoint

Fill in the blank.

1. Content complexity refers to the level of cognitive demand associated with _____ and curriculum.

2. In reading, determining the author's purpose is level _____ (1, 2, 3, or 4) complexity.

3. In social studies, conducting a study of local natural resources is level _____ (1, 2, 3, or 4) complexity.

4. In math, solving a simple linear equation is level _____ (1, 2, 3, or 4) complexity.

Checkpoint Answers

1. standards

2. 3

3. 4

4. 2

Lesson Cycle Model

The **lesson cycle model** follows the adage: "Tell them what you're going to say, say it, and then tell them what you said" (Kizlik, 2014). Although there are variations of the model, basically, it consists of the following components:

- **Focus (or anticipatory set):** The teacher gains students' attention, explains the instructional objective(s) of the lesson, communicates the expectations for the lesson, and links the lesson objective to students' prior knowledge.
- **Explanation:** The teacher presents new information related to the lesson's instructional objective using various techniques such as demonstrating and modeling skills, giving examples and nonexamples of concepts, and stating and applying academic rules.
- **Check for understanding:** The teacher observes and questions students to determine the degree to which they understand the concepts and essential information presented in the explanation component of the lesson. Checking for understanding is frequent and ongoing throughout the lesson. The teacher provides clarification and specific feedback to reinforce learning and to avert misunderstandings.
- **Guided practice:** The teacher monitors and scaffolds students' learning as they apply the new knowledge or skills.

- **Closure:** The teacher "wraps up" the lesson by reviewing with the students the instructional content that was presented in the lesson.
- **Independent practice:** The students apply the new knowledge or skills without assistance from the teacher. Independent practice is usually given as homework.
- **Reteach and extend:** The teacher has planned (1) additional instruction using an alternative strategy for students who fail to achieve the instructional objective, and (2) new learning experiences for students who are ready to extend their learning.

Checkpoint

Fill in the blank.

1. One purpose of the focus component of the lesson cycle model is to gain students' _____.
2. Checking for understanding is _____ throughout the lesson.
3. During guided practice, the teacher _____ and scaffolds students' learning as they apply the new knowledge or skills.

Mark as true or false.

4. _____ (a) Giving examples and nonexamples is an appropriate teacher action during the explanation component of the lesson cycle model.

   _____ (b) During guided practice, students work alone, without teacher assistance.

Checkpoint Answers

1. attention
2. ongoing
3. monitors
4. (a) true; (b) false

5E Model

The **5E model** (also called the **learning cycle model**) follows the principle that students learn best when they are provided opportunities to construct their own understandings of concepts by building on prior knowledge and by actively engaging in the learning experience. The five *E*s are the following:

- **Engage:** The teacher engages students' attention and stimulates motivation to learn by helping students relate the content to their prior knowledge and to their own personal interests and experiences.
- **Explore:** Students work together, usually in pairs or small groups, to get directly involved with the phenomena and materials. The teacher becomes a facilitator, providing support as the students engage in active inquiry.
- **Explain:** Students support each other's understandings as they communicate their findings and discuss their ideas, observations, questions, and predictions.
- **Extend/elaborate:** Students expand on the concepts learned, make connections to other related concepts, and apply their understandings to real-world settings.
- **Evaluate:** In Florida, the last *E* is more directly about assessment than evaluation. According to *Successful Strategies for Learner-Centered Classrooms and Their Management* (available at www.scps.k12.fl.us/Portals/2/LA_Best%20Practices/Successful%20Strategies%20for%20Learning-Centered%20Classrooms%20and%20Their%20Management.pdf), in the learner-centered classroom, assessment should be shared between the teacher and the students and should include "both self- and peer-assessment as well as teacher assessment" (p. 2).

The 5E model is not incompatible with the lesson cycle model. On the contrary, the two models overlap (for instance, engage and focus are essentially the same in both models), and both are designed to accomplish learning objectives.

Checkpoint

Fill in the blank.

1. The 5E model is designed to help students _____ their own understandings of concepts.
2. One purpose of the engage component of the 5E model is to gain students' _____.
3. During the explore component of a 5E lesson, the teacher's role is as a _____.

Mark as true or false.

4. _____ (a) During the explain component of a 5E lesson, the teacher is doing most of the explaining.

   _____ (b) The 5E model is most consistent with a behaviorist point of view.

Checkpoint Answers

1. construct
2. attention
3. facilitator
4. (a) false; (b) false

Cooperative Learning

Cooperative learning instruction allows students to assume responsibility for their own learning as they work together to complete a project or activity. It provides students with opportunities to develop interpersonal and small-group social skills through a variety of group formats. These skills are lifelong abilities that are vital for the democratic decisions of citizenship and the teamwork required in the workplace. Moreover, cooperative learning instruction enables learners to further develop their creative and critical thinking skills by requiring them to engage in brainstorming, problem solving, decision making, negotiation, and so on. Additionally, students are able to examine their own values, attitudes, and forms of social behavior and to consider alternative points of view.

Planning for cooperative learning group activities requires teachers to focus on teacher-student interaction, student-teacher interaction, student-student interaction, task specification and materials, roles, and expectations. Although there are variations in the application of the cooperative learning concept, according to Johnson and Johnson (1994), the five critical attributes of cooperative learning are the following:

- **Positive interdependence:** Everyone's success depends on the success of everyone else in the group.
- **Individual accountability:** Everyone in the group has to contribute and learn.
- **Group processing of social skills:** Group functioning is frequently monitored and adjusted to improve group effectiveness.
- **Face-to-face promotive interaction:** Group members facilitate and help each other by committing personal resources, encouragement, and assistance to others to achieve group goals.
- **Effective interpersonal interaction:** Group members regularly use interpersonal skills such as using appropriate tone, voice level, and turn-taking to show respect for others.

The main purpose underlying cooperative learning methods is to encourage students to help each other learn. Group members take responsibility for their own learning and for one another's learning. Teachers intervene only when necessary. The positive interdependence that is an essential component of cooperative learning is a strong motivating factor for students. Students perceive that the group "sinks or swims" together. The group incentive structure allows all students—even those who have a history of limited academic success—an opportunity to succeed, which can be highly motivating to students. Commonly, group membership should extend over a period of time to allow for intergroup responsibility and collaboration to build, although group membership should not be permanent for the entire year. Cooperative learning group activities are learner-centered, with the teacher functioning as both a facilitator to promote effective group functioning and as an academic resource.

In the *Florida Curriculum Framework: Elementary Program* (1998), the FLDOE listed the following benefits of cooperative learning:

- Fosters interdependence and pursuit of mutual goals and rewards
- Develops communication and leadership skills
- Increases participation of shy students (including ELLs and ESE learners)
- Produces higher levels of student achievement, thus increasing self-esteem
- Fosters respect for diverse abilities and perspectives
- Allows students with special talents to operate as peer tutors to others in the group (p. 411)

In addition, research indicates that, in particular, minority students, at-risk students, and students with a physical or mental disability benefit from involvement in cooperative learning instruction.

Despite these benefits, critics have challenged the use of cooperative learning strategies with gifted students, arguing that high-achieving students are penalized by working in mixed-ability cooperative learning groups. They complain that high achievers feel used and frustrated by low achievers who are not motivated to perform well (National Association for Gifted Children, 2009). Nevertheless, ample research indicates that high-achieving students learn as much in cooperatively structured classes as they do in traditional classes, as long as group goals and individual accountability are incorporated into activities (Slavin, 2008). Furthermore, they benefit socially from the opportunity to work collaboratively with and help others who are not their intellectual peers. Even so, high achievers should also be given opportunities to work cooperatively with other high achievers or on independent projects.

Numerous research supports the positive outcomes for all students when cooperative learning is used. Specifically, Marzano et al. (2000) identified cooperative learning as a high yield instructional strategy (see "Marzano's High Yield Instructional Strategies" in Chapter 3 for a discussion of this topic). However, adequate training for teachers and students is necessary in order for cooperative learning to be implemented successfully. Teachers who want to use cooperative learning groups should do the following:

- Arrange the classroom furniture to support group interaction.
- Assign students to groups to ensure a mix of gender, ethnicity, linguistic level, and academic ability.
- Select tasks that students will find interesting, meaningful, and challenging and that genuinely require group effort to accomplish.
- Determine group size based on the tasks and goals for the group. For most activities, particularly problem-solving activities, groups of two to four work best.
- Present objectives as group objectives and communicate expectations clearly.
- Assign each group member a job or role.
- Make expectations of group behavior clear.
- Teach socials skills necessary for working with others (before and during activities).
- Make sure everyone understands what he or she is expected to do to make the group function well.
- Monitor group processes during activities.
- Monitor individual social skills during activities.
- Reward the group for successful completion of the task.
- Assess both group and individual performance.
- Assess group participation and cooperation using self-assessment, peer assessment, and teacher assessment.
- Always incorporate group goals and insist on individual accountability.
- Apply cooperative learning in a consistent and systematic manner but do not overuse it.

Four special types of cooperative learning described in the *Florida Curriculum Framework: Elementary Program* (1998) are

- **Jigsawing:** Group members become experts on an assigned topic that they then teach to others, after reorganizing into different groups, so that eventually all members of the class know all the content.
- **Corners:** Group members meet in a designated corner of the room to discuss an assigned topic and then teach it to the rest of the class.
- **Think, pair, and share:** First, students work individually on an assigned problem-solving task; next, they pair with a partner to discuss and revise; and finally, they share their results with the entire class.
- **Debate:** Students work in teams to research a topic and formulate persuasive arguments supporting their viewpoints on an issue. Then they present their arguments in a teacher-determined format and structure.

Checkpoint

Fill in the blank.

1. Positive interdependence means everyone's success _____ on the success of everyone else.

2. Cooperative learning group activities are _____ (learner-centered, teacher-centered).

3. In jigsawing, group members become _____ on an assigned topic.

Mark as true or false.

4. _____ (a) Cooperative learning produces higher levels of student achievement.

   _____ (b) Students in cooperative learning groups should be similar with respect to their academic abilities.

Checkpoint Answers

1. depends

2. learner-centered

3. experts

4. (a) true; (b) false

Developmentally Appropriate Practice

Teachers enhance students' development and learning by using developmentally appropriate practice. **Developmentally appropriate practice** (DAP) refers to a framework that takes into account the typical patterns of physical, social, and cognitive development of students in order to optimize student learning and to promote social growth. According to the National Association for the Education of Young Children (NAEYC), developmentally appropriate practice should be based on the following elements:

- What is known about child development and learning: Knowledge of age-related human characteristics that permits general predictions within an age range about what activities, materials, interactions, or experiences will best promote learning and development
- What is known about the strengths, interests, and needs of each individual student in the group to be able to adapt to and be responsive to inevitable individual variation
- What is known about the social and cultural contexts in which students live to ensure that learning experiences are meaningful, relevant, and respectful for the students and their families

Further, the NAEYC offers 12 principles of child development and learning that inform developmentally appropriate practice in early childhood (birth through age 8). Following is a simplified version of the 12 principles as they would relate to the FTCE PEd Test:

- Domains of students' development—physical, social, emotional, and cognitive—are interrelated. Development in one domain can limit or facilitate development in others.

- Development occurs in a relatively predictable sequence, with later abilities building on those previously acquired.

- Variation in development occurs among students and within different areas for an individual student. Each student is a unique person with an individual pattern and timing of growth, and this individual variation should be expected and valued.

- Development proceeds in predictable directions toward greater complexity, organization, and internalization.

- Early experiences, either positive or negative, are cumulative in the sense that those that occur most often usually have more effect.

- Each student's development and learning occur in and are influenced by the sociocultural context of the family, educational setting, community, and broader society.

- The interplay between biological maturation and physical and social experiences impacts development and learning.

- Students are products of both heredity and environment, and these forces are interrelated.

- Most of the time, teachers should give students tasks that, with effort, they can accomplish, and present them with content that is accessible at their level of understanding. At the same time, development advances when, in a supportive context, students experience challenges just beyond their current level of mastery.

- Students exhibit a variety of learning needs. They benefit when teachers select the best strategy to use in a learning situation.

- Play is an important vehicle for young children's social, emotional, and cognitive development. (See the section "Types of Play" that follows for a discussion of play.)

- Students develop and learn best in a learning environment in which they are part of a community where they are safe and valued, their physical needs are met, and they feel psychologically secure. (See Chapter 2 for additional discussion on learning environments.)

Checkpoint

Fill in the blank.

1. Developmentally appropriate practice refers to a framework that takes into account the _____ patterns of physical, social, and cognitive development of students.

2. Development occurs in a relatively _____ sequence.

3. Students learn best when they are part of a nurturing _____.

Mark as true or false.

4. _____ (a) A teacher should never give a student a task above the student's current level of mastery.

   _____ (b) Play is inappropriate in early-childhood classrooms and should be reserved for the playground.

Checkpoint Answers

1. typical

2. predictable

3. community

4. (a) false; (b) false

Types of Play

Gestwicki (1999) characterized **play** as pleasurable, spontaneous, self-motivated, and freely chosen activity. The NAEYC strongly advocates play as an important component of developmentally appropriate practice in early childhood because play supports children's cognitive, physical, emotional, and social development.

Piaget (in Gestwicki, 1999) identified three categories of increasing sophistication of play:

- **Functional play:** Commonly occurs from birth to age 2 and involves movement and sensory exploration of the environment (for example, a toddler banging on a toy piano)
- **Symbolic play:** Usually begins around age 2 and involves using materials or objects to represent things (for example, a preschooler using a block to represent a telephone) or engaging in imaginary roles (for example, kindergarteners playing store)
- **Games with rules play:** Commonly begins near school age and involves the ability to agree upon and abide by rules (for example, children playing "Simon Says")

Note: See the section "Piaget" later in this chapter for an additional discussion of Piaget's theories.

Parten (in Gestwicki, 1999) identified five progressive stages of play:

- **Onlooker play:** A child watches other children play, but does not join in.
- **Solitary play:** A child plays alone.
- **Parallel play:** Children play side-by-side, engage in similar activities, and might mimic each other, but they do not play together and interact very little.
- **Associative play:** Children play similar activities side-by-side with interaction such as talking or sharing, but with little joint focus.
- **Cooperative play:** Children play as a group of two or more with more complex social interaction (for example, conversations, turn-taking, and choosing sides) and with a common focus.

Checkpoint

Fill in the blank.

1. Assuming imaginary roles is _____ play.
2. A child works alone on a puzzle. This type of play is _____ play.
3. Two children work together on a puzzle. This type of play is _____ play.

Mark as true or false.

4. _____ (a) Play has an important role in early-childhood classrooms.

   _____ (b) Making a fort with blocks is symbolic play.

Checkpoint Answers

1. symbolic
2. solitary
3. cooperative
4. (a) true; (b) true

Physical Characteristics of Children and Adolescents

Physical development of children proceeds from head to toe in what is called a **cephalocaudal progression.** This progression means motor ability develops from the top down. Infants are first able to control their heads, then their shoulders, then their arms, and, finally, their legs and feet. While this is taking place, growth and motor ability are also developing in a **proximodistal progression,** from the central axis of the body outward. Trunk and shoulder movements occur before separate arm movements. Hand and finger control comes last. Variations in physical development are to be expected since growth and development are related to heredity, nutrition, and other health factors. Some common (but not absolute) developmental milestones at various ages are shown in the following chart.

Physical Development Chart

Age	Milestones
3	Walk without watching feet; run smoothly; walk up and down stairs with assistance, alternating feet; balance on one foot for 5 to 10 seconds; use a slide without assistance; throw and catch objects; build towers with blocks; manipulate Play-Doh/clay; work simple puzzles; copy circles; push buttons to turn on/off; spread with knife; button and unbutton large buttons; wash hands unassisted
4	Walk heel to toe; walk backward, toe to heel; jump forward 5 to 10 times without falling; gallop smoothly; walk up and down stairs alone, alternating feet; turn somersaults; throw ball overhand; catch bounced ball; cut on line; print some letters; copy squares and rectangles; fold paper and crease it to make objects when shown; make simple drawings; pour well from small pitcher; lace shoes, but not tie bow; wash and dry hands; button, zip, and snap clothes; cut easy foods with knife
5	Run with ease; run on toes; skip; hop a distance on one foot; skip on alternate feet; easily balance on one foot; run and kick moving ball; catch large ball in two hands; print words and numerals; cut with scissors; copy triangles; dress self completely; tie bow; brush teeth independently; grip pencil correctly; use paste and glue appropriately; begin to color within lines
6–7	Run, jump, skip, and hop easily (gross-motor skills); view an entire page because eyes can track in a full circle; outgrow farsightedness, which is common up to age 6, but still not ready for sustained close work; draw realistic pictures; have better eye-hand coordination than previously; copy diamonds; can do small printing by age 7; have increased skill in handling tools and materials; lose baby-like contours and features; lose front teeth; grow mainly in the arms, legs, and face; girls ahead of boys in development and physical achievement
8–10	Show endurance in physical activities such as running and swimming; perform activities that require control of small muscles of body, hands, feet, and eyes (fine-motor skills); give attention to details; write in cursive; onset of adolescent growth spurt in girls; quiet growth period for boys; by 9, some girls overtake boys in size, but not in strength; girls more mature than boys
11–13	Easily perform activities that require fine-motor skills, especially girls; show improved motor development and coordination, especially boys; have longer and leaner faces; have most of permanent teeth; pubescent stage for girls; onset of adolescent growth spurt for boys; peak of growth spurt for girls; awkwardness in girls typical; girls reach puberty before boys; (some) early maturing girls self-conscious; boys ahead of girls in physical achievement
Adolescents	Have rapid, but irregular, gain in height and weight, especially boys; might be clumsy because body parts grow at different rates; have high energy, especially boys; experience restlessness due to hormonal changes; develop secondary sex characteristics; might be completely physically mature before others of the same age have begun puberty; early maturing boys larger and perform better athletically; (some) late maturing boys self-conscious and experience low self-esteem; early maturing girls comfortable with pubertal changes and sometimes develop a precocious interest in boys

Note: See the section "Psychosocial Characteristics of Children and Adolescents" in Chapter 2 for a discussion of psychosocial developmental characteristics of children and adolescents.

Checkpoint

Fill in the blank.

1. Before about age 6, children's eyesight tends to be _____.

2. In the period from ages 8 to 10, the adolescent growth spurt begins in _____ (girls, boys).

3. In the period from ages 11 to 13, the adolescent growth spurt begins in _____ (girls, boys).

Mark as true or false.

4. _____ (a) By age 4, most children draw realistic pictures.

   _____ (b) Adolescence is a time of rapid, but irregular, height and weight gain.

Checkpoint Answers

1. farsighted
2. girls
3. boys
4. (a) false; (b) true

Piaget

Jean Piaget (in Slavin, 2008) proposed that learning involves three basic processes: *assimilation, accommodation,* and *equilibration.* **Assimilation** involves fitting new information into existing mental structures, which Piaget called **schema. Accommodation** requires modifying current schema or creating new schema in order to take the new data or information into account. When children encounter new data or information, they experience **disequilibrium,** a cognitive conflict, so to speak, until they can either assimilate or accommodate it and, thus, achieve equilibrium. Piaget believed that disequilibrium is an unnatural state and, therefore, all learners seek equilibrium through either assimilation or accommodation when disequilibrium occurs. The process of reaching equilibrium is **equilibration.** Piaget saw the construction of meaning inherent in equilibration as the essence of learning.

Additionally, Piaget asserted that children eventually acquire three types of knowledge:

- **Physical knowledge:** Developed from physical interaction with objects
- **Logical-mathematical knowledge:** Developed from recognizing logical relationships between objects and ideas
- **Social knowledge:** Developed through custom or social convention

Piaget spent a lifetime observing children and the ways they think in learning situations. He concluded that children do not think like adults, nor do they see the world as adults do. According to Piaget, **cognition,** or thinking, is an active and interactive process that develops in stages. The stages of cognitive development are predictable, but the ages of children entering them may vary.

The first stage, **sensorimotor,** begins at birth and continues until about age 2. During this stage, learning is through the senses and motor development and through trial and error. Children learn to distinguish themselves from the external world. They discover the beginning of independence through cause and effect, learn imitative behavior, and develop **object permanence,** which means they learn that objects continue to exist even when the objects are no longer visible, such as knowing that a ball that rolled behind a piece of furniture did not "disappear."

During the **preoperational** stage, from ages 2 to 6, children are highly imaginative, and they enjoy games of pretend. They see the world from their own points of view **(egocentric),** focus on one aspect of a situation **(centration),** are rapidly developing language, and are beginning to acquire some reasoning ability, although they do not infer beyond what they see. Of particular significance is the development of **symbolic thought**—the ability to mentally represent objects, events, and actions—as evidenced through the use of language and make-believe play. This period is also characterized by what children lack—**reversibility,** the ability to mentally reverse an operation, and **conservation,** the ability to recognize that number, length, quantity, area, mass, weight, and volume of objects has not necessarily changed even though the appearance of these objects might have changed. They also have difficulty distinguishing appearances from reality.

In the **concrete operational** stage, ages 7 to 11, children develop the ability to take another's point of view **(decenter)** and no longer have problems with centration, conservation, reversibility, and distinguishing appearances from reality. They can sort objects into multiple categories and, based on more than one aspect, can think of the whole and its parts simultaneously **(class inclusion),** and can arrange objects in sequential order **(seriation).** They can reason logically to solve concrete problems, can reason and make inferences about reality, and can infer beyond what they see. They are able to logically reason that if *A* is related to *B* and *B* is related to *C,* then *A* is related to *C* **(transitivity).** They acquire the ability to think about and solve problems mentally but still need concrete experiences and physical actions to make mental connections. They can think about their own thinking and use metacognitive strategies. Even though they can reason logically (for example, from cause to effect) with concrete objects, they have difficulty with abstract reasoning and hypothetical thinking.

The last stage of development, **formal operational,** begins at about age 12 and continues to adulthood. Adolescents who reach this stage begin to think more easily about **abstract concepts,** things they cannot touch or see. They can develop hypotheses, organize information, test hypotheses, and solve problems. They also can reason both deductively and inductively, make generalizations, and critically analyze the thinking of others. However, for most young adolescents, Piaget's concrete operational stage is predominant, although frequently an adolescent functions at the concrete operational stage for some topics (such as mathematical problem solving) and the formal operational stage for other topics (such as civil rights). Teachers should not assume that all adolescents are at the same stage developmentally or that an individual student functions at the same level in all situations. Whether all people achieve formal operational thinking at this or any other stage is still a major question.

In addition to his stages of cognitive development, Piaget postulated two stages of moral development (Slavin, 2008):

- Younger children are in the **heteronomous morality** stage. In this stage, children see rules as unbreakable and unchangeable—even if everyone agrees to change them. They obey rules for fear of punishment; when very young, they will tattle on rule breakers.
- Older children are in the **autonomous morality** stage. In this stage, children develop autonomy and are willing to challenge rules. They recognize that punishment is not always automatic and that rules exist by mutual agreement and can be changed with the consent of participants.

Checkpoint

Fill in the blank.

1. _____ (Accommodation, Assimilation) involves fitting new information into existing mental structures.

2. A child who recognizes that objects continue to exist even when the objects are no longer visible has acquired _____ (two words).

3. A kindergarten child who tattles on rule breakers is in Piaget's _____ (autonomous, heteronomous) morality stage.

Mark as true or false.

4. _____ (a) Before about age 7, children have difficulty taking the perspective of others.

_____ (b) High school teachers should assume that their students have achieved formal operational thinking.

Checkpoint Answers

1. Assimilation

2. object permanence

3. heteronomous

4. (a) true; (b) false

Bruner

Like Piaget, Jerome Bruner (in Reinhartz and Beach, 1997) viewed learning as a process of constructing meaning by building on prior understandings. He believed that children learn best when tasks are presented to them at their appropriate level of development through a discovery-oriented approach. He proposed three modes through which children can learn based on their level of cognitive development:

- Up to about age 6, children primarily learn through the **enactive mode,** which involves interacting with objects in their environment.
- Elementary children (ages 6 through 11) can learn through the **iconic mode,** which involves the use of images or graphic illustrations to convey concepts.
- Older students and adults (ages 11 and above) can learn through the **symbolic mode,** which involves using symbols and words to represent concepts.

According to Bruner, when a concept is first introduced to students, teachers should structure the presentation of the concept so that it proceeds from enactive to iconic to symbolic mode. For instance, in science, students might first build models of simple molecules, next draw pictures of molecules, and finally, write the symbolic representation of molecules.

Checkpoint

Fill in the blank.

1. Bruner viewed learning as a process of _____ meaning by building on prior understandings.
2. Up to about age 6, children primarily learn through the _____ (enactive, iconic, symbolic) mode.
3. The _____ (enactive, iconic, symbolic) mode involves using symbols and words to represent concepts.

Mark as true or false.

4. _____ (a) Bruner was an advocate of discovery learning.

_____ (b) According to Bruner, when introducing concepts, teachers should start with the symbolic representation of the concept.

Checkpoint Answers

1. constructing
2. enactive
3. symbolic
4. (a) true; (b) false

Vygotsky

Lev Vygotsky's 1978 work is based on the premise that learning cannot be understood without consideration of its cultural and social context. Gestwicki (1999) expressed Vygotsky's view of learning by saying, "Social engagement and collaboration with others is [sic] the powerful force that transforms children's thinking" (p. 39). Terms associated with Vygotsky's theory of cognitive development are *self-regulation, private speech, zone of proximal development,* and *scaffolding* (Slavin, 2008).

Self-regulation is the ability to learn and solve problems on one's own without assistance.

Private speech is the self-talk learners use to monitor and guide themselves as they work through a problem or complete a learning task.

The **zone of proximal development** is the gap between a student's independent level of problem-solving ability and the student's potential level of problem-solving ability that can be achieved with assistance from an adult or more capable peer (Gestwicki, 1999).

When students are learning in their zone of proximal development, **scaffolding** is the support and assistance provided for learning and problem solving, such as verbal cues or prompts, visual highlighting, diagrams, checklists, reminders, modeling, partially completed learning charts or tasks, and examples. Scaffolding is more intense and frequent at first but should be diminished as learners become self-regulated.

Checkpoint

Fill in the blank.

1. The self-talk learners use to monitor and guide themselves as they work through a problem is _____ (two words).

2. The zone of proximal development is the gap between a student's independent level of problem-solving ability and the student's _____ level of problem-solving ability that can be achieved with assistance.

3. Vygotsky described the support and assistance provided for learning and problem solving as _____.

Mark as true or false.

4. _____ (a) According to Vygotsky, learning is enhanced by social interaction.

   _____ (b) Scaffolding should be diminished as learners become self-regulated.

Checkpoint Answers

1. private speech

2. potential

3. scaffolding

4. (a) true; (b) true

Ability Levels

Teachers need to be aware of the characteristics of both high-ability and struggling learners. As with all students, high-ability students come to school with unique characteristics and abilities and are from various ethnic, cultural, and socioeconomic backgrounds. According to Gallagher (1994), teacher identification of high-ability students can be influenced by the erroneous belief that a high-ability student must fit the "perfect" student model (that is, performs well in school, behaves appropriately, turns in work on time, and so forth). However, not all high-ability students perform well in school. Students of high ability might conceal their potential for various reasons, such as peer pressure or cultural norms to "fit in" and not be different. Teachers need to be sensitive to these issues and strive to overcome them by nurturing a climate in the classroom that fosters a positive attitude toward learning.

Generally, when motivated, high-ability learners can sustain concentration for lengthy periods, comprehend readily, learn quickly and retain what is learned, show initiative in their classwork, set high standards for themselves, and express themselves very well, both orally and in writing (Council for Exceptional Student Education, 1990). They are ready for fast-paced, very abstract instruction and learn better in environments in which they are given a measure of control over their learning options. They need learning experiences that are challenging, meaningful, and appropriate to their needs and abilities. In particular, when working with students identified as gifted, effective teachers recognize that gifted students need opportunities to interact and work with the other students in the class, but that they also need time to work alone and with other high-ability students to pursue topics to higher levels of cognitive challenge (see "Professional Conduct with ESE Students" in Chapter 6 for an additional discussion about gifted students).

Struggling learners are students who, for a variety of reasons, are at risk of academic failure and might drop out of school at some point. In 2011, Section 1003.413 (2)(a), Florida Statutes (F. S.) stated struggling learners need "the highest-quality teachers and dramatically different, innovative approaches to teaching and learning." These students are not incapable of learning, but they are (usually) concrete thinkers who need structured environments. Moreover, they need opportunities to experience academic success on assignments they perceive as meaningful and challenging. To make this aim a reality, good teachers differentiate instruction to meet their learning needs (see the section "MTSS PS/RtI" later in this chapter for a discussion of differentiation).

Good teachers are sensitive and caring in their interactions with students of varying abilities. They avoid disparate treatment toward students who are perceived to be high or low achievers, rather aiming to treat all students fairly. In their studies of classrooms, Good and Brophy (2002) identified the following disparate treatment behaviors by teachers:

- Give high achievers preferential seating.
- Seat low achievers away from the teacher.
- Isolate low achievers from high achievers.
- Use fewer nonverbal cues with low achievers during instruction.
- Call on high achievers more frequently than low achievers.
- Wait longer for responses from high achievers.
- Fail to use probes with low achievers when they attempt a response.
- Criticize low achievers for incorrect responses more often.
- Praise high achievers for correct public responses more often.
- Praise low achievers for inadequate public responses.
- Provide low achievers with less useful feedback.
- Lower standards for low achievers.
- Interrupt low achievers' performances more frequently.
- Talk negatively about low achievers more often.
- Punish off-task behavior of low achievers, but more frequently ignore it in high achievers.

To make instruction effective for all students, teachers need to take into account students' diverse learning needs and must make a conscious effort to avoid disparate treatment based on students' ability levels. It is not unusual for teachers to have a wide range of ability levels in their classrooms. Too much whole-group instruction in such classrooms is likely to be ineffective because the instruction could be too advanced for some students and too easy for others.

Checkpoint

Fill in the blank.

1. High-ability students need opportunities to work _____ and also with other high-ability students.

2. Struggling students need frequent, corrective _____.

3. Struggling students are usually _____ (abstract, concrete) thinkers.

Mark as true or false.

4. _____ (a) It is appropriate for students to be given responsibility for their own learning.

   _____ (b) Whole-group instruction usually works well in mixed-ability classes.

Checkpoint Answers

1. alone

2. feedback

3. concrete

4. (a) true; (b) false

Gender Patterns

Gender equity is an important initiative in the nation and in the State of Florida. In planning for instruction, teachers need to recognize that although boys and girls are equally capable of academic achievement, learned patterns of gender differences might be exhibited in their classrooms. To counteract such patterns, teachers should first check themselves to make sure they are not exhibiting stereotypical behavior toward students and then build safeguards into their lessons that include

- monitoring group activities to make sure both boys and girls assume various roles during activities.
- modeling acceptance of nonstereotypical behaviors and attitudes.
- bringing in both male and female guest speakers who have "nontraditional" careers.
- openly discussing gender stereotyping with students, when necessary.
- encouraging students to strive for excellence in all subject areas.
- consciously endeavoring to provide equitable opportunities for boys and girls alike.

Checkpoint

Fill in the blank.

1. Boys and girls are _____ capable of academic achievement.
2. Teachers should encourage students to strive for excellence in _____ subject areas.
3. Teachers should consciously endeavor to provide _____ opportunities for boys and girls alike.

Mark as true or false.

4. _____ (a) Gender equity is an important issue in Florida.

   _____ (b) High school teachers should encourage students to consider careers traditionally associated with their gender roles.

Checkpoint Answers

1. equally
2. all
3. equitable
4. (a) true; (b) false

Learning Styles

Researchers such as Rita and Kenneth Dunn (2006) have suggested that effective teachers should consider their students' learning styles in order to facilitate academic achievement. **Learning style** is the manner in which an individual perceives and processes information in learning situations. Knowledge of learning style theory may help teachers in designing educational conditions in which most students are likely to learn. According to Dunn and Dunn, classrooms can be designed to either stimulate or inhibit learning for students based on their individual learning style needs related to the following:

- The environmental setting in which learning opportunities are presented—includes room temperature, lighting, noise level, and type of seating (for example, desks, chairs, or tables)
- Personal characteristics of the learner—includes motivation, persistence, responsibility, and preference with regard to structure

- The social setting in which learning opportunities are presented—includes grouping arrangement (for example, individual, pairs, small groups, or teams) and teacher interaction patterns
- Physiological factors that impact the learner—includes modality preference (see the section "Modality Preferences" that follows for a discussion of this topic), food/drink intake, time of day, and mobility opportunities

Furthermore, Dunn and Dunn maintained that psychological characteristics of the student influence the student's ability to learn. These psychological characteristics include *impulsivity/reflectivity inclination* and *brain hemisphericity.*

Kagan's (1966) work on **impulsivity/reflectivity** concluded that individuals are consistent in the way they process information and the speed with which they do it. **Impulsive** students tend to work and make decisions quickly. They respond to situations often with the first thought that occurs to them, regularly finishing assignments and tests before everyone else. **Reflective** students ponder all the alternatives carefully before responding, working cautiously and deliberately. Impulsive students tend to concentrate on speed, but reflective students concentrate more on accuracy.

Brain hemisphericity refers to the tendency to be either **right-brain dominant** or **left-brain dominant** in learning style. In theory, each hemisphere of the brain is associated with certain thinking traits and, therefore, certain learning styles. Considerable research has been done that supports the notion that people who are left-brain dominant learn in different ways than do right-brain-dominant people. The terms *left-brained, analytic,* and *deductive* and the terms *right-brained, global,* and *inductive* are often used interchangeably to describe learners based on their brain hemispheric orientation. The following table summarizes the characteristics of the different types of learners using these labels.

Type of Learner	Characteristics
Left/analytic/deductive learner	Thinks from part to whole Processes thought logically and analytically Approaches problem solving systematically Is skillful at reasoning deductively Depends on words and language for meaning Readily follows verbal instructions Prefers lessons that proceed in a step-by-step logical order Prefers structured assignments Is independent Prefers quiet, bright lighting, and formal seating when working Might not think of himself/herself as creative
Right/global/inductive learner	Thinks from whole to part Processes thought holistically Approaches problem solving randomly with visual, nonverbal strategies (for example, drawing a picture) Is skillful at reasoning inductively Sees patterns and relationships Prefers to see the big picture before exploring the small details Prefers instructions that are graphically presented or modeled Learns better when images and pictures augment text Can work on several parts of a task at the same time Likes group work and social activities Likes music/sound, dim lighting, and relaxed seating when working Engages in creative activities

Everyone is a whole-brained person but, usually, with a preference for receiving information through either the left or right hemisphere. Neither preference is in any way superior to the other, although instruction in most public schools in the United States has traditionally favored left-brain-dominant students.

Other well-known learning style classifications are *field independence/field dependence, concrete/abstract learning,* and *multiple intelligences.* (See the sections "Field Independence–Field Dependence," "Gregorc's Mind Styles," and "Multiple Intelligences" later in this chapter for discussions on these topics.)

Checkpoint

Fill in the blank.

1. Generally, learners who prefer to see the big picture before engaging in a learning activity are _____ (right-brain-dominant, left-brain-dominant) learners.

2. Learners who approach problem solving systematically are _____ (right-brain-dominant, left-brain-dominant) learners.

3. A brightly lit classroom would appeal to _____ (right-brain-dominant, left-brain-dominant) learners.

Mark as true or false.

4. _____ (a) Impulsive students ponder all the alternatives carefully before responding.

   _____ (b) Instruction in most public schools in the United States has traditionally favored left-brain-dominant students.

Checkpoint Answers

1. right-brain-dominant

2. left-brain-dominant

3. left-brain-dominant

4. (a) false; (b) true

Modality Preferences

Educators usually refer to the predominant way a student takes in information through the five primary senses (sight, hearing, smell, taste, and touch) as **sensory modality strength.** Students who prefer to learn by seeing or reading something are **visual** learners; students who learn best by listening are **auditory** learners; and students who prefer to learn by touching objects, by feeling shapes and textures, and by moving things around are **tactile/kinesthetic** learners. Some students have a single modality strength (visual, auditory, or tactile/kinesthetic), while others have combination, or mixed, modalities. Children with mixed modality strengths usually are able to process information efficiently no matter how it is presented. In contrast, children with single modality strengths might experience difficulties when instruction is presented outside the scope of their modality strength. Most students eventually learn to adjust when the instructional material is not consistent with their modality preference. However, most educators agree that planning for those learners who are visual, auditory, tactile/kinesthetic, or a combination of these is critical if teachers are to help all learners be successful. The following chart describes the three types of learners.

Description of Learners

Auditory Learner	Visual Learner	Kinesthetic/Tactile Learner
Is talkative	Notices small details	Needs to move around
Likes to make people laugh	Has good spatial memory	Wants to feel and touch things
Is a good storyteller	Enjoys drawing pictures	Has good motor skills
Enjoys listening activities	Enjoys illustrated books	Enjoys doing things manually

Description of Learners (*continued*)

Auditory Learner	Visual Learner	Kinesthetic/Tactile Learner
Memorizes easily	Likes to work puzzles	Likes taking things apart
Can deliver oral messages accurately	Remembers faces	Likes to use concrete objects when learning
Is easily distracted	Has trouble remembering oral instructions	Avoids reading
Enjoys being in charge	Dislikes speaking before a group	Sometimes appears immature in behavior

This next chart contains guidelines for working with auditory, visual, and kinesthetic/tactile learners.

Ways to Accommodate

Auditory Learner	Visual Learner	Kinesthetic/Tactile Learner
Read directions orally.	Use graphic aids (pictures, images, graphs, charts, and so on).	Use hands-on activities.
Use repetition.	Use videos and PowerPoint presentations.	Use manipulatives and other tactile materials.
Have learners read aloud.	Use models and demonstrations.	Use outdoor activities.
Use music activities.	Encourage learners to draw or illustrate.	Keep learners physically active.
Use read-alouds.	Use memory and concentration games.	Use role playing and simulations.
Have learners verbalize while reading.	Play "what's missing?" games.	Use dramatic play and puppetry.
Have learners act as peer tutors.	Use puzzles.	Use musical instruments.
Use taped lessons.	Use art activities.	Associate concepts with movement activities.
Use group activities.	Provide time for independent work.	Allow freedom for physical movement by the learner.

Checkpoint

Fill in the blank.

1. Role playing and simulations are most beneficial for _____ (auditory, visual, kinesthetic/tactile) learners.

2. Reading directions aloud will help _____ (auditory, visual, kinesthetic/tactile) learners the most.

3. Students who prefer to learn by seeing or reading something are _____ (auditory, visual, kinesthetic/tactile) learners.

Mark as true or false.

4. _____ (a) Visual learners prefer group activities.

_____ (b) Auditory learners are talkative.

Checkpoint Answers

1. kinesthetic/tactile

2. auditory

3. visual

4. (a) false; (b) true

Field Independence–Field Dependence

The work of Witkin & Goodenough (1981) on **field independence–field dependence** closely paralleled brain hemisphericity findings. These researchers described learners as **field independent** (having the ability to perceive objects without being influenced by the background) and **field dependent** (having the ability to perceive objects as a whole rather than as individual parts). Characteristics of field-independent and field-dependent learners are summarized in the following chart.

Type of Learner	Characteristics
Field independent	Processes information in parts Might focus on specific parts, rather than see the whole Passive in social situations Tends to be less influenced by peers Likes working alone Chooses fields like math, science, and engineering
Field dependent	Processes information holistically Has difficulty separating specific parts from a situation or pattern Able to see relational concepts Active in social situations Tends to be influenced by suggestions from others Likes to work in groups Chooses fields requiring interpersonal, nonscientific orientation, such as history, art, or social work

Checkpoint

Fill in the blank.

1. Teachers who plan social events for students should keep in mind that _____ (field-independent, field-dependent) learners are likely to be passive during the event.

2. Math and science fields are preferred by _____ (field-independent, field-dependent) learners.

3. Group work appeals to _____ (field-independent, field-dependent) learners.

Mark as true or false.

4. _____ (a) Field-dependent learners process information holistically.

   _____ (b) Field-independent learners are very susceptible to peer pressure.

Checkpoint Answers

1. field-independent

2. field-independent

3. field-dependent

4. (a) true; (b) false

Gregorc's Mind Styles

Gregorc's (2002) Mind Styles model considers the predominant way learners prefer to process and organize information for learning. To perceive information, **concrete learners** rely on physically experiencing it; in contrast, **abstract learners** are able to process symbolic, abstract representations of information. To organize information, **random organizers** tend to chunk information in no particular order, and **sequential organizers** use a linear, step-by-step organizational approach. These classifications give rise to four types of learners as described in the following chart.

Type of Learner	Learning Preferences
Concrete-sequential	Enjoys hands-on, linearly sequenced learning
Concrete-random	Enjoys hands-on, exploratory learning
Abstract-sequential	Enjoys abstract, logically sequenced, analytical learning
Abstract-random	Enjoys mentally challenging activities in an informal environment

Checkpoint

Fill in the blank.

1. Using manipulatives would appeal to _____ (concrete, abstract) learners.

2. Solving written abstract equations would appeal to _____ (concrete, abstract) learners.

3. Being given step-by-step directions would appeal to _____ (random, sequential) organizers.

Mark as true or false.

4. _____ (a) Working in an unorganized environment would be difficult for a concrete-sequential learner.

   _____ (b) Working in a restricted environment would be difficult for an abstract-random learner.

Checkpoint Answers

1. concrete

2. abstract

3. sequential

4. (a) true; (b) true

Multiple Intelligences

Howard Gardner (1983) proposed the theory of **multiple intelligences** (Davis et al., 2012). In his most recent works, he suggested that humans have eight intelligences:

- **Verbal-linguistic intelligence:** The ability to use and produce words
- **Logical-mathematical intelligence:** The ability to do math, recognize patterns, and problem-solve
- **Visual-spatial intelligence:** The ability to form images and pictures in the mind
- **Body-kinesthetic intelligence:** The ability to use the body in physical activities

- **Musical-rhythmic intelligence:** The ability to recognize musical and rhythmic patterns and sounds
- **Intrapersonal intelligence:** The ability to know oneself
- **Interpersonal intelligence:** The ability to work cooperatively with other people
- **Naturalistic intelligence:** The ability to understand and work in the natural world

Multiple intelligences inform teachers that students can be smart in many ways. Teachers whose practices reflect the theory of multiple intelligences learn to look at learners from eight different viewpoints. They recognize that students have less anxiety and can learn better when the learning task is congruent with their strengths and abilities. For example, in social studies, verbal-linguistic learners would prefer to debate about a historical event, but body-kinesthetic learners would prefer to act it out.

The popularity of Gardner's theory persists among teachers despite criticism of the theory from both psychologists and educators. These detractors contend that Gardner's definition of intelligence is too broad and that some of the so-called "intelligences" are simply talents or personality traits.

Checkpoint

Fill in the blank.

1. Having students create a human graph will appeal to _____ intelligence.
2. Drawing a map of the setting of a story will appeal to _____ intelligence.
3. Using a familiar tune to teach math rules will appeal to _____ intelligence.

Mark as true or false.

4. _____ (a) Students with strong interpersonal intelligence will enjoy group activities.

   _____ (b) Students with strong visual-spatial intelligence tend to think in images rather than in words or sounds.

Checkpoint Answers

1. body-kinesthetic
2. visual-spatial
3. musical-rhythmic
4. (a) true; (b) true

Behaviorism and Constructivism

When designing instruction, teachers need a strong knowledge base of how students learn. Numerous studies have been conducted on the factors that affect learning. Behaviorism and constructivism are two learning theories that can be applied to Instructional Design and Planning.

Behaviorism is a learning theory based on using immediate consequences to either weaken or strengthen a learner's observable response. A **consequence** is a pleasant or unpleasant effect that follows a behavior and influences whether it will occur again. Other key ideas associated with behaviorism include *positive* and *negative reinforcement, intrinsic* and *extrinsic reinforcers, extinction, reinforcement schedule,* and *shaping.*

The appropriate use of **reinforcement,** which is a pleasant consequence that follows a behavior, is an essential strategy associated with a behavioristic approach to learning. The idea is that students' accomplishments and appropriate behavior should be rewarded not only with good grades but also with other rewards and incentives: attention, public recognition (such as public displays of good work), tangible rewards (such as stickers, stars, and stamps), extra privileges, and so forth. The basic principle of reinforcement is that students will continue good behaviors that are reinforced and discontinue undesirable behaviors when they are not reinforced.

Reinforcers are either **extrinsic reinforcers,** which are reinforcers that are external to a student such as tangible rewards or grades, or **intrinsic reinforcers,** which are reinforcers that come from within a student such as a personal enjoyment of problem solving. When using extrinsic reinforcement, most teachers prefer to use **positive reinforcement,** in the form of things given to students (such as tangible rewards or special privileges), rather than **negative reinforcement,** which is removal from a situation perceived by the student to be unpleasant (such as a night off from doing homework). In either case, teachers need to use reinforcers that are perceived as desirable by students. For example, elementary students might enjoy getting stickers as rewards, but high school students would prefer the reward of free time or getting to see a movie for their good behavior. Teachers should use reinforcement to inform students about what they are doing right. Reinforcement should be given contingent on specific student behaviors and should be awarded in such a way that it helps to develop intrinsic motivation and other natural reinforcers of desirable student performance. (See the section "Motivational Strategies" in Chapter 3 for a discussion of intrinsic motivation.)

Extinction is the process of weakening and eventually eliminating the occurrence of a behavior usually through the removal or withholding of reinforcement. The **schedule of reinforcement,** which is the frequency with which reinforcement is given, influences the response rate of a behavior and, furthermore, its resistance to extinction. Slavin (2008) explained that behaviors that are reinforced on a **variable, unpredictable schedule** tend to have steady, high response rates and be resistant to extinction, while behaviors that are reinforced on a **fixed, predictable schedule** have uneven response rates and drop off quickly after reinforcement is removed.

Shaping uses positive reinforcement upon successful completion of incremental steps along the way toward a desired learning goal or behavior to change a student's behavior. Teachers might use shaping to teach a complex skill by using reinforcement of step-by-step procedures.

Punishment is characterized as *positive* or *negative.* **Positive punishment** involves giving an undesirable consequence (for example, extra work) in order to deter undesirable behavior. **Negative punishment** involves taking away a desirable reward (for example, free time) in order to deter undesirable behavior. Do not confuse punishment, which penalizes students and, is, thus, perceived negatively by them, with negative reinforcement, which is a type of reward that is perceived positively by students. Teachers should avoid using punishment in their classrooms because it puts in jeopardy the safe, supportive learning environment that is essential for facilitating student learning. (See Chapter 2 for additional discussion on learning environments.)

Behavioristic lessons often involve direct instruction. Teachers gain attention, activate prior knowledge, and present explicit information about the lesson content and structured models that demonstrate the knowledge or skill. They scaffold students' understanding, often with examples and nonexamples, and provide clarification and immediate feedback. (See "Instructional Methods" in Chapter 3 for further discussion of direct instruction.) Research supports the use of a direct instruction model when teaching reading (see Chapter 8, "Literacy Strategies," for a full discussion of evidence-based reading instruction).

Evolving from the works of John Dewey, Jean Piaget, Lev Vygotsky, and other proponents of child-centered methods, **constructivism** is a learner-centered approach to teaching that emphasizes teaching for understanding, predicated on the concept that students construct knowledge by making connections between present learning experiences and the existing knowledge they already possess. Teachers must establish learning environments that provide experiences from which learners can construct meaning based on what they already know. Constructivist teachers help learners to reinvent their knowledge, thus creating new understandings. To develop understanding about a concept, students need to see the whole picture and also need to be able to break it down into its various parts. Constructivist teachers take a whole-to-parts approach, with the content organized around broad concepts. When students break down a concept into parts, they can understand how the parts fit together because they know what the whole looks like.

In constructivist lessons, teachers intentionally help students connect new learning to prior understandings, foster a view of learning as a personally meaningful pursuit, promote a sense of responsibility for one's own learning, and encourage exploration, problem solving, inquiry, and discovery in individual and collaborative settings.

Constructivist teachers recognize the power of group dynamics and the "critical role of social groups in the development of understanding" (FLDOE Bureau of School Improvement, 2006, *Learning Theories and Their Implications to Teaching and Teachers,* p. 1). They use a variety of collaborative strategies such as cooperative learning groups, teaming, and pairing, along with class discussions to create a rich environment of productive communication and interactive problem solving and inquiry.

Constructivist learning encourages students to think creatively and critically, to consider carefully, to make decisions, and to reflect. Students are actively engaged—often in collaborative groups—in seeking answers to questions and solutions to actual or authentic problems. They reflect on their ideas and communicate them as a regular part of instruction and are provided with opportunities to discover principles on their own. Student autonomy and initiative are encouraged. Learning is negotiated between the teacher and the students. This practice results in decreasing the number of activities controlled by the teacher, thus empowering the students to assume responsibility for their own learning.

Checkpoint

Fill in the blank.

1. The appropriate use of _____, which is a pleasant consequence that follows a behavior, is an essential strategy associated with behaviorism.

2. Giving gold star stickers is an example of using _____ (intrinsic, extrinsic) reinforcers.

3. Taking away a desirable reward is an example of _____ (positive, negative) punishment.

4. Constructivist teachers establish learning environments that provide experiences from which the learner can _____ meaning based on what the learner already knows.

5. In constructivist classrooms, students are encouraged to assume _____ for their own learning.

Mark as true or false.

6. _____ (a) Detention is an example of negative reinforcement.

_____ (b) In Florida, cognitive psychology approaches are not as acceptable as approaches grounded in behaviorism.

_____ (c) Constructivist approaches are mainly teacher-centered.

Checkpoint Answers

1. reinforcement

2. extrinsic

3. negative

4. construct

5. responsibility

6. (a) false; (b) false; (c) false

MTSS PS/RtI

Florida's **Multi-Tiered System of Supports (MTSS)** is an integrated data-driven model of academic and behavioral instruction and intervention. Two statewide MTSS projects are Problem Solving/Response to Intervention (PS/RtI) and Florida's Positive Behavior Support/RtI for Behavior (FLPBS RtI:B). As a term, **RtI** is the change in performance or behavior that results from an intervention (Gresham, 2003). **PS/RtI** is a data-based decision-making model that enables educators to match instruction and/or intervention to learners' areas of specific need as soon as those needs become apparent. Similarly, **FLPBS RtI:B** addresses problem student behaviors using Positive Behavior Support (PBS) within the framework of an RtI model (see "FLPBS RtI:B" in Chapter 2 for a discussion of this topic).

The basic premise of MTSS PS/RtI is for students to receive an array of high-quality, research-based instruction and/or interventions in multi-tiered learning situations (all students, small-group, or one-on-one) to increase the expectation that they will achieve district grade-level/subject area proficiency levels. Differentiating instruction in a three-tiered model that uses increasingly "intense" (increased time, smaller group size, narrower focus) instruction and support based on **ongoing progress monitoring (OPM)** and data analysis is the framework for MTSS PS/RtI.

Tier 1 (Universal) instruction provides general core academic instruction to all students in whole-group or small-group settings in the general education classroom. Differentiated instruction occurs based on students' diverse learning abilities. Instructional time for a particular content/subject area is based on district standards, which must comply with state guidelines/regulations. On average, 80 percent of students are expected to achieve academic success (that is, achieve district grade-level/subject area expectations) with Tier 1 instruction.

Tier 2 (Targeted) instruction is targeted, supplemental skills-focused instruction that uses evidence-based interventions. It is delivered to only small groups (of three to five students). Students are grouped for this supplemental instruction based on common academic needs identified through the use of formal and informal assessment data. They receive Tier 2 instruction (in addition to their Tier 1 instruction) to help them catch up. It must be integrated with Tier 1 content and grade-level expectations. Tier 2 instruction can be provided in the general education classroom by the general education teacher or by a supplemental instruction teacher; or it can be provided outside of the general education classroom. The number of minutes of instruction must be greater than the number of minutes typically provided to students for that skill focus. On average, 15 percent of students might need Tier 2 interventions.

Tier 3 (Intensive) instruction uses the most intensive, evidence-based interventions and support. Usually, Tier 3 instruction is provided to students individually or in very small groups (of two or three students). The interventions for these students focus on skills that assessment data indicate are the greatest barriers to their learning. Candidates for Tier 3 instruction are students who are most at risk of failure and need concentrated instruction. Compared to Tiers 1 and 2, Tier 3 instruction has the most instructional time, smallest group size (often, one student), and narrowest skills focus. It also provides extensive opportunities for practice, error correction, and feedback. On average, about 5 percent of students might need Tier 3 interventions when assessments show that Tier 1 instruction and Tier 2 instruction have not resulted in the student achieving desired learning goals.

Teachers should be aware that the three tiers describe different instructional levels of help that students need at some particular time. These are not instructional categories that students are locked into. Instead, the levels of support a student receives will increase or decrease if the student's level of need changes.

A principal idea behind MTSS PS/RtI is that proactive continuous progress monitoring of students' performance and delivery of appropriate support and interventions should be an ongoing part of the educational experience of all Florida students, from kindergarten through graduation. Instead of waiting until students fail when they are typically too far behind to reach grade-level expectations through interventions normally available in public schools, MTSS PS/RtI procedures identify and begin interventions early, monitor frequently, and modify based on student response to intervention. A data collection and assessment system is used to inform decisions at the different tier levels.

In addition, an essential feature of MTSS PS/RtI is a problem-solving process that is implemented across the tier levels. Four critical questions drive the ongoing problem-solving cycle: "What is the problem?", "Why is this happening?", "What are we going to do about it?", and "How well are interventions working?" The goal of the process is to improve the effectiveness of instruction/interventions to maximize achievement of positive outcomes for students.

MTSS PS/RtI is a significant initiative in Florida. The FLDOE has set up an MTSS website (www.florida-rti.org/) that provides up-to-date information and innovative resources for educators in Florida. The goal is "to ensure consistent movement toward maximizing student achievement" (www.florida-rti.org/, accessed 2014). Schools are held accountable for implementing MTSS PS/RtI and must document that interventions for students are delivered with fidelity and appropriate intensity (FLDOE, 2013e).

Checkpoint

Fill in the blank.

1. MTSS PS/RtI involves _____ instruction and/or interventions to meet the diverse needs of learners.

2. The basic premise of MTSS PS/RtI is that all students must receive high-quality, _____ instruction in multi-tiered learner situations.

3. MTSS PS/RtI uses a _____-tier delivery system.

Mark as true or false.

4. _____ (a) A principal idea behind MTSS PS/RtI is that waiting until students fail is the most effective way to determine appropriate interventions.

   _____ (b) MTSS PS/RtI is only for students with disabilities.

Checkpoint Answers

1. matching

2. research-based

3. three

4. (a) false; (b) false

Accommodations for Students with Disabilities

The Individuals with Disabilities Education Act (IDEA 2004, revised in 2007) and Chapter 6A-6 (FAC) require teachers in Florida to provide needed modifications and accommodations to students with disabilities. **Modifications** are changes in what a student is expected to learn and may include changes to content, requirements, and expected level of mastery (Rule 6A-6.03028(2)(f), FAC), which might, at graduation, result in the awarding of a special diploma to the student receiving the modifications. **Accommodations** are changes that are made in how the student accesses information and demonstrates performance (Rule 6A-6.03028(2)(e), FAC). Accommodations are the adaptations that need to be made so that ESE students with disabilities can participate in the general curriculum as fully as possible and, thus, be eligible for a standard diploma. When providing accommodations, teachers should avoid making the ESE learner feel singled out or stigmatized. (See "Professional Conduct with ESE Students" in Chapter 6 for further discussion of ESE students.)

The focus of this section is on accommodations. Students eligible for accommodations are those with physical or mental disabilities who are students in ESE with an Individual Educational Plan (IEP) or who qualify under Section 504 of the Rehabilitation Act of 1973 and have 504 plans. State Board of Education Rule 6A-6, FAC, gives the following categories for exceptionalities:

- **Students with intellectual disabilities:** Have significantly below average general intellectual and adaptive functioning (that is, the skills necessary to function at home, at school, and in the community) manifested during the developmental period, with significant delays in academic skills. (Rule 6A-6.03011, FAC)

- **Students with speech impairments:** Have disorders of speech sounds, fluency, or voice that interfere with communication, adversely affect performance and/or functioning in the educational environment, and result in the need for exceptional student education. (Rule 6A-6.03012, FAC)

- **Students who are deaf or hard of hearing:** Have a hearing loss aided or unaided, that impacts the processing of linguistic information and adversely affects performance in the educational environment. The degree of loss may range from mild to profound. (Rule 6A-6.03013, FAC)

- **Students who are visually impaired:** Include the following: (a) a student who is blind, has no vision, or has little potential for using vision; (b) a student who has low vision. (Rule 6A-6.03014, FAC)

- **Students who are physically impaired with orthopedic impairment:** Have a severe skeletal, muscular, or neuro-muscular impairment. The term includes impairments resulting from congenital anomalies (for example, including but not limited to skeletal deformity or spina bifida) and impairments resulting from other causes (for example, including but not limited to cerebral palsy or amputations). (Rule 6A-6.030151, FAC)

- **Students who are physically impaired with other health impairment:** Have a limited strength, vitality, or alertness, including a heightened alertness to environmental stimuli, resulting in limited alertness with respect to the educational environment, that is due to chronic or acute health problems. This includes but is not limited to asthma, attention deficit disorder or attention deficit hyperactivity disorder, Tourette syndrome, diabetes, epilepsy, a heart condition, hemophilia, lead poisoning, leukemia, nephritis, rheumatic fever, sickle cell anemia, and acquired brain injury. (Rule 6A-6.030152, FAC)

- **Students with traumatic brain injury:** Have an acquired injury to the brain caused by an external physical force resulting in total or partial functional disability or psychosocial impairment, or both, that adversely affects educational performance. The term applies to mild, moderate, or severe open or closed head injuries resulting in impairment in one or more areas such as cognition; language; memory; attention; reasoning; abstract thinking; judgment; problem solving; sensory, perceptual, and motor abilities; psychosocial behavior; physical functions; information processing; or speech. The term includes anoxia due to trauma. The term does not include brain injuries that are congenital, degenerative, or induced by birth trauma. (Rule 6A-6.030153, FAC)

- **Students with emotional/behavioral disabilities:** Have persistent (are not sufficiently responsive to implemented evidence-based interventions) and consistent emotional or behavioral responses that adversely affect performance in the educational environment that cannot be attributed to age, culture, gender, or ethnicity. (Rule 6A-6.03016, FAC)

- **Students with specific learning disabilities:** Have a disorder in one or more of the basic learning processes involved in understanding or using language, spoken or written, that may manifest in significant difficulties affecting the ability to listen, speak, read, write, spell, or do mathematics. Associated conditions may include but are not limited to dyslexia, dyscalculia, dysgraphia, or developmental aphasia. A specific learning disability does not include learning problems that are primarily the result of a visual, hearing, motor, intellectual, or emotional/behavioral disability, Limited English Proficiency, or environmental, cultural, or economic factors. (Rule 6A-6.03018, FAC)

- **Students with autism spectrum disorder:** Have a disorder from a range of pervasive developmental disorders that adversely affects a student's functioning and results in the need for specially designed instruction and related services. Autism spectrum disorder is characterized by an uneven developmental profile and a pattern of qualitative impairments in social interaction, communication, and the presence of restricted repetitive and/or stereotyped patterns of behavior, interests, or activities. These characteristics may manifest in a variety of combinations and range from mild to severe. Autism spectrum disorder may include autistic disorder, pervasive developmental disorder not otherwise specified, Asperger's disorder, or other related pervasive developmental disorders. (Rule 6A-6.03023, FAC)

According to the *Accommodations Manual: How to Select, Administer, and Evaluate Use of Accommodations for Instruction and Assessment of Students with Disabilities,* 2nd Edition (Thompson, Morse, Sharpe, and Hall, 2005), accommodations may be made in four general ways:

- **Presentation accommodations:** The adaptive ways information and tests are presented to students. For instance, for learners with visual impairments, use large print; books, text, or notes on tape; peer or adult readers; note-takers; preferential seating; magnifying devices; DVDs and CDs; large-key calculators; or devices that use synthesized speech (for example, "talking" calculators, text-to-speech technology). For learners who are deaf or hard of hearing, use visuals and graphics, gestures and visual cues, note-takers, sign language interpreters, audio amplifying devices, and/or speech-to-text technology. For learners who are easily distracted, use prearranged cues and signals, checklists and agendas, highlighters, and written step-by-step instructions. For learners who have trouble comprehending material, provide graphic organizers and overviews, vocabulary lists, and checklists; use repetition, paraphrasing, and summarizing; use concrete materials and hands-on activities; and use peer helpers and cooperative learning groups.

- **Response accommodations:** The adaptive ways students are allowed to complete assignments and tests. For instance, for learners with visual impairments, allow the use of personal note-takers, Braillers, large-key calculators, and devices with an audio component (for example, talking calculators or thermometers), and accept oral responses, as well as responses through a scribe, on tape, and/or through speech-to-text technology. For learners who are deaf or hard of hearing, allow the use of sign language interpreters, word processors, visual organizers, and/or spelling and grammar assistive devices. For learners who have physical impairments and those who have speech and language impairments, allow the use of scribes, assistive communication devices, and/or tape recorders. For learners who have specific learning disabilities, allow the use of word processors, spelling and grammar assistive devices, word prediction software, written notes, math tables and formula sheets, and/or calculators.

- **Setting accommodations:** The adaptive ways to change the setting to make completion of assignments and tests more appropriate for the student. For instance, for learners with visual impairments and those who are deaf or hard of hearing, change location to reduce distractions to the student and to surrounding students or to provide access to special equipment. For learners who have physical impairments, change location to provide access to special equipment. For learners who are easily distracted, change location to reduce distractions and/or use white noise or music to mask sounds in the environment.

- **Timing and scheduling accommodations:** The adaptive ways to alter time constraints and scheduling to be more appropriate for the student. For most categories, give extended time based on the needs of the student. For learners who have trouble concentrating, build in frequent breaks and/or split assignments or tests into subparts and give at different times or on different days (p. 14).

It is important to note that in order for an accommodation to be allowed on a statewide assessment, the accommodation must be specified on the IEP or 504 plan and used regularly in classroom instruction and assessment. Furthermore, parents must be informed about and their permission obtained for any accommodation not allowed on statewide assessments. For instance, students cannot use spell checkers or grammar checkers when taking the statewide assessments.

Note: See the section "Learning Environment Accommodations for Learners in Exceptional Student Education (ESE)" in Chapter 2 for a discussion of accommodations for students with disabilities that affect their behavior in the classroom.

Checkpoint

Fill in the blank.

1. Modifications are changes in _____ a student is expected to learn.

2. Accommodations are changes in _____ a student accesses information and demonstrates performance.

3. In order for an accommodation to be allowed on a statewide assessment, the accommodation must be specified on the IEP or 504 and used _____ in classroom instruction and assessment.

Mark as true or false.

4. _____ (a) Teachers are required by law to make accommodations for students with disabilities.

    _____ (b) Giving students extended time is an example of an accommodation.

Checkpoint Answers

1. what

2. how

3. regularly

4. (a) true; (b) true

Selecting Technology

Technology includes projectors, interactive whiteboards, computers, scanners, printers/copiers, sophisticated calculators, digital gaming, social networking technologies, e-readers, webcams, smart phones, iPads, software/apps, DVDs, CDs, TV, and the Internet. Teachers must learn to use these tools effectively. They should be knowledgeable and selective in choosing the appropriate technology for instructional purposes.

Advanced technology adds new dimensions to teaching and learning. Instead of writing with pen and paper, students can use word processors with spell checkers, grammar checkers, and thesauruses to create written documents such as letters, themes, essays, and research papers. An advantage of word processing is that corrections and revisions can be made without retyping the entire document. Simulation software creates an interactive, reality-based environment. It allows the user to explore, investigate, and problem-solve in a simulated real-life setting. Spreadsheets can perform mathematical or statistical calculations on data and create graphs, charts, and other data summaries. They can be used by teachers for making grade books and by students for recording data from experiments or inventory for a make-believe company. Scanners can convert graphics into digitized images. Students can access resource material like multimedia encyclopedias on CDs or use interactive apps and software packages. They also can link up to other resources and to students at other schools in the state, country, and world via the Internet.

Technology can help teachers create learning environments that change and interact with students' needs. **Assistive technology** (any item, piece of equipment, or product system, whether acquired commercially off the shelf, modified, or customized) can be used to increase, maintain, or improve the functional capabilities of children with disabilities (Section 34, Code of Federal Regulations). **Computer assisted instruction (CAI)** can be used for individualized instruction. CAI sequences content into small units of information and provides immediate feedback to the student on the student's grasp of the content, thereby allowing the student to monitor progress while proceeding through the program. **Blended learning** is a term applied to an education program in which students learn in part in a traditional school setting and in part through online learning.

Technology in the classroom can benefit students by

- offering more control and involvement in the learning process.
- making learning more interesting.
- promoting investigative skills.
- serving as an access to almost unlimited sources of information.
- developing skills to measure, monitor, and improve performance.
- enabling communication with people from many parts of the world, bringing the sights, sounds, and thoughts of another language and culture into the classroom.
- providing opportunities to apply knowledge to simulated or real-life projects.
- developing readiness for a high-tech world of work.

Source: *Secondary Physical Education Curriculum Guide, 2003–2004, Brevard Public Schools*

Technology literacy is a must for Florida teachers. They need to have a sound understanding of the nature and operation of technology systems and be proficient in the use of technology both for accomplishing teacher tasks and enhancing learning opportunities for their students. For example, they should know basic computer terminology; be able to solve routine hardware and software problems; be able to save and move files; be able to use word processing, database, and spreadsheet software; be able to import graphics and images; be able to use e-mail to send and receive messages and attachments; be able to use scanners, digital/streaming video, and digital cameras; be able to create simple web pages; and be able to efficiently use the Internet as a resource in their classrooms for performing their professional duties (such as accessing and recording student data) and for professional development. Furthermore, teachers need to know Internet safety issues (see the section "Professional Responsibility Regarding Internet Safety" in Chapter 6 for a discussion of this topic). Finally, even though devices, apps, software, and so on might come highly recommended, teachers should heed the caveat "Buyer beware!" and personally preview technology for the classroom before using it.

Checkpoint

Fill in the blank.

1. Teachers should be knowledgeable and selective in choosing _____ technology.

2. An advantage of using word processing in writing is that corrections and revisions can be made without _____ the entire document.

3. Technology can help teachers create a learning environment that changes and interacts with students' _____.

4. In blended learning, students learn in part in a traditional school setting and in part through _____ learning.

5. Teachers should personally _____ technology for the classroom before using it.

Checkpoint Answers

1. appropriate

2. retyping

3. needs

4. online

5. preview

Summary

In summary, effective planning is a thoughtful, decision-making process. Effective teachers have a strong foundational knowledge of human development and learning theories, and they apply this knowledge to create learning environments in which students engage in active, purposeful, and developmentally appropriate learning. They understand that as students mature, they progress through cognitive, psychosocial, and physical developmental stages. Moreover, effective teachers recognize that students' developmental characteristics affect their performance in school; therefore, the teachers design instruction based on an understanding of how students learn that is responsive to the varied characteristics of students in their classrooms.

Sample Questions

1. Which of the following would be the most appropriate way to express the action element of an instructional objective?

   A. The student will understand the solar system.
   B. The student will be aware of the solar system.
   C. The student will recite the names of the planets.
   D. The student will know the names of the planets.

2. A first-grade teacher begins a science lesson on the effect of heat on matter by placing an egg in boiling water and asking students to predict how it will differ from an uncooked egg if both eggs are broken open. Beginning the lesson in this way is likely to promote learning by

   A. stimulating students' interest in the topic of the lesson.
   B. encouraging students to examine a problem systematically.
   C. creating a temporary sense of disbelief in the students.
   D. providing students with the conceptual framework for the lesson.

3. "Given examples of 10 mammals, the student will be able to classify 9 out of 10 correctly as herbivore, carnivore, or omnivore." This statement is an example of a(n)

   A. affective objective.
   B. cognitive objective.
   C. psychomotor objective.
   D. reflective objective.

4. Which of the following instructional strategies is most compatible with a behaviorist point of view?

   A. discovery learning
   B. project-based learning
   C. inquiry learning
   D. direct instruction

5. A teacher makes a student remain in the classroom during a school pep rally as a consequence for inappropriate behavior. This measure is an example of which of the following?

   A. positive reinforcement
   B. negative reinforcement
   C. positive punishment
   D. negative punishment

Answer Explanations for Sample Questions

1. **C.** Notice that you must select the answer choice that is the *most* appropriate way to express the action element of an instructional objective. Choice **C** is the correct response. The statement in **C** contains the action verb *recite,* so it is the most appropriate way to express the action element of an instructional objective. Eliminate **A, B,** and **D** because these statements do not contain action verbs.

2. **A.** Choice **A** is the correct response. Beginning the lesson with the egg demonstration is likely to promote learning by stimulating students' interest in the topic of the lesson. The other answer choices are not supported by the information given in the question.

3. **B.** The statement in the question is an example of an instructional objective. Instructional objectives are classified as affective, cognitive, or psychomotor. Eliminate **D** because this choice is not a type of lesson objective. Eliminate **A** because affective objectives involve feelings and dispositions. Eliminate **C** because psychomotor objectives involve physical activity on the part of the student. Cognitive objectives involve thinking capabilities such as classifying mammals as herbivores, carnivores, or omnivores. Therefore, **B** is the correct response.

4. **D.** Notice that you must select the answer choice that is *most* compatible with a behaviorist point of view. Of the instructional strategies given in the answer choices, direct instruction is the one that is most compatible with a behaviorist point of view. Thus, **D** is the correct response. The instructional strategies given in the other answer choices are compatible with a constructivist point of view.

5. **D.** Staying in the classroom instead of going to a pep rally is an undesirable consequence, so eliminate **A** and **B** because reinforcement is a desirable consequence. Eliminate **C** because positive punishment involves giving an undesirable consequence (for example, extra work). Choice **D** is the correct response because negative punishment involves taking away a desirable reward (for example, going to a pep rally) in order to deter undesirable behavior.

Competency 2: Learning Environments

Competency Description and Key Indicators

According to the *Competencies and Skills Required for Teacher Certification in Florida*, 20th Edition (available at www.fldoe.org/asp/ftce/pdf/ftce20edition.pdf), **Competency 2** of the FTCE PEd Test addresses **Learning Environments** as follows:

> *Knowledge of appropriate student-centered learning environments*

Key indicators:

- Select and use appropriate techniques for organizing, allocating, and managing the resources of time, space, and attention in a variety of learning environments (e.g., face-to-face, virtual).
- Apply appropriate strategies and procedures to manage individual student behaviors and group dynamics.
- Use effective techniques for communicating high expectations to all students.
- Evaluate and adapt the learning environment to accommodate the needs and backgrounds (i.e., cultural, home language, family) of all students.
- Apply relevant techniques for modeling appropriate oral and written communication skills.
- Determine skills and practices that encourage innovation and foster a safe climate of openness, inquiry, equity, and support for all students.
- Apply information and communication technologies to maintain a student-centered learning environment.
- Identify assistive technologies that enable all students to effectively communicate and achieve their educational goals.

Overview

Effective teachers know how to establish **Learning Environments** that maximize the potential for students' academic success and behavior self-management. The teachers understand how to involve their students in classroom communities whose members are responsible, cooperative, and mutually encouraging. The learning environments are developmentally appropriate and designed to make students feel safe and secure.

This chapter provides a general review of Learning Environments with sample questions and explanations at the end of the chapter. Checkpoint exercises are found throughout the review material. These exercises give you an opportunity to practice what you just learned. The answers to the Checkpoint exercises are found immediately following the set of exercises. When doing the Checkpoint exercises, you should cover up the answers. Then check your answers when you've finished the exercises. The sample questions at the end of this chapter are multiple-choice questions that are similar to what you might expect to see on the FTCE PEd Test. The answer explanations for the sample questions are provided immediately after the questions.

Effective Classroom Management

The key to being a successful classroom manager is *planning* and *preplanning*. **Planning** means being prepared each day with lesson plans and everything needed to implement those plans. **Preplanning** means going through each lesson mentally from a student's point of view and anticipating explanations, information, and directions needed in order to carry out the lesson successfully. Teaching well-planned lessons using evidence-based instructional strategies that actively engage students in learning is a powerful way to deter undesirable student behavior.

Effective managers are able to secure the cooperation of students, maintain their involvement in instructional tasks, and attend to the clerical or business duties of the classroom quickly and smoothly. They are courteous and respectful; they maximize academic learning time; and, in discipline situations, they ensure at all times that the dignity of the student, even the seriously disruptive student, is preserved. Furthermore, the classroom environment is organized and predictable, providing an overall secure structure in which maximum student learning can take place.

Good classroom managers facilitate the development of responsibility and self-regulation in students. They welcome student participation in developing classroom rules and procedures and engage students' assistance in resolving problems and conflicts in the classroom (for example, through class meetings and conflict resolution). The feeling is cultivated that the classroom is the students' classroom and that each student has a definite responsibility in helping determine and maintain the standards by which it functions. Within this collaborative context, clear, appropriate, consistent, and fair expectations for student behavior are established and students are held accountable to age-appropriate standards of acceptable behavior. The classroom incentives/rewards and consequences system is fair, equitable, and consistent with school-wide standards. Meaningful consequences for inappropriate behavior are decided upon and adhered to. Responses to student misconduct are fair and equitable without regard to students' personal characteristics such as race, ethnicity, sex, English Language Learner (ELL) or Exceptional Student Education (ESE) status, migrant or homeless status, national origin, sexual orientation, or religion.

Successful classroom managers are skilled both in preventing behavior problems and in dealing appropriately with them when they do arise. When dealing with problems, they listen to and acknowledge students' feelings and frustrations and respond with respect. They guide students to resolve conflicts and model skills that encourage students to solve problems constructively. They help students to come to the realization that conflict can be positive and that, when handled appropriately, can promote improved relationships among students. Moreover, they encourage parents* to become active partners in promoting and reinforcing appropriate behavior.

*Note: By Florida school law, a *parent* is either or both parents, a guardian, or any person in a parental relationship to a student or who has charge over a student in place of the parent.

When talking with a student who has misbehaved, teachers need to make sure that the student knows that he or she has done something that is unacceptable, and they should ask for an explanation from the student. It is important that the student understands why the behavior is unacceptable and cannot be tolerated. Teachers should be careful to talk about the behavior, not the student. Effective teachers describe what they saw, how they feel about it, how it affects others, and what needs to be done. They try to get the student to accept responsibility for the misbehavior and to agree not to commit the offense again. In some cases, the teacher might need to help the student develop a plan for changing his or her behavior so that it becomes acceptable. In other words, good teachers use students' mistakes as learning opportunities in the caring atmosphere of a warm, supportive classroom environment.

Creating and managing smoothly functioning learning communities is central to the work of teachers. Effective teachers use a variety of ways of flexibly grouping students for instruction and interventions that support collaboration and interaction among students. At appropriate times, students have opportunities to work as a whole class, in small groups, and individually. When teachers are working with small groups, they need to be clear about directions and expectations. Additionally, they need to spend time moving through the room and checking on the groups so that they can offer reinforcement and feedback to students about their academic work as well as their group process skills. (See the section "Ability Grouping" later in this chapter for further discussion of appropriate grouping practices.)

Students want structure and need limits. They also expect teachers to treat them with dignity and be consistent and fair in enforcing classroom rules. The following guidelines for classroom management have been gleaned from USDOE (www.ed.gov/) and FLDOE (www.fldoe.org/) online materials and the works of Cotton (1993), Slavin (2008), and Brophy (1983):

- Align classroom procedures and rules with school-wide expectations.
- Involve students in creating age-appropriate classroom rules and fair, meaningful consequences for infractions.
- Teach classroom rules and procedures at the beginning of the year.

- Give reasons for consequences when going over the rules.
- Set clear standards and limits for classroom behavior.
- Apply the established rules and standards for behavior consistently and equitably.
- Learn students' names by the end of the first day and use their names regularly.
- Establish norms for everyday activities so that students know, for example, the appropriate voice level for various situations, how to make transitions, how to get help, and how to turn in homework.
- Initially, work with the whole class and use activities with low content demand and high emphasis on procedures while students are adjusting to classroom rules and procedures.
- Use well-planned lessons and a variety of teaching strategies in varied learning settings—whole class, small group, or individual.
- Adapt instruction to meet students' needs and special characteristics (for example, learning style, modality, and strength).
- Begin lessons promptly and provide transitions between activities.
- Use signals (bell, clapping pattern) for transitions.
- Give explicit directions so that students know what to do and how to do it.
- Anticipate problems and try to prevent or minimize the effect of their occurrence.
- Make sure that all students have access to instructional materials.
- Maintain instructional momentum at a brisk, but appropriate, pace.
- Include all students in class discussions, showing respect and sensitivity to each student.
- Elicit students' cooperation, and praise them when they give it.
- Promote students' development of internal locus of control.
- Monitor student behavior and provide feedback to students about what they are doing correctly and what they still need to work on.
- Approach off-task students promptly and privately to avoid power struggles and possible negative impact on the classroom learning environment.
- Be quick to stop or redirect misconduct.
- Whenever possible, begin with the least intrusive intervention to stop or redirect misconduct.
- Use a variety of verbal and nonverbal signals to stop misconduct.
- If a discipline situation involving a "perpetrator" and a "victim" occurs, immediately stop the perpetrator's actions, but then do what is necessary to take care of the victim.
- When a student misbehaves, focus on the misconduct, not on the student.
- Make sure that students who misbehave know what they did wrong, why the behavior is unacceptable, and what appropriate behavior should have occurred in place of the misbehavior.
- Use incidences of misconduct to teach appropriate behavior.
- If discipline in a student's home is inconsistent with classroom rules, explain to the student that obeying the rules at school is necessary, but do so with sensitivity and respect for the student's home culture.
- Consider placing students with behavior problems in peer tutoring arrangements, either as tutors or tutees, as appropriate.
- Model positive behavior and constructive conflict resolution.
- Encourage students to assume responsibility for their own behavior.
- Explicitly teach (for example, through modeling and role playing) self-monitoring and self-regulating behaviors.
- Be a good listener.
- Elicit ideas from students on how to prevent and stop misconduct.
- Contact parents and elicit their help and support for appropriate classroom behavior.
- Be warm and friendly toward students.

- Show students you have a sense of humor, but do not make fun of students.
- Communicate high expectations to all students.
- Make sure that the classroom is physically comfortable.
- Make appropriate accommodations in the learning environment for learners in Exceptional Student Education (ESE) who have disabilities. (See the section "Learning Environment Accommodations for Learners in Exceptional Student Education (ESE)" later in this chapter for a discussion on this topic.)
- Avoid punitive discipline measures such as writing students' names on the board or other public display, taking away privileges, or assigning extra work.
- Avoid using threats, bribes, or coaxing to elicit appropriate behavior.
- Avoid sarcasm and put-downs.
- Avoid giving long lectures to students who misbehave.
- Never react to student misbehavior in anger.
- Never embarrass, humiliate, or disparage a student.
- Never harass or discriminate against a student.
- Be on the alert for bullying, intimidation, sexual harassment, alcohol or tobacco use, or other behaviors that threaten school safety.
- Make students aware of building procedures to follow in case of an emergency.
- Maintain a safe and orderly environment in a manner consistent with federal and state statutes. (See the section "Important Statutes Related to Classroom Management" later in this chapter for a discussion of this topic.)

Checkpoint

Fill in the blank.

1. Good classroom managers facilitate the development of _____ and self-regulation in students.
2. Teachers' responses to student misconduct should be fair and _____ without regard to students' personal characteristics.
3. Good teachers use students' mistakes as _____ opportunities.

Mark as true or false.

4. _____ (a) A well-planned lesson is a deterrent to misconduct.

   _____ (b) Teachers should make a practice of giving long lectures to students who misbehave.

Checkpoint Answers

1. responsibility
2. equitable
3. learning
4. (a) true; (b) false

Procedures and Rules

Procedures are guidelines for regular daily routines (transitions, homework policy, turning in papers, bathroom policy, and so on). **Rules** specify behavior expectations (be respectful, be responsible, be safe). When developing their classroom procedures and rules, it is imperative that teachers use their school's universal (school-wide) behavior expectations. Students need to understand and experience that the entire school community is working together to create a positive, safe, and productive learning environment.

Teachers need to spend time at the beginning of the school year teaching students procedures and rules of the classroom and school. Procedures and rules should be explicitly taught using modeling, role playing, and practicing with monitoring and feedback. Thereafter, teachers should monitor compliance and frequently model expected behaviors. They should regularly review procedures and rules with students to keep them fresh (i.e., after breaks/holidays). In grades 5 through 10, disciplinary aspects of classroom management become more pronounced, so consistent enforcement of behavior standards is critical. In grades 11 and 12, most students have passed through the oppositional phase of adolescence, although the teacher still will need to reinforce expected appropriate behavior. Students at risk of academic failure, regardless of grade level, need explicit orientation to and frequent review of classroom rules and procedures.

All students need to be made aware of and to practice building-level procedures that should be followed for campus emergencies, including life-threatening emergencies such as weapon use and hostage situations. By state law, the district school board must "formulate and prescribe policies and procedures for emergency drills and for actual emergencies, including but not limited to fires, natural disasters, and bomb threats, for all the public schools of the district which comprise grades K-12. District school board policies shall include commonly used alarm system responses for specific types of emergencies and verification by each school that drills have been provided as required by law and fire protection codes" (Section 1006.07 (4)(a), F. S.). Teachers should make sure they know the specific codes and procedures that are used on their particular campuses for emergencies.

Effective teachers post classroom rules that are fair and appropriate for the grade level. For the rules to be effective, the students must know the rules and their consequences, and the teacher must enforce the rules consistently and impartially. Consequences should be **logical** (that is, clearly related to the behavior violation) and **proportional** (that is, matched to the severity of the infraction). In general, rules should be positively stated and, to foster retention by students, should number no more than five.

With regard to discipline, effective teachers are proactive rather than reactive. They anticipate when misconduct is likely to occur and take action beforehand to prevent or limit its occurrence. When a discipline situation does arise, effective classroom managers are quick to stop or redirect off-task or inappropriate behavior. They use the least intrusive means—for instance, dealing with potentially serious disruptions early by using eye contact, moving around the room, or providing short, quiet comments to a disruptive student, and talking privately with students who misbehave to avoid power struggles and to prevent face-saving gestures from students. Stronger measures are used only when the teacher has exhausted all other options to curtail misbehavior. Nevertheless, when a disruption or behavior threatens the maintenance of a safe and orderly classroom environment, a teacher should send the student to an appropriate administrator along with an **office discipline referral (ODR)** form that contains a written description of the incident.

Teachers should avoid using harsh or punitive discipline measures. Epstein et al. (2008) recommended that "teachers adopt an overall positive and problem-solving approach … because harsh or punitive discipline is not effective in increasing the likelihood of appropriate behavior and tends to elicit student resentment and resistance" (p. 34). (See the section "Important Statutes Related to Classroom Management" later in this chapter for information about legal issues related to handling disruptive discipline incidents.)

Checkpoint

Fill in the blank.

1. Students at risk of academic failure need _____ orientation to classroom rules and procedures.

2. With regard to discipline, effective teachers are _____ rather than reactive.

3. Harsh or punitive discipline tends to elicit student resentment and _____.

Mark as true or false.

4. _____ (a) Consequences should be logical and proportional.

   _____ (b) Teachers should use punitive-based discipline so that students will know that the teachers are in charge.

Checkpoint Answers

1. explicit
2. proactive
3. resistance
4. (a) true; (b) false

FLPBS RtI:B

Florida's Positive Behavior Support Response to Intervention for Behavior (FLPBS RtI:B) is an initiative, supported by Florida's Multi-Tiered System of Supports (MTSS), to create and sustain positive, safe, and productive learning environments in schools. School-wide FLPBS RtI:B is a three-tiered framework that uses data, problem solving, and decision making to provide a continuum of evidence-based interventions based on students' behavioral needs. Defining features of school-wide FLPBS RtI:B include

- explicit teaching of appropriate school behaviors.
- adequate time for students to practice appropriate school behaviors.
- progress assessment and program decisions based on data collected about student behavior.
- appropriate interventions validated by research.
- systematic monitoring of student progress.
- collaborative cooperation among school staff, families, and community members.

(Source: Florida Advisory Committee to the United States Commission on Civil Rights, 2011)

At Tier 1 (Universal), supports are applied to all students and are designed to promote positive behavior and prevent behavioral problems. Teachers' classroom management plans should be built upon and support the Tier 1 (school-wide) behavior expectations. For instance, teaching students the school-wide expectations and reinforcing students for displaying appropriate behaviors is a Tier 1 intervention that occurs at the classroom level. At Tier 2 (Group), research-based interventions are provided to small groups of students who need additional support beyond that provided in Tier 1. Tier 2 interventions should be easy to administer to small groups of students, with minimal time and staff involvement. At Tier 3 (Individual Student), focused, intensive interventions are provided to individual students. Tier 3 supports include the implementation of a **behavior implementation plan (BIP)** based on a **functional behavioral assessment (FBA).** The BIP is composed of individualized, assessment-based intervention strategies and requires more resources and staff time. Consequently, it provides a means for addressing the needs of individual students in a more comprehensive manner.

Checkpoint

Fill in the blank.

1. FLPBS RtI:B is a _____-tiered framework.
2. FLPBS RtI:B includes _____ teaching of appropriate school behaviors.
3. FLPBS RtI:B Tier 1 supports are designed to promote positive behavior and _____ behavioral problems.

Mark as true or false.

4. _____ (a) Tier 1 supports are applied to all students.

   _____ (b) Teachers' classroom management plans should be built upon and support the Tier 1 behavior expectations.

Checkpoint Answers

1. three

2. explicit

3. prevent

4. (a) true; (b) true

Praise

Praise, if used appropriately, can be a valuable tool for teachers. It is a way for teachers to inform students about what the students are doing right. Teachers should praise students frequently, especially students in early-childhood classrooms and low-performing students who are struggling. However, some experts contend that indiscriminate praise can have undesirable effects in the classroom. They assert that some teachers overuse global, nonspecific praise (for example, "Good job" or "Great") to the point that it becomes meaningless to students. Specific praise for desired performance and behavior is more powerful. Here are some guidelines for effectively using praise in the classroom.

Effective Praise

- Specifies the behavior or accomplishment that is worthy of praise—for example, "You did a very good job punctuating the sentences correctly on the quiz."
- Is genuine, honest, and not given randomly.
- Is given in a natural, not exaggerated, voice.
- Is most effective when done privately, rather than publicly in front of the whole class.
- Is given for effort and persistence as well as for accomplishments.
- Is given for risk taking and bold thinking, regardless of the "correctness" of the ideas—for example, "That is very good thinking about this issue, Dante."
- Is done in a way that encourages intrinsic motivation—for example, "You must feel pleased that you were able to name the planets from memory."
- Attributes success to effort (rather than to ability or luck).
- Implies that present success leads to high expectations for future successes.

Ineffective Praise

- Is global ("Good job," "Nice work") rather than specific.
- Is given indiscriminately, with little thought to meaning.
- Is reserved for only strong or correct responses from students.
- Rewards participation rather than the value of the effort or accomplishment.
- Attributes success to external forces rather than to the student's ability—for example, "You were lucky to get so many questions correct. Good job!"
- Is used publicly as a control technique—for example, "I like the way that Kelsey is paying attention while I'm talking."
- Suggests that the behavior or performance deserves praise because it pleases the teacher—for example, "I'm so happy that you finished your assignment on time."
- Fosters a climate in which students feel manipulated by the teacher.
- Creates a competitive climate in which students compare themselves to others in the classroom.
- Is overused to the point of being meaningless.

The amount of praise that teachers give students for appropriate behavior should substantially exceed the amount of reprimands they give to students. Research indicates that a ratio of about four to one for positive over corrective statements can improve students' academic and behavioral outcomes (Epstein et al., 2008). It is also a good idea to use the "Pause, Prompt, Praise" technique. If a student is struggling, *pause* (instead of assisting right away) to give him or her "think time" to figure out a correct response or to correct an error. If the student continues to struggle, then *prompt* with suggestions/hints or helpful questions to scaffold successful performance. When the student responds correctly, recognize his or her effort and achievement by offering meaningful, specific *praise*.

Checkpoint

Fill in the blank.

1. Praise should be _____, not global.

2. Teachers should avoid overusing global, nonspecific praise because it can become _____ to students.

3. Using praise to foster competition among students is a _____ (good, poor) practice.

4. "Good job" is an example of _____ (effective, ineffective) praise.

Checkpoint Answers

1. specific

2. meaningless

3. poor

4. ineffective

Teacher Expectations

Teacher expectations is a term used to describe a teacher's opinion of the likelihood that students will be successful. Research suggests that a teacher's attitude about students' abilities is an important classroom climate variable that is significantly related to student success. Teachers who exhibit high expectations toward their students have students who actually perform better. This phenomenon is often referred to as a **self-fulfilling prophecy,** which means that teachers get what they expect from students. Teachers who expect students to be successful have confidence in their students' abilities and treat them accordingly. This positive climate fosters students' belief in themselves and increases their ability to achieve.

Sometimes teachers unconsciously, rather than explicitly, convey low expectations to students. For example, a teacher might ask lower-level questions to at-risk students or minority students. This teacher behavior can send the message that the teacher believes these students are not capable of answering higher-level questions. Researchers have found a number of factors that influence how teachers perceive students. They warn that these potential sources of bias might result in disparate teacher expectations—for example:

- Socioeconomic status (SES)—lower expectations for lower-SES students
- Gender—lower expectations for elementary boys because of their slower maturation; lower expectations for girls in upper grades because of sex-role stereotyping
- Ethnicity—lower expectations for minorities
- Previous academic performance/standardized test scores—lower expectations for low performers

Teachers should monitor their interactions with students to make sure that they are communicating high expectations for all their students. Some ways are to

- promote the importance of education and each student's capacity for academic achievement.
- set realistic goals for students that can be achieved with effort, and recognize students when they are successful.

- adopt incentives that encourage individual progress toward a high, challenging, yet attainable, standard of performance, instead of emphasizing competition.
- clearly communicate goals and objectives to students and their responsibilities for attainment.
- be explicit about the teacher's expectations for learning and behavior and reiterate these expectations throughout the school year.
- provide regular, constructive feedback to students and information about grading criteria.
- engage all students in thought-provoking, challenging activities while avoiding diluted instruction for lower achievers.
- base academic grades on the measurement of students' performance according to established learning criteria (that is, the Next Generation Sunshine State Standards and benchmarks).
- adopt flexible behavior standards that allow students to interact when engaged in learning.
- for cooperative learning, use heterogeneous grouping practices, instead of separating high-achieving students from low achievers.

Checkpoint

Fill in the blank.

1. Teacher expectations are significantly related to student _____.

2. Teachers should adopt incentives that encourage individual progress rather than emphasize _____.

3. For cooperative learning, teachers should use _____ (heterogeneous, homogeneous) grouping practices.

Mark as true or false.

4. _____ (a) A self-fulfilling prophecy means that if a teacher expects little from students, the teacher is likely to get little.

_____ (b) To convey high expectations to low achievers, a teacher should set challenging, but attainable, performance standards.

_____ (c) Grouping low-ability students together provides a risk-free environment that makes them feel like they can succeed.

Checkpoint Answers

1. success

2. competition

3. heterogeneous

4. (a) true; (b) true; (c) false

Socioeconomic Status

Slavin (2008) contended that, in the United States, the culture of our schools reflects mainstream, middle-class values. Payne (2006) agreed and maintained that this circumstance results in a *hidden curriculum* that economically disadvantaged students must navigate without explicitly knowing it exists. Researchers have found that middle socioeconomic status (SES) teachers often have low expectations for low-SES students, which, in turn, might result in low achievement for these students. Indeed, on average, children from lower-SES backgrounds are likely to be less successful in school than are children from middle-SES backgrounds. Slavin (2008) made the point that teachers should be aware that often, economically disadvantaged students are also educationally disadvantaged in the typical school environment.

Slavin (2008) and Payne (2006) explained that economically disadvantaged students (on average) are less likely to be as well prepared when entering school as students from the middle or upper classes, and their upbringings often emphasize behaviors and values different from those expected of them in school (such as individuality and future time orientation). They are less likely to respond to delayed reinforcement, less willing to compete, and more oriented toward cooperation with other students and individualized contact with the teacher. Even the way parents of lower-SES children communicate with their children tends to differ from that of middle-SES parents. Lower-SES mothers generally give more commands and less-clear directions. Payne (2006) suggested that teachers can be successful with economically disadvantaged students if the teachers do two things:

- Help the students develop the ability to deal with abstract representational systems.
- Develop a relationship of mutual respect and trust with the students.

One group of economically disadvantaged students that needs conscientious attention from teachers is students from homeless families. By federal law, all school districts are required to provide a free appropriate public education to homeless children. Furthermore, the law explicitly states that school districts "must ensure that homeless students are not segregated or stigmatized due to their homelessness" (McKinney-Vento Act, 2001).

Checkpoint

Fill in the blank.

1. Often, economically disadvantaged students are also _____ disadvantaged in the typical school environment.

2. Teachers need to help economically disadvantaged students develop the ability to deal with _____ representational systems.

3. Researchers have found that middle-SES teachers often have _____ (high, low) expectations for low-SES students.

Mark as true or false.

4. _____ (a) The hidden curriculum reflects middle-class values and behaviors.

_____ (b) By law, school districts must ensure that homeless students are segregated from other students.

Checkpoint Answers

1. educationally

2. abstract

3. low

4. (a) true; (b) false

Kounin

Based on an observational study of 80 elementary classrooms, Jacob S. Kounin (in Cotton, 1993) determined that the responses to classroom disruptions of unsuccessful classroom managers compared to those of successful classroom managers were not dramatically different. Instead, asserted Kounin, the difference between the two groups was that successful classroom managers, unlike unsuccessful classroom managers, were proactive in preventing disruptions before they occurred. He went on to identify specific classroom management skills associated with effective prevention of classroom disruptions:

- **Withitness:** Being aware of what is happening in the classroom at all times
- **Overlapping:** Being able to do more than one thing at a time, such as moving to stand beside a student who is off-task, answering a question from another student, and monitoring cooperative learning groups, all simultaneously

- **Group alerting:** Being able to keep students' attention on the learning task
- **Momentum:** Being able to keep instruction moving at a brisk pace
- **Smoothness:** Being able to effect smooth transitions between activities
- **Exploiting the ripple effect:** Skillfully using the phenomenon that occurs, for example, when a teacher reminds an off-task student to get back to work and all other off-task students also return to their assigned task

Checkpoint

Fill in the blank.

1. According to Kounin, the main difference between successful and unsuccessful classroom managers is that successful classroom managers are _____ in preventing disruptions before they occur.

2. A teacher who is able to give instructions and distribute materials at the same time is exhibiting _____.

3. A teacher who redirects an off-task student when the teacher's attention appears to be focused elsewhere is exhibiting _____.

Mark as true or false.

4. _____ (a) Kounin found that successful classroom managers were significantly better at handling disruptions than unsuccessful classroom managers.

   _____ (b) Successful classroom managers know how to stop misconduct before it starts.

Checkpoint Answers

1. proactive
2. overlapping
3. withitness
4. (a) false; (b) true

Physical Layout

Successful classroom managers are skilled both in preventing behavior problems and in dealing appropriately with them. They arrange the physical layout of the room so that they can see the students from anywhere in the classroom. They know that the physical arrangement of the classroom influences the way teachers and students feel, think, and behave. Classroom furniture might consist of desks or tables and chairs. The seating arrangement can determine the kind and extent of interactions that will take place in the classroom.

Clusters of three to five desks or students seated at small tables promote social contact and interaction. Students can easily share materials, have group discussions, and work together on assignments. This arrangement is particularly appropriate when teachers want to use cooperative learning activities.

Teachers who want their students to exchange ideas know that the more the students see each other, the more they will be involved in discussions. Thus, for whole-group settings, circles and U-shaped designs promote discussion. Teachers who use these arrangements usually place their own desks in an out-of-the-way place or in a corner.

Arranging desks in rows is particularly appropriate for teacher-centered instruction. Rows tend to reduce the interaction among students and make it easier for them to work individually. Rows also direct the students' attention toward the teacher. Teachers who use this type of physical arrangement typically place their desks in front of the room where they are easily visible.

Where students are seated in the classroom can also influence participation patterns. Planned seating is better than random seating. When desks are arranged in rows, students who are seated in the front and center are in the **action zone.** These students interact most frequently with the teacher. Students who are seated in the back and corners tend to participate less. Some evidence indicates that teachers might communicate differently with students, depending on where the students are seated. Students in the action zone receive a more permissive and interactive style of communication, while students in the back and corners receive more lecturing and one-way communication.

Effective teachers arrange and change the environment as needed to encourage learning. They make sure that movement in the classroom and acquisition of materials can occur with little disruption; that students can see and be seen by the teacher; and that students can see the whiteboard/SMART Board, projector screen or display screen, and so forth, when necessary. They are also aware that an accessible and barrier-free environment is necessary for students with physical disabilities.

Checkpoint

Fill in the blank.

1. The seating arrangement can determine the kind and extent of _____ that will take place in the classroom.

2. Social contact and interaction are promoted by _____ arrangements.

3. Seating students in rows directs the students' attention toward the _____.

Mark as true or false.

4. _____ (a) Putting desks in a U-shaped design minimizes interaction.

   _____ (b) Students in the action zone usually get most of the teacher's attention.

Checkpoint Answers

1. interactions
2. cluster
3. teacher
4. (a) false; (b) true

Ability Grouping

Education experts in Florida agree that MTSS PS/RtI—differentiated instruction that allows within-class, skills-based grouping situations based on student assessment data—leads to higher student achievement, particularly since continuous monitoring and feedback are essential components of the MTSS PS/RtI process (see the section "MTSS PS/RtI" in Chapter 1 for a discussion of this topic). However, teachers should avoid careless use of ability grouping. Grouping practices can affect students' perceptions of themselves and their own worth and, thus, impact student behavior. A 1988 Carnegie Foundation report, *An Imperiled Generation,* summarized the harmful effects of ability grouping. The report concluded that such grouping has a devastating impact on how teachers think about students and how students think about themselves. The results of this report still hold true. The following are concerns to consider about ability grouping:

- It carries a social stigma.
- It promotes negative feelings about school for low-achieving students.
- It consistently hinders academic progress for average and low-achieving students.
- It often widens the gap between high- and low-achieving students.

According to Slavin (2008), the harmful effects of ability grouping for low-ability students are pronounced, including low expectations for their achievement and behavior, less instruction time resulting in less learning, less opportunity to experience higher-level topics, and lowered self-esteem, all of which have a stigmatizing effect on these students. These findings are particularly disturbing when one considers that low socioeconomic children tend to score below average on the types of assessment that are often used to assign students to ability groups. If the ability grouping system is very rigid, not providing for frequent reassessment of students and regrouping, poor and minority students are likely to be tracked into an inferior educational experience.

In contrast, both high-ability and low-ability learners can benefit academically and socially in mixed-ability cooperative learning groups that incorporate group goals and individual accountability (Slavin, 2008). The positive results that can accrue for low-achieving students placed in such groups include improved self-image and willingness to learn. This result occurs, in part, because the low-achieving students receive group assistance and support and, not insignificantly, because they are allowed to experience a more challenging curriculum. Nonetheless, teachers should monitor cooperative group interactions to ensure that students with high academic ability are not treated more favorably by the group as a whole than the low-ability students in the group, and that all students are expected to contribute to group success. Mixed-ability grouping benefits high-ability learners by providing opportunities for these students to socialize and work with students of various abilities and traits. (See the section "Cooperative Learning" in Chapter 1 for additional discussion of cooperative learning groups.)

Checkpoint

Fill in the blank.

1. Grouping practices can affect students' _____ of themselves.

2. Grouping by ability has a negative effect on the academic performance of _____ (low-ability, high-ability) students.

3. Low socioeconomic students tend to score _____ (above, below) average on assessments that are used to assign students to ability groups.

Mark as true or false.

4. _____ (a) When within-class ability groups are used, frequent reassessment should take place as students progress.

   _____ (b) A risk of using a rigid ability grouping system is that poor and minority students are likely to be tracked into an inferior educational experience.

Checkpoint Answers

1. perceptions

2. low-ability

3. below

4. (a) true; (b) true

Psychosocial Characteristics of Children and Adolescents

Children enter school with a variety of psychological and social characteristics. Teachers need to be aware that these characteristics have great variability across age groups and cultures. Nevertheless, understanding and dealing with children's and adolescents' behavior can be enhanced when teachers have knowledge of general developmental characteristics. Some common psychosocial characteristics for various age groups are shown in the following chart.

Psychosocial Characteristics of Children and Adolescents

Age	Characteristics
3	Have acquired self-identity; aware of own gender and that of others; will play with other children instead of beside them; beginning to understand that others have feelings, although unable to take the perspective of others; will share toys; learning to take turns; are becoming more self-reliant; need more personal attention; like silly humor; like repetitive activities; might develop irrational fears; have short attention spans
4	Can describe self in simple terms; have developed racial/cultural identity; are self-centered; enjoy group activities; might have imaginary friends; tend to play with same-sex peers and to select commonly gender-identified toys and might exclude the other sex; like jokes and silly humor; enjoy the security of repetitive activities; need warm personal attention; have increased attention span; generally, boys prefer active play and are more aggressive and boisterous; generally, girls prefer quieter play with one or two others; girls set up rules for play, boys are less organized
5	Enjoy the security of repetitive activities; want to be accepted by adults; engage in gender-specific forms of play; can play simple board games; will share and take turns but are still very self-centered; are very individualistic; tend to tattle on others (as they become aware of right and wrong); choose own friends; like same-sex friends with same interests; engage in cooperative play; like practical jokes; have an interest in the world outside their own; very inquisitive about their surroundings; appear to live in a world of make-believe and imagination; are spontaneous and uninhibited
6–7	Can take the perspective of others; tend to overestimate their abilities; are highly competitive (cheating at games common); are highly imaginative and enjoy imitating; like warm personal attention; need encouragement and acceptance from adults; choose same-sex peers as friends at school; neighborhood friends might be mixed; are imaginative in their play; interested in games and rules; show social give-and-take; have a growing social interest; begin to want to "fit in"
8–10	Become more realistic about their abilities; are very curious; have well-established racial/ethnic prejudices, which are resistant to change; are somewhat self-conscious; need encouragement and acceptance from adults; prefer group activities to independent work; are interested in what's happening in the world; have social life focused around family; rely on opinions of family members in forming attitudes; choose same-sex friends; feel pressure to conform to others of same age, especially in terms of dress; might use inappropriate language; might develop hero worship of family member or media/sports figure
11–15 (young adolescents)	Often resistant toward parent/adult authority and will challenge adult authority; need understanding and support from parents and others; have social life shifted in focus from family to friends; are intensely curious; interested in investigating real-life problems; easily offended and sensitive to criticism; concerned about their physical appearance; often preoccupied with self (**adolescent egocentrism**); feel like they are "on stage," others watching and judging them (**imaginary audience**); like to work with peers; have a strong need for approval, especially from peers (**peer pressure**); have a strong desire to belong to a group; want to be different, but "fit in" at same time; very loyal to peer-group values; tend to form cliques; interested in opposite sex; choose friends who are like themselves; have both male and female friends; like trends; are generally idealistic; turn to friends for advice and understanding but rely on family when making major decisions; experience mood swings; believe their personal situation is unique (**personal fable**), that no one else understands them; believe that bad things happen to other people, not to them (**invincibility fable**), so will engage in risky behavior; have difficulty coping with being "caught" between childhood and adulthood; girls have strong need to be liked by boys; girls more susceptible to becoming obsessed with pop culture figures

Psychosocial Characteristics of Children and Adolescents (*continued*)

Age	Characteristics
16–18 (older adolescents)	Show decreased resistance to authority; are beginning to be less influenced by adolescent egocentrism, imaginary audience, and personal fable; need understanding and support from parents and others; interested in opposite sex and dating; are comfortable with their sexuality; still very concerned with their appearance; choose friends who are like themselves; have male and female friends; tend to keep same friends and form cliques; often form a close relationship with a "significant other" and tend to be strongly influenced by this person (especially true of girls); have increased personal autonomy; will still test boundaries and engage in risky behavior (especially true of boys); turn to trusted friends (male or female) for advice and understanding, but rely on family when making major decisions; interact with their parents as people; interested in investigating real-life problems and topics that are personally meaningful; interested in the future; value support of their families; girls more mature than boys

Checkpoint

Fill in the blank.

1. By age _____, children have acquired gender identity.

2. By no later than age _____, children have well-established racial/ethnic prejudices.

3. Younger adolescents are very susceptible to _____ pressure.

Mark as true or false.

4. _____ (a) A 6-year-old child will tend to overestimate his or her abilities.

   _____ (b) Younger adolescents tend to be less rebellious than older adolescents.

Checkpoint Answers

1. 3

2. 10

3. peer

4. (a) true; (b) false

Kohlberg and Gilligan

Lawrence Kohlberg (1981) studied the ways children (and adults) reason about rules that govern their moral behavior. After conducting a long series of studies with children and adults, Kohlberg concluded that moral development occurs in a specific sequence of stages, regardless of culture. He identified six stages of moral reasoning, which he grouped into the following three levels.

Preconventional Level (Birth to 9 Years)	Conventional Level (10 to 15 Years)	Postconventional Level (16 to Adulthood)
Stage 1: **Punishment-Obedience Orientation.** Rules are obeyed to avoid punishment. Accepts rules, but internalization of moral values is lacking.	Stage 3: **Good Boy–Nice Girl Orientation.** Good behavior is doing what others expect and whatever is approved by them. Accepts and respects authority. Peer acceptance is needed.	Stage 5: **Social Contract Orientation.** What's right is defined in terms of standards that have been agreed upon by the whole society. Obeys rules, but might question them. Recognizes that rules are subject to change if outdated. Respects rights of others.

(*continued*)

Preconventional Level (Birth to 9 Years)	Conventional Level (10 to 15 Years)	Postconventional Level (16 to Adulthood)
Stage 2: **Instrumental-Relativist Orientation.** What's right is whatever satisfies one's own needs and occasionally the needs of others. Behaves to get a reward.	Stage 4: **Law-Order Orientation.** Good behavior is doing one's duty, respecting authority, and obeying the laws of society. Regardless of the circumstances, it is wrong to break rules.	Stage 6: **Universal Ethical Principle.** What's right is a decision of one's conscience according to ethical principles. Ethical principles are abstract concepts such as justice, equality, and the dignity of all people.

Carol Gilligan (1982) took issue with Kohlberg's theory of moral development, contending that it failed to take into consideration obvious gender differences. According to Gilligan, when making moral decisions, men and boys rely on their sense of fairness and justice more often than women and girls. On the other hand, women and girls respond from a caring perspective and sense of responsibility to others more often than men and boys.

Checkpoint

Fill in the blank.

1. A person who obeys the rules to avoid punishment is in Kohlberg's _____ stage of moral development.

2. A person who obeys the rules out of a desire to please others is in Kohlberg's _____ stage of moral development.

3. According to Gilligan, women and girls respond to moral decisions from a _____ perspective.

Mark as true or false.

4. _____ (a) Kohlberg believed that moral development occurs in a specific sequence of stages.

   _____ (b) A person who breaks the rules to follow his or own conscience is in Kohlberg's law-order orientation of moral development.

Checkpoint Answers

1. punishment-obedience orientation

2. good boy–nice girl orientation

3. caring

4. (a) true; (b) false

Erikson

Erik Erikson (1968) developed a life-cycle conception of personality development. According to him, people go through a series of major crises as they proceed through life. At each stage, there is a critical social crisis. How the individual reacts to each future crisis is determined by earlier development and by adjustment to social experiences. The stages are as follows:

- **Trust versus mistrust (birth to 18 months):** During this first stage, an infant whose basic physical needs are met and who feels loved and secure will develop feelings of trust. Otherwise, the seeds of mistrust will be firmly planted.

- **Autonomy versus doubt (18 months to 3 years):** During the second stage, children should be allowed to explore, make simple choices, and learn to control themselves as autonomy is experienced. Otherwise, feelings of self-doubt will prevail.

- **Initiation versus guilt (3 to 6 years):** Children need to develop a confident attitude about their own actions and abilities. It is important that they have opportunities to initiate activities and engage in real and make-believe play. Also, in this period, children need to develop a comfortable sense of their gender identity. Nurturing and reinforcing children's sense of initiative at this stage will help build a firm foundation for the next stages and diminish feelings of guilt for following their own initiatives.

- **Industry versus inferiority (6 to 12 years):** Numerous skills are acquired at this stage, and children seemingly cannot learn fast enough. If they experience satisfaction and success with the completion of tasks they are assigned or initiate, they will feel good about themselves and develop a sense of industry rather than inferiority.

- **Identity versus role confusion (12 to 18 years):** The changes that take place during this state of adolescence bring about a major shift in personal development. This is the time of transition from childhood to adulthood, when adolescents are developing a sense of identity. They often struggle with self-doubt and question, "Who am I?" When they are able to know themselves, they have a sense of who they are and are comfortable with their own identity. If this does not happen, a sense of role confusion can result.

- **Intimacy versus isolation (young adulthood):** This is the period when young adults are able to make a commitment to another person, to a cause, or to a career. They are able to give a sense of direction to their lives. Otherwise, they feel isolated from the rest of the world.

- **Generativity versus stagnation (middle adulthood):** Concern with future generations and child rearing is the main focus of this stage. People should continue to grow in this stage and become less selfish; if they don't, stagnation sets in, and they become self-absorbed or self-indulgent, caring for no one.

- **Integrity versus despair (late adulthood):** Those who reach the final stage find themselves looking back on their lives with a feeling of satisfaction or with a sense of despair about how life turned out for them—or somewhere in between these two conditions. Coming to terms with one's life and accepting one's failures as well as successes lead to ego integrity. Anguishing over lost opportunities and dreading poor health and death lead to despair.

Checkpoint

Fill in the blank.

1. According to Erikson, an infant whose basic physical needs are met and who feels loved and secure will develop feelings of _____.

2. According to Erikson, between the ages of 3 and 6, children are in the process of developing a sense of _____.

3. According to Erikson, adolescents are in the process of developing a sense of _____.

Mark as true or false.

4. _____ (a) Preschoolers want to take actions that assert themselves.

   _____ (b) Being successful in school contributes to a child's sense of industry.

Checkpoint Answers

1. trust

2. initiative

3. identity

4. (a) true; (b) true

Learning Environment Accommodations for Learners in Exceptional Student Education (ESE)

Teachers need to use appropriate management strategies for learners in ESE who have disabilities, are easily distracted, have difficulty completing work, or have difficulty controlling their behavior. The Florida Department of Education (FDOE) publication *Accommodations, Assisting Students with Disabilities* Third Edition (Beech, 2003) offers guidelines for making accommodations to the learning environment for these students. The following chart summarizes the guidelines.

ESE Learner Difficulty	Suggested Accommodations
Short attention span	Minimize classroom distractions; seat away from windows, doors, materials center, and noisy machinery; use white noise or soft music to neutralize distracting noise; provide planned opportunities for physical movement (for example, running errands, erasing the board, or passing out materials); break tasks into smaller chunks; have a private area where the student can voluntarily go when needed.
Working in large groups	Preview activities so the student will know what to expect; recruit and train a peer helper to sit next to the student to help him or her know what to do and stay on-task.
Working in small groups	Spend time explicitly teaching the student (through modeling and role playing) how to share responsibility, how to plan with others, and so on; assign roles to the students in the group, including the ESE learner; recruit and train a peer helper to join the student's group and help the student stay on-task.
Working independently	Make sure the task is one the student wants to do and understands how to do; offer a choice of tasks and use hands-on activities frequently; use computer assisted instruction or learning centers with easy-to-follow directions (which are illustrated for younger students); recruit and train a peer helper to repeat and explain directions and give assistance when the teacher is unavailable.
Controlling his/her own behavior	Provide a structured environment with predictable routines; use a cueing system, agreed upon with the student, to signal transitions; make sure the student understands the class rules and consequences by having the student role-play (on a regular basis) examples of appropriate and inappropriate behaviors; as with other students, use meaningful consequences that escalate in severity depending on the seriousness of the infraction and/or the number of times it is repeated; monitor the student's compliance with the rules and provide constructive feedback and positive reinforcement; communicate regularly with the student's parents and elicit their support of positive behavior; if ordinary measures fail to yield success, contact the ESE teacher for assistance.

Checkpoint

Fill in the blank.

1. A student who has a short attention span will be helped by minimizing classroom _____.

2. Providing a learning center is a way to accommodate a student who has difficultly working _____.

3. A student who has difficulty controlling his or her own behavior needs _____ routines.

Mark as true or false.

4. _____ (a) When a student has difficulty working in a small group, the teacher should teach the student group process skills.

   _____ (b) Peer helpers do not need to be trained.

Checkpoint Answers

1. distractions
2. independently
3. predictable
4. (a) true; (b) false

Maslow's Hierarchy of Needs

Classrooms should be inviting, attractive places where students feel welcome, comfortable, secure, and safe. A teacher who creates such a climate is providing a learning environment that encourages and motivates students to be successful, thus creating good feelings of self-worth. That teacher is also meeting some important needs of the students.

According to Abraham Maslow (1954), all human beings have certain needs that must be met. These needs are listed in a hierarchy as follows:

- **Physiological needs,** such as food and shelter
- **Safety needs,** such as a predictable environment and security from harm
- **Belongingness and love needs,** such as affection and affiliation with others
- **Esteem needs,** such as self-respect, worthiness, and gaining approval and recognition
- **Self-actualization needs,** such as self-fulfillment and personal achievement

Maslow explained that everyone has an innate desire to achieve self-actualization, the highest level of needs; however, lower-level needs must be satisfied before higher-level needs can be met. He described physiological, safety, belongingness and love, and esteem needs as **deficiency needs** and contended that motivation to learn is hampered when these needs are not satisfied. The implication is that a hungry child or a child who is worried about a family problem such as divorce or illness likely will not be interested in the lesson topic, or even be attentive in the classroom, for that matter. The charge for teachers is to strive to keep the learning environment conducive to student learning by being on the alert for situations where deficiency needs are not being met and to do what they can to assist the student or students in satisfying those needs.

Checkpoint

Fill in the blank.

1. Food and shelter are examples of _____ needs, which fall under deficiency needs.
2. Self-respect is an example of _____ needs, which fall under deficiency needs.
3. Personal achievement is an example of _____ needs.

Mark as true or false.

4. _____ (a) According to Maslow, a student will have difficulty learning if deficiency needs have not been satisfied.

   _____ (b) According to Maslow, everyone has an innate desire to achieve self-actualization.

Checkpoint Answers

1. physiological
2. esteem
3. self-actualization
4. (a) true; (b) true

Important Statutes Related to Classroom Management

Following is a list of federal and Florida Statutes (current in 2014) related to classroom management that teachers in Florida should know:

Section 6A-5.065 (2)(2b)(FAC) requires that teachers consistently manage individual and class behaviors through a well-planned management system.

Section 1003.32 (1)(F. S.) gives teachers authority for control and discipline of their students and mandates that teachers must keep good order in the classroom. Teachers are authorized to undertake any of the following actions:

(a) Establish classroom rules of conduct.
(b) Establish and implement consequences, designed to change behavior, for infractions of classroom rules.
(c) Have disobedient, disrespectful, violent, abusive, uncontrollable, or disruptive students removed from the classroom for behavior management intervention.
(d) Have violent, abusive, uncontrollable, or disruptive students directed for information or assistance from appropriate school or district school board personnel.
(e) Assist in enforcing school rules on school property, during school-sponsored transportation, and during school-sponsored activities.
(f) Request and receive information as to the disposition of any referrals to the administration for violation of classroom or school rules.
(g) Request and receive immediate assistance in classroom management if a student becomes uncontrollable or in case of emergency.
(h) Request and receive training and other assistance to improve skills in classroom management, violence prevention, conflict resolution, and related areas.
(i) Press charges if there is a reason to believe that a crime has been committed on school property, during school-sponsored transportation, or during school-sponsored activities.
(j) Use reasonable force, according to standards adopted by the State Board of Education, to protect himself or herself or others from injury.
(k) Use corporal punishment according to school board policy and at least the following procedures, if a teacher feels that corporal punishment is necessary:
　(1) The use of corporal punishment shall be approved in principle by the principal before it is used, but approval is not necessary for each specific instance in which it is used. The principal shall prepare guidelines for administering such punishment, which identify the types of punishable offenses, the conditions under which the punishment shall be administered, and the specific personnel on the school staff authorized to administer the punishment.
　(2) A teacher or principal may administer corporal punishment only in the presence of another adult who is informed beforehand, and in the student's presence, of the reason for the punishment.
　(3) A teacher or principal who has administered punishment shall, upon request, provide the student's parent with a written explanation of the reason for the punishment and the name of the other adult who was present.

Section 1003.32 (2)(F. S.) requires teachers to

(a) set and enforce reasonable classroom rules that treat all students equitably.
(b) seek professional development to improve classroom management skills when data show that they are not effective in handling minor classroom disruptions.
(c) maintain an orderly and disciplined classroom with a positive and effective learning environment that maximizes learning and minimizes disruption.
(d) work with parents and other school personnel to solve discipline problems in their classrooms.

Section 1003.32 (3)(F. S.) empowers a teacher to send a student to the principal's office to maintain effective discipline in the classroom and to recommend an appropriate consequence consistent with the student code of conduct. The principal is required to employ the teacher's recommended consequence or a more serious disciplinary action if the student's history of disruptive behavior warrants it. If the principal determines that a lesser disciplinary action is appropriate, the principal should consult with the teacher prior to taking disciplinary action.

Section 1003.32 (4–5)(F. S.) empowers a teacher to remove from class a student whose behavior the teacher determines interferes with the teacher's ability to communicate effectively with the students in the class or with the ability of the student's classmates to learn. Each district school board, each district school superintendent, and each school principal shall support the authority of teachers to remove disobedient, violent, abusive, uncontrollable, or disruptive students from the classroom. This statute prohibits the principal from returning the student to that teacher's class without the teacher's consent unless a placement review committee (composed of a principal-selected member of the school staff and two teachers, one selected by the school's faculty and one selected by the teacher who has removed the student) determines that such placement is the best or only available alternative.

Section 1003.32 (7)(F. S.) provides that a teacher who removes 25 percent of his or her total class enrollment is required to complete professional development to improve classroom management skills.

Section 1006.11 (F. S.) provides that, except in the case of excessive force or cruel and unusual punishment, a teacher is not civilly or criminally liable for any action carried out in conformity with the State Board of Education and district school board rules regarding the control, discipline, suspension, and expulsion of students.

Section 6A-10.081 (FAC) provides that teachers should make a reasonable effort to protect a student from conditions harmful to learning and/or to the student's mental and/or physical health and/or safety; should not intentionally expose a student to unnecessary embarrassment or disparagement; should not harass or discriminate against any student on the basis of race, color, religion, sex, age, national or ethnic origin, political beliefs, marital status, handicapping condition, sexual orientation, or social and family background; and should make a reasonable effort to ensure that each student is protected from harassment or discrimination.

Section 1006.147 (F. S.) prohibits bullying or harassment of any student or employee of a public K-12 school. Bullying includes cyberbullying and means systematically and chronically inflicting physical hurt or psychological distress on one or more students and may involve teasing; social exclusion; threat; intimidation; stalking; physical violence; theft; sexual, religious, or racial harassment; public or private humiliation; or destruction of property. Cyberbullying means bullying through the use of technology or any electronic communication. Harassment means any threatening, insulting, or dehumanizing gesture, use of data or computer software, or written, verbal, or physical conduct directed against a student or school employee that places a student or school employee in reasonable fear of harm to his or her person or damage to his or her property; has the effect of substantially interfering with a student's educational performance, opportunities, or benefits; or has the effect of substantially disrupting the orderly operation of a school.

Section 1003.03 (1)(F. S.) specifies that the maximum number of students in core-curricula courses assigned to a teacher are as follows: (1) prekindergarten through grade 3, 18 students; (2) grades 4 through 8, 22 students; and (3) grades 9 through 12, 25 students.

The Individuals with Disabilities Education Act (IDEA, 2007) and Section 504 of the Rehabilitation Act (1973) mandate that classrooms must accommodate students with disabilities.

Checkpoint

Fill in the blank.

1. Florida law mandates that teachers must keep good _____ in the classroom.

2. Under Florida law, a teacher can have a disruptive student _____ from the classroom.

3. Under Florida law, teachers can use _____ force against students to protect themselves or others from harm or injury.

Mark as true or false.

4. _____ (a) Corporal punishment is illegal in Florida public schools.

   _____ (b) The maximum number of students in core-curricula courses assigned to a third-grade teacher is 25 students.

Checkpoint Answers

1. order

2. removed

3. reasonable

4. (a) false; (b) false

Summary

In summary, Florida teachers understand that the goal of classroom management is to maximize student achievement. Effective classroom managers understand their responsibilities in regard to the learning environment. They strive to build a positive physical, social, and intellectual environment that is conducive to learning and responsive to students' needs and characteristics. They value and respect all students and treat them with dignity and respect at all times.

Sample Questions

1. A middle school teacher has been assigned to a class that has a wide range of socioeconomic and cultural backgrounds. Most of the students have had varied school experiences with little or no success. Which of the following approaches at the beginning of the school year would best promote a productive learning environment in the classroom?

   A. Initially have students work independently and then incorporate group activities after students have adjusted to classroom routines.
   B. Select one or two students who will take responsibility for monitoring the behavior of peers and helping to maintain order in the classroom.
   C. Adopt a punitive-based discipline plan and enforce it consistently and fairly.
   D. Explicitly teach classroom procedures and rules, including those that seem self-evident (for example, how to disagree with peers).

2. A newly hired fourth-grade teacher wants the students to work in cooperative learning groups, but the teacher is reluctant to use group activities because the students are too noisy when it's time to transition from whole-class to group instruction. The best way for the teacher to improve the situation is to

   A. give free time to students who move into groups quietly.
   B. spend time teaching students how to transition from whole-class to group activities.
   C. assign roles to the members of the groups.
   D. hold a class meeting to discuss the importance of keeping the noise in the classroom at a reasonable level.

3. A second-grade boy behaves in school to avoid getting into trouble. The boy is probably in which of Kohlberg's stages of moral development?

   A. punishment-obedience orientation
   B. instrumental-relativist orientation
   C. good boy–nice girl orientation
   D. law-order orientation

4. A seventh-grade boy is worried because his father just got laid off from work. This situation is most closely related to which of the following types of needs?

   A. physiological needs
   B. safety needs
   C. belongingness and love needs
   D. esteem needs

5. Under Florida law, a teacher who removes 25 percent of his or her total class enrollment

    A. is required to complete professional development to improve classroom management skills.

    B. must be placed immediately on probation by the principal.

    C. will have his or her license permanently revoked.

    D. is required to meet with the parents of the removed students to work out a plan for readmitting the students to the teacher's class.

Answer Explanations for Sample Questions

1. **D.** Eliminate **B** because students should not be put in charge of classroom discipline. Eliminate **C** because teachers should use positive discipline approaches. Now you must choose between **A** and **D.** Choice **A** is a tempting response because students should not work in groups until they have learned appropriate group behaviors; however, the teacher is usually working with the class as a whole rather than having the students work independently, before group activities begin. At the beginning of the school year, teachers should explicitly teach classroom and school procedures and rules to all students. In particular, students at risk for academic failure benefit from explicit instruction in classroom procedures and rules. Thus, **D** is the correct response.

2. **B.** Eliminate **C** because this measure has impact only after students are in groups, not when they are transitioning into group work. Eliminate **A** and **D** because while these measures might result in quieter transitioning, neither would be as effective as explicitly teaching students how to transition from whole-class to group activities. Thus, **B** is the correct response. At the beginning of the school year, successful classroom managers establish and teach classroom procedures (including how to make transitions) to create smoothly functioning learning communities.

3. **A.** Choice **A** is the correct response. When children are in the stage of punishment-obedience orientation, they obey rules to avoid punishment. Eliminate **B, C,** and **D** because these stages are higher levels of moral development than what is indicated by the situation described in the question.

4. **B.** The boy's sense of security about his home situation is threatened, so his safety needs are not being met. Thus, **B** is the correct response. Eliminate **A, C,** and **D** because none of the needs in these answer choices is as closely aligned with the situation given in the question stem as is the need in **B.**

5. **A.** Choice **A** is the correct response. Under Florida law, a teacher who removes 25 percent of his or her total class enrollment is required to complete professional development to improve his or her classroom management skills. Eliminate **B, C,** and **D** because these measures do not reflect Florida law. The measure in **C** is an outcome that could eventually occur, but there is no guarantee that it *will* occur. (Don't read too much into a question.)

Competency 3: Instructional Delivery

Competency Description and Key Indicators

According to the *Competencies and Skills Required for Teacher Certification in Florida*, 20th Edition (available at www.fldoe.org/asp/ftce/pdf/ftce20edition.pdf), **Competency 3** of the FTCE PEd Test addresses **Instructional Delivery** as follows:

> *Knowledge of instructional delivery and facilitation through a comprehensive understanding of subject matter*

Key indicators:

- Use motivational strategies to engage and challenge all students.
- Apply appropriate instructional practices for developing content area literacy.
- Analyze gaps in students' subject matter knowledge in order to improve instructional delivery.
- Assess and adapt instruction to address preconceptions and misconceptions of subject matter.
- Relate subject matter to life experiences and across disciplines.
- Apply techniques for developing higher-order critical thinking skills.
- Select varied strategies, resources, and appropriate technology for relevant and comprehensible instruction.
- Identify differentiated instructional practices based on assessment of learning needs, individual differences, and continuous student feedback.
- Determine and apply techniques to provide feedback in order to promote student achievement.
- Apply appropriate subject area activities to accommodate learning needs, developmental levels, and experiential backgrounds of all students.

Overview

Instructional Delivery denotes the instructional activities and strategies that teachers use to communicate subject matter knowledge in a manner that enables students to learn. High-quality, effective teachers are essential to students' success in the classroom. Effective teachers use instructional methods that motivate students, activate their prior knowledge, and engage them in meaningful learning. They incorporate the materials and technologies of the content area in learning activities for students. Moreover, they use research-based differentiated instructional practices based on identified student learning needs and individual differences.

This chapter provides a general review of Instructional Delivery with sample questions and explanations at the end of the chapter. Checkpoint exercises are found throughout the review material. These exercises give you an opportunity to practice what you just learned. The answers to the Checkpoint exercises are found immediately following the set of exercises. When doing the Checkpoint exercises, you should cover up the answers. Then check your answers when you've finished the exercises. The sample questions at the end of this chapter are multiple-choice questions that are similar to what you might expect to see on the FTCE PEd Test. The answer explanations for the sample questions are provided immediately after the questions.

Motivational Strategies

All human beings are born with a natural curiosity and desire to learn (Gestwicki, 1999). Unfortunately, many students show little or no excitement about school learning. A primary objective of an effective teacher is to stimulate in pupils the desire, or motivation, to learn. **Motivation** is the willingness or desire of a student to exhibit a behavior such as productively engaging in a learning experience. Teachers are challenged to tap into students' innate urges to learn by using teaching strategies that influence students' motivation. Research on motivation has focused on topics such as *intrinsic* and *extrinsic motivation, reinforcement*, and *achievement motivation.*

Sometimes, a student wants to learn something just for the sake of learning it. We say this student wants to learn because of **intrinsic motivation.** The desire to learn originates within the student and stems from the student's intellectual curiosity, attitudes, beliefs, and needs regarding the learning task. Brain research indicates that teachers who make learning relevant and personally meaningful to students, give them choices in what they learn and how they learn it, and provide learning experiences in which students are actively engaged often will find that students become intrinsically motivated to learn.

If a desire to learn does not arise from within a student, the teacher may need to stimulate **extrinsic motivation** by using external reinforcement (see the section "Behaviorism and Constructivism" in Chapter 1 for a discussion of reinforcement) in the form of rewards or incentives to engage the student in learning. In extrinsic motivation, the emphasis is on external factors that students find desirable. Teachers who reward students with stickers or stars, public recognition, privileges, or special treats are capitalizing on extrinsic motivation.

However, teachers should be aware that a great deal of reinforcement occurs in students when they do something well, regardless of whether they receive tangible rewards or incentives from the teacher. The satisfaction and accomplishment that students feel for success in school and gaining the respect of their teachers and peers are potent reinforcers. Jensen (1998) pointed out that, biologically, "the limbic system ordinarily rewards cerebral learning with good feelings on a daily basis" (p. 65). In light of this internal reward system, some experts suggest tangible rewards can negatively impact intrinsic motivation when the reinforcement is given for tasks that students have a high interest in doing anyway. Moreover, students' reactions to external rewards vary from student to student, depending on the personal characteristics and previous experiences of the student. Jensen argued that external rewards are unfair because an external reward that motivates one student will not necessarily motivate another student. However, when students are successful in a learning task, "nearly all students will respond positively in their unique biological ways" (Jensen, 1998, p. 65). Given these concerns, experts (e.g., Gersten et al., 2009) suggest that when tangible rewards are used to stimulate student learning, teachers can gradually discontinue the use of rewards because students' successes will trigger intrinsic rewards.

A noteworthy exception to the cautions given here about external rewards or incentives is Marzano's evidence-based strategy of *reinforcing effort and providing recognition,* which research indicates positively affects students' level of engagement in learning tasks (see the section "Marzano's High Yield Instructional Strategies" later in this chapter for a discussion of this topic). Teachers should be purposeful in helping students relate their successes to their efforts in achieving those successes (see the section "Attributions and Locus of Control" later in this chapter for further discussion of this topic). Marzano et al. (2000) stated that "Believing that effort will affect level of achievement can serve as a powerful motivational tool that students can apply to any situation" (p. 54). Recognition, particularly verbal praise that is specific, honest, and credible to the student, is an external reinforcer that has been shown to increase intrinsic motivation—even after giving praise is discontinued (see the section "Praise" in Chapter 2 for guidelines on effective praise). Also, timely feedback—even when it is self-managed, as in interactive computer instructional programs—that informs students about what they are doing correctly and what they still need to work on strongly increases intrinsic motivation.

Achievement motivation is the tendency to strive for success and choose goal-oriented, success/failure activities. Students high in achievement motivation want and expect to succeed, and when they fail, they try harder. In some cases, students may have a strong desire to achieve, but they may be more controlled by the need to maintain a positive self-image, so they seek achievement by avoiding failure. Failure avoiders tend to choose either very easy or very difficult tasks, the reasoning being that they will likely succeed at the easy task. If they fail at the difficult task, they can attribute the failure to the difficulty level of the task, rather than to their own lack of ability.

Teachers' behavior and demeanor in the classroom can also affect student motivation. Kindsvatter et al. (1996) pointed out that highly motivating teachers are enthusiastic, energetic, exciting, and stimulating. When such teachers introduce lessons, they focus students' attention on the learning activity, communicate clearly the purposes of activities, and stimulate students to get involved. During lessons, they move around the classroom, vary voice level and quality, use instructional variety, change pace during the lesson, and use gestures (such as okay signs), facial expressions (such as smiles), body movements (such as nods), and other nonverbal signals to create a presence in the classroom that excites students to learn. In addition, their questioning techniques are student-oriented and nonjudgmental.

Here are some guidelines based on ideas of experts, particularly the work of Jensen (1998), for intrinsically motivating students to learn:

- Remove threats—such as lack of resources, language barriers, text difficulty, and uncomfortable environmental conditions—that discourage engagement in learning.
- Make sure students have sufficient background knowledge for the content presented.
- Relate subject content to students' interest and experiences.
- Appeal to students' natural curiosity, desire for fun, and need for social interaction.
- Be alert to an increase in student interest or curiosity and capitalize on it.
- Involve students in choosing and planning their learning activities.
- Help students set goals for learning that are achievable with effort.
- Use a variety of instructional strategies that address various learning preferences.
- Use hands-on, minds-on activities in which students are actively engaged in learning.
- Use role playing, simulation, drama, debate, games, rituals, celebrations, and so on to evoke positive emotional involvement of students.
- Be sure students understand your expectations and how to meet those expectations.
- Affirm and encourage students' efforts and involvement.
- Build frequent, constructive feedback into learning activities.
- Maintain a warm, supportive atmosphere.
- Model desired behavior (enthusiasm, interest, curiosity, and so on).

Note: See the section "Maslow's Hierarchy of Needs" in Chapter 2 for a discussion of understanding motivation from the standpoint of a hierarchy of needs.

Checkpoint

Fill in the blank.

1. In intrinsic motivation, the desire to learn is based on factors that are _____ (external, internal) to the learner.

2. In extrinsic motivation, the emphasis is on _____ (external, internal) factors that students find desirable.

3. Relating content to students' interest and experiences is a way to stimulate _____ (extrinsic, intrinsic) motivation.

Mark as true or false.

4. _____ (a) Students high in achievement motivation want and expect to succeed.

   _____ (b) Teachers' behavior and demeanor in the classroom have little impact on student motivation.

Checkpoint Answers

1. internal
2. external
3. intrinsic
4. (a) true; (b) false

Instructional Methods

Not only must teachers know what they are teaching, but they also must know how to teach it. This means using a wide range of instructional methods and materials based on knowledge of content pedagogy and characteristics of the learners. The instructional objective and the needs of the students will determine which methods teachers use.

Some of the instructional methods teachers might select when teaching are *direct instruction; lecture method; constructivist instruction; discovery learning; inquiry-based learning; project-based learning* and *problem-based learning; thematic learning; reciprocal teaching; simulations, role playing, and games; differentiated instruction; individualized instruction; independent student centers; peer tutoring;* and *interdisciplinary instruction.* In some instances, these methods overlap. For example, discovery learning, inquiry-based learning, project-based learning, and problem-based learning fall under the umbrella of constructivist instruction.

Direct Instruction

Direct instruction is a teacher-led (but student-centered) instructional strategy in which the teacher as a subject-matter expert provides systematic and explicit instruction, followed by monitored and guided student practice, to ensure that students are making progress toward mastery of specific skills and content. It emphasizes teacher control of all classroom events and the presentation of highly structured lessons, enhanced by focused teacher-student interactions. Teacher modeling is used extensively (see the section "Modeling" later in this chapter for a discussion of this topic). Lessons are arranged sequentially into small steps and move from the simple to the more complex. The teacher provides and elicits from students examples and nonexamples to enhance understanding. Feedback is immediate and constructive, and reteaching occurs as needed. The teacher checks for understanding at key points in the lesson and adjusts scaffolding based on student feedback. A primary goal is to foster independent learning in students. Stemming from this goal, direct instruction incorporates a gradual release of responsibility—the teacher models first, then guides students in shared practice, and finally provides opportunities for students to apply a skill or complete an activity independently.

In Florida, by law and in accordance with evidence-based research, reading skills are taught using systematic, explicit, scaffolded, and data-driven instruction (Rule 6A-6.053, FAC). That is, reading is taught through direct instruction. Teachers sequence reading skills to provide application and practice of previously taught skills and differentiate according to individual student needs in whole-group, small-group, or one-on-one settings (see Chapter 8, "Literacy Strategies," for further discussion of reading instruction in Florida).

Direct instruction is appropriate for all learners. Slavin (2008) noted that "Direct instruction is particularly appropriate for teaching a well-defined body of information or skills that all students must master." He went on to say, "It is less appropriate when … exploration, discovery, and open-ended objectives are the object of the lesson" (p. 222). In fact, by design, direct instruction does not rely on students being able to discover important concepts and skills. It prepares students for independent higher order comprehension by systematically and explicitly teaching strategies for text reading and critical thinking skills.

To be clear, research consistently points to direct instruction as a highly effective instructional method. It is not a traditional lecture or simply a teacher presentation of information; and it is not drill, nor does it focus on rote learning. Rather, it consists of carefully crafted and executed teacher actions, whose primary goal is to equip students with strategies that support independent and efficient learning.

The steps of direct instruction are incorporated into the lesson cycle model, which was developed by Madeline Hunter. (See the section "Lesson Cycle Model" in Chapter 1 for a description of the components of this model.)

Lecture Method

In the traditional **lecture method,** the teacher uses one-way communication to attempt to convey knowledge to the learner orally. The recommended length of time for teacher lectures is 10 to 15 minutes. The lecture method is not a common approach at the elementary level, where it definitely should be avoided; however, it is often seen at the secondary level—despite research findings that indicate it is one of the least effective teaching strategies, as measured by enduring effect. Evidence suggests that teaching by lecturing results in superficial learning, low-level simple recall, or no learning at all on the part of students. Furthermore, the traditional lecture method promotes passive rather than active learning and is the least effective instructional method at all grade levels. Most knowledge and skills can be better learned by active engagement of the learner than by listening to someone talk about them. Nevertheless, teachers continue to use the lecture method, most likely because it has the advantage that the teacher can organize facts and ideas and present them in an orderly way with a minimum amount of time and effort. If learning from a lecture is to be improved, the lecture needs to be an interactive process in which the learners are given opportunities to respond, ask questions, and react to the speaker's point of view.

Constructivist Instruction

Constructivist instruction is based on the constructivist belief "that learning is an active process [in which prior knowledge plays a powerful role], that it has social aspects, and that it is context specific" (FLDOE Bureau of School Improvement, 2006, p. 1) (see the section "Behaviorism and Constructivism" in Chapter 1 for additional discussion on constructivism). Collaboration and the teacher's guidance and support, often in the form of scaffolding, are essential features of constructivist instruction. Additionally, Brooks and Brooks (1993) offer the following principles that guide constructivist instruction:

- Encourage and accept student autonomy and initiative.
- Use raw data and primary sources along with manipulative, interactive, and physical materials.
- Use cognitive terminology such as *classify, analyze, predict,* and *create* when framing tasks.
- Allow student input to drive lessons, shift instructional strategies, and alter content.
- Find out about students' understandings of concepts before sharing your own understandings of those concepts.
- Encourage students to engage in dialogue, both with the teacher and with one another.
- Encourage student inquiry by asking thoughtful, open-ended questions and encouraging students to ask questions of each other.
- Seek elaboration of students' initial responses.
- Engage students in experiences that might engender contradictions to their initial hypotheses and then encourage discussion.
- Allow sufficient wait time after posing questions.
- Provide time for students to construct relationships and create metaphors.
- Use instructional strategies that nurture students' natural curiosity (pp. 103–117).

Constructivist instruction is exemplified in the 5E model (see the section "5E Model" in Chapter 1 for a detailed description of this model).

Discovery Learning

Discovery learning is designed to encourage students to be active learners while exploring new concepts, developing new skills, and figuring things out for themselves. It promotes and capitalizes on the natural curiosity of the learner. The supposition behind discovery learning is that active manipulation, thinking, and reasoning will enhance the students' understanding and increase the likelihood that they will develop appropriate generalizations and concepts.

Inquiry-based Learning

Inquiry-based learning is a process in which students engage when they have identified a problem to be solved. The process involves the awareness of a problem, generating possible solutions, developing a hypothesis, gathering data and testing the hypothesis, analyzing and interpreting the data, and drawing conclusions and making generalizations. Inquiry-based learning requires students to use critical thinking skills including scientific thinking, higher-order thinking (analysis, synthesis, and evaluation), logical reasoning, and decision making.

Project-based Learning and Problem-based Learning

In both **project-based learning** and **problem-based learning,** students investigate real-world problems and then share their findings. Investigations, which are often interdisciplinary in nature, might last over a period of several weeks. The main difference in the two strategies is that in project-based learning, students create a presentation as an end-product to the investigation, whereas in problem-based learning, students present their results, but an end-product might or might not be required. Project-based learning promotes in-depth study of a topic by an individual student, a small group, or even the whole class. Problem-based learning allows students to identify a problem of interest to them. The teacher helps students select an appropriate topic and facilitates students as they assign roles and responsibilities for members of a group focused on exploring the same problem. Both project-based learning and problem-based learning challenge students to plan and organize their own learning and to use problem-solving and decision-making skills.

Thematic Learning

Thematic learning results when a teacher designs one or more lessons around a central theme or topic. The theme can be an **intradisciplinary** (within a discipline) or an **interdisciplinary** (involving two or more disciplines) topic. Thematic learning helps students see relationships between and among concepts. Themes are selected for breadth and depth of coverage, their relevance to students' interests and experiences, and to convey information in connected, meaningful ways.

Reciprocal Teaching

Reciprocal teaching, developed by Palincsar and Brown (1984), is designed to increase students' reading comprehension. It consists of an interactive dialogue between the teacher and students that includes four steps: summarizing, generating questions, clarifying, and predicting.

Simulations, Role Playing, and Games

Simulations, role playing, and games are designed to allow students to learn through their experiences in a learning activity. **Simulation** is a learning experience designed to reflect reality. Students might set up a mock business, pretend to play the stock market, reenact a historic event, and so on. In **role playing,** students act out characters or situations based on real-world models. Role playing is a necessary part of simulations. Students must act out the roles they assume in the simulation. Simulations also can be computer- and/or web-based. **Games** are learning experiences that have rules and involve students in competitive situations, having winners and losers. Games, too, can be computer-based and/or web-based. Teachers can find numerous well-designed, educational games on the Internet. In addition, teachers have available a wide array of commercially produced computer simulations and games for the various subject areas. Advantages associated with simulations, role playing, and games are as follows:

- They are student-centered.
- They engage students' interest and motivation.
- Students learn by doing.
- They provide a realistic context.
- They allow for risk-taking in a safe environment.
- They promote creative and critical thinking, including decision making and problem solving.
- They provide opportunities for students to practice social and communication skills.

Differentiated Instruction

Differentiated instruction is the practice of matching instruction to students' needs. In Florida, differentiated instruction is implemented through Florida's Multi-Tiered System of Supports (MTSS) Problem-Solving/Response to Intervention (PS/RtI) process (see the section "MTSS PS/RtI" in Chapter 1 for a discussion of this topic).

Individualized Instruction

Individualized instruction is characterized by a shift in responsibility for learning from the teacher to the student. Effective individualized instruction is tailored to meet an individual student's interests, needs, and abilities, with consideration given to the appropriateness of the content. Individualized instruction can take various forms, such as independent study or peer tutoring. It can be as simple as allowing a student to complete the same lessons as the rest of the students but at a different pace, or modifying the objective requirements for a particular student. A technology-based strategy for individualizing instruction is **computer assisted instruction (CAI).** In CAI, the student interacts with the computer and proceeds at his or her own speed. CAI software is commonly classified into these categories: (1) drill and practice, (2) tutorial, (3) simulation, (4) problem solving, and (5) utility programs (robles.callutheran.edu/~crowe/software.html).

Independent Student Centers

Independent student centers are carefully designed, designated places in the classroom where students can go to explore and learn, either individually or with others, using a variety of materials and resources. Independent student centers are an effective way to differentiate instruction to meet the diverse needs of learners in the classroom. Teachers in the upper elementary grades, middle school, and high school set up independent student centers for exploration of topics or for practice, extension of concepts previously learned, and focused intervention. Independent student centers (or simply **learning centers**) are an essential feature of the early-childhood environment. Besides skills-focused reading centers, classrooms might have listening, creative writing, math, science, computer, dramatic play, spelling, block, and art centers. Some guidelines for early-childhood centers include the following:

- Noisy centers should be separated from quiet centers.
- Centers should be self-contained with all materials labeled, including both print and a picture representation, and easily accessible (no higher than eye level).
- Rules and procedures for using centers should be developed in conjunction with students and clearly understood by them.
- Centers should be previewed (with demonstration and modeling) by the teacher one at a time in the whole-class setting.
- Each center should have a posted chart with brief verbal instructions illustrated with **pictograms** (drawings or symbols depicting an activity) telling what to do in that center.
- Usually no more than four to six children should be in a particular center at any given time.
- Books and writing material should be incorporated into activity centers.
- Children should be given choices when selecting centers to go to at any given time.

Peer Tutoring

In **peer tutoring,** a trained student tutor teaches a same-age classmate or a younger student. According to Slavin (2008), both same-age tutoring and cross-age tutoring have been found to be effective. Research indicates that both the tutor and the tutee have increased academic achievement; however, it is highly important that tutors are trained beforehand and monitored during tutoring. The goal of peer tutoring is for both students to have academic gains; neither should feel burdened or frustrated by this instructional method.

Interdisciplinary Instruction

Interdisciplinary instruction is the result when teachers combine several disciplines into one or more lessons. At the elementary level, it is very common for teachers to identify the primary discipline, such as reading or social studies, and then incorporate other subject areas into the lesson. At the middle and secondary levels, it is common for teachers from different disciplines to form interdisciplinary teams that collaboratively plan integrated learning activities. Information and activities from other disciplines are used to illustrate, elaborate, and enrich the learning. The information should be practical and relevant to real life. The premise behind the interdisciplinary approach is that the world is not divided into distinct subject-area compartments, so teachers should design instruction that reflects the complexity of the real world in order to prepare students for life.

Checkpoint

Fill in the blank.

1. In direct instruction, the teacher provides systematic and _____ instruction.

2. Collaboration and the teacher's _____ and _____ are essential features of constructivist instruction.

3. Reciprocal teaching is designed to increase students' reading _____.

Mark as true or false.

4. _____ (a) Discovery learning is most compatible with a behaviorist point of view.

   _____ (b) Learning centers are an essential feature of an early-childhood classroom.

Checkpoint Answers

1. explicit

2. guidance, support

3. comprehension

4. (a) false; (b) true

Marzano's High Yield Instructional Strategies

In *What Works in Classroom Instruction* (2000), Marzano et al. identified nine evidence-based instructional strategies that have the "highest probability of enhancing student achievement" across students, grade levels, and subject areas (p. 4). These nine strategies have come to be known as "Marzano's High Yield Instructional Strategies." The following table contains a summary of the strategies.

Strategy	Brief Description	Remarks	Classroom Tools/Tasks
Identifying similarities and differences	Involving students in (teacher-led or student-directed) comparing, classifying, creating metaphors, and creating analogies	Model and scaffold activities until students become comfortable with the processes. Thereafter, monitor student-directed activities and assist/scaffold, when needed.	Venn diagrams, T-charts, comparison charts, classification tables and diagrams, teacher-led (modeled)/student-led metaphor tasks, teacher-scaffolded analogy tasks/student-directed analogy tasks
Summarizing and note taking	Involving students in teacher-scaffolded or student-directed activities in which students distill information for later review, analysis, and synthesis	Explicitly teach summarizing and note taking using think-alouds. Provide rules for summarizing (e.g., omit trivial details, use texting "shorthand"). Show students various formats for note taking. When taking notes, more is better. However, discourage verbatim note taking.	Subject notebook/journal entries, outlines, think-alouds, graphic organizers, teacher-created specialized summary frames (narrative, definition, problem/solution, etc.), teacher-prepared notes or outlines, reciprocal teaching

(*continued*)

Strategy	Brief Description	Remarks	Classroom Tools/Tasks
Reinforcing effort and providing recognition	Using teacher-directed or student-directed practices that convey to students the influence of effort on achievement; using teacher-directed practices that provide contingency-based rewards/praise for specific accomplishments	Explicitly teach students about the value of effort using personal examples or familiar stories. Make reward/praise contingent on specific accomplishments. Link rewards/praise to student effort (not just to completing work). Avoid global, meaningless praise. Gradually discontinue tangible rewards when no longer needed.	Effort-achievement charts/rubrics, pause-prompt-praise technique, symbolic tokens of recognition, tangible rewards, quality teacher praise See the section "Praise" in Chapter 2 for a detailed discussion of this topic.
Homework and practice	Using activities/assignments that extend students' learning and/or improve skill proficiency	Have a written homework policy. Provide clear instructions and well-structured assignments for homework. Grade homework and provide specific feedback. Provide class time for guided practice and well-structured independent practice *before* students try skills at home. Avoid giving "busy work" for homework or practice.	Assignments, journal reflections, speed and accuracy charts, focused practice, guided practice, independent practice See the section "Homework" in Chapter 4 for a detailed discussion of this topic.
Nonlinguistic representation	Using visual, mental, and concrete/hands-on representations/activities to represent concepts	Explicitly involve students in creating visual, mental, and concrete representations.	Graphic organizers, drawings/pictures, pictographs, mental imagery, physical models, realia, kinesthetic activities See the section "Graphic Organizers" later in this chapter for a detailed discussion of this topic.
Cooperative learning	Organizing student-led small group activities in which students work together on a collective task that has been clearly defined and explained. Students are expected to help each other learn, rather than to depend solely upon the teacher.	Explicitly teach students cooperative learning social skills. Use a variety of grouping criteria (e.g., random assignment, birthday month). Avoid grouping according to ability. Use small groups (3–4 students). Assign each group member a role or job. Monitor group processes and social skills during activities. Avoid overusing cooperative learning.	Group problem solving, group projects, jigsawing, think-pair-share, reader's theater, debate, corners See the section "Cooperative Learning" in Chapter 1 for a detailed description of this instructional strategy.
Setting goals and providing feedback	Providing opportunities for students to set learning targets personalized from teacher established broad learning goals; giving criterion-referenced feedback	Make goals specific but flexible. Explicitly teach students how to set goals and keep track of their own progress. Provide frequent, timely, specific feedback that explains what is correct and what is incorrect. Let students provide feedback for themselves and others.	Goal-setting guidelines, K-W-L charts (see page 87), contracts, progress monitoring forms, information rubrics, processes and skills rubrics, self-assessment, peer feedback

(continued)

Strategy	Brief Description	Remarks	Classroom Tools/Tasks
Generating and testing hypotheses	Engaging students in making and testing informed predictions/ guesses	Use structured tasks to explicitly teach students the process of generating and testing hypotheses. Ask students to explain their thinking.	Systems analysis tasks, problem-solving tasks, historical investigation, invention process, experimental inquiry, decision making, inductive and deductive techniques
Cues, questions, advance organizers*	Facilitating students' recall of what they already know about a topic	Ask questions that evoke analytical thinking. Give explicit cues about the topic. Focus on what's important.	K-W-L charts (see page 87), advance organizers, cues (hints)/ guiding questions about the lesson, think-alouds, anticipation guides, skimming for information, vocabulary activities.

*Called "Activating Prior Knowledge" in Marzano et al. (2000), but since renamed in Classroom Instruction That Works (Dean et al., 2012).

Checkpoint

Fill in the blank.

1. Marzano's High Yield Instructional Strategies work across students, grade levels, and _____ areas.

2. Venn diagrams are useful when identifying _____ and _____.

3. Rewards and/or praise should be contingent on _____ accomplishments.

Mark as true or false.

4. _____ (a) Effort is unrelated to achievement.

   _____ (b) Using cooperative learning every day in the same classroom is problematic.

Checkpoint Answers

1. subject

2. similarities; differences

3. specific

4. (a) false; (b) true

Attributions and Locus of Control

Attributions are the causes students assign to their successes or failures. The following four attributions are used most frequently:

- **Ability:** For example, the student might say/think, "I failed because I'm just not smart."
- **Effort:** For example, the student might say/think, "I succeeded because I tried really hard."
- **Task difficulty:** For example, the student might say/think, "I failed because the test was too hard."
- **Luck:** For example, the student might say/think, "I passed the test because I guessed right."

Locus of control reflects the degree to which students feel they have power over forces in their lives. Students with an **internal locus of control** believe that events they experience are under their own control. These students attribute their successes to their own effort or ability. When students have an **external locus of control,** they believe that they are under the control of other people or forces outside themselves. These students attribute their successes to luck and their failures to factors that they have no control over (for example, task difficulty). Researchers believe that students will be more likely to engage in learning activities when they attribute success or failure to things they can control, like their own effort or lack of it, rather than to forces over which they have little or no control, such as luck or outside forces. Teachers should help students, especially at-risk learners, link their successes to something they did to contribute to their success. When this occurs, the students develop **self-efficacy,** meaning they believe in their own ability to be successful.

Checkpoint

Fill in the blank.

1. Attributions are the _____ students assign to their successes or failures.

2. Locus of control reflects the degree to which students feel they have _____ over forces in their lives.

3. A student who says, "I failed the test because there were a lot of trick questions on it," likely has an _____ (external, internal) locus of control.

Mark as true or false.

4. _____ (a) Internal locus of control is linked to self-confidence.

   _____ (b) A teacher should be concerned if a student attributes failure on a test to bad luck.

Checkpoint Answers

1. causes

2. power

3. external

4. (a) true; (b) true

Modeling

Modeling is a powerful way to communicate intended learner outcomes to students. In modeling, the teacher demonstrates a skill (for example, solving a mathematical equation) or learning strategy (for example, using self-monitoring) that students will be expected to do automatically. Usually, the teacher articulates his or her thought processes (thinks aloud), and engages students in imitation of the skill or learning strategy. Modeling is followed by guided practice to help students learn to use the skill or strategy on their own.

Students can learn knowledge and skills, appropriate behaviors, and positive attitudes from teacher modeling. No matter the age of the student, explicit modeling is an effective way to help students know what to do and how to do it, from simple skills such as routine classroom procedures, to complex cognitive tasks such as analyzing a poem. Teachers model the intended learner outcome, and then give students opportunities to practice it. This strategy provides the structure to assignments that students often need to help them focus in a productive way. Of course, teachers should avoid being overly prescriptive when using modeling for assignments in which creativity and flexibility of thought are expected.

Furthermore, teachers should know that everything they do in front of students is a type of modeling. Indeed, modeling can impact students' thinking and behaviors to such a high degree that teachers have a responsibility to make sure they are being positive role models for their students. They can use this implicit modeling to encourage motivation and foster positive values (for example, kindness and respect) in their students.

Checkpoint

Fill in the blank.

1. Modeling is a powerful way to _____ intended learner outcomes to students.

2. Modeling provides the _____ to assignments that students often need to help them focus in a productive way.

3. Teachers should know that everything they do in front of students is a type of _____.

4. Teachers can use implicit modeling to encourage motivation and foster positive _____.

Checkpoint Answers

1. communicate

2. structure

3. modeling

4. values

Verbal Communication

Effective teachers are effective communicators. Teachers continually send messages to students and receive messages from them. They use language that is appropriate to students' developmental levels and social and linguistic backgrounds. They model and emphasize to students that the critical elements of verbal communication are

- accuracy of language.
- accuracy of information.
- standardization of language.
- clearly defined expectations.

Because communication is critical to the learning process, teachers need to be effective speakers. Not only are the words themselves important, but so is the way in which the words are said. Changes in voice loudness, rate, tone, inflection, and pitch can change the meaning of words and the emphasis of the message. Projection of the voice so it can be heard by all students is also necessary.

Written communication of teachers should be "logical and understandable ... with appropriate grammar, spelling, and sentence structure" (Rule 6A-10.095(4), FAC). This requirement should be reflected in all written communications with students, parents*, administrators, community members, and others. For instance, when teachers prepare written instructions for students, the instructions should be clear and easy to follow. Performing or visualizing what students are expected to do is an effective way to make sure that all necessary details are included.

*Note: By Florida school law, a *parent* is either or both parents, a guardian, or any person in a parental relationship to a student or who has charge over a student in place of the parent.

Whenever written instructions are presented to students, they should be communicated orally as well. This approach accommodates different learning styles in the classroom, while providing the written instructions to which the students can refer as they complete the assigned task. Asking students to repeat directions or to chorus important steps or cautions will help ensure that the instructions are communicated effectively. If students are working in groups, giving the group leader the task of reading the instructions aloud before students begin is another effective way to communicate the instructions orally. When appropriate, graphic representation, modeling, or demonstration should be included to enhance understanding. In particular, previewing centers and modeling the instructions for centers is critical for centers in early-childhood classrooms. Early-childhood teachers commonly use pictograms (pictorial representations of instructions), which are an effective way to provide directions for centers. Finally, students should be given an opportunity to ask questions about the instructions for clarification.

Asking questions is another component of verbal communication. Questions should be determined by the lesson objectives. Questions should be clear and should yield student responses—even though students' answers might not always be correct. Effective teachers provide supportive feedback to incorrect student responses. Questions can be categorized as convergent (closed-ended) or divergent (open-ended), depending on whether the teacher is seeking knowledge of information or is trying to generate ideas and stimulate thinking, respectively. If a teacher wants to determine the level of student learning, a focusing question is appropriate. To increase student interaction, a teacher will ask a prompting question. In order to clarify or justify an answer, a probing question is used.

Note: See the sections "Leading Class Discussions" and "Skillful Questioning" later in this chapter for additional discussion on questioning.

Checkpoint

Fill in the blank.

1. Teachers continually send messages to students and _____ messages from them.

2. The critical elements of verbal communication are accuracy of language, accuracy of information, standardization of language, and clearly defined _____.

3. Florida law mandates that teachers should use appropriate _____, _____, and sentence structure.

4. Questions should be determined by the lesson _____.

Checkpoint Answers

1. receive
2. expectations
3. grammar; spelling
4. objectives

Nonverbal Communication

The importance of nonverbal communication should not be underestimated. Most experts contend that nonverbal communication speaks louder than words. Nonverbal communication includes vocal cues, eye contact, facial expressions, gestures, body language, proximity, and dress.

Vocal cues include such vocal elements as tone, pitch, tempo, loudness, and inflection. Teachers who speak in a monotone are often perceived as boring and uninteresting. When teachers modulate their voices and speak in an animated manner, students are more likely to listen and be interested in the teacher's message. Research suggests that people who use a fast tempo in speech are perceived as intelligent and dynamic, while those who use a slow tempo are perceived as kind and people-oriented. However, listeners usually prefer a tempo that is similar to their own, so adopting a moderate tempo would be a safe course for a teacher.

Eye contact is an indication of a person's openness to communication. During a conversation, a speaker will make direct eye contact to signal that another person can speak. When a teacher is asking questions, as a general rule, students who know the answers look at the teacher; those who don't avoid eye contact. Furthermore, in "Six Ways to Improve Your Nonverbal Communications," Ritts and Stein (2011) maintained that eye contact with students increases a teacher's credibility and conveys warmth and concern. In some cultures, eye contact is used as an indicator of a person's veracity, with a direct gaze indicating truthfulness and an averted gaze, dishonesty. Research does not support this view; furthermore, a direct gaze is considered disrespectful in some cultures. Notwithstanding, teachers often use a stern look as a nonverbal cue to signal students to stop inappropriate behaviors.

Facial expressions can send positive or negative nonverbal messages. Smiling is a powerful nonverbal cue that conveys approval, warmth, friendliness, and approachability. When students are confused or don't understand, they might frown or look perplexed. A raised eyebrow might signal skepticism. A sneer might mean hostility.

Gestures such as pointing and illustrating with limbs and other body parts are forms of nonverbal communication. Speakers who fail to use gestures often appear wooden and boring.

Body language indicates the listener's respect for the speaker and interest in the speaker's message. Head nodding and leaning slightly forward convey respect and attention, but turning away or slouching show disrespect and lack of interest.

Proximity refers to the physical distance separating individuals. Teachers can use closeness to increase student interaction or discourage inappropriate student behavior. At the same time, teachers should be aware of cultural norms of personal space and should be on the alert for signals (such as leaning back or backing away) that students are being made to feel uneasy because the teacher is invading their personal space. Another aspect of proximity is vertical distance, with a higher level conveying more authority than a lower level. Generally, teachers will improve communication with students, especially younger students, by making an effort to get on eye level with the student (for example, getting on one knee to talk with a young child).

Dress is an often overlooked form of nonverbal communication. During the first weeks of school, when students are forming their first impressions of teachers, it is particularly important that teachers dress appropriately. Teachers who dress professionally are perceived as competent and capable. Moreover, to establish credibility, teachers should avoid dressing like their students.

Students as well as teachers communicate nonverbally. Teachers need to "hear" the messages students are sending them by nonverbal communication. If there is a discrepancy between the verbal and nonverbal message, teachers should pay closer attention to the nonverbal message because it is usually more valid. Using these cues, instruction can be adjusted as needed.

Checkpoint

Fill in the blank.

1. In general, nonverbal messages are _____ (less, more) powerful than verbal messages.

2. Teachers who speak in a _____ are often perceived as boring and uninteresting.

3. Eye contact with students _____ (decreases, increases) a teacher's credibility.

4. When speaking with a preschooler, a teacher could improve communication by getting on _____ (two words) with the student.

Checkpoint Answers

1. more

2. monotone

3. increases

4. eye level

Leading Class Discussions

Teachers need to take advantage of what students can learn in social situations such as class discussions and, in so doing, focus on developing communities of learners in their classrooms (FLDOE, 2003). Teachers who intend to make frequent use of class discussion can promote effective use of the discussion format by establishing rules and directly teaching procedures for proper discussion behavior and turn-taking to students.

In classrooms, most discussions and conversations are spontaneous and informal. However, sometimes teachers need to bring students together to process information, discuss an activity, brainstorm ideas, resolve a conflict, and so on. Teachers can use these occasions as opportunities to assess student learning and evaluate students' thinking. Class discussions also provide students with an opportunity to learn how to share and disagree about ideas in an intellectually productive way.

When a formal discussion is warranted, the discussion must have a purpose that is aligned with the teacher's goals and objectives for the subject at hand. The discussion needs to be well planned without being scripted. The teacher should have in mind questions and prompts that will elicit critical thinking from the students about the topic of discussion. However, this preparation does not mean that the teacher does most of the talking. Teachers should avoid the initiation-response-evaluation (IRE; Mehan, 1979) pattern in which the teacher asks a question and then provides an evaluation (such as "Yes, that's correct") of a student's response. On the contrary, teachers should aim to facilitate discussions that are sustained by student-initiated questions and ideas and that allow students to assume ownership of the classroom discourse.

Teachers play key roles as facilitators of classroom discussions, with the goal being to orchestrate student-to-teacher, student-to-student, and teacher-to-student interactions in ways that actively engage students in the discussion topic and allow them to use critical thinking skills. In other words, teachers set the stage for interactions without dominating the discussion. Appropriate techniques for leading class discussions are *posing questions, active listening, identifying relevant information, probing, prompting or asking leading questions, redirecting*, and *drawing inferences*.

During class discussions, **posing questions** is a crucial skill that teachers use to provide focus to the discussion and elicit and extend students' reasoning and critical thinking. Skilled facilitators use **divergent questions** (open-ended questions that allow many correct responses) to engage students in higher-level thinking and generate ideas, reactions, or opinions (for example, "What would our world be like without paper?"). Facilitators employ **convergent questions** (closed-ended questions that have a limited number of correct responses) to obtain facts, obtain specific information, check for understanding, ask for a different opinion, or, when appropriate, direct the discussion toward consensus (for example, "Does everyone agree with that solution?"). In general, active classroom discourse is best promoted by the use of open-ended questions. Asking too many closed-ended questions tends to make the discussion overly teacher-centered and stifles creative and critical thinking on the part of students. Artful teachers are purposeful in their questioning to ensure an appropriate mixture of convergent and divergent thinking.

Active listening is listening behavior that indicates to the speaker you are paying attention and hearing the speaker's message. Active listening skills include **repetition** (repeating the speaker's message), **paraphrasing** (putting the speaker's message in your own words to check for understanding), **summarizing** (stating key points of the speaker's message), and **asking questions** to clarify the content of the message or the speaker's intent. Additionally, active listeners use tone, voice level, and nonverbal behaviors such as eye contact, facial expressions, attentive body language, and proximity to indicate respect and interest in the responses and contributions of others. Teachers should foster active listening skills in students by modeling those skills when listening to others.

Identifying relevant information is "extract[ing] major ideas or themes from the statements of others," as explicitly stated in Florida law (Rule 6A-10.095(6), FAC). During classroom discussions, teachers should periodically point out key ideas and relevant information that have been brought forth. Sometimes, writing/displaying major ideas or themes on the whiteboard/SMART Board is an effective way to accomplish this task. Besides helping students recognize the main ideas that have been generated, this practice sends the message to students that their ideas are valued and important to their learning.

Probing is the technique of eliciting more information from students, often for the purpose of clarifying students' contributions or obtaining justification for their answers. Probing is a device that teachers use to help students clarify their own understandings. When students make errors, probing can be used to help them self-correct their mistakes. (See the section "Correcting Student Errors" in Chapter 4 for additional discussion on this topic.) Probing can be verbal (for example, "Please elaborate on what you mean by that") or nonverbal (for example, head nodding, direct eye contact). Creating a climate of trust and respect is essential when teachers use probing. Otherwise, students might become defensive or feel interrogated. Modeling respect for students' ideas and conveying an expectation that students are obliged to state their ideas clearly and defend them, when necessary, is crucial.

Prompting or asking leading questions is the technique of providing hints or suggestions to encourage students to keep trying and not give up. Deciding when to let a student struggle and when to offer assistance is based on the teacher's judgment of the student. Regardless, the teacher should not move on to a different student or switch to an easier question. It is imperative that the student at hand be given sufficient **wait time** to think and formulate ideas before the teacher prompts or leads the student. Research regarding wait time indicates that the desire to avoid "empty silence," a cultural norm in American culture, can cause a teacher to become uncomfortable and unable to wait at least 3 seconds for students' responses, even though waiting for students to respond communicates positive expectations for them and results in more thoughtful responses, thereby enhancing achievement. When a student cannot answer a question after an appropriate amount of time, the teacher can best support the student's learning by providing one or more prompts to help him or her summon up a correct response.

Redirecting is the technique of posing a question or prompt to students for a response or to add new insights. Most often, this technique is used by skilled facilitators to invite the class to respond to a question addressed to the teacher—for example, "That's a good question. Let's ask the class for ideas about that." Redirecting might also involve extending a student's partial contribution by asking another student for additional insights—for example, "Marisa, can you add to what Brendan said?"

Drawing inferences is the process of reaching conclusions based on implications from students' input. Drawing inferences is a step beyond summarizing, which is limited to ideas that were explicitly stated in the discussion. Inferencing involves drawing logical conclusions from the students' contributions. Of course, teachers should solicit assistance from the class in formulating conclusions and strive to obtain consensus about conclusions drawn.

Here are some guidelines that will promote productive classroom discussions.

Before Discussions

- Guide students to establish rules and procedures.
- Use an advance organizer to prepare students.
- When appropriate, role-play proper discussion behaviors and turn-taking.
- Arrange the furniture/desks to facilitate discussion (for example, in a U-shape or circle).

During Discussions

- Establish and model a norm of respect for others and their contributions.
- Use strategies that are age-appropriate and sensitive to cultural background, exceptionality, and learning preferences to ensure participation by all students.
- Reinforce participation with both verbal and nonverbal cues.
- Encourage and reinforce student-to-student exchanges.
- Use questions geared to lesson objectives.
- Ask the question and give sufficient wait time before calling on a student.
- Be comfortable with silence; give students time to think and formulate ideas.
- Avoid answering your own questions.
- Refrain from modifying a student's contribution to reflect your own ideas.
- Be honest, but use tact when correcting student errors.
- Keep the discussion on track by tactfully deflecting trivial or irrelevant questions.
- Be alert for nonverbal cues from students that signal lack of interest, frustration, and so on.
- Monitor your own nonverbal communication to make sure you are sending inviting signals.
- Use techniques to discourage monopolizers.

- Avoid taking sides when disagreements arise.
- Avoid put-downs or sarcasm.

After Discussions

- Involve students in reflecting on what they learned from the discussion.
- Ask students to assess their participation in the discussion.
- Make notes about what to do differently next time to improve the discussion format.

Checkpoint

Fill in the blank.

1. In classroom discussions, it is important that _____ do most of the talking.

2. In general, active classroom discourse is best promoted by the use of _____ (closed-ended, open-ended) questions.

3. Listening in a way that indicates to the speaker that you are paying attention and hearing the speaker's message is _____ listening.

4. "From what you've read, what are the pros and cons on this issue?" is an example of a _____ (convergent, divergent) question.

5. "That is an interesting question. Class, how would you respond?" is an example of _____.

6. Head nodding is a nonverbal cue that can be used when _____ for additional information.

Checkpoint Answers

1. students
2. open-ended
3. active
4. divergent
5. redirecting
6. probing

Skillful Questioning

In crafting their questions for a lesson, class discussion, or other activity, Florida teachers must give thoughtful attention to the cognitive complexity associated with the content they are teaching. The questions they develop for their classrooms should be aligned with the content complexity levels for the NGSSS benchmarks that the teachers are teaching (see the section "Levels of Content Complexity" in Chapter 1 for a discussion on this topic). Low-complexity questions rely mainly on recall of information, moderate-complexity questions require concrete reasoning or problem solving, and high-complexity questions should elicit abstract reasoning and higher-order thinking skills.

Teachers will find it helpful to use Bloom's Taxonomy of higher-order thinking skills—knowledge, comprehension, application, analysis, synthesis, and evaluation—when developing questions. **Knowledge-level thinking** involves recalling or remembering information. **Comprehension-level thinking** involves interpreting previously learned material. **Application-level thinking** involves applying knowledge to produce a result. **Analysis-level thinking** involves subdividing knowledge to show how it fits together. **Synthesis-level thinking** involves putting together ideas or elements to form a whole. **Evaluation-level thinking** involves judging the quality of an idea or solution. The following table contains a list of question types based on Bloom's Taxonomy.

Question Type	Student Activities	Typical Words	Examples
Knowledge/Factual	Remembering, memorizing, recognizing, recalling	Who, what, where, when, how, find, label, relate, tell, define, list, name	Who is the current president of the United States? Name the parts of speech.
Comprehension	Grasping the meaning, interpreting, translating from one medium to another, describing, explaining	Summarize, interpret, explain, illustrate, outline, rephrase, translate, estimate	In your own words, what does the term *popular sovereignty* mean? Summarize the plot of the story.
Application	Applying information to produce some result, problem solving	Apply, construct, select, choose, produce, classify, develop, solve, demonstrate, model	How many numbers between 1 and 20 are prime? Classify the animals in the list as herbivores, carnivores, or omnivores.
Analysis	Identifying motives, making inferences, finding evidence to support, comparing, breaking into component parts	Analyze, compare, contrast, simplify, examine, diagram, break apart, identify, specify, infer, predict	What are the main ways that butterflies and moths are different? Specify the steps you would use to test your theory.
Synthesis	Creating something new, writing proofs, making predictions, recognizing patterns, putting parts together to create an original whole	Compile, create, predict, combine, construct, design, develop, invent, propose, problem-solve, adapt	What rule describes the pattern shown between the two variables? Create an alternate ending for the story.
Evaluation	Stating an opinion, making value judgments, drawing conclusions	Evaluate, judge, form an opinion, critique, decide, justify, prove, prioritize, rate, assess, recommend, conclude	What is your opinion about the Supreme Court decision in *Lau v. Nichols?* Decide what you liked best about the learning activity and justify your response.

Additionally, according to research, giving students extended time in which to respond during questioning better enables them to give more comprehensive responses involving higher levels of thinking. Therefore, teachers who want their students to think at higher levels need to become comfortable with pauses and extended silence. Questions that are meant to engage mental processing beyond simple recall or recognition require ample time for students to formulate responses. Here are some further guidelines for using questioning to promote higher-order thinking in the classroom:

- Establish a climate of trust, openness, and risk-taking in the classroom.
- Model respect for students and provide recognition for their efforts.
- Provide many opportunities for student involvement during questioning.
- Ask the question and provide sufficient wait time (no less than 3 seconds) for thought.
- Evaluate the level of difficulty of your questions.
- Ask more divergent than convergent questions.
- Ask more analysis, synthesis, and evaluation questions than lower-level questions.
- Ask speculative and "What if?" questions.
- Ask questions that motivate students to detect and scrutinize assumptions.

- Ask questions that challenge students to examine their own ideas and beliefs.
- Ask questions that stimulate curiosity.
- Ask questions that encourage original and flexible thinking.
- Ask questions that prompt imagination and exploration of alternatives.
- Ask questions that require students to make connections among concepts that might, on the surface, appear unrelated.
- Ask students to identify key ideas and issues and to evaluate their relevance.
- Use probing to help students clarify their thinking.
- Use prompting to encourage students to keep trying or to assist students in modifying their responses.
- Redirect students' questions to the class.
- Use students' responses to make a point or to stimulate additional discussion.
- Encourage students to ask questions of each other.
- Encourage students to ask questions that challenge you, the textbook, or other students.
- Be nonjudgmental in your response to students' answers to higher-level questions.
- Avoid the following:
  - Giving up on a student by asking an easier question or moving on to another student.
  - Being rude or sarcastic, or making fun of students' responses.
  - Using nonverbal cues (for example, a frown) that show judgmental reactions to students' responses.
  - Answering your own questions.
  - Asking nonspecific questions such as "Are there any questions?" or "Does everyone understand?"
  - Asking questions that give away answers.

Checkpoint

Fill in the blank.

1. Subdividing knowledge to show how it fits together requires _____-level thinking.

2. Giving students extended time in which to respond during questioning better enables them to give more comprehensive responses involving _____ levels of thinking.

3. Questions that encourage students to keep trying are _____ questions.

Mark as true or false.

4. _____ (a) Skillful questioning plays a vital role in fostering students' critical and creative thinking skills.

   _____ (b) To check for understanding, a teacher should ask, "Are there any questions?"

Checkpoint Answers

1. analysis

2. higher

3. prompting

4. (a) true; (b) false

Graphic Organizers

Graphic organizers are visual depictions of the interrelationships among abstract concepts or illustrations of processes. They are powerful instructional tools that help students understand concepts and organize their thinking by putting information into a logical, easy-to-read visual format. Graphic organizers are naturally conducive to learning for visual learners, but research indicates other students also show improved learner achievement when teachers use graphic organizers. Furthermore, according to Brooks-Young (2006), "students who regularly use visual learning strategies show improvement in reading comprehension, problem-solving skills, ability to organize and express their thoughts, and identifying patterns and relationships in content" (p. 1). Moreover, their retention of content is enhanced. The following chart lists some common graphic organizers and how they can be used.

Graphic Organizer	Brief Description	Uses
K-W-L chart	A visual representation of the K-W-L process in the form of a chart with three columns headed "What We Know," "What We Want to Know," and "What We Learned." Before a learning episode on a topic, students brainstorm on what they know about the topic and what they want to know about it. The information is listed in the proper column. After the learning episode, the students identify what they learned, and the information is listed in the proper column. Next, the students compare the information under "What We Want to Know" with what is listed under "What We Learned."	To activate prior knowledge To set a purpose for learning To provide a structure for learning
Web	A visual picture that shows connections of words or phrases to a topic. The teacher lists the topic and circles it, and then from the students' contributions builds a web-like structure that links words or phrases to the central circled topic.	To activate prior knowledge To show connections within a topic To identify key vocabulary To help students organize their thoughts (for example, for a writing activity)
Concept map or semantic map	A visual picture that shows the interrelationships among concepts. The teacher lists a central concept and then assists students in identifying a set of associated concepts. Related concepts are linked and, sometimes, words or short phrases are added to explain the connections.	To help students organize their knowledge To show the interrelationships among concepts
Venn diagram	A visual depiction of the commonalities and differences among concepts or entities. Overlapping circles are drawn to represent each concept/entity. Students brainstorm common characteristics, which are listed in the proper intersections (overlapping areas), and differences, which are listed in the respective circles, but outside the intersections.	To facilitate contrast and comparison of concepts To help students see relationships To help students organize their thinking To foster higher-level thinking skills
Decision tree	A tree-like diagram of actions and their expected outcomes or consequences	To facilitate decision making To develop students' predicting skills To help students organize their thinking

87

(*continued*)

Graphic Organizer	Brief Description	Uses
Cause-effect chart	A chart showing a series of events or actions and their expected outcomes or consequences	To facilitate decision making To develop students' predicting skills To help students organize their thinking
Flowchart	A visual depiction of a sequence of events or a process	To foster logical thinking skills To develop skill in organizing information To facilitate planning To foster attention to detail
Story tree	A tree-like structure in which each main branch represents a major element of a story (plot, setting, and so on). On the branches, students add questions (in the shape of clumps of leaves) that they should ask themselves as they read to evaluate that particular element.	To guide students' critical evaluation of a work of literature To help students organize their thinking To foster self-questioning skills To promote evaluation-level thinking

When students are first introduced to a graphic organizer, a good practice is for the teacher to model how to properly use it, stopping frequently to check for understanding. Once the students are familiar with various organizer types, then the teacher can merely remind them of the organizer before the learning experience. But, at first, if the organizer is a new type, then, just as with any new learning, explaining and modeling is critical.

Traditionally, graphic organizers are produced on whiteboards, transparencies, or large sheets of paper. Brooks-Young (2006) pointed out that a downside to this approach to using graphic organizers is that creating, editing, revising, and saving work can sometimes be problematic. To overcome these limitations, teachers are moving toward the use of electronic graphic organizers such as Inspiration, Kidspiration, and Cmap Tools. These innovative tools are "inexpensive, easy to use, and address the roadblocks of their offline counterparts" (Brooks-Young, 2006, p. 2).

Checkpoint

Fill in the blank.

1. Graphic organizers are _____ depictions of the interrelationships among abstract concepts or illustrations of processes.

2. A graphic organizer that fosters logical thinking skills is a _____.

3. A graphic organizer that shows actions and their expected outcomes or consequences is a _____ tree.

Mark as true or false.

4. _____ (a) Students show improved learner achievement when teachers use graphic organizers.

_____ (b) Teachers should prepare graphic organizers in advance to save academic learning time.

Checkpoint Answers

1. visual

2. flowchart

3. decision

4. (a) true; (b) false

Critical and Creative Thinking

Effective teachers recognize the importance of fostering critical and creative thinking in their students. By design, teachers use adroit questioning and their knowledge of levels of content complexity and Bloom's Taxonomy to stimulate these higher-order thinking skills in their students. In addition, teachers demonstrate and model critical and creative thinking and provide numerous opportunities for students to engage in activities (for example, problem solving and brainstorming) that foster critical and creative thinking.

Critical Thinking

Critical thinking is the mental process of making reasoned judgments and reaching objective conclusions by analyzing, organizing, comparing, synthesizing, logically examining, challenging, and evaluating assumptions and evidence. Students might learn isolated information, but without the application of critical thinking to that information, actual understanding is minimal. As Schafersman (1991) asserted, teachers transmit the subject content, but "often fail to teach students how to think effectively about this subject matter; that is, how to properly understand and evaluate it. This second ability is termed critical thinking" (p. 1). In Florida, early and intentional instruction in critical thinking for students was mandated by Standard 4 of Goal 3 of Florida's School Improvement and Accountability Act of 1991. Research indicates that critical thinking can be taught and that explicit instruction in critical thinking results in increased student academic performance.

Teachers need to be aware of characteristics of critical thinkers they can build on to advance the development of critical thinking skills in their classrooms. The following personality characteristics of critical thinkers have been gathered from the works of Brookfield (1991), Cotton (1993), Paul et al. (1990), and Schafersman (1991): Critical thinkers tend to be curious, flexible, fair-minded, independent, humble, confident, honest, skeptical, analytical, cautious, and intellectually persistent. Other characteristics identified by these authors are that critical thinkers

- identify and challenge assumptions underlying beliefs, behaviors, or issues.
- recognize and explore alternatives to their present ways of thinking.
- challenge standardized or bureaucratic ways of doing things.
- question the credibility of sources of information.
- consider how context affects beliefs, behaviors, or issues.
- recognize and prioritize key ideas.
- use evidence to make plausible inferences or predictions or to reach conclusions or make decisions.
- determine what evidence is material and relevant to an argument or issue.
- distinguish fact from opinion.
- recognize bias and vested interest.
- recognize faulty reasoning and misuse of information.
- perceive anomalies, discrepancies, or contradictions.
- evaluate issues, arguments, ideas, or interpretations using self-formulated criteria.
- sometimes ask impertinent questions or suggest disquieting ideas.
- anticipate reactions to questions or suggestions.
- are self-confident and trust their own judgment.
- "hold true to hard-won beliefs and commitments" (Brookfield, 1991, p. 23).

On the surface, some of these characteristics might appear at odds with traditional classroom situations. However, effective teachers know how to balance their responsibility to regulate and control student behavior with the need to create a classroom climate that encourages critical thinking. Here are some ideas for the classroom, gathered from Brookfield (1991), Cotton (1993), Paul et al. (1990), Schafersman (1991), and the FLDOE:

- Provide an atmosphere that respects and values personal expression.
- Provide a climate that is open and conducive to "thinking for oneself."

- Create an environment that supports critical inquiry.
- Establish a culture of high expectations and encouragement.
- Explicitly explain and model higher-order thinking skills (analysis, synthesis, and evaluation) for students and provide opportunities for students to practice the skills.
- Create tasks that require students to become proficient in using critical thinking to solve problems and make decisions.
- Nurture attitudes of persistence and perseverance when students are problem-solving.
- Require students to clarify and defend their solutions or conclusions.
- Use skillful questioning (for example, to create cognitive disequilibrium) that incites critical thinking.
- Provide opportunities for students to put critical thinking skills into practice within a group setting.
- Provide ample time for critical thinking to take place.

Creative Thinking

Creative thinking is the mental process of generating new ideas, recognizing and finding solutions to problems, and making informed decisions. It involves originality of thinking. Young children are naturally creative. They play pretend games, make up stories, and freely express themselves in other ways. Encouraging and nurturing this natural inclination is important to students' academic success. As they progress through the grades, students are expected to generate creative ideas in a variety of situations, such as developing alternative solutions or perspectives to a complex problem.

Teachers need to be aware of characteristics of creative thinkers that they can build on to promote creative thinking in their classrooms. The following personality characteristics of creative thinkers have been gleaned from the works of Brookfield (1991) and Davidson (2003): Creative thinkers tend to be curious, optimistic, confident, open-minded, flexible, tolerant of ambiguity, persistent, independent, uninhibited, excitable, eager, and sociable as well as being risk-takers, nonconformists, holistic learners, and divergent thinkers. Other characteristics identified by these authors are that creative thinkers

- have interests in a wide range of fields but can also be intensely absorbed in one area.
- persevere unrelentingly when problem-solving.
- can look at a situation from multiple perspectives.
- are willing to consider new ideas and seek out opposing viewpoints.
- make novel or unique connections between seemingly unrelated things or ideas.
- find unusual solutions to problems.
- use metaphors or analogies to frame concepts and ideas, when appropriate.
- reject standardized or bureaucratic ways of doing things.
- sometimes ask impertinent questions or suggest disquieting ideas.
- do not see the world as absolute and unchangeable.
- are future-oriented and embrace change as a positive dynamic.
- are self-confident and trust their own judgment.

As in the case for critical thinkers, on the surface, some of these characteristics might appear at odds with traditional classroom situations. However, effective teachers know how to balance their responsibility to regulate and control student behavior with the need to create a classroom climate that encourages creative thinking. Here are some ideas for the classroom, gathered from Davidson (2003), Wilson (2004), and the FLDOE:

- Provide an atmosphere that respects and values personal expression.
- Provide a climate that encourages questioning, exploration, experimentation, and intellectual risk-taking.
- Engage students in generating ideas in a variety of situations, such as in brainstorming or using graphic organizers.
- Create tasks that require students to become proficient in using creative processes to solve problems.

- Nurture attitudes of persistence and perseverance when students are problem-solving.
- Use skillful questioning that evokes creative thinking.
- Allow students to pose their own problems and devise their own approaches to problem solving.
- Encourage students to develop open-ended and innovative projects.
- Allow students to collaborate with others to get feedback and support for their ideas.
- Provide ample time for creativity to flourish.
- Demonstrate and model creative thinking.
- Avoid micromanaging, hovering over students, restricting choices, rewarding students excessively, emphasizing competition, and pressuring students.

Checkpoint

Fill in the blank.

1. Critical thinkers identify and _____ assumptions.
2. Critical thinkers can distinguish fact from _____.
3. To promote critical thinking, teachers should require students to clarify and _____ their solutions or conclusions.
4. Teachers should _____ explain and model higher-order thinking skills.
5. Young children are _____ creative.
6. Creative thinkers can look at a situation from _____ perspectives.
7. To promote creative thinking, teachers should provide an atmosphere that respects and values _____ expression.

Mark as true or false.

8. _____ (a) Creative thinkers see the world as absolute and unchangeable.

   _____ (b) Rewarding students excessively stifles creativity.

Checkpoint Answers

1. challenge
2. opinion
3. defend
4. explicitly
5. naturally
6. multiple
7. personal
8. (a) false; (b) true

Brainstorming

Brainstorming is a learning activity in which students generate ideas around a specific topic of interest. It is an effective way to engage students in creative thinking. The two main rules of brainstorming are the following:

- Any idea is acceptable.
- Criticism of the ideas of others is forbidden.

Brainstorming can be an individual, small-group, or whole-class activity. Before teachers engage students in group brainstorming, teachers should prepare students by having them discuss the rules of brainstorming and how they will implement the rules during the activity. Often, teachers find it helpful to have students role-play active listening and turn-taking before brainstorming begins. During brainstorming, the teacher or a designated recorder writes down the ideas or key points. Teachers should monitor and facilitate the process without imposing their own ideas on students. Ample time should be allotted for the activity so that students have time to think in divergent ways. Repetitive responses or the slowing down of the flow of ideas signal that it is time to end the session. After group brainstorming, the ideas are organized, prioritized, and summarized.

Brainstorming can be used for various purposes. For instance, before beginning a lesson, teachers can use brainstorming to activate prior knowledge about the lesson topic. They can use a brainstorming session to help the class reach consensus on a problem in the classroom. Additionally, students can be encouraged to brainstorm as a pre-activity to reading, when beginning the writing process, or when they are engaged in problem solving.

Benefits of brainstorming are that it

- reveals background information and knowledge of a topic.
- discloses misconceptions.
- helps students relate existing knowledge to content.
- strengthens communication skills.
- fosters creative thinking and problem solving (*Florida Curriculum Framework*, 1998, p. 430).

Checkpoint

Fill in the blank.

1. Brainstorming is an effective way to engage students in _____ thinking.

2. During a brainstorming session, criticism of the ideas of others is _____.

3. Teachers can use brainstorming to _____ students' prior knowledge about the lesson topic.

Mark as true or false.

4. _____ (a) During brainstorming sessions, "wild" ideas are acceptable.

   _____ (b) Before engaging students in brainstorming, teachers should make sure that students understand the rules of brainstorming.

Checkpoint Answers

1. creative

2. forbidden

3. activate

4. (a) true; (b) true

Metacognition

Metacognition is the process of thinking about and monitoring one's own thinking. It refers to a person's awareness of, reflection on, understanding of, and control over his or her mental operations. Successful learners are adept at using metacognition. For instance, they know how to use mental self-talk for the following metacognitive strategies:

- **To set a purpose for learning:** Why do I need to learn this? Why is this task important? What will I gain from doing this? What is my learning goal for this task?

- **To plan for learning:** How can I organize my thoughts for accomplishing this task? What resources do I need? How much time do I need? What should I do first?

- **To select learning strategies that are suited to the learning task:** What is the best way to learn this? What other strategies might I consider? What strategies have worked for a similar task in the past?

- **To monitor their progress:** What am I learning? Am I understanding? Am I concentrating? What am I thinking right now? Is this strategy working for me? What help do I need? What difficulties am I having? Where can I find information to help me? Why did I do that? What makes sense to do next? Am I making progress toward my learning goal?

- **To make adjustments and modifications when they are making what they perceive as insufficient progress toward achieving learning goals:** What should I change? Should I give up on this approach? Would another strategy work better? Should I start over?

- **To assess their learning:** What do I understand? What do I not understand? What did I accomplish? What do I still need to work on? Did I achieve my learning goal?

Often, successful learners automatically and unconsciously use this mental self-questioning. At the same time, they have the conscious ability to take charge of their learning. In other words, successful learners know "how to learn." In contrast, struggling students seldom demonstrate metacognitive abilities on their own. They need explicit training and guidance on how to learn. From the works of Thamraksa (2005) and Armbruster et al. (2001), explicit instruction of metacognitive strategies can be achieved through the following step-by-step process:

1. **Direct explanation:** The teacher explains a metacognitive strategy, why the strategy is helpful, and when to use it.

2. **Modeling:** The teacher models the strategy and how to apply it by doing a "think-aloud"—saying his or her mental self-talk aloud for the students to hear.

3. **Guided practice:** The students practice the strategy under the direct guidance and feedback of the teacher.

4. **Application:** While the teacher monitors, the students are given multiple opportunities in individual and group situations to apply and practice the strategy on their own, with automaticity being the ultimate goal.

Checkpoint

Fill in the blank.

1. Successful learners set a _____ for learning.

2. Struggling students seldom demonstrate _____ abilities on their own.

3. When teachers are modeling metacognitive strategies, they say their self-talk _____.

Mark as true or false.

4. _____ (a) Metacognition is the process of thinking about and monitoring one's own thinking.

   _____ (b) Struggling learners need explicit instruction in metacognitive strategies.

Checkpoint Answers

1. purpose

2. metacognitive

3. aloud

4. (a) true; (b) true

Logical Reasoning

Logical reasoning involves the higher-level thinking processes that are used to make decisions or draw conclusions. There are two basic ways of reasoning to reach conclusions: *inductive reasoning* and *deductive reasoning*.

Inductive reasoning is the process of drawing a general conclusion based on one or more examples. When using inductive reasoning, you look at specific examples and try to identify a pattern or trend that fits the given examples in order to determine a general rule. For instance, you might observe the coldness of a number of ice cubes and conclude (through inference) that all ice cubes are cold.

In contrast, **deductive reasoning** is the process of using an accepted rule to draw a conclusion about a specific example. When using deductive reasoning, you apply a general rule to a specific case. For instance, you might start by knowing that all rectangles are parallelograms and conclude (through implication) that a square is a parallelogram because a square is a rectangle. **Syllogistic reasoning** (for example, "All rectangles are parallelograms. A square is a rectangle. Therefore, a square is a parallelogram.") and **conditional reasoning** (for example, "If a figure is a rectangle, then the figure is a parallelogram. A square is a rectangle; therefore, a square is a parallelogram.") are types of deductive reasoning.

Knowing the difference between inductive and deductive reasoning is essential to evaluating arguments. An **argument** is a course of reasoning offered in support of a position. When inductive reasoning is used in an argument, inferences are used to support the position of the person making the argument. When deductive reasoning is used, accepted truths or generalizations are applied to support the favored position.

Because inductive arguments are based on observations and examples, the validity of their conclusions is always open to question. When students are evaluating inductive arguments, they should be encouraged to consider the reliability of the evidence, whether generalizations are adequately supported, and whether the inferences made are honest and reasonable. **Hasty generalization** (generalizing from a few atypical examples), **faulty analogy** (assuming that because two things are alike in some respects, they are alike in all respects), and **false cause** (assuming that a first thing caused a second thing because the first thing preceded the second thing in time) are examples of faulty reasoning that students should be taught to be watchful for when evaluating arguments.

Deductive arguments use assumed generalizations or premises to logically arrive at conclusions. If the premises are true and the logic is sound, then the conclusion of the argument is valid. When students are evaluating deductive arguments, they should be encouraged to consider the credibility and reasonableness of the premises and the soundness of the logic used. They should look for premises that are based on half-truths, exaggerated claims, or propaganda. Also, two well-known illogical pitfalls that students need to be made aware of are affirming the consequent and denying the antecedent. **Affirming the consequent** refers to assuming the first part of a conditional statement must be true when the second part is true. Here is an example: "If a person smokes, then he or she will have breathing difficulties. Tara has breathing difficulties; therefore, Tara is a smoker." This line of reasoning is illogical because Tara's breathing difficulties might be unrelated to smoking; in fact, Tara might not be a smoker at all. **Denying the antecedent** refers to assuming that when the first part of a conditional statement is not true, then the second part of the statement must also be false. Here is an example: "If a person smokes, then he or she will have breathing difficulties. Tara does not smoke; therefore, Tara does not have breathing difficulties." This reasoning is illogical because Tara might have breathing difficulties that are caused by something unrelated to smoking.

Checkpoint

Fill in the blank.

1. Reasoning from the specific to the general is _____ reasoning.

2. Reasoning from the general to the specific is _____ reasoning.

3. A course of reasoning offered in support of a position is called a(n) _____.

4. The validity of the conclusions of inductive arguments is always _____ to question.

Checkpoint Answers

1. inductive

2. deductive

3. argument

4. open

Problem Solving

Problem solving is a systematic and usually cyclical process. One commonly used problem-solving approach (based on the work *How to Solve It* by G. Polya, 1957) consists of the following four steps:

1. Identify and clarify the problem.

2. Brainstorm possible ways to solve the problem and devise a plan.

3. Carry out the plan.

4. Look back to see whether the problem has been solved.

Of course, in practice, problem solving seldom occurs in a sequential, step-by-step manner. Problem solvers often revisit previous steps, skip steps, and even start over. This strategy has traditionally been associated with problem solving in mathematics; however, it is applicable across the curriculum as a systematic approach to resolving problems or issues.

The importance of developing students' problem-solving skills cannot be overemphasized. Problem-solving ability is critical to students' success in school and is an essential tool for the enjoyment of a full, productive, and satisfying life. Teachers should, by design, structure the learning environment to promote a climate conducive to problem solving and provide students with numerous individual and group opportunities to engage in problem-solving activities. Benefits associated with problem solving include the following:

- It promotes critical and creative thinking skills.
- It develops logical reasoning skills.
- It facilitates reflective thinking.
- It motivates students' interest in the content.
- It promotes students' understanding and retention of concepts.
- It provides an opportunity for students to discover new ways of thinking.
- It enhances students' self-confidence.
- It gives students a sense of empowerment.

Checkpoint

Fill in the blank.

1. The first step in problem solving is to _____ and clarify the problem.

2. In practice, problem solving seldom occurs in a _____, step-by-step manner.

3. Problem-solving ability is critical to students' _____ in school.

Mark as true or false.

4. _____ (a) Problem solving promotes students' retention of concepts.

   _____ (b) Problem solving sharpens students' critical thinking skills.

Checkpoint Answers

1. identify

2. sequential

3. success

4. (a) true; (b) true

Scientific Inquiry

Scientific inquiry (or laboratory investigation) is the process used by scientists to obtain reliable and valid information about the world we live in. It has five main steps:

1. **Define the problem:** Pose a thoughtful question about a topic or variable of interest.

2. **Research the topic:** Look up what others have found out about the topic or variable.

3. **Formulate a hypothesis:** Make an educated guess about an aspect of the topic or variable.

4. **Gather evidence:** Design and perform an investigation to test the hypothesis; collect data about the hypothesis.

5. **Draw conclusions:** Analyze the data collected and decide whether the hypothesis is supported or not supported by the results.

Laboratory investigations benefit students by

- helping them visualize concepts and participate in learning processes.
- letting them experience the way some scientists work.
- giving them a chance to learn that some questions might have one or more answers or possibly no answer.
- developing their scientific process skills.
- fostering critical and creative thinking (*Florida Curriculum Framework*, 1998, p. 432).

Obviously, as in problem solving, the practice of science seldom occurs in a lock-step fashion. Scientists often revisit previous steps, skip steps, and even start over. Furthermore, "scientific argumentation is a necessary part of scientific inquiry and plays an important role in the generation and validation of scientific knowledge.... Not only does science require creativity in its methods and processes, but also in its questions and explanations" (Science Next Generation Sunshine State Standards, 2008, FLDOE).

Teachers should guide students in evaluating the plausibility of claims or interpretations from scientific investigations. Students should be made aware that only when investigators use well-designed studies can conclusions that are reliable and valid be drawn. **Well-designed studies** investigate issues that are clear and unambiguous; clearly define populations of study; use randomization in selecting representative samples of adequate size; use well-defined variables of interest; control outside factors, such as extraneous variables; and avoid **bias,** an unintentional or, perhaps, deliberate study flaw that favors particular results and that could jeopardize the validity of conclusions.

Checkpoint

Fill in the blank.

1. The first step in scientific inquiry is to define the _____.

2. A _____ is an educated guess.

3. A study flaw that favors particular results is called _____.

4. Teachers should guide students in evaluating the _____ of claims from scientific investigations.

Checkpoint Answers

1. problem

2. hypothesis

3. bias

4. plausibility

Multiple Learning Styles and Teaching

Effective teachers are keenly aware of learning style differences. They know that if all students are to be successful, teachers must understand that students learn in different ways. Nevertheless, some critics suggest that teachers should disregard students' learning styles and that, instead, students should learn to adapt to the teachers' styles. These critics seem to be disregarding the research that indicates that certain learning style characteristics are biological in nature and that, in the short run, learning styles are remarkably resistant to change. Perhaps the most reasonable approach for teachers is to

- recognize that some students' behaviors are manifestations of the students' learning styles (such as needing to see the big picture before focusing on details) and should not automatically be viewed negatively.
- cater to individual styles as much as possible, particularly at first.
- use a mix of teaching styles so that students with different learning styles will have an opportunity to learn in their preferred style at least occasionally.
- teach students how to function in situations when the teaching style does not match their own learning style.

The FLDOE Bureau of School Improvement (2006) suggested the following teaching strategies for working with diverse learners:

- Incorporate multimedia and multimodality instructional activities.
- Assess students' preferred ways of receiving instruction and implement learning experiences that incorporate students' preferences.
- Help students to recognize their learning styles, to understand why they do what they do in learning situations, and to use this information to improve their ability to learn.
- When possible, give students choices in how they will engage in learning opportunities.
- Prior to instructional experiences, set a clear purpose for learning and provide a general overview of material to be learned.
- Use advance organizers (K-W-L charts, webs, semantic maps, and so on) to facilitate students' ability to link new learning to prior knowledge.
- Group in various ways for learning activities.
- Use a combination of self-directed and teacher-led activities.
- Allow sufficient time for students to process information and experiences.
- Revisit challenging learning tasks using different approaches.
- Use a variety of review and reflection strategies to close learning experiences.
- Provide immediate, consistent, and informative feedback.
- Assess students through a variety of procedures and activities.
- Use assessment that is aligned with the instructional experiences.
- Evaluate learning experiences in terms of attainment of learning goals, observed student behavior, and student involvement.
- While continuing to provide instruction in familiar, comfortable, and successful ways, gradually introduce students to learning experiences that require students to learn in new ways (p. 2).

Finally, effective teachers recognize that it is important for students to assume ownership for their learning. Teachers who actively involve their students in the learning process create a climate of mutual trust, respect, and accountability.

See the section "Learning Styles" in Chapter 1 for a fuller discussion of this topic.

Checkpoint

Fill in the blank.

1. Advance organizers are useful for activating students' _____ knowledge.

2. Students need sufficient _____ to process information and experiences.

3. Teachers should use a _____ of assessment strategies.

Mark as true or false.

4. _____ (a) In the short run, learning styles are resistant to change.

   _____ (b) It is inappropriate for teachers to introduce students to new ways of learning.

Checkpoint Answers

1. prior
2. time
3. variety
4. (a) true; (b) false

Technology Literacy

The No Child Left Behind Act of 2001 requires that every student be technology-literate by the end of the eighth grade. This federal mandate means it is more critical than ever that Florida teachers have **technology literacy.** "Technology literacy is the ability to responsibly use appropriate technology to communicate; solve problems; and access, manage, integrate, evaluate, and create information to improve learning in all subject areas and to acquire lifelong knowledge and skills in the 21st century" (FLDOE, 2003, *Document 1: Florida Technology Literacy Profile*, www.fldoe.org/bii/Instruct_Tech/downloads/FLTechLiteracyProfile.pdf).

Technology literacy is important because, according to the National Association for the Education of Young Children, research indicates that, when used appropriately, technology has positive effects on children's cognitive and social abilities. For instance, technology in the classroom

- offers more control and involvement in the learning process.
- makes learning more interesting.
- promotes investigative skills.
- serves as an access to almost unlimited sources of information.
- develops skills to measure, monitor, and improve performance.
- enables communication with people from many parts of the world, bringing the sights, sounds, and thoughts of another language and culture into the classroom.
- provides opportunities to apply knowledge to simulated or real-life projects.
- develops readiness for a high-tech world of work.

Source: *Secondary Physical Education Curriculum Guide,* Brevard County Public Schools (secondarypgms.brevard.k12.fl.us/PE/Sec%20PE%20Curric%20Guide%202009.pdf)

Recognizing the significance of technology literacy for teachers and students, the International Society for Technology in Education (www.iste.org/) developed the **National Education Technology Standards (NETS).** The NETS have been adopted or adapted by most states, including Florida. A technology-literate teacher

- is able to identify and solve routine hardware and software problems that occur during everyday use.
- keeps up-to-date on changes in technologies and their effects on the workplace and society.
- follows legal and ethical guidelines when using technology and discusses consequences of misuse with students.
- uses appropriate technology tools (for example, content-specific software, graphing calculators, and web tools) to support learning and research.
- uses productivity/multimedia tools and peripherals to support personal productivity, group collaboration, and learning throughout the curriculum.
- is able to use technology resources to design, develop, publish, and present products (for example, PowerPoint presentations, web pages, and videotapes) that demonstrate and communicate curriculum concepts to audiences inside and outside the classroom.
- collaborates with colleagues, experts, and others using interactive communication tools to investigate curriculum-related problems, issues, and information, and to develop solutions or products for audiences inside and outside the classroom.
- is able to investigate and evaluate the accuracy, relevance, appropriateness, comprehensiveness, and bias of electronic information sources.
- selects and uses appropriate technology tools and resources to accomplish a variety of tasks and solve problems. Understands concepts underlying hardware, software, and connectivity, as well as practical applications of technology to learning and problem solving (FLDOE, *Document 1: Florida Technology Literacy Profile*, 2003).

Technology literacy is a must for Florida teachers. They need to have a sound understanding of the nature and operation of technology systems and be proficient in the use of technology for both accomplishing teacher tasks and enhancing learning opportunities for students. However, to use technology to its maximum potential in the teaching and learning process, teachers need support and training from colleagues and administrators.

Checkpoint

Fill in the blank.

1. The No Child Left Behind Act of 2001 requires that every student be technology-literate by the end of _____ grade.

2. Research indicates that, when used appropriately, technology has _____ (positive, negative) effects on children's cognitive and social abilities.

3. Florida teachers should exhibit legal and _____ behaviors when using information and technology.

Mark as true or false.

4. _____ (a) Technology literacy is an option for Florida teachers.

   _____ (b) The National Association for the Education of Young Children is opposed to the use of technology in schools.

Checkpoint Answers

1. eighth

2. positive

3. ethical

4. (a) false; (b) false

Summary

In summary, effective teachers seek out and use research-based instructional methods, strategies, and procedures to deliver instruction so that students of all capabilities are able to understand the content. They use explicit and systematic instruction, as needed, and model and scaffold student learning for optimum outcomes. They recognize that critical thinking must be an integral part of every student's school experience. They are aware that higher-order thinking is stimulated when learners are given opportunities to reflect, challenge, discuss, generate ideas, and problem-solve. They use this understanding to structure learning environments that encourage intellectual risk-taking and critical thinking.

Sample Questions

1. A kindergarten teacher sets up a new learning center and posts illustrated directions to explain how students are expected to use the center. Which of the following would be most effective in ensuring that the students understand the directions for the center?

   A. Before students go to the center, introduce the center to the students and model how to follow the directions given.

   B. Before students go to the center, tell them to be sure to consult the directions when they are in the center.

   C. Make sure that students go to the center in pairs, so that they can work together to figure out what to do.

   D. Praise students when they follow the directions for the center without asking for clarification from the teacher.

2. A teacher can convey high expectations to a low-achieving student by

   A. accepting and praising all work.

   B. setting challenging but attainable performance standards that can be achieved with effort.

   C. using a lower grading standard that better reflects the student's abilities.

   D. modeling creative and critical thinking when working with the student.

3. As a student is talking, the teacher leans forward slightly and smiles at the student. This teacher behavior is an example of

   A. prompting.

   B. active listening.

   C. praising.

   D. redirecting.

4. Which of the following is a common characteristic of critical thinkers?

   A. skepticism

   B. boastfulness

   C. conceit

   D. self-consciousness

5. Which of the following activities would best promote students' creative thinking skills?

   A. In math, listing the prime numbers between 1 and 100.

   B. In reading, identifying the main idea in a paragraph.

   C. In science, designing an experiment to test brands of fertilizer.

   D. In language arts, underlining all the adjectives in a selection of text.

6. Which of the following tasks related to a book that third-grade students have read requires higher-order thinking skills?

   A. Students discuss similarities and differences between the protagonist and the antagonist.
   B. Students play-act episodes from the book.
   C. Students identify and describe the characters in the book.
   D. Students summarize the plot of the story.

Answer Explanations for Sample Questions

1. **A.** For early-childhood learners, teachers should preview centers and model the instructions for the children. Therefore, **A** is the correct response. Eliminate **B** and **C** because these approaches would not be as effective as the approach given in **A.** Eliminate **D** because this answer choice is not aligned with the question because it does not address how the teacher will help ensure that students understand the directions.

2. **B.** Eliminate **A** and **C** because these practices would convey low expectations to the student. Eliminate **D** because it is not aligned with the question. Setting challenging but attainable performance standards that can be achieved with effort is an effective way for a teacher to convey high expectations to a low-achieving student. Thus, **B** is the correct response.

3. **B.** The behaviors of leaning forward and smiling are nonverbal cues, which often are used in active listening. Thus, **B** is the correct response. The other answer choices are incorrect because these communication techniques require verbal communication.

4. **A.** Critical thinkers tend to be skeptical. Thus, **A** is the correct response. The characteristics in the other choices are not typical of critical thinkers.

5. **C.** Eliminate **A, B,** and **D** because these activities do not involve originality of thinking. Choice **C** is the correct response because in this activity the student must create the design for the experiment.

6. **A.** Eliminate **B, C,** and **D** because these tasks require only comprehension-level thinking, a lower-level thinking skill. Engaging in a discussion of the similarities and differences between the protagonist and the antagonist will require students to use analysis-level thinking, a higher-order thinking skill. Thus, **A** is the correct response.

Competency 4: Assessment

Competency Description and Key Indicators

According to the *Competencies and Skills Required for Teacher Certification in Florida*, 20th Edition (available at www.fldoe.org/asp/ftce/pdf/ftce20edition.pdf), **Competency 4** for the PEd Test addresses **Assessment** as follows:

Knowledge of various types of assessment strategies for determining impact on student learning

Key indicators:

- Analyze assessment data from multiple sources to guide instructional decisions.
- Select formative and summative assessments that match learning objectives leading to student mastery.
- Use a variety of assessment tools to monitor student progress, achievement, and learning gains.
- Determine appropriate assessments and testing conditions to accommodate learning styles and varying knowledge levels of students.
- Identify ways to share the importance and outcomes of student assessment data with students and stakeholders.
- Use technology to organize and integrate assessment data.

Overview

Assessment is a process in which information about students' progress toward learning outcomes and performance standards is collected. The purpose of assessment is to promote student learning and development. Assessment should be systematic and ongoing in the classroom in both formal and informal ways. Effective teachers know that assessment is most useful when it aims to help students by identifying their unique strengths and needs so as to inform teacher planning and instruction.

This chapter provides a general review of Assessment with sample questions and explanations at the end of the chapter. Checkpoint exercises are found throughout the review material. These exercises give you an opportunity to practice what you just learned. The answers to the Checkpoint exercises are found immediately following the set of exercises. When doing the Checkpoint exercises, you should cover up the answers. Then check your answers when you've finished the exercises. The sample questions at the end of this chapter are multiple-choice questions that are similar to what you might expect to see on the FTCE PEd Test. The answer explanations for the sample questions are provided immediately after the questions.

Effective Classroom Assessment

The most effective classroom assessment practices are those that are aligned directly with curriculum and instruction and focus on student learning. Skillful teachers use a variety of assessment approaches, such as observation, documentation of students' talk, interviews, anecdotal notes, collections of students' work over time, traditional teacher-made tests, self-assessment, peer assessment, and appropriate performance assessments to find out how well students know, understand, and are able to apply the state curriculum. Key questions to ask about any classroom assessment are

- Does the assessment constitute developmentally appropriate measures?
- Does the assessment align with state curriculum and grade-level standards?
- Does the assessment provide multiple and varied ways for students to demonstrate understanding?

- Does the assessment provide sufficient data/information for differentiating instruction and/or providing interventions?
- Does the assessment provide sufficient data/information to determine whether instruction or interventions are effective?
- Does the assessment reflect the instructional program, the teaching resources, and the instructional method?

Effective teachers are aware that careful, thoughtful, and age-appropriate assessment is important for all students, especially for students identified as English Language Learners (ELLs) and those receiving Exceptional Student Education (ESE) services. Teachers use information collected through assessment to make decisions about students' learning strengths and needs. Additionally, assessment results are communicated to students and parents* in a timely manner.

*Note: By Florida school law, a *parent* is either or both parents, a guardian, or any person in a parental relationship to a student or who has charge over a student in place of the parent.

Checkpoint

Fill in the blank.

1. Teachers should use a _____ of assessment approaches.
2. Assessment should align with state _____ and grade-level standards.
3. Assessment should reflect the instructional _____.
4. Teachers use assessment data to _____ instruction and/or provide interventions.

Checkpoint Answers

1. variety
2. curriculum
3. method
4. differentiate

Testing Terminology to Know

If a method of assessment is to be valuable to a teacher in making important decisions about children, it must have reliability and validity and be unbiased. **Reliability** refers to the consistency of a measurement over time and repeated measurements. If a teacher gives alternate forms of the same test periodically over several months and the students' performance scores remain relatively the same, the test has reliability. **Validity** has to do with whether the assessment instrument measures what it is supposed to measure. Validity can be determined by comparing a test score against some separate or independent observation of whatever is being measured. If a teacher wants to measure math skills, the test must measure math skills, not reading skills. The teacher also can compare the daily or weekly grades of students to their test scores. If they are similar, then the test probably has validity. An **unbiased** test is one that does not unfairly favor a particular group. For instance, a test that uses references that are unfamiliar to minority cultural groups might give an unfair advantage to the dominant cultural group. Thus, such a test would be **biased.**

A **standardized test** is one that has been carefully constructed and field-tested so that, ideally, it has a high degree of reliability and validity. Directions for taking the test and conditions for administering and scoring it are uniform and rigorously monitored. A **norm-referenced test** (such as the National Assessment of Educational Progress) is one that assesses students by comparing their performance to that of a norm group. Usually, the norm group is representative of students of the same age or grade level as the test-takers. A **criterion-referenced test** assesses students by comparing their performance to a predetermined level of mastery. Florida's statewide, standardized assessments are criterion-referenced tests (see the section "K-12 Statewide, Standardized Assessment Program" later in this chapter for a discussion of statewide assessments). An advantage of criterion-referenced tests over norm-referenced tests is their diagnostic, placement, and remediation use. Teachers in Florida are expected to analyze student performance data to address remediation needs of individual students. Disaggregation of the data (that is, separating it) by subject, gender, race, and so on must be used by schools and teachers to identify groups of students needing remediation/interventions.

All teachers need to be familiar with the terms *mean, median,* and *mode,* known as **measures of central tendency.** These measures are used frequently for determining certain information in assessment data. When you have a set of scores, the **mean** is determined by adding all the scores and dividing this sum by the total number of scores that were added. The **median** is the midpoint when the scores are listed from lowest to highest (or highest to lowest). The **mode** is the score (or scores) that occurs most frequently. Measures of central tendency should have the same units as those of the data values from which they are determined. If no units are specified, as in test scores, then the measure of central tendency will not specify units.

All three of these measures provide a way to describe the typical or average score. The mean is usually the best indicator of the average; however, when a few scores are either very high or very low compared to the rest of the scores, the median is a better choice to use for the average. If a large number of the scores are the same, the mode can be used to report which score or scores occurred most often—but only if used in conjunction with the mean and/or median. The mode should not be used as the only measure of central tendency for summarizing assessment data.

Although measures of central tendency are important for describing data sets, their interpretation is enhanced when the spread or dispersion about the central value is known. **Measures of variability** are used to describe the amount of spread. Two important measures of variability are the range and the standard deviation. The **range** is the simplest measure of variability. It is the greatest score minus the least score in a set of scores. The range should have the same units as those of the data values from which it is computed. If no units are specified, then the range will not specify units.

The range gives some indication of the spread of the scores, but its value is determined by only two scores. A measure of variability that takes into account all the scores is the standard deviation. The **standard deviation** is a measure of the dispersion of a set of data values about the mean of the data set. The more the data values vary from the mean, the greater the standard deviation, meaning that the data set has more spread. The standard deviation should have the same units as those of the data values from which it is computed. If no units are specified, then the standard deviation will not specify units. The standard deviation is used extensively in education, particularly with the normal curve and standardized tests.

Other measures used to describe assessment data are percentiles and quartiles. The *P*th **percentile** is a value at or below which *P* percent of the data fall. For example, the median is the 50th percentile because 50 percent of the data falls at or below the median. **Quartiles** are values that divide an ordered data set into four portions, each containing approximately one-fourth of the data. Twenty-five percent of the data values are at or below the **first quartile** (also called the **25th percentile**); 50 percent of the data values are at or below the **second quartile** (also called the **50th percentile**), which is the same as the median; and 75 percent of the data values are at or below the **third quartile** (also called the **75th percentile**).

The **interquartile range** is another measure of the spread of a data set. To compute the interquartile range, you first compute the first quartile (Q_1) and third quartile (Q_3) of the data set. The **interquartile range (IQR)** is the difference between the first and third quartiles; that is, $IQR = Q_3 - Q_1$. The IQR contains the center 50 percent of the data. It gives you an indication of how much the data values "stretch" from the center of the data.

The **raw score** is (most commonly) the total number of correct responses on an assessment. For a constructed response test, the raw score is the sum of the scorer's ratings assigned to a test-taker's responses.

The **z-score** for a raw score is its distance in standard deviations from the mean of the scores on the assessment. To compute a z-score, use the following formula:

$$\text{(raw score–mean)} \div \text{(standard deviation)}$$

A **percentile rank** is a derived score used to rank a student's performance in relation to a specific group (for example, a representative sample of Florida students at the same grade level). The **percentile rank** of a student's score is based on the percentage of scores in the comparison group that are the same or lower than it. For instance, if 74 percent of the comparison group are the same or lower than a student's score, the student's percentile rank is 74th. *Tip*: A percentile rank is NOT the percentage of items answered correctly.

Stanine scores usually are derived from percentiles and compare test performance using nine intervals that are numbered in order from 1 to 9. The 5th stanine is the middle interval, and corresponds to the interval between the 40th and 60th percentiles. Stanine scores from 1 to 3 are below average, 4 to 6 are average, and 7 to 9 are above average.

A **grade equivalent score** is used to describe a student's performance in comparison to the performance of an average student at a specified grade level. Be careful interpreting grade equivalent scores when taking the PEd Test. For instance, suppose that a fourth-grade student receives a grade equivalent score of 6.2 on a reading assessment. This student's score reflects performance on the reading assessment matching the estimated performance of an average student in the second month of sixth grade on the *same* assessment. The score does *not* mean that the fourth-grader is ready for sixth-grade reading material. Grade equivalent scores range from the beginning of kindergarten (K.0) to the ninth month of grade 12 (12.9).

The **effect size** expresses in standard deviations the difference between the increased or decreased achievement of an experimental group (a group of students who were exposed to an intervention) with that of a control group (a group of students who were not exposed to the intervention). This means that if the effect size computed for a specific study is 1.0, the average score for students in the experimental group is 1.0 standard deviation higher than the average score of students in the control group. A useful aspect of an effect size is that it can be easily translated into percentile gains. By consulting a statistical conversion table for translating effect sizes to percentile gains, you can determine that an effect size of 1.0 represents a percentile gain of about 34 points. This means that the performance of the average student who received the intervention was 34 percentile points higher than the average student who did not.

Checkpoint

Fill in the blank.

1. If a test measures what it purports to measure, the test has _____.

2. Florida's standard deviation is a measure of the dispersion of a set of data values about the _____ of the data set.

3. A vocabulary test that includes terms specific to a particular socioeconomic group is likely to yield _____ results.

Mark as true or false.

4. _____ (a) The statewide, standardized assessments are criterion-referenced tests.

   _____ (b) A median score of 75 on a history test in a class of 22 students means 11 students scored at or below 75.

   _____ (c) A grade equivalent score of 7.6 obtained by a fourth-grader on a standardized math test means that the fourth-grader can do math at the seventh-grade level.

Checkpoint Answers

1. validity

2. mean

3. biased

4. (a) true; (b) true; (c) false

Formative and Summative Assessment

Two broad categories of assessment are formative and summative. **Formative assessment** occurs before and during instruction. It is critical to teachers' instructional decision making. Formative assessments include *screening, diagnostic, progress monitoring*, and various *informal classroom assessments*. **Summative assessment** occurs after instruction has taken place at the end of an instructional unit, regular grading period, or school year. Summative assessments include *outcome assessments* and *report cards*.

Formative Assessment

Screening assessments are administered to all students (that is, statewide, district-wide, school-wide, grade-level, or classroom). These assessments typically are given at three points during the school year: at the beginning of the year (BOY or baseline), at midyear (MOY), and at the end of the year (EOY). Screening assessments are brief and easy-to-administer measures of critical skills and concepts. They provide information for differentiating instruction and for measuring core instruction and the effectiveness of interventions. For instance, according to FLDOE guidelines, if a student receiving interventions maintains his or her baseline level or moves to a higher level of risk at midyear, the additional interventions or his or her implementation were not effective and should be modified or changed. To comply with state law (Section 1002.69 (1), F. S.), public schools in Florida administer the state-adopted Florida Kindergarten Readiness Screener (FLKRS). FLKRS measures important skills that form the basis for early success in reading and provides information about whether the child demonstrates age-appropriate development.

Diagnostic assessments are administered (usually individually) to selected students for the purpose of identifying learning strengths and weaknesses with critical skills and concepts. They provide specific information that can be used to customize instruction and/or interventions for particular students. The Diagnostic Reading Assessment (DAR) is an example. The DAR is administered individually to assess a student's relative strengths and weaknesses in nine key areas of reading.

Progress monitoring assessments are regularly administered (that is, **dynamic, ongoing**) assessments used to evaluate students' academic progress for the purpose of making data-based decisions regarding instruction and interventions. Progress monitoring should occur routinely (weekly, biweekly, or monthly) and use valid and reliable assessments that are sensitive to small changes in student academic performance. The frequency should increase for Tier 2 and Tier 3 students (see "MTSS PS/RtI" in Chapter 1 for a discussion of multi-tiered instruction). Data from progress monitoring assessments provide information about whether a student's or group's level of performance is progressing at an acceptable rate toward a year-end standards-aligned outcome goal. A student's **level of risk** is assessed based on the extent of discrepancy between the student's actual level of performance and the performance of peers who are achieving benchmarks. The Dynamic Indicators of Basic Early Literacy Skills (DIBELS) Oral Reading Fluency (ORF) test for accuracy and fluency in reading is an example of a progress monitoring assessment.

Informal classroom assessments include teacher observations, anecdotal records, classroom questioning, checklists, guided practice, student activities, portfolios and work samples, projects and products, teacher-made quizzes and tests, and homework. The information obtained can be used to guide reteaching, adjust instruction and/or interventions, vary the pace of instruction, or adjust the curriculum. Typically, these measures are not standardized or normed, but they can be used in conjunction with formal standardized assessments to **triangulate data** (that is, using two or more different data sources) to corroborate results.

Formative assessment also includes student **progress reports,** which report students' grades to date, usually at the mid-grade reporting period. By Florida law, parents must receive accurate and timely information regarding their child's academic progress and must be informed of ways they can help their child to succeed in school (Section 1002.20, F. S.). This requirement helps parents and their student monitor whether the student's learning in particular subject areas is progressing at an acceptable rate.

Summative Assessment

Outcome assessments include the end-of-year statewide, standardized assessments; standardized norm-referenced tests; and end-of-grading period assessments. Data from these assessments are used to evaluate the effectiveness of the instructional program. The end-of-year assessments are used in determining whether schools, school districts, and the state have made adequate yearly progress (AYP) for the requirements of the No Child Left Behind Act of 2001 (NCLB). Also, by law, Florida students must participate in the National Assessment of Educational Progress (NAEP) or a similar national assessment program (Section 1008.22 (2), F. S.). The NAEP, also known as "the nation's report card," is a nationwide assessment of what students know and can do in various subject areas. Individual student scores are not reported for the NAEP. Local districts also give a variety of nationally norm-referenced tests such as the California Achievement Test (CAT) and the Iowa Test of Basic Skills (ITBS).

Report cards are summative assessments that reflect a student's academic performance relative to established learning criteria. By Florida law, students and parents must receive student report cards on a regular basis. The report cards must "clearly depict and grade the student's academic performance in each class or course, the student's conduct, and the student's attendance" (Section 1003.33 (1)(a–c), F. S.). The FLDOE (2006) points out that parents use report cards to find out how well their child is doing and whether the child needs additional help in school, and that students use them to evaluate their progress and set future goals. Therefore, report card grades need to provide valid and meaningful information about a student's academic performance, which (by law) must be based upon examinations, written papers, class participation, and other academic performance criteria.

Checkpoint

Fill in the blank.

1. Assessment that occurs at the end of an instructional unit is _____ assessment.

2. Formative assessments that are designed to identify a student's strengths and weaknesses are _____ assessments.

3. Progress reports are a type of _____ assessment.

4. In addition to the student's academic performance, Florida law requires that report cards clearly depict and grade the student's _____ and _____.

Checkpoint Answers

1. summative

2. diagnostic

3. formative

4. conduct; attendance

K-12 Statewide, Standardized Assessment Program

The Florida Bureau of K-12 Assessment oversees the statewide, standardized assessment program. The primary goal of the state-mandated program is to measure students' knowledge of and skills in the state-mandated core curricular content as required by Florida law (Section 1008.22, F. S.).

The **statewide, standardized assessment program** consists of computer-based, criterion-referenced assessments designed to assess the annual learning gains of Florida's K-12 students toward achieving the Next Generation Sunshine State Standards (NGSSS). The statewide, standardized **end of course (EOC)** assessments test students in Algebra 1, Geometry, Biology 1, U.S. History, and Civics. By law, a student's performance on a statewide EOC subject assessment constitutes 30 percent of the student's final course grade for that subject (Section 1008.22, F. S.). Accommodations for state-mandated assessments (e.g., large print, braille, one-item-per-page, and paper-based versions of computer-based tests) are provided to students with disabilities who require allowable accommodations as specified in their Individual Educational Plans (IEPs) or Section 504 plans.

For the statewide assessments, students receive a **scale score,** derived from the raw test score. Based on the scale score, an **achievement level,** ranging from 1 (lowest) to 5 (highest), is reported. Descriptions of the achievement levels (in 2014 per FLDOE) are the following:

Level 5: Indicates mastery of the assessment's content.

Level 4: Indicates above-satisfactory success with the assessment's content.

Level 3: Indicates satisfactory success with the assessment's content, but performance was inconsistent.

Level 2: Indicates limited success with the assessment's content.

Level 1: Indicates inadequate success with the assessment's content.

Students who score in level 3, 4, or 5 are performing at or above expectations. Students who score in level 1 or 2 are performing below expectations. For a student who performs below expectations on statewide assessments in reading and/or mathematics, school districts must develop (in consultation with the student's parent) and implement an individualized progress monitoring plan (PMP) or state-approved equivalent plan. The PMP is designed to assist the student in meeting state (and district) expectations for proficiency in reading and/or mathematics. Based on diagnostic assessments to determine the nature of the student's difficulties and areas of academic need, the PMP specifies strategies for appropriate instruction and/or interventions (Section 1008.25 (4), F. S.). A third-grade student who scores below level 2 on the statewide assessment in reading must be retained, unless the student is exempt from mandatory retention for good cause (Section 1008.25 (5), F. S.).

Checkpoint

Fill in the blank.

1. Florida's state-mandated assessments are _____-based assessments.

2. By law, a student's performance on a statewide EOC subject assessment constitutes _____ percent of the student's final course grade for that subject.

3. School districts must provide appropriate remedial instruction to students who perform _____ expectations on statewide assessments.

Mark as true or false.

4. _____ (a) The assessments used in Florida's statewide, standardized assessment program are norm-referenced assessments.

_____ (b) Level 1 is the highest achievement level for the statewide assessments.

Checkpoint Answers

1. computer

2. 30

3. below

4. (a) false; (b) false

Alternative Classroom Assessment

Effective teachers integrate assessment into everyday classroom practice and real contexts. As an alternative to traditional assessments (see the section "Traditional Assessments" that follows), they employ multiple measures, including more authentic classroom assessments of students such as performance observations (in person, by videotape and/or audiotape), work samples (tests, papers, and projects), process observations and products, interviews, and portfolios. **Authentic assessment** incorporates real-life application tasks and enables the teacher to directly assess meaningful and complex educational performances. Authentic assessment is sometimes called **performance assessment** or **process/product assessment.** Performance assessments have long been used in the assessment of music, art, drama, and physical education. Process/product assessments are usually more evident in science, math, social studies, and language arts. In theory, authentic assessment is more likely to possess validity than traditional assessment methods because it allows the teacher to directly observe what the student has learned. Following are some commonly used authentic classroom assessment methods.

Instructionally embedded assessment (also called **teacher observation**) uses systematic observational methods along with checklists, interviews, and questioning while students are engaged in learning activities. This assessment approach is particularly essential in early-childhood classrooms in order to provide developmentally appropriate curricula and instruction. According to Gestwicki (1999), "Teachers observe children's performance and activity during real interest center times, group work, and literacy experiences. They have conversations with children to gain additional insights into their style, rate, and interest in learning.… Teachers do all of this over periods of time, so that they put together a consistent picture or pattern about a particular child, rather than a single observation that may or may not be representative of the child's actual accomplishment or ability" (p. 291).

A **portfolio** is a meaningful collection of student work. It provides various and comprehensive summaries of student performance in particular contexts. Portfolio assessment requires students to collect and reflect on examples of their work and provide documentation of what they can do. Teachers also can select pieces of a student's work to include in the portfolio. Keeping a portfolio is one of the best ways for students to engage in assessing their progress over time.

Projects or **products** include stories, essays, drawings, models, audio recordings, videos, PowerPoint presentations, and other mechanisms that allow students to demonstrate their acquisition of knowledge and skills.

A **checklist** of skills or performances is an assessment tool that can be used by teachers or students to monitor learning.

Conferences and **interviews** provide an opportunity for the teacher to discuss and question a student about what the student knows and is able to do. These methods also can be used between students.

Journals and **notebooks** provide a way for students to respond in writing to a prompt by the teacher and to reflect on their own learning.

Two other popular assessment methods used by teachers are student self-assessment and peer-assessment. **Student self-assessment** is performed by the student. Students can assess themselves in many ways, such as grading their own papers, group participation, and portfolio assessment. **Peer assessment** is assessment by students of their classmates' products or performances. Generally, student self-assessment and peer assessment lack validity due to factors such as the assessor's immaturity and lack of expertise. Nevertheless, students benefit from involvement in self-assessment and peer assessment because these forms of assessment give students opportunities to develop their critical thinking and evaluation-level thinking skills.

Checkpoint

Fill in the blank.

1. Authentic assessments incorporate _____ application tasks.

2. In theory, authentic assessment is more likely to possess _____ than traditional assessment methods.

3. A meaningful collection of student work is commonly called a _____.

4. In order to provide developmentally appropriate curricula and instruction in early-childhood classrooms, _____ (two words) assessment is particularly essential.

Checkpoint Answers

1. real-life

2. validity

3. portfolio

4. instructionally embedded

Traditional Assessments

Traditional assessment is a term used to describe a traditional teacher-made test composed of true-false, multiple-choice, matching, fill-in-the-blank, or essay (commonly called constructed response) questions. Traditional assessments can provide valuable information about students' grasp of rules, facts, information, and concepts.

When designing a test, teachers must decide what form the test questions will take. In selecting a format for the test, teachers need to consider the degree of objectivity of the test questions. **Objective** questions depend less on teacher judgment when grading, and **subjective** questions require more teacher judgment in the scoring process. In general, multiple-choice, matching, fill-in-the-blank, and true-false questions are considered objective. Constructed response and essay questions fall into the subjective category. To reduce inconsistency in grading, teachers should try to design tests so that subjectivity in grading is minimized. Following are some guidelines for writing the various test question types.

True-False Questions

A true-false question requires students to decide whether a statement is true or false.

Here is an example:

Directions: Read each question and decide whether it is true or false. Write the letter corresponding to your answer in the blank provided.

> **1.** _____ George Washington was the first president of the United States.
>
> **A.** True
>
> **B.** False

The correct answer is **A.**

Advantages: True-false questions are easy to write, can be used to test a lot of content efficiently, and are easy to grade.

Disadvantages: Writing nontrivial questions is a challenge. Most true-false questions test at lower cognitive levels. Student guessing is a problem. True-false tests have little diagnostic value.

Following are some guidelines for construction.

Teachers should DO the following:

- Write questions based on the significant ideas they've presented—important facts, principles, and concepts.
- Make sure that each question tests one, and only one, main idea, not a combination of several ideas.
- Write questions so that the main idea in the statement is readily apparent to the student.
- Use simple, easy-to-understand language.
- Write simple, clear statements.
- Write statements that have sufficient information to clearly indicate whether the statement is true or false.
- Write questions that are completely true or completely false, not partially true or partially false.
- Make the length of the questions, whether true or false, about the same.
- Cite the source when the question contains material based on opinion.
- Try to include questions that test beyond lower levels of thinking.
- Write clear and specific directions.
- Include about the same number of true questions and false questions on a test.

Teachers should AVOID the following:

- Using statements copied from the book
- Using ambiguous language
- Stating questions negatively
- Using giveaway words like *always* or *never* that help students decide the correctness or incorrectness of the statement
- Using tricky questions or questions for which the correct answer relies on a trivial detail
- Using statements that could be read in more than one way
- Falling into a pattern for the correct answer

Multiple-Choice Questions

A multiple-choice question requires students to select the correct or best answer from a number of possible options.

Here is an example:

Directions: Read each question and select the best response. Write the letter corresponding to your answer in the blank provided.

1. _____ What is the area, in square inches, of a square that measures 5 inches on a side?	
A. 10	
B. 20	
C. 25	
D. 50	

The correct answer is **C**.

Advantages: Multiple-choice questions can be used to test at lower and higher cognitive levels and are easy to grade.

Disadvantages: Preparing a well-crafted multiple-choice question is time-consuming. Coming up with plausible *distractors* (incorrect answer choices) is difficult. Writing stems that present situations briefly is challenging.

Following are some guidelines for construction.

Teachers should DO the following:

- Write questions based on the significant ideas they've presented—important facts, principles, and concepts.
- Make sure that each question tests one, and only one, main idea.
- Use no more than five answer choices.
- Put the answer choices in a logical order (for example, alphabetically or from least to greatest).
- Use simple, easy-to-understand language.
- Write brief, concise question stems.
- Make sure that all answer choices agree grammatically with the question stem.
- Make sure that all answer choices are parallel in construction.
- Write question stems that have sufficient information to clearly indicate the correct answer.
- Write distractors that make sense and are plausible to students.
- Write distractors that are based on common misconceptions or errors.
- Make sure that the distractors are clearly wrong or inadequate.
- Make sure that one question does not help in answering another question.
- Cite the source when the question contains material based on opinion.
- Include questions that test higher levels of thinking.
- Write clear and specific directions.

Teachers should AVOID the following:

- Using statements copied from the book
- Using ambiguous language
- Stating questions negatively
- Using giveaway words like *always* or *never* that help students eliminate incorrect answer choices
- Using *none of the above, none of these, not given*, or *all of the above* as a final answer choice
- Falling into a pattern when placing the correct answer choice in the questions

Matching Questions

A matching question requires students to match a list of items with a set of answer choices based on a relationship between the items listed and their matching answer choices (for example, countries with their capitals or terms with their characteristics).

Here is an example:

Directions: Match the state with its capital. Write the letter corresponding to your answer in the blank provided.

_____ **1.** Arkansas		**A.**	Albuquerque
_____ **2.** California		**B.**	Austin
_____ **3.** Louisiana		**C.**	Baton Rouge
_____ **4.** New Mexico		**D.**	Houston
_____ **5.** Texas		**E.**	Little Rock
		F.	Sacramento
		G.	Santa Fe

The correct answers are 1-E; 2-F; 3-C; 4-G; 5-B.

Advantages: Matching questions are easy to write, can be used to test a lot of content efficiently, are easy to grade, and are a quick way to check students' recognition of relationships.

Disadvantages: Most matching questions test at the recall level of thinking. Writing short, succinct answer choices is sometimes challenging. Coming up with plausible extra incorrect choices is sometimes difficult. As students complete the matching, guessing can enter into selecting answer choices.

Following are some guidelines for construction.

Teachers should DO the following:

- Write questions based on the significant ideas they've presented—important facts, principles, and concepts.
- Use a list of items that are similar in content.
- Write matching answer choices that are short in length.
- Put both the list of items and the answer choices on the same page in two columns.
- Use numbers to identify the items in the first column and uppercase letters to identify the answer choices in the second column.
- Use no more than 10 to 12 answer choices.
- Include one or two extra answer choices that do not match up, or let answer choices be used more than once.
- Write directions that are clear and specific (for example, "Write the letter corresponding to your answer in the blank provided."). Tell whether answer choices might be used more than once.

Teachers should AVOID the following:

- Listing items in the two columns so that they match up in a predictable manner
- Writing questions that rely on recall of trivial or insignificant details

Fill-in-the-Blank or Completion Questions

A fill-in-the-blank or completion question requires students to fill in a blank with one word or a brief answer.

Here is an example:

Directions: Fill in the blank with the correct response.

> **1.** The author of *Great Expectations* is _____.

The correct answer is **Charles Dickens.**

Advantages: Fill-in-the-blank questions are fairly easy to write, can be used to test a lot of content efficiently, and minimize student guessing.

Disadvantages: Most fill-in-the-blank questions test at lower cognitive levels. Writing questions that elicit only the desired correct answer is challenging. Deciphering students' writing can be a problem (when the test is paper-based, as is common for teacher-made tests). Subjectivity might enter into the scoring of responses. Deciding how to score unanticipated correct answers must be addressed.

Following are some guidelines for construction.

Teachers should DO the following:

- Write questions based on the significant ideas they've presented—important facts, principles, and concepts.
- Make sure that each question tests one, and only one, main idea.

- Write questions for which only key words or important concepts, rather than trivial words, should be placed in the blanks.
- Use simple, easy-to-understand language.
- Write questions that have sufficient information to clearly indicate one correct answer.
- Write questions that have one word or a short phrase as the correct answer.
- Make sure that one question does not help in answering another question.
- Cite the source when the question contains material based on opinion.
- Include questions that test higher levels of thinking.
- Try to put the question blank at or near the end of the question.
- Make all blanks the same length.
- Use no more than two blanks in a question.
- Leave ample space for writing the answer.
- Write clear and specific directions.

Teachers should AVOID the following:

- Using statements copied from the book
- Using ambiguous language
- Stating questions negatively
- Using tricky questions or questions for which the correct response relies on recall of a trivial detail
- Using statements that could be read in more than one way

Constructed Response (or Essay) Questions

A constructed response question requires students to write an extended response to a question or prompt.

Here is an example:

Directions: In the space provided, write a well-organized 250- to 300-word response addressing the following prompt:

Compare and contrast the Norse gods with the Roman gods.

Advantages: Constructed response questions are fairly easy to write, allow the teacher to test at higher cognitive levels of thinking, allow students more opportunity to express themselves in their own way, and minimize student guessing.

Disadvantages: Constructed response questions are time-consuming for the student to answer; thus limiting the number per test. Not as much content can be assessed with this type of question. Deciphering students' writing can be a problem (when the test is paper-based, as is common for teacher-made tests). Grading students' responses is time-consuming and difficult to do fairly and reliably.

Following are some guidelines for construction.

Teachers should DO the following:

- Write questions/prompts based on the significant principles and concepts they've presented.
- Write clear, specific, and unambiguous questions/prompts.
- Use introductory phrases such as *explain in your own words, describe the similarities and differences between, compare and contrast, present an argument for or against,* and *list and describe the major causes of.*
- Write questions/prompts that address higher levels of thinking.

- Write questions/prompts that students can reasonably answer in the time allotted.
- Write clear and specific directions.
- Allow students to use word processing to construct responses, if feasible.
- Use a rubric or scoring guide (see the sample scoring guide that follows) and explain it to students *before* they write their constructed responses.
- Give a separate grade for mechanical skills.

Teachers should AVOID the following:

- Using broad questions/prompts
- Grading when tired or sleepy

Sample Constructed Response Scoring Guide

All constructed response questions will be assessed using a holistic rating scale ranging from 0 to 4 points.

4 points: The response indicates that the writer has a complete understanding of the topic. The response is accurate, complete, and fulfills all requirements of the task. The writer demonstrates control in the development of ideas and clearly specifies supporting details.

3 points: The response indicates that the writer has an understanding of the topic. The response is accurate, complete, and fulfills all requirements of the task, but the writer's attempts to develop supporting details are not fully realized.

2 points: The response indicates that the writer has a partial understanding of the topic. The response is essentially correct, but the writer does not maintain focus on the topic. Development and organization are largely incomplete or unclear.

1 point: The response indicates that the writer has a very limited understanding of the topic. The response is largely inaccurate and incomplete. Development and organization are very weak and incoherent.

Score of 0: The response is off-topic, too short to score, or otherwise unscorable at a level of 1 or above.

The key to preparing good teacher-made tests is ensuring that they accurately reflect what has been taught. Teachers should try to make sure that content that was given more emphasis in class is given more weight on the test. Research on the effectiveness of testing has consistently found that tests promote learning (Slavin, 2008). This is especially true if what is to be learned is tested soon after it is introduced. The most effective tests are those given frequently and at consistent intervals. Furthermore, frequent cumulative tests result in more learning than infrequent tests or tests given only on content covered since the last test.

Planned review and practice activities before testing also are important. These activities might include games, role-playing, simulations, computer-based exercises, hands-on practice assignments, self-checks, or quizzes. Review activities and materials should be logical extensions of instruction and should involve frequent feedback from the teacher. Most of the time, reviews should be done in pairs or groups to encourage active engagement and communication among students. Frequent short reviews, spaced over time, are more effective than concentrated practice. Moreover, weekly or monthly reviews of previously learned material will help students' retention.

Checkpoint

Fill in the blank.

1. A teacher-made multiple-choice test is a type of _____ (nontraditional, traditional) assessment.
2. Most often, true-false questions test at _____ (higher, lower) cognitive levels.
3. Fill-in-the-blank questions reduce the opportunity for students to _____ correctly.

Mark as true or false.

4. _____ (a) When writing test questions, teachers should write questions based on the significant ideas they have presented.

_____ (b) Most often, matching questions test lower levels of thinking.

_____ (c) Research has consistently found that testing promotes learning.

Checkpoint Answers

1. traditional

2. lower

3. guess

4. (a) true; (b) true; (c) true

Homework

Another way for teachers to find out what students have learned is through homework assignments. Homework is a research-based, high yield instructional strategy (Mazano et al., 2000). Studies indicate that carefully prepared and implemented homework assignments positively impact student achievement. In the elementary and middle school grades, students should be given homework to help them develop good study habits, develop positive attitudes toward school, and realize that learning is something that happens not only at school but also at home. By the time students reach high school, the purpose of giving homework is primarily to improve their academic achievement. Further, homework is a valuable tool that allows parents to monitor their child's learning activities.

When homework is given as independent practice, it should

- be viewed as an integral part of instruction.
- be appropriate for the ability and maturity level of the students.
- be closely tied to what was taught in class.
- have a clearly articulated purpose.
- be worthwhile (not meaningless worksheets).
- be coordinated with what the students' other teachers are requiring them to do.
- be given immediately after presentation of the subject matter.
- be given frequently as a means of extending learning beyond the classroom.
- be carefully prepared and accompanied by concise written instructions, if needed.
- be clearly understood by the students before they leave class.
- be frequently checked orally in class.
- be checked and returned to students in a timely manner, when collected.
- be returned with feedback that informs the students about what they are doing correctly and what they still need to work on.
- be successfully completed by most of the students.
- *never* be given as punishment.

For elementary school students, homework assignments should be short and require only materials commonly found in the students' homes. As a general rule, a reasonable time expectation for homework is approximately ten times a student's grade level in minutes (for example, a first grader would spend 10 minutes, a sixth grader 60 minutes). For middle school students, homework assignments can be longer, taking from 1 to 2 hours per night. These students might also be assigned voluntary homework. These assignments should involve tasks that students of middle school age are intrinsically motivated to do (for example, assignments that use pop-culture technology). In high school, teachers should assign homework on a regular basis. It is not unreasonable to expect homework assignments in high school to call for materials not commonly found in the students' homes and to take several hours to complete. For most high school students, 7 to 15 hours of homework per week is suitable. Marzano et al. reported that, in general, homework has increased influence on students' learning, as they progress through the grades.

Regardless of grade level, teachers should have written homework policies (that might be obtained from the school or district). Students and parents should be provided copies of a teacher's homework policy, and the parent should be asked to return signed acknowledgement of receipt of the policy. For students in elementary and middle-school, the teacher should provide parents information about assignments and elicit their support to encourage completion of homework and monitor their child's study time. When a student consistently fails to complete homework assignments, parental contact is essential, and an appropriate plan to remediate the problem should be developed in consultation with the student, parent, and teacher. This plan should be appropriate to the student's needs and home environment.

Checkpoint

Fill in the blank.

1. Feedback on homework should inform students about what they are doing correctly and what they still need to _____ (two words).

2. In the elementary and middle school grades, two reasons students should be given homework are to help them develop good _____ habits and positive _____ toward school.

3. In high school, it is not unreasonable to expect students to do 7 to _____ hours of homework per week.

Mark as true or false.

4. _____ (a) Homework should be offered only on a voluntary basis.

   _____ (b) An hour a day of homework is suitable for children in first grade.

   _____ (c) When students misbehave, giving homework as punishment is appropriate.

Checkpoint Answers

1. work on

2. study; attitudes

3. 15

4. (a) false; (b) false; (c) false

Correcting Student Errors

In order for students to learn, they need to know whether what they are doing is correct. Validating students' correct responses with appropriate reinforcement such as simple acknowledgment, class agreement, or specific praise makes students aware of their own understanding. Teachers should provide timely, specific feedback based on clear and appropriate criteria. Feedback informs the students about what they are doing correctly and what they still need to work on. Moreover, teachers know how to help students use feedback to manage and direct their own learning.

When students respond incorrectly, the teacher uses a variety of strategies such as probing, restating or rephrasing the question, or asking a leading question to encourage students to take chances and keep trying. When possible, the teacher should try to find something positive to point out about the student's response prior to pointing out errors, even if it is simply to commend the student for trying.

To correct student errors, teachers use strategies that include constructive feedback, modeling, providing an explanation of additional information, or probing by asking additional questions. Corrections often provide the opportunity to discuss common errors associated with the situation. For some teachers, it is not easy to criticize students; however, teachers can be honest without humiliating or disparaging students. Providing criticism is important so that the student and the other students do not internalize misinformation or become perplexed about key concepts. Often probing, prompting, or asking a follow-up question can result in the student self-correcting his or her own error, thereby taking the responsibility for correction from the teacher and placing it on the student.

With regard to correcting students' verbal communication errors, generally teachers should avoid publicly pointing out grammatical mistakes—especially when students are very young or English Language Learners (ELLs). Accepting students' efforts and rephrasing them correctly when responding will be less likely to inhibit speech production. At the same time, teachers should make sure that students know they are expected to use grammatically correct constructions. Besides modeling correct usage, the teacher—even in content areas other than English language arts—can hold class discussions about common errors the teacher has observed. This approach will communicate high expectations from the teacher and help all students develop improved language skills.

Checkpoint

Fill in the blank.

1. Students need to know when they make _____.
2. "Let me rephrase the question for you" is a way a teacher can encourage a student to keep _____.
3. Teachers should try to find something _____ to say about a student's response prior to pointing out errors.
4. "Will you explain how you got that answer?" is an example of probing that could lead to a student _____ his or her own error.

Checkpoint Answers

1. errors
2. trying
3. positive
4. self-correcting

Study Skills and Test-Taking Strategies

To help students achieve success on assessments, teachers should identify and sequence learning activities that support study skills and test-taking strategies. For instance, students benefit from explicit guidance on how to study. Teachers should help students learn how to set goals for learning, monitor their learning, assess their own progress, and self-check their understanding. Using modeling, demonstrations, think-alouds, and other explicit instructional techniques, teachers can show students what works, why it works, and when to use it. These skills include how to

- take notes in class.
- listen and mentally process what they hear in class.
- write summaries.
- use self-questioning and answering.
- proofread and evaluate work.
- analyze a math problem or reading assignment.
- preview and make predictions about what they are learning.

- put confusing points into their own words (paraphrase).
- use mental imagery to help them remember.
- use mnemonic devices such as acronyms, rehearsal, and chunking to enhance memorization and recall. (See Appendix B for definitions of these terms.)
- use analogies to link new information to prior knowledge.
- use graphic organizers to make concepts meaningful.
- manage and organize their study time.

Teachers need to be aware that students also need explicit help on how to prepare for and take tests. The following tips are given in *Helping Your Child with Test-Taking—Helping Your Child Succeed in School*, a publication of the U.S. Department of Education Office of Communications and Outreach (2005):

- Plan ahead. Start studying for the test well in advance. Make sure that you understand what material the test will cover. Try to make connections about what will be on the test and what you already know. Review the material more than once.
- Don't cram the night before. This will likely increase your anxiety, which will interfere with clear thinking. Get a good night's sleep.
- When you get the test, read the directions carefully before you begin work. If you don't understand how to do something, ask the teacher to explain.
- Look quickly at the entire test to see what types of questions are on it (multiple choice, matching, true-false, essay). See whether different questions are worth different numbers of points. This will help you to determine how much time to spend on each part of the test.
- If you don't know the answer to a question, skip it and go on. Don't waste time worrying about one question. Mark it, and if you have time at the end of the test, return to it and try again (p. 1).

Also, teachers should not assume that all students are experienced with the various formats of standardized and classroom tests. In particular, English Language Learners (ELLs) who come from other countries might be unfamiliar with the types of test formats commonly used in Florida schools and might need to be taught, for example, how to fill in an answer form for a multiple-choice test or take a computer-based test.

Checkpoint

Fill in the blank.

1. Students benefit from _____ guidance on how to study.
2. Students can use analogies to link new information to _____ knowledge.
3. Cramming the night before a test is not a good idea because it likely will increase _____.
4. ELLs who come from other countries might be _____ with the types of test formats commonly used in Florida schools.

Checkpoint Answers

1. explicit
2. prior
3. anxiety
4. unfamiliar

Assessment Guidelines

The State of Florida expects teachers to adhere to accepted guidelines regarding assessment. The following assessment guidelines are derived from Zemelman, Daniels, and Hyde (2005) and the FLDOE (2006):

- Focus on the important ideas, rather than on trivial details.
- Most of the time, use assessment that is formative, not summative, and then use the information to evaluate the effectiveness of instruction, differentiate instruction, and plan future instruction or interventions.
- Use a variety of assessment measures, gathered over time, that allow students multiple ways to demonstrate what they have learned.
- Use assessments at short, frequent intervals to monitor learning and adjust instruction.
- Provide constructive feedback regarding assessments in a timely manner.
- Use authentic assessment more often than traditional tests and quizzes.
- Use self-assessment and peer assessment regularly.
- Integrate assessment into instruction (as in teacher-student conferences) rather than separate from it.
- Use criterion-referenced grading—that is, grading in comparison to established learning criteria (for example, grade-level benchmarks for the Next Generation Sunshine State Standards).
- Base academic grades on academic performance only.
- Do not use work habits, neatness, perceived effort, conduct, or improvement as factors in determining academic grades.
- Convey information about factors such as effort, work habits, behavior, or improvement through comments for these elements in reports to students and parents.
- Avoid competitive grading systems such as "grading on the curve"—that is, grading a student's performance in comparison to the performance of other students.
- Invite parent input with regard to the assessment process and report card format.

Additionally, in *Where We Stand on Curriculum, Assessment, and Program Evaluation*, the National Association for the Education of Young Children (2003) offers the following indicators of effective assessment practices:

- Ethical principles guide assessment practices.
- Assessment instruments are used for their intended purposes.
- Assessments are appropriate for ages and other characteristics of children being assessed.
- Assessment instruments are in compliance with professional criteria for quality.
- What is assessed is developmentally and educationally significant.
- Assessment is used to understand and improve learning.
- Assessment evidence is gathered from realistic settings and situations that reflect children's actual performance.
- Assessments use multiple sources of evidence gathered over time.
- Screening is always linked to follow-up.
- Use of individually administered, norm-referenced tests is limited.
- Staff and families are knowledgeable about assessment.

You should consciously consider these guidelines when answering questions involving assessment on the FTCE PEd Test.

Checkpoint

Fill in the blank.

1. Assessment should not focus on _____ details.

2. Teachers should use _____ assessment more often than traditional tests and quizzes.

3. Assessment should be developmentally _____.

4. Teachers should use multiple sources of evidence gathered over _____.

Checkpoint Answers

1. trivial

2. authentic

3. appropriate

4. time

Summary

In summary, assessment is critical to effective decision making in schools. Assessments at all levels (state, district, school, classroom) provide information about student learning to assist educators in meeting students' needs. Teachers assess their students for a number of reasons: to gain understanding of their skills and knowledge, assign grades, make decisions about what to teach, find out which students need extra help and which students need to be challenged more, and so forth. Effective teachers keep track of their students' progress, hold students accountable for their work, and differentiate instruction to improve student learning. The assessment process is vital to successful schools and classrooms.

Sample Questions

1. Ms. Nguyen, a history teacher, teaches at a school in which most of the students have a different ethnic background from her own. She is concerned that she might disadvantage students by unintentionally giving assessments that are biased. To minimize potential bias in her assessments, Ms. Nguyen should

   A. have a lead teacher critically review her tests to look for biased items.
   B. use only multiple-choice tests, so that the students do not have to construct responses.
   C. make sure the content and terminology used in the tests reflect the students' ethnic backgrounds.
   D. use tests developed by the publisher of the state-adopted history textbook.

2. Mr. Stark, a fifth-grade teacher, meets with a student's parents. The student's grade equivalent score on a standardized mathematics exam is 7.4. Based on this result, the parents want to know whether their child can spend part of the day at a middle school receiving mathematics instruction with a seventh-grade class. Which of the following responses would be most appropriate for Mr. Stark to make?

   A. Offer to set up a computerized tutorial in the classroom to teach the seventh-grade mathematics standards to the child.
   B. Explain that the student's score indicates the student's level of performance on fifth-grade level, not seventh-grade level, mathematics.
   C. Suggest that the child go to after-school seventh-grade mathematics tutorials at the middle school.
   D. Agree to arrange for the child to attend a seventh-grade mathematics class.

3. A fourth-grade teacher is using an Internet activity to introduce adding decimals. To best assess whether the Internet activity is successful in promoting students' understanding of adding decimals, the teacher should

   A. informally observe and question students as they do the activity.
   B. give a test and compare the grades of the students currently in the class to those from students in past classes to see if there is an improvement.
   C. give a pop quiz the next day to see what students learned.
   D. after the activity, conduct one-on-one interviews with the five highest-achieving students to see whether they grasp the concept of adding decimals.

4. Which of the following assessment methods is most appropriate for assessing student mastery of content in a high school history class at midyear?

   A. administering a standardized achievement test
   B. giving a diagnostic test
   C. giving a teacher-made test
   D. using peer assessment

Answer Explanations for Sample Questions

1. **C.** Eliminate **A** because this action reflects a failure on Ms. Nguyen's part to recognize the time constraints of the lead teacher. Eliminate **B** because this action would shortchange the students. Eliminate **D** because the publisher-developed tests might not be aligned with the curriculum and instruction in Ms. Nguyen's classroom. To ensure that her tests do not unfairly favor a particular ethnic group, Ms. Nguyen should make sure that the content and terminology used in the tests reflect the students' ethnic backgrounds. Thus, **C** is the correct response.

2. **B.** Grade equivalent scores can easily be misinterpreted, especially by parents. Mr. Stark should explain to the parents that the score indicates the student's level of performance on fifth-grade level, not seventh-grade level, mathematics. Thus, **B** is the correct response. The responses in the other answer choices would be inappropriate because these responses reflect incorrect interpretations of the student's grade equivalent score.

3. **A.** Eliminate **B** because a comparison of current students to past students would not take into account the differences in the two groups. Eliminate **C** because some students might be thrown into a state of confusion or anxiety by the surprise quiz and, thus, be unable to demonstrate their true understanding of addition of decimals. Eliminate **D** because, by choosing only the five highest-achieving math students, the teacher is not getting a good range of the entire class's understanding of addition of decimals. By informally observing and questioning the students during the activity, the teacher can most accurately determine whether the Internet activity is helping the students understand the concept of adding decimals. Thus, **A** is the correct response.

4. **C.** Eliminate **A** because a standardized achievement test is a norm-referenced test, which means that it assesses students by comparing their performance to that of a norm group; more important, the items on the test are only a sample of the whole subject area, so the test would not necessarily show whether the students have mastered the history content taught in the teacher's classroom. Eliminate **B** because diagnostic assessments usually are administered individually. Eliminate **D** because this assessment method is not a reliable way to determine whether students have mastered content. A teacher-made test is the most appropriate way to assess the students' mastery of history content at midyear. Thus, **C** is the correct response.

Competency Description and Key Indicators

According to the *Competencies and Skills Required for Teacher Certification in Florida*, 20th Edition (available at www.fldoe.org/asp/ftce/pdf/ftce20edition.pdf), **Competency 5** of the FTCE PEd Test addresses **Continuous Improvement** as follows:

> *Knowledge of relevant continuous professional improvement*

Key indicators:

- Determine relevant and measurable professional development goals to strengthen the effectiveness of instruction based on educator and students' needs.
- Analyze and apply data-informed research to improve instruction and student achievement.
- Use a variety of data, independently and in collaboration with colleagues, to evaluate learning outcomes, adjust planning, and continuously improve and reflect upon the effectiveness of lessons and practices.
- Identify ways to collaborate with home, school, and other stakeholders to foster communication and obtain resources in order to support diverse student learning and continuous improvement.
- Select and determine appropriate professional growth opportunities and reflective practices to improve teacher performance and impact student learning.
- Analyze the implementation of professional development experiences and application to the teaching and learning process.
- Choose appropriate professional growth opportunities in technology for the design and delivery of instruction to impact student learning.

Overview

Continuous Improvement is the process of engaging in professional learning. Good teachers are reflective practitioners who know the value and importance of continuous improvement. They ask themselves, "What can I do better? How can I effect positive change in my students?" They make use of reflective journaling, professional organizations, and professional growth opportunities to enhance their professional knowledge and skills in an ongoing endeavor to improve teaching performance and achieve positive learning outcomes for students. They accept their responsibilities as professionals and collaborate with colleagues in professional learning communities to create a school culture that enhances student learning.

This chapter provides a general review of Continuous Improvement with sample questions and explanations at the end of the chapter. Checkpoint exercises are found throughout the review material. These exercises give you an opportunity to practice what you just learned. The answers to the Checkpoint exercises are found immediately following the set of exercises. When doing the Checkpoint exercises, you should cover up the answers. Then check your answers when you've finished the exercises. The sample questions at the end of this chapter are multiple-choice questions that are similar to what you might expect to see on the FTCE PEd Test. The answer explanations for the sample questions are provided immediately after the questions.

The School Community Professional Development Act

The driving force for continuous improvement for teachers in Florida is the School Community Professional Development Act (Section 1012.98, F. S.). This state law specifies that the "purpose of the professional development system is to increase student achievement, enhance classroom instructional strategies that promote rigor and relevance throughout the curriculum, and prepare students for continuing education and the workforce." This act requires that districts develop and submit for approval by the Florida Department of Education (FLDOE) a professional development system that meets the following requirements:

- Links professional learning activities to
  - student achievement data.
  - analyses of instructional strategies and methods that support rigorous, relevant, and challenging curricula for all students.
  - school discipline data.
  - school environment surveys.
  - assessments of parental satisfaction.
  - performance appraisal data of teachers, managers, and administrative personnel.
  - other performance indicators to identify school and student needs that can be met by improved professional performance (Section 1012.98 (4)(b), F. S.).
- Provides in-service activities coupled with appropriate follow-up support that primarily focus on
  - analysis of student achievement data.
  - ongoing formal and informal assessments of student achievement.
  - identification and use of enhanced and differentiated instructional strategies that emphasize rigor, relevance, and reading in the content areas.
  - enhancement of subject content expertise.
  - integrated use of classroom technology that enhances teaching and learning.
  - classroom management.
  - parent involvement.
  - school safety (Section 1012.98 (4)(b), F. S.).
- Includes a master plan for in-service activities that must
  - be based on input from district and school educators.
  - use the latest available student achievement data and research to enhance rigor and relevance in the classroom.
  - be aligned to and support the school-based in-service plans and school improvement plans.
  - be updated annually by September 1.
  - be approved by the district school board annually by October 1 (Section 1012.98 (4)(b), F. S.).
- Requires school principals to establish and maintain for each teacher an Individual Professional Development Plan (IPDP) that must
  - be related to specific performance data for the students to whom the teacher is assigned.
  - define the in-service objectives.
  - define specific measurable improvements expected in student performance as a result of the in-service activity.
  - include an evaluation component that determines the effectiveness of the professional development plan (Section 1012.98 (4)(b), F. S.).

These requirements are consistent with research and guidelines offered by professional organizations such as the American Federation of Teachers (AFT) and the National Staff Development Council (NSDC). Furthermore, they are aligned with the federal No Child Left Behind (NCLB) Act, which defines high-quality professional development activities as those that

- improve and increase teachers' knowledge of academic subjects.
- are integral to broad school-wide and district-wide educational improvement plans.
- give teachers the knowledge and skills to help students meet challenging state academic standards.
- improve classroom management skills.
- are sustained, intensive, and classroom-focused.

- are not one-day or short-term workshops.

- advance teacher understanding of effective instructional strategies that are supported by scientifically based research.

- are developed with extensive participation of teachers, principals, parents*, and administrators (Title IX, Section 9101 (34)).

*Note: By Florida school law, a *parent* is either or both parents, a guardian, or any person in a parental relationship to a student or who has charge over a student in place of the parent.

The intent of the School Community Professional Development Act is to ensure that professional learning implemented in Florida's public schools is effective in assisting the school community in improving student achievement. The law requires that the FLDOE design methods by which the state and districts will evaluate and improve their professional development systems. The evaluation must include an annual assessment of data that indicate student progress or lack of progress. If the data indicate progress, then best practices are to be identified by the FLDOE. If lack of progress is indicated, then the FLDOE will investigate the causes, provide technical assistance, and require the district to employ a different approach to professional development.

By Rule 6A-5.071, the state evaluation system follows the Florida Professional Development System Evaluation Protocol 2010, Third Cycle, 2010–14 (available at www.fldoe.org/profdev/pdf/pdsprotocol.pdf). The protocol system is based on a set of standards that reflects the requirements of Florida laws as well as that of the National Staff Development Council Standards for Staff Development. At the educator level, the protocol organizes 18 standards under four strands:

- Planning
- Learning
- Implementing
- Evaluating

The Florida Department of Education Professional Development System Evaluation Protocol Reviewers Guide, Third Cycle, 2010–14 (Protocol, 2010–14), is available at www.fldoe.org/profdev/pdf/pdsreviewers.pdf.

Checkpoint

Fill in the blank.

1. According to the School Community Professional Development Act, a district's professional development system must be designed around a focus on increased _____ (student, teacher) achievement.

2. Principals are required by law to establish and maintain for each _____ (student, teacher) an Individual Professional Development Plan (IPDP).

3. The evaluation of a district's professional development system must include an annual assessment of data that indicates _____ (student, teacher) progress or lack of progress.

4. The four strands of the Florida Professional Development System Evaluation Protocol 2010 are _____, _____, _____, and _____.

Mark as true or false.

5. _____ (a) An appropriate professional development offering by a district would be one that focuses on technology.

_____ (b) The intent of the School Community Professional Development Act is to ensure that professional learning implemented in Florida's public schools is effective in assisting the school community in improving student achievement.

_____ (c) One-day or short-term workshops are recommended by the federal No Child Left Behind Act.

Checkpoint Answers

1. student

2. teacher

3. student

4. planning; learning; implementing; evaluating

5. (a) true; (b) true; (c) false

Planning

The **planning** strand consists of the *individual needs assessment, administrator review*, and the *IPDP* standards (Protocol, 2010–14).

Planning of the professional learning for an IPDP begins with an **individual needs assessment** conducted by the teacher. The purpose of this standard is to ensure that teachers "consider the academic progress of their students in determining what professional learning they need that will increase the learning of their students" (Protocol, 2010–14). As part of the decision-making process, the teacher reviews disaggregated classroom achievement and behavior data in addition to considering school initiatives, the school improvement plan, school and team goals, and needs related to certification, particularly certificate renewal needs. (See the section "Certification Needs" later in this chapter for additional discussion on this topic.)

Disaggregated classroom data are data from a teacher's students that are broken down by subgroups according to student characteristics. For teachers of students in grades 3 through 11, the most relevant data that should be disaggregated and examined are their students' results from the statewide, standardized assessment program. The disaggregation might be by racial/ethnic group, by English Language Learner (ELL) or Exceptional Student Education (ESE) status, by gender, or by other appropriate categories. Usually, for statewide data, districts generate the classroom-level disaggregated data for teachers. For other classroom data, teachers might disaggregate the data themselves. For example, a district might break down a fourth-grade teacher's statewide results by the achievement level obtained in each subject area. Another example is disaggregating the performance of a teacher's students by racial/ethnic categories to determine whether all groups are making satisfactory learning gains.

After the teacher has identified professional development needs, the teacher meets with the principal for an **administrative review** to determine any additional professional learning needs based on school-level priorities or identified through the teacher appraisal process. (See the section "Teacher Appraisal" later in this chapter for additional discussion of this topic.) This standard ensures that teachers meet individually with the principal to review the IPDP as it is being developed. The principal can use the administrative review meeting as an opportunity to review the progress of the teacher's students toward higher achievement and to discuss plans for long-term continuous improvement (Protocol, 2010–14).

The **IPDP** standard requires the teacher to develop an Individual Professional Development Plan (IPDP). The IPDP must plainly show the relationship of the professional learning to performance data of the teacher's students, contain clearly defined professional learning objectives that delineate measurable student performance improvements expected as a result of the professional learning for those students assigned to the teacher, specify changes in the teacher's practices resulting from professional learning, and include a plan for evaluating the effectiveness of the professional learning toward improving achievement of the students assigned to the teacher (Protocol, 2010–14).

Checkpoint

Fill in the blank.

1. Planning of the professional development for an IPDP begins with a _____ assessment.

2. Disaggregated data are data that are broken down by _____.

3. In the administrative review, the teacher meets with the principal to review the _____.

4. The IPDP must include a plan for evaluating the effectiveness of the professional learning toward improving _____ of the students assigned to the teacher.

5. The IPDP must plainly show the _____ of the professional learning to performance data of the teacher's students.

Checkpoint Answers

1. needs

2. subgroups

3. IPDP

4. achievement

5. relationship

Learning

The **learning** strand consists of the *learning communities, content focused, learning strategies, sustained professional learning, use of technology, time resources,* and *coordinated records* standards (Protocol, 2010–14).

The **learning communities** standard requires the teacher to participate in professional learning communities. A **Professional Learning Community (PLC)** is a formal, organized group of faculty who share common student achievement goals and meet on a regular basis during the school day to identify practical ways to improve learning and teaching practices. The group collectively reviews student data to guide development of more effective instructional strategies and identify needs for professional learning to achieve joint learning goals of the group. The rationale for the learning communities standard is that teachers will learn more when they can relate the learning to what they do in the classroom in a practical way. Grade-level or subject area collaborative groups that regularly meet primarily for the purposes of joint planning and discussion of student needs do not constitute a learning community. Collaborative groups are considered PLCs if they contribute to a culture of continuous improvement by studying and researching new practices, investigating new curricular programs, examining the impact of school initiatives, and sharing their findings with other school faculty. For instance, a **Lesson Study Group (LSG)** is a PLC that meets regularly to strengthen lesson planning through a highly structured process, the **Lesson Study Cycle** (scheduling and planning, teaching and observing, debriefing, re-teaching, and reflecting), with the goal of improving instructional effectiveness and maximizing student learning (Protocol, 2010–14).

The **content focused** standard requires that the professional learning that a teacher receives is research- and/or evidenced-based and directly related to the needs of the teacher in terms of the grade level and subject taught. Furthermore, the professional learning must directly relate to one or more of the following areas specified in Section 1012.98 (4)(b) (F. S.): analysis of student achievement data; ongoing formal and informal assessments of student achievement; identification and use of enhanced and differentiated instructional strategies that emphasize rigor, relevance, and reading in the content areas; enhancement of subject content expertise; integrated use of classroom technology that enhances teaching and learning; classroom management; parent involvement; and school safety. Although a professional learning choice does not have to address all of these areas, professional learning that is not related to at least one of these areas is unacceptable. Teachers may satisfy the professional learning requirement of the law in a number of ways; however, it is imperative that professional learning activities consistently result in improved academic achievement of students in the teachers' respective classrooms. Teachers should select activities that are directly related to their teaching assignments and to the needs and characteristics of their students. Teachers are not limited to district- or campus-based professional learning; they might also choose to participate in appropriate professional learning opportunities offered by the Adult and Community Educators (ACE) of Florida organization, colleges, universities, or other approved organizations (Protocol, 2010–14).

The **learning strategies** standard requires facilitators of the professional learning that teachers receive to use and model (in the professional learning sessions) effective research- and/or evidence-based instruction. Facilitators should teach the teachers using the same strategies and techniques that teachers are expected to use with their students in the classroom. They should model the skills they want the teachers to acquire, provide opportunities for the teachers to practice the skills, and provide feedback to the teachers on their performance of the skills during the professional learning sessions. Facilitators should avoid lectures and other types of passive learning (Protocol, 2010–14).

The **sustained professional learning** standard requires rigor and intensity in the professional learning in which teachers participate. The professional learning that is most likely to improve student achievement is sustained over an extended period of time and through multiple sessions over multiple days. No longer are one-day workshops and short-term training the norm for professional learning. Experts on professional learning have long contended that such quick-fix measures seldom succeed in effecting lasting change in what teachers do in their classrooms. Sustained, intense professional learning is needed to ensure mastery by the teachers of the content, techniques, and strategies that they are expected to acquire in the professional learning sessions. Ideally, teachers will have opportunities to practice the skills learned in their own classrooms while they are participating in the professional learning (Protocol, 2010–14).

The **use of technology** standard requires that various forms of technology be used to present (or deliver) professional learning activities to teachers, and moreover, that the technology used supports and enhances teachers' professional learning. Without exaggeration, the use of technology has revolutionized professional learning activities for teachers. Technology provides varied ways for teachers to observe and experience new learning. Professional learning facilitators can use interactive video/ SMART Boards, DVDs, PowerPoint presentations, computer programs, computer-based simulations, graphing calculators, dynamic mathematical software, document cameras, podcasts, and numerous other technology-based ways to enhance delivery of professional learning and support instruction. When the professional learning topic is a particular type of technology, hands-on practice with the technology is essential. The Internet has greatly expanded the use of technology in professional learning by providing online opportunities. Other distance learning media are online courses and interactive television broadcasts. Current law requires school districts to "Provide for delivery of professional development by distance learning and other technology-based delivery systems to reach more educators at lower costs" (Section 1012.98 (4)(b) F. S.) (Protocol, 2010–14).

The **time resources** standard requires that the teacher's workday includes sufficient time to implement planned professional learning. It isn't uncommon for time resources to be an issue when it comes to professional learning for teachers. Most teachers feel that finding time to complete planned professional learning is difficult. School district administrators need to be creative in finding ways to provide more time for professional learning, such as early release days. At a minimum, teachers should have 30 hours per year, during the school day, that are designated for professional learning and be required to attend professional learning sessions on those days (Protocol, 2010–14).

Finally, **coordinated records** is an important standard of effective professional learning. According to this standard, teachers need to be able to easily access the information in district-maintained records of their professional learning activity, including the in-service points awarded for the successful completion of the professional learning so that they can make informed decisions with regard to their professional learning needs. According to Rule 6A-5.071, FAC, 1 hour of professional learning participation equates to 1 in-service point, 1 semester hour of college credit equates to 20 in-service points, and ¼-hour of college credit equates to 13⅓ in-service points. Districts need to make concerted efforts to keep the records up-to-date and information easily accessible to teachers. Knowing the current in-service points they've earned toward recertification is important to teachers' careers (Protocol, 2010–14).

Checkpoint

Fill in the blank.

1. Collaborative groups are considered learning communities if they contribute to a culture of _____ improvement.

2. Professional learning is most likely to be used in the classroom when the content is relevant to the _____ of the teachers.

3. Professional learning facilitators should teach the teachers using the _____ strategies and techniques that teachers are expected to use with their students in the classroom.

4. The professional learning that is most likely to improve student achievement is sustained over a(n) _____ period of time and through multiple sessions over multiple days.

5. At a minimum, teachers should have _____ hours per year, during the school day, that are designated for professional learning.

6. One semester hour of college credit equates to _____ in-service points.

Checkpoint Answers

1. continuous

2. needs

3. same

4. extended

5. 30

6. 20

Implementing

The **implementing** strand consists of the *implementation of learning, coaching and mentoring*, and *web-based resources and assistance* standards (Protocol, 2010–14).

The **implementation of learning** standard requires teachers to transfer the knowledge and skills acquired in professional learning to their classroom practices with students. If this does not occur, then participating in professional learning is pointless, because, in the final analysis, higher student achievement is the primary goal of professional learning. A key idea of the standard is that teachers should actually use in their classrooms what they learned through engagement in professional learning (Protocol, 2010–14).

The **coaching and mentoring** standard requires that professional learning facilitators or other qualified personnel provide follow-up support and assistance to teacher participants through coaching and mentoring. The rationale for this standard is that teachers are more likely to use newly acquired skills and knowledge if they have ongoing follow-up assistance as they apply the professional learning in their own classrooms. Coaches and mentors are highly skilled individuals who provide guidance (often, one-on-one in teachers' classrooms or, more recently, through webcams) to help teachers correctly implement the new strategies and techniques presented in professional learning. Joyce and Showers (2003) contended that coaching/mentoring is an important component of professional learning. Coached/mentored teachers tend to practice skills more often and retain them longer than uncoached/unmentored teachers, are more likely to explain the new strategies to their students and make appropriate adaptations to the professional learning received to better meet the needs of students than uncoached/unmentored teachers, and are more likely to have a clearer understanding of the new skills and knowledge than uncoached/unmentored teachers. Schools should ensure that this crucial support and assistance is maintained until teachers feel they have mastered the newly acquired knowledge and skills (Protocol, 2010–14).

The **web-based resources and assistance** standard requires districts to provide teachers with web-based resources and assistance to support implementation of professional learning. These are efficient and, usually, economical ways for districts to provide support while teachers try out newly acquired skills and knowledge in their classrooms. For instance, to provide support related to the professional learning completed by teachers, districts can maintain websites that contain useful information, help desks, and links to helpful resources; set up online discussion forums; and disseminate information through newsletters or social networking technologies. Additionally, professional learning facilitators might share their contact information and invite participants to text or e-mail them for assistance regarding the professional learning received (Protocol, 2010–14).

Checkpoint

Fill in the blank.

1. Professional learning must be used in teachers' _____ in order to impact student achievement.

2. Teachers are more likely to use new skills and knowledge on an ongoing basis in their classrooms if they have _____ in trying out the new skills and knowledge.

3. Coached teachers tend to practice skills _____ (less, more) often than uncoached teachers.

4. An efficient way for districts to provide follow-up support for professional learning is through _____ resources and assistance.

Checkpoint Answers

1. classrooms

2. assistance

3. more

4. web-based

Evaluating

The **evaluating** strand consists of the *implementing the plan, changes in educator practice, changes in students, evaluation methods,* and *use of results* standards (Protocol, 2010–14).

The **implementing the plan** standard requires the teacher to provide convincing evidence of participation in a meeting with the principal (or the principal's designee) to conduct an evaluation of the degree to which the IPDP was implemented as written. Before conclusions about the impact of the planned professional learning are drawn, verification that the teacher participated in and completed the planned professional learning must be confirmed (Protocol, 2010–14).

The **changes in educator practice** standard requires the teacher to provide convincing evidence of reviewing the impact of professional learning on the teacher's practice and professional growth. How teachers go about documenting the changes in their practice varies. Methods could include gathering work samples such as lesson plans or videos of lesson presentations, using peer observations, or assembling portfolios that document improvements in educator practices that are a direct result of professional learning. Some principals might require teachers to submit written evidence such as lesson plans in which they incorporated the newly acquired knowledge and skills. Principals might use formal observations including **walk-throughs** (that is, structured visits to teachers' classrooms using checklists) to check on teachers' application of new skills. Principals also might use administrative reviews, interviews with students and other teachers, and examination of students' work to verify that teachers have used the new skills and knowledge in the classroom (Protocol, 2010–14).

The **changes in students** standard requires teachers to provide convincing evidence that professional learning had a positive impact on student achievement gains as measured by classroom assessment data. Unquestionably, the changes in students standard is the most important component of the evaluating strand. Professional learning that does not contribute to improvement in student success is a waste of time and resources for schools and teachers. Moreover, Florida law requires documentation that professional learning resulted in increased student achievement. Based on the documentation, principals must determine to what extent the measurable, observable performance gains expected as a result of the professional learning were attained (Protocol, 2010–14).

The **evaluation methods** standard requires the teacher to assess the impact of professional learning by using data collected through standardized achievement measures and other valid and reliable measures of student achievement and behavior. Documentation of the effect of professional learning on student performance might be achieved through the use of statewide assessments, standardized achievement tests, district-wide assessments, progress monitoring assessments, teacher-made tests, portfolios of student work, checklists of student mastery of skills, and other appropriate measures (Protocol, 2010–14).

The **use of results** standard requires the teacher to provide convincing evidence that the results from the IPDP evaluation is consistently used as part of continuous professional improvement to develop the next year's IPDP and to revise professional learning goals. Professional learning that fails to produce positive student change when implemented should be discontinued. Additionally, information obtained in the evaluation process should be used as part of the needs assessment for planning the IPDP for the subsequent school year.

Checkpoint

Fill in the blank.

1. A teacher's IPDP should be implemented as _____.

2. Unquestionably, "changes in _____" is the most important component of the evaluating strand.

3. Florida law requires documentation that professional learning resulted in _____ student achievement.

4. Information obtained in the IPDP evaluation process should be used as part of the needs assessment for _____ the IPDP for the subsequent school year.

Checkpoint Answers

1. written

2. students

3. increased

4. planning

Certification Needs

All classroom teachers in Florida must hold valid Florida teaching certificates. The Florida Legislature has established criteria for certification that ensures that teachers in Florida are professionally qualified. Further, the legislature has established a renewal process that teachers must adhere to in order to retain their certifications. According to 1012.585, F. S., to renew professional certificates—which are valid for 5 years—teachers must earn the equivalent of a minimum of 120 in-service points during each renewal period. College credit earned at an accredited or approved institution or community or junior college may be used to renew the professional certificate, with the requirement that a grade of at least C or the equivalent shall be earned in each course used for the renewal of a certificate. A grade of pass shall be acceptable under the pass-or-fail grading system (Rule 6A-4.0051, FAC).

For each area of specialization to be retained on a certificate, a teacher must earn at least 60 in-service points in the specialization area with the latitude that points earned through professional learning in some special topics such as literacy, ESE or limited proficiency in English strategies, drug abuse, child abuse and neglect, dropout prevention, and so on (as listed in 1012.585 (2), F. S.) may be applied toward a specialization area. Additionally, in place of in-service points, a teacher can renew a specialization area by passing a State Board of Education–approved subject area test or through national board certification in the subject area.

A teacher who is teaching out-of-field is required to participate in a certification or professional learning program designed to provide the teacher with the competencies required for the teaching assignment. By Florida law, when a district has any teacher teaching out-of-field, the parents of all students in the class shall be notified in writing of such assignment (Section 1012.42, F. S.).

Checkpoint

Fill in the blank.

1. All classroom teachers in Florida must hold _____ Florida teaching certificates.

2. The Florida Legislature has established criteria for certification that ensures that teachers in Florida are professionally _____.

3. Professional certificates are valid for _____ years.

4. To renew professional certificates, teachers must earn the equivalent of a minimum of _____ in-service points during each renewal period.

5. When a district has any teacher teaching out-of-field, the _____ of all students in the class shall be notified in writing of such assignment.

Checkpoint Answers

1. valid

2. qualified

3. 5

4. 120

5. parents

FEAPs

The Florida Educator Accomplished Practices (FEAPs) are set forth in Rule 6A-5.065 (FAC) as Florida's core standards for effective educators. The FEAPs were established in 1998 and revised in 2010. These standards form the foundation for the state's teacher preparation programs, educator certification requirements, and school district instructional personnel appraisal systems. Specifically, the eight competencies for the PEd Test are derived from the FEAPs.

The FEAPs are based upon three essential principles:

- The effective educator creates a culture of high expectations for all students by promoting the importance of education and each student's capacity for academic achievement.
- The effective educator demonstrates deep and comprehensive knowledge of the subject taught.
- The effective educator exemplifies the standards of the profession.

Effective teachers apply the foundational principles through the following six FEAPs:

- **Instructional Design and Lesson Planning:** Applying concepts from human development and learning theories, the effective educator consistently
  - aligns instruction with state-adopted standards at the appropriate level of rigor.
  - sequences lessons and concepts to ensure coherence and required prior knowledge.

- designs instruction for students to achieve mastery.
- selects appropriate formative assessments to monitor learning.
- uses diagnostic student data to plan lessons.
- develops learning experiences that require students to demonstrate a variety of applicable skills and competencies.

- **The Learning Environment:** To maintain a student-centered learning environment that is safe, organized, equitable, flexible, inclusive, and collaborative, the effective educator consistently
    - organizes, allocates, and manages the resources of time, space, and attention.
    - manages individual and class behaviors through a well-planned management system.
    - conveys high expectations to all students.
    - respects students' cultural, linguistic, and family backgrounds.
    - models clear, acceptable oral and written communication skills.
    - maintains a climate of openness, inquiry, fairness, and support.
    - integrates current information and communication technologies.
    - adapts the learning environment to accommodate the differing needs and diversity of students.
    - utilizes current and emerging assistive technologies that enable students to participate in high-quality communication interactions and achieve their educational goals.

- **Instructional Delivery and Facilitation:** The effective educator consistently utilizes a deep and comprehensive knowledge of the subject taught to
    - deliver engaging and challenging lessons.
    - deepen and enrich students' understanding through content area literacy strategies, verbalization of thought, and application of the subject matter.
    - identify gaps in students' subject matter knowledge.
    - modify instruction to respond to preconceptions or misconceptions.
    - relate and integrate the subject matter with other disciplines and life experiences.
    - employ higher-order questioning techniques.
    - apply varied instructional strategies and resources, including appropriate technology, to provide comprehensible instruction, and to teach for student understanding.
    - differentiate instruction based on an assessment of student learning needs and recognition of individual differences in students.
    - support, encourage, and provide immediate and specific feedback to students to promote student achievement.
    - utilize student feedback to monitor instructional needs and to adjust instruction.

- **Assessment:** The effective educator consistently
    - analyzes and applies data from multiple assessments and measures to diagnose students' learning needs, informs instruction based on those needs, and drives the learning process.
    - designs and aligns formative and summative assessments that match learning objectives and lead to mastery.
    - uses a variety of assessment tools to monitor student progress, achievement, and learning gains.
    - modifies assessments and testing conditions to accommodate learning styles and varying levels of knowledge.
    - shares the importance and outcomes of student assessment data with the student and the student's parents.
    - applies technology to organize and integrate assessment information.

- **Continuous Professional Improvement:** The effective educator consistently
    - designs purposeful professional goals to strengthen the effectiveness of instruction based on students' needs.

- examines and uses data-informed research to improve instruction and student achievement.
- uses a variety of data, independently and in collaboration with colleagues, to evaluate learning outcomes, adjust planning, and continuously improve the effectiveness of the lessons.
- collaborates with the home, school, and larger communities to foster communication and support student learning and continuous improvement.
- engages in targeted professional growth opportunities and reflective practices.
- implements knowledge and skills learned in professional development in the teaching and learning process.
- **Professional Responsibility and Ethical Conduct:** Understanding that educators are held to a high moral standard in a community, the effective educator adheres to the Code of Ethics and the Principles of Professional Conduct of the Education Profession of Florida and fulfills the expected obligations to students, the public, and the education profession (Rule 6A-5.065, FAC).

Checkpoint

Fill in the blank.

1. The FEAPs are Florida's core standards for _____ educators.

2. An essential principle of the FEAPs is that an effective educator should demonstrate deep and _____ knowledge of the subject taught.

3. Teachers should use _____ student data to plan lessons.

4. Teachers should convey _____ expectations to all students.

5. Teachers should use student _____ to monitor instructional needs and to adjust instruction.

6. Teachers should use a _____ of assessment tools to monitor student progress, achievement, and learning gains.

7. Teachers should use _____ research to improve instruction and student achievement.

8. Teachers should understand that educators are held to a high _____ standard in a community.

Checkpoint Answers

1. effective

2. comprehensive

3. diagnostic

4. high

5. feedback

6. variety

7. data-informed

8. moral

Teacher Appraisal

Section 1012.34 (F. S.) requires districts to implement the following:

- A teacher appraisal system that uses student performance as the single greatest component of teachers' evaluations
- A teacher contract system that continues or terminates contracts based on teacher performance evaluations

The act requires that each district's teacher appraisal system must be designed to support effective instruction and student achievement and must be approved by the FLDOE.

The teacher appraisal system must differentiate among four levels of performance:

- Highly effective
- Effective
- Needs improvement or, for instructional personnel in the first three years of employment or in the first year of a new teaching assignment, developing
- Unsatisfactory

The performance evaluation criteria for classroom teachers must include the following:

- **Student performance:** At least 50 percent of the evaluation must be based on data and indicators of student learning growth assessed annually by state assessments or, for subjects and grade levels not measured by the state assessments, by district assessments. The student learning growth portion of the evaluation must include growth data for students assigned to the teacher over the course of at least three years. If less than three years of data are available, the school district must include the years for which data are available and may reduce the percentage of the evaluation based on student growth to not less than 40 percent.
- **Instructional practice:** The evaluation criteria must include indicators based on each of the FEAPs adopted by the State Board of Education.
- **Professional responsibilities:** This criterion must include other professional responsibilities and employment requirements.

Measurement of **student growth in learning** is through a formula adopted by the State Board of Education based on statewide assessment results. The formula takes into account each student's prior academic performance, grade level, and subject. In the development of the formula, the Commissioner of Education must consider other factors, including but not limited to a student's attendance record, disability status, or student English Language Learner status. The formula must not set different expectations for student growth based on gender, race, ethnicity, or socioeconomic status.

Each teacher must be appraised by the principal (or the principal's designee) at least once a year. Newly hired teachers in a district must be evaluated twice in the first year of teaching in the district. Before the appraisal takes place, the principal must fully explain the criteria and procedures associated with the appraisal process to the teacher. The principal prepares a written report and submits it to the teacher no later than 10 days after the appraisal takes place. The principal then discusses the report with the teacher. The teacher has the right to prepare a written response to the principal's report, and the response becomes a permanent attachment to the teacher's personnel file.

The principal must submit the written appraisal report to the school district superintendent for the purpose of reviewing the employee's contract. If the teacher is not performing his or her duties in a satisfactory manner, the teacher is placed on performance probation after the principal has delivered to the teacher a written notice of unsatisfactory performance that explicitly describes the unsatisfactory performance. The principal must confer with the teacher, make recommendations, and provide assistance and professional learning training to help the teacher correct deficiencies related to the teacher's unsatisfactory performance. The teacher is expected to correct the deficiencies within 90 calendar days (excluding school holidays and vacation periods) or risk having the super-intendent recommend that the teacher's contract be terminated. However, the teacher is entitled to procedural safe-guards such as appealing a termination recommendation by the superintendent and requesting a hearing before the school board, which might delay termination and extend the prescribed time period for correction of deficiencies. Notwithstanding, the determination of the district school board shall be final as to the sufficiency or insufficiency of the grounds for termination of employment.

Checkpoint

Fill in the blank.

1. A district's teacher appraisal system must use student performance as the single _____ component of the teacher's evaluation.

2. A district's teacher compensation system must award salary increases based on sustained student _____.

3. A district's teacher contract system must award contracts based on student _____.

4. A district's teacher appraisal system must be designed to support effective instruction and _____ achievement.

5. At least _____ percent of the teacher performance evaluation must be based on data and indicators of student learning growth for teachers who have been teaching for at least three years.

6. Each teacher must be appraised by the principal at least _____ per year.

7. The principal must submit a written report of a teacher's appraisal to the teacher no later than _____ days after the appraisal takes place.

8. If a teacher is not performing his or her duties in a satisfactory manner as identified by the principal's appraisal, the teacher is placed on performance _____.

Checkpoint Answers

1. greatest
2. performance
3. performance
4. student
5. 50
6. once
7. 10
8. probation

Reflective Practitioners

Research studies have identified certain characteristics that are essential for effective teaching. The studies found that effective teachers are clear about instructional goals and accept responsibility for student learning; choose, adapt, and use materials effectively; have a firm command of subject matter and teaching strategies; motivate students by communicating expectations to students; incorporate higher-level thinking skills; develop empathy, rapport, and personal interactions with students; and integrate instruction with other subject areas. Furthermore, effective teachers possess personality characteristics that include enthusiasm, warmth, supportiveness of students, sensitivity, interest in people, flexibility, and self-confidence. In addition, researchers maintain that effective teachers are **reflective practitioners** (meaning, they monitor and assess whether their teaching is effective).

Reflective practitioners understand that reflection and self-evaluation are important, and recognize that their own personal factors—both positive (enthusiasm, warmth, commitment to student success, and so on) and negative (negative attitudes, biases, low self-concept, and so on)—affect their effectiveness in the classroom. Before, during, and after a lesson, they are observing whether students are learning, and they adjust the lesson accordingly. They are constantly making decisions based on observed student needs. They ask themselves such questions as the following: Is this the best teaching strategy to use for this lesson and these students? Is what I'm doing working? Am I being supportive and sensitive toward my students? This process is known as **reflective teaching.** Reflective teaching helps teachers become proactive in their teaching practices and develop self-confidence in their ability to promote student learning.

Some teachers keep a daily or weekly journal of their thoughts and feelings to facilitate reflection and self-evaluation. They regularly reflect on what they did, and then think about what they can do better. A **reflective journal** is an authentic and effective way for teachers to identify strengths, challenges, and potential problems. It also provides a means for a teacher to look back and see progress over time.

Besides reflective journaling, teachers can use a number of other ways to examine their teaching. For instance, some teachers assess themselves by videotaping or audiotaping lessons for later reviewing and critiquing of their instructional performance. Asking a colleague or mentor to observe in the teacher's classroom is another way to obtain helpful insights. This idea can be extended into a partnership with another teacher, in which the two teachers share ideas and provide feedback on one another's teaching.

Checkpoint

Fill in the blank.

1. Researchers maintain that effective teachers are _____ practitioners, meaning that they monitor and assess whether their teaching is effective.

2. Reflective teaching helps teachers become _____ in their teaching practices.

3. A reflective journal is a(n) _____ and effective way for teachers to identify strengths, challenges, and potential problems.

Checkpoint Answers

1. reflective

2. proactive

3. authentic

Role with Parents

In 2003, the Florida Legislature passed the Family and School Partnership for Student Achievement Act, Section 1002.23 (F. S.), to enhance the involvement of parents in their children's educational progress. This act is intended to "provide a framework for building and strengthening partnerships among parents, teachers, principals, district school superintendents, and other personnel."

The person with the most opportunities to build positive parent-school partnerships is the classroom teacher. Teachers can be effective public relations agents by reaching out to their students' parents. Positive telephone calls, notes, and newsletters throughout the year to all parents telling of class happenings and their children's achievements will be welcomed and appreciated. Parents should feel free to visit the school at any time. They can be invited to attend student performances and to become involved in school activities. They will care about the school when they feel ownership of it. This dynamic can be further enhanced when teachers invite parents to be on-site volunteers or at-home volunteers. Among other things, parents can serve as tutors; share a specific skill, talent, interest, or hobby; read to students or listen to them read; make bulletin boards; set up centers or labs; perform clerical tasks; help with special activities; or serve as aides and room mothers/fathers. If parents indicate that they feel unqualified or incapable of being involved in their child's education, it is very important that the teacher emphasize to the parents that they are the experts when it comes to their own child.

The art of communicating with parents is an integral part of being an effective teacher. Communication between the school and the home should be purposeful and ongoing. Teachers and parents share responsibility for creating a working relationship that fosters student learning. When parents participate and are involved in their child's learning, the child has a greater chance of success. Moreover, research suggests that parents' expressed belief about their child's academic abilities and potential for achievement significantly affects the child's perceptions of his or her own competence and learning potential, regardless of the child's age.

An important way that teachers communicate with parents is through parent-teacher conferences. The nature of parent-teacher conferences might differ depending upon the age and grade level of the student. Parents are usually more involved in their child's education during the early grades than at the middle or high school levels, when students assume more responsibility for their own educational development. Traditionally, conferences take place at the school where the parents and teacher can meet face to face. Nowadays, conferences can also be through telephone calls and via computer. For busy parents whose schedules make it difficult to set up a mutually convenient time for a conference, these virtual formats might be the best way to "meet." When scheduling a conference time, the teacher should use a written form, giving the parents some time options as well as alternative days if possible. They should allow ample time for parents to complete the form and return it. Following are some general guidelines for parent conferences.

Preparing for the Conference

- Schedule the conference at a definite day and time.
- Inform the principal.
- Invite the student to attend the conference, if appropriate and the parents agree.
- Provide parents with topics to be discussed prior to the conference.
- Have a written conference agenda to keep you on task.
- Anticipate questions you think parents might have.
- Gather information/materials that are pertinent to the conference objective (for example, samples of the student's work, anecdotal records, cumulative record).
- Make sure that the setting for the conference is warm and inviting.
- Make sure that the seating is comfortable and arranged so that there are no physical barriers between you and the parents (for example, don't sit behind a desk).
- Arrange to have an interpreter, if needed.
- Ask the principal (or the principal's designee) to attend if you anticipate difficulties.

During the Conference

- Think of the conference as partnering with parents to help the student.
- Greet the parents warmly and offer refreshments.
- Introduce yourself using your first and last name.
- Be professional at all times.
- Stay poised and focused.
- Be respectful of and sensitive to the parents' cultural and social background.
- Establish and maintain eye contact (unless you sense doing so makes the parents feel uncomfortable, defensive, or hostile).
- Be an active and empathetic listener and encourage parental input.
- Address the parents often by name.
- Use language and terminology that parents can easily understand. Avoid jargon.
- Paraphrase parents' comments to avoid misunderstandings or miscommunication, especially when dealing with parents whose home language is one other than English.
- Be tactful, but honest and sincere.
- Respect confidentiality.
- Avoid comparing the student to his or her siblings.
- Stay away from psychological references as to why the student is not doing well. Avoid "diagnosing" or "labeling" the student.

- Avoid downplaying problems when explaining difficulties to parents.
- Avoid discussing other students.
- Avoid becoming defensive if parents question your judgment. Keep in mind that it is normal for parents to be protective of their child.
- Share any notes taken and review them with parents, summarizing key points.
- Collaboratively develop a student-parent-teacher plan.
- Suggest what parents can do to help at home.
- Set a timetable for contacting parents with a follow-up report.
- Explain to parents the procedures and practices that will be followed.
- Arrange to provide the parents and student (if appropriate) with a written copy of the plan.
- Schedule another conference, if warranted.
- Invite parents to visit the school and participate in activities.
- Accentuate the positive. Always begin and end on a positive note.

After the Conference

- Engage in self-reflection and evaluation. (What went well? What didn't?)
- Review notes and comments and file them for future reference.
- Document, date, and file what was proposed.
- Send the mutually agreed-upon plan to parents and give a copy to the student.
- Write a personal note or e-mail to the parents, thanking them for their time and informing them when you will contact them with an update.
- Have a positive contact with the student as soon as possible to dispel any fears and to reassure him or her.

During the school year, continue the communication in the form of weekly or monthly telephone calls, e-mails, or notes. A positive phone call will be appreciated by parents who have received only negative reports in the past. The campus policy handbook will usually contain suggestions for communicating with parents. The handbook should also inform you of what kinds of records of contact to keep.

Another way teachers can build positive relationships with parents is by helping them understand their child's statewide assessment results. Many parents have only rudimentary knowledge of assessment terms and concepts, so statewide assessment reports can be confusing. (See the section "K-12 Statewide, Standardized Assessment Program" in Chapter 4 for a discussion of this topic.)

Checkpoint

Fill in the blank.

1. Parents' expressed beliefs about their children's academic abilities _____ (do, do not) affect students' perceptions of their own competence.

2. The seating for a parent-teacher conference should be arranged so that there are no physical _____ between the teacher and the parents.

3. If parents indicate to a teacher that they feel unqualified to help their child with school, the teacher should emphasize to the parents that they are the _____ when it comes to their own child.

Mark as true or false.

4. _____ (a) In a parent conference, it is best to start off explaining the problem so as not to waste the parents' time.

   _____ (b) To alleviate parents' anxiety, a teacher should tell them that other students have similar problems.

Checkpoint Answers

1. do

2. barriers

3. experts

4. (a) false; (b) false

Role on Collaborative Teams

In their roles as professionals, teachers often serve on collaborative teams such as *Individual Educational Plan (IEP) teams, Educational Plan (EP) teams, Section 504 plan (504) teams, Child Study Teams (CSTs), English Language Learner (ELL) [also known as Limited English Proficient (LEP)] Committees, interdisciplinary teams, subject area teams, School Advisory Councils (SACs)*, and *School-Based Management (SBM) teams.* Florida teachers also serve as members of *Professional Learning Communities (PLCs), Lesson Study Groups (LSGs)*, and *Reading Leadership Teams (RLTs).* PLCs and LSGs are discussed in the section "Learning" earlier in this chapter. RLTs are discussed in Chapter 8.

Under the Individuals with Disabilities Education Act (IDEA), the **IEP team** is the group of individuals who make decisions about the services and accommodations or modifications provided to a student with a disability. The IEP team must include the parents of the student, at least one regular education teacher of the student (provided the student is participating in a regular education classroom), at least one special education teacher of the student, a representative of the school who is qualified to provide or supervise the provision of special services, an individual who can interpret evaluation results, the student (if appropriate), and other individuals who might be of help in designing and reviewing the IEP. Parents may invite a person who, in their judgment, has "knowledge or special expertise" about the child. The IEP documents the student's present levels of performance, establishes annual goals for the student, and specifies which special services and supports are needed, including accommodations and modifications, for the student to advance toward attaining the annual goals. The regular education teacher is a full participant in the development of the IEP, including the determination of intervention strategies and accommodations, appropriate supplementary aids and services, and program modifications. The IEP team must meet at least once a year to review the IEP. IEPs may be reviewed more frequently as needed (for example, if a parent or teacher requests a review). Every IEP meeting must include a discussion of the least restrictive environment (LRE) appropriate for the student. A student's services can be changed only during an IEP meeting. A copy of the IEP must be accessible to each of the student's teachers, who must follow it as written.

The **EP team** is the group of individuals who make decisions about the ESE services provided to students identified as gifted. The EP team must include the parents of the student, at least one regular education teacher of the student, at least one teacher of the gifted program, a representative of the school who is qualified to provide or supervise the provision of special services, an individual who can interpret evaluation results, the student (if appropriate), and other individuals who might be of help in designing and reviewing the EP. The EP documents the student's present levels of performance, establishes goals for the student, and specifies which special services and supports are needed for the student to advance toward and achieve his or her goals. The EP team must meet at least once every 3 years for students in kindergarten through grade 8 and at least once every 4 years for students in grades 9 through 12. EPs may be reviewed more frequently as needed (for example, if a parent or teacher requests a review). A student's services can be changed only during an EP meeting. A copy of the EP must be accessible to each of the student's teachers, who must follow it as written (Rule 6A-6.030191, FAC).

A Section 504 plan is designed to ensure that students with physical or mental disabilities that substantially limit a major life activity are provided with the same opportunity as other students without disabilities to learn at school (Section 504 of the Rehabilitation Act of 1973). The team that determines a student's eligibility for special services under Section 504 writes the plan and is called the **504 team** for the student. Although Section 504 regulations do not mandate the composition of the 504 team, they require that placement decisions be "made by a group of persons, including persons knowledgeable about the child, the meaning of the evaluation data, and the placement options." They suggest that teams should include teachers, school counselors, school nurses, related services providers, and school psychologists, if appropriate.

When a parent, teacher, or other member of the school staff raises a concern about a student's behavior or academic progress, a **CST** is assembled to collect and review information about the student to decide how best to meet the student's educational needs. In most cases, the process actually begins with a meeting between the student's parents and the teacher, and thereafter, if further intervention seems warranted, the CST is organized. The CST process facilitates the identification of struggling students and the determination of appropriate RtI interventions and/or referrals for evaluations. The student might be eligible for ESE or other services. Even if a child does not meet eligibility requirements, the CST considers what strategies might best help the student to be successful in school. In Florida schools, the CST might be called the Pupil Assistance Team (PAT), Student Assistance Team (SAT), Educational Planning Team (EPT), Teacher Support Team (TST), Intervention Assistance Team (IAT), Student Services Team (SST), or Student Support Team (SST), among others.

Under the Florida Consent Decree, an **ELL (or LEP) Committee** is a team of individuals who are responsible for overseeing an English Language Learner's English for Speakers of Other Languages (ESOL) program. The committee is composed of the ESOL teacher or teachers, the home language teacher (if any), and an administrator (or designee), plus other members such as school counselors, school social workers, school psychologists, or other educators as appropriate for the situation. The parents would also be invited to attend any committee meetings. (See Chapter 7, "Teaching English Language Learners (ELLs)," for additional discussion on this topic.)

An **interdisciplinary team** (also called a **grade-level team**) consists of two or more teachers from different subject areas who collaboratively plan for the students they commonly instruct. Usually, these teachers share a common planning period and meet frequently on a regular basis to plan the curriculum and discuss the progress and needs of their students. The advantages of interdisciplinary teams include the following: Members provide an expanded pool of ideas and solutions to problems; members can plan collaboratively and coordinate instructional activities; members can discuss and decide on year-long curriculum objectives, goals, and timelines; members provide support and guidance for each other; beginning teachers have the benefit of experienced teachers' advice and help; members tend to work harder on improving instructional quality; members help substitute teachers when a team member is absent; members can collaborate in dealing with individual students; and students are provided a coordinated curriculum with an opportunity to see interdisciplinary connections.

It is common for middle school and secondary school faculty who teach the same basic subject areas to meet on a regular basis as **subject area teams** to share ideas and problem-solve about concerns related to their subject areas. Subject area teams collaboratively plan and sequence instructional activities and tests for their disciplines.

The **SAC** is a state-mandated advisory group composed of the principal, teachers, educational support staff, parents, and business and other community members, who are representative of the ethnic, racial, and economic communities served by the school. The SAC's primary duties are assisting in the preparation and evaluation of the **School Improvement Plan (SIP)** and in the preparation of the school's annual budget and plan (Section 1001.452, F. S.). The **SIP** is a state-mandated, written plan developed by the SAC that addresses school goals (Section 1008.42 (18)(a), F. S.). The SIP helps schools focus on setting measurable and attainable objectives consistent with the state's education priorities. SACs should meet regularly and have action-oriented agendas guided by long- and short-term goals.

The **SBM team** is composed of the principal, teachers, parents, and other community members. SBM decentralizes authority and gives more power to individual schools. Decision making regarding the school budget, hiring and job responsibilities of faculty and staff, and curriculum programs is placed at the school level, rather than at the district level. The advantages of SBM are improved teacher morale, better alignment of financial and instructional resources with instructional goals, increased quantity and quality of communication among stakeholders, greater flexibility for schools in meeting the needs of their students, and more realistic budget setting and increased financial prudence.

Checkpoint

Fill in the blank.

1. The IEP team is the group of individuals who make decisions about the services and accommodations or modifications provided to a student with a _____.

2. The EP team must meet at least once every _____ years for students in kindergarten through grade 8 and at least once every _____ years for students in grades 9 through 12.

3. A(n) _____ team consists of two or more teachers from different subject areas who collaboratively plan for the students they commonly instruct.

Mark as true or false.

4. _____ (a) If a teacher feels an ESE student's IEP is not appropriate, it is not necessary for the teacher to consult the IEP team before changing the plan.

   _____ (b) Parents of ESE students who are gifted are not full participants on their child's EP team.

Checkpoint Answers

1. disability

2. 3; 4

3. interdisciplinary (or grade-level)

4. (a) false; (b) false

Professional Organizations

Another way for teachers to improve their practice is to become members of professional organizations associated with their fields of interest such as the following:

- National Association for the Education of Young Children (NAEYC); www.naeyc.org/
- International Reading Association (IRA); www.reading.org/
- National Council of Teachers of English (NCTE); www.ncte.org/
- National Council of Teachers of Mathematics (NCTM); www.nctm.org/
- National Science Teachers Association (NSTA); www.nsta.org/
- National Council for the Social Studies (NCSS); www.socialstudies.org/
- National Council for Agriculture Education (The Council); www.ffa.org/thecouncil/Pages/index.html
- National Academy of Sciences (NAS); www.nasonline.org/
- American Alliance for Health, Physical Education, Recreation, and Dance (AAHPERD); www.aahperd.org/

Joining professional organizations provides an opportunity for teachers to keep abreast of the latest research and innovative practices in their areas of expertise by networking with other professionals, attending conferences and workshops, and subscribing to professional journals.

Other noteworthy groups are the following:

- The National Education Association (NEA); www.nea.org/
- American Federation of Teachers (AFT); www.aft.org/
- ASCD (Association for Supervision and Curriculum Development); www.ascd.org/
- Florida Association of Teacher Educators (FATE); www.fate1.org/
- Florida Education Association (FEA); feaweb.org/

Checkpoint

Fill in the blank.

1. A way for teachers to improve their practice is to become members of professional organizations associated with their _____ of interest.

2. The major benefit of joining a professional organization is that it provides an opportunity to keep abreast of the latest _____ and innovative practices.

Checkpoint Answers

1. fields

2. research

Summary

In summary, continuous improvement of teachers is an ongoing process in Florida. The Florida Legislature has enacted legislation to ensure the quality of professional learning in public education in the state. A rigorous system is in place that demands student progress as a result of professional learning activities offered by school districts. In addition, legislation by Florida lawmakers has made student achievement the cornerstone of the teacher appraisal system.

Besides engaging in required and voluntary professional learning opportunities, teachers grow professionally by reflecting on their practice, sharing ideas, and collaborating with colleagues. They also benefit from joining professional organizations and attending professional conferences.

Sample Questions

1. The school district is planning in-service activities for the coming school year. Which of the following would be an appropriate topic for an in-service activity?

   A. important Supreme Court decisions
   B. highlights of the Individuals with Disabilities Act
   C. prevention-oriented Internet safety
   D. understanding Florida's school accountability system

2. Which of the following is the most important reason a teacher should engage in professional learning?

   A. to satisfy recertification requirements
   B. to avoid being placed on professional probation
   C. to have opportunities to interact with other professionals
   D. to acquire skills and knowledge that will enhance student learning

3. A student's grandfather is invited by a parent to attend the student's IEP team meeting. During the meeting, the grandfather responds to questions directed to the parent. How should the school personnel on the team deal with this situation?

   A. They should continue with the meeting without comment to either the grandfather or the parent about the grandfather's behavior.
   B. They should ask the parent whether the parent wants the grandfather to continue to answer questions directed to the parent.
   C. They should ask the grandfather to leave the meeting.
   D. They should stop the meeting and speak privately with the parent about the grandfather's behavior.

Answer Explanations for Sample Questions

1. **C.** According to Section 1012.98, F. S., appropriate professional learning should focus primarily on the content areas specified by Florida law: analysis of student achievement data; ongoing formal and informal assessments of student achievement; identification and use of enhanced and differentiated instructional strategies that emphasize rigor, relevance, and reading in the content areas; enhancement of subject content expertise; integrated use of classroom technology that enhances teaching and learning; classroom management; parent involvement; and school safety. Only **C** meets this requirement.

2. **D.** Eliminate **B** because it is a poor reason for engaging in professional learning. Choice **C** is a reason that a teacher might want to engage in professional learning, but it is not an important reason. Choice **A** is an important reason for a teacher to engage in professional learning, but it is not the most important reason. According to Florida law, the most important reason for a teacher to engage in professional learning is to acquire skills and knowledge that will enhance student learning. Thus, **D** is the correct response.

3. **A.** Choice **A** is the correct response. The school personnel on the team should continue with the meeting without comment to either the grandfather or the parent about the grandfather's behavior. The school team members must assume that the parent feels the grandfather has knowledge or special expertise regarding the student since the parent invited him. The action given in **C** would be a violation of the parent's rights under IDEA. The actions given in **B** and **D** are inappropriate and could possibly be construed as violations of the parent's rights as well.

Competency Description and Key Indicators

According to the *Competencies and Skills Required for Teacher Certification in Florida,* 20th Edition (available at www.fldoe.org/asp/ftce/pdf/ftce20edition.pdf), **Competency 6** of the FTCE PEd Test addresses **Professional Conduct** as follows:

> *Knowledge of the Code of Ethics and Principles of Professional Conduct of the Education Profession in Florida*

Key indicators:

- Apply the Code of Ethics and Principles of Professional Conduct to realistic professional and personal situations.
- Identify statutory grounds and procedures for disciplinary action, the penalties that can be imposed by the Educational Practices Commission against a certificate holder, and the appeals process available to the individual.
- Apply knowledge of rights, legal responsibilities, and procedures for reporting incidences of abuse, neglect, or other signs of distress.
- Identify and apply policies and procedures for the safe, appropriate, and ethical use of technologies.
- Determine and apply the appropriate use and maintenance of students' information and records.

Overview

Professional Conduct refers to a teacher's conduct as a certified professional educator. To promote and govern professional behavior of teachers in Florida, the state has adopted the Code of Ethics of the Education Profession in Florida and Principles of Professional Conduct for the Education Profession in Florida, which are jointly referred to as the Code of Ethics and Principles of Professional Conduct for the Education Profession in Florida (Code of Ethics and Principles of Professional Conduct). The Code of Ethics and Principles of Professional Conduct addresses professional attitudes and concerns and ethical conduct toward students, the public, and the profession of education. Any teacher who is charged with and found guilty of violating any part of the Code of Ethics and Principles of Professional Conduct is subject to having his or her teaching certificate revoked or suspended.

This chapter provides a general review of Professional Conduct as the term applies to teachers in Florida with sample questions and explanations at the end of the chapter. Checkpoint exercises are found throughout the review material. These exercises give you an opportunity to practice what you just learned. The answers to the Checkpoint exercises are found immediately following the set of exercises. When doing the Checkpoint exercises, you should cover up the answers. Then check your answers when you've finished the exercises. The sample questions at the end of this chapter are multiple-choice questions that are similar to what you might expect to see on the FTCE PEd Test. The answer explanations for the sample questions are provided immediately after the questions.

Code of Ethics

The Code of Ethics (6A-10.080, FAC) is stated in three parts as given here:

- The educator values
  - the worth and dignity of every person.
  - the pursuit of truth.

- devotion to excellence.
- acquisition of knowledge.
- the nurture of democratic citizenship.

Essential to the achievement of these standards are the freedom to learn and to teach and the guarantee of equal opportunity for all.

- The educator's primary professional concern will always be
  - for the student.
  - for the development of the student's potential.

The educator will, therefore, strive for professional growth and will seek to exercise the best professional judgment and integrity.

- Aware of the importance of maintaining the respect and confidence of one's colleagues, of students, of parents*, and of other members of the community, the educator strives to achieve and sustain the highest degree of ethical conduct.

*Note: By Florida school law, a *parent* is either or both parents, a guardian, or any person in a parental relationship to a student or who has charge over a student in place of the parent.

Checkpoint

Fill in the blank.

1. By state law, a teacher's primary professional concern will always be for the _____ and the development of the _____ potential.
2. By state law, teachers must value the pursuit of _____.
3. By state law, teachers must value the nurturing of _____ citizenship.
4. By state law, teachers must strive for _____ growth.

Checkpoint Answers

1. student; student's
2. truth
3. democratic
4. professional

Principles of Professional Conduct: Obligation to the Student

Under the Principles (Rule 6A-10.081 (3), FAC), the obligation to the student requires that the educator

- shall make reasonable effort to protect the student from conditions harmful to learning and/or to the student's mental health and/or safety.
- shall not unreasonably restrain a student from independent action in pursuit of learning.
- shall not unreasonably deny a student access to diverse points of view.
- shall not intentionally suppress or distort subject matter relevant to a student's academic program.
- shall not intentionally expose a student to unnecessary embarrassment or disparagement.
- shall not intentionally violate or deny a student's legal rights.

- shall not harass or discriminate against any student on the basis of race, color, religion, sex, age, national or ethnic origin, political beliefs, marital status, handicapping condition, sexual orientation, or social and family background, and shall make reasonable effort to ensure that each student is protected from harassment or discrimination.

- shall not exploit a relationship with a student for personal gain or advantage.

- shall keep in confidence personally identifiable information obtained in the course of professional service, unless disclosure serves professional purposes or is required by law.

Checkpoint

Fill in the blank.

1. Teachers should not intentionally expose a student to unnecessary _____ or disparagement.

2. Teachers should allow students to have access to _____ points of view.

3. Teachers should not intentionally violate a student's legal _____.

Mark as true or false.

4. _____ (a) Teachers should be committed to openness and objectivity.

   _____ (b) Discrimination on the basis of marital status is not addressed in the Principles of Professional Conduct for the Education Profession in Florida.

Checkpoint Answers

1. embarrassment

2. diverse

3. rights

4. (a) true; (b) false

Principles of Professional Conduct: Obligation to the Public

Under the Principles (Rule 6A-10.081 (4), FAC), the obligation to the public requires that the educator

- shall take reasonable precautions to distinguish between personal views and those of any educational institution or organization with which the individual is affiliated.

- shall not intentionally distort or misrepresent facts concerning an educational matter in direct or indirect public expression.

- shall not use institutional privileges for personal gain or advantage.

- shall accept no gratuity, gift, or favor that might influence professional judgment.

- shall offer no gratuity, gift, or favor to obtain special advantages.

Checkpoint

Fill in the blank.

1. Teachers should refuse to accept gratuities, _____, or favors that might influence their professional judgment.

2. When speaking publicly, teachers should not intentionally distort facts concerning a(n) _____ matter.

3. Teachers should avoid using their professional positions for _____ gain or advantage.

Mark as true or false.

4. _____ (a) It is ethical for teachers to present their personal views as the views of the school personnel where they teach.

_____ (b) Teachers should be committed to honesty in their professional behavior.

Checkpoint Answers

1. gifts

2. educational

3. personal

4. (a) false; (b) true

Principles of Professional Conduct: Obligation to the Profession of Education

Under the Principles (Rule 6A-10.081 (5), FAC), the obligation to the profession of education requires that the educator

- shall maintain honesty in all professional dealings.
- shall not on the basis of race, color, religion, sex, age, national or ethnic origin, political beliefs, marital status, handicapping condition if otherwise qualified, or social and family background deny to a colleague professional benefits or advantages or participation in any professional organization.
- shall not interfere with a colleague's exercise of political or civil rights and responsibilities.
- shall not engage in harassment or discriminatory conduct that unreasonably interferes with an individual's performance of professional or work responsibilities or with the orderly processes of education or that creates a hostile, intimidating, abusive, offensive, or oppressive environment; further, the educator shall make reasonable effort to ensure that each individual is protected from such harassment or discrimination.
- shall not make malicious or intentionally false statements about a colleague.
- shall not use coercive means or promise special treatment to influence professional judgments of colleagues.
- shall not misrepresent his or her own professional qualifications.
- shall not submit fraudulent information on any document in connection with professional activities.
- shall not make any fraudulent statement or fail to disclose a material fact in his or her own or another's application for a professional position.
- shall not withhold information regarding a position from an applicant or misrepresent an assignment or conditions of employment.
- shall provide upon the request of the certificated individual a written statement of specific reasons that lead to the denial of increments, significant changes in employment, or termination of employment.
- shall not assist entry into or continuance in the profession of any person known to be unqualified in accordance with these Principles of Professional Conduct for the Education Profession in Florida and other applicable Florida Statutes and State Board of Education rules.
- shall self-report within 48 hours to appropriate authorities (as determined by district) any arrests/charges involving the abuse of a child or the sale and/or possession of a controlled substance. Such notice shall not be considered an admission of guilt nor shall such notice be admissible for any purpose in any proceeding, civil or criminal, administrative or judicial, investigatory or adjudicatory. In addition, the educator shall self-report any conviction, finding of guilt, withholding of adjudication, commitment to a pretrial diversion program, or entering of a plea of guilty or nolo contendere for any criminal offense other than a minor traffic violation within 48 hours after the final judgment. When handling sealed and expunged records

disclosed under this rule, school districts shall comply with the confidentiality provisions of Sections 943.0585 (4)(c) and 943.059 (4)(c), Florida Statutes (F. S.).

- shall report to appropriate authorities any known allegation of a violation of Florida School Code or State Board of Education Rules as defined in Section 1012.795 (1), F. S.
- shall seek no reprisal against any individual who has reported any allegation of a violation of Florida School Code or State Board of Education Rules as defined in Section 1012.795 (1), F. S.
- shall comply with the conditions of an order of the Education Practices Commission imposing probation, imposing a fine, or restricting the authorized scope or practice.
- shall as the supervising administrator, cooperate with the Education Practices Commission in monitoring the probation of a subordinate.

Checkpoint

Fill in the blank.

1. Teachers must not _____ their professional qualifications.

2. A teacher should not assist an applicant whom the teacher knows is _____ in gaining employment in the profession.

3. Teachers must self-report within _____ hours to appropriate authorities any arrests/charges involving the abuse of a child.

Mark as true or false.

4. _____ (a) Teachers must report alleged violations of the Code of Ethics and Principles of Professional Conduct for the Education Profession in Florida.

_____ (b) Teachers must not make fraudulent statements against a colleague.

Checkpoint Answers

1. misrepresent

2. unqualified

3. 48

4. (a) true; (b) true

Disciplinary Action

The section presents information (current in 2014) about statutory grounds and procedures for disciplinary action, the penalties that can be imposed by the Educational Practices Commission against an educator certificate holder, and the appeals process available to a teacher in the State of Florida.

Under Section 1012.33 (1)(a) and (4)(c), F. S., a school district can suspend or dismiss a teacher at any time during the school year for "just cause." **Just cause** for dismissal includes but is not limited to

- immorality.
- misconduct in office.
- gross insubordination.
- willful neglect of duty.
- drunkenness.
- conviction of a crime involving moral turpitude.
- incompetence.

Whenever such charges are made, the district school board may suspend the teacher without pay; but, if the charges are not sustained, the teacher shall be immediately reinstated, and his or her back salary shall be paid (Section 1012.33 (4)(c).

In the case of incompetence, teachers are given an opportunity to remediate before charges of incompetence are filed. The teacher is given

- notification that deficiencies, which might lead to disciplinary action, exist.
- a written, detailed explanation of the deficiencies, along with recommendations for remediation.
- assistance in the form of a plan developed with the help of the principal.
- reasonable time to complete the remediation (Section 1012.34 (4), F. S.).

If remediation does not occur in the designated time period, charges of incompetence are filed, and the teacher is then subject to suspension or revocation of his or her certificate.

The Education Practices Commission (EPC) oversees disciplinary actions taken against the certificate of an educator certified to teach in Florida. The EPC is composed of 25 members who are nominated by the commissioner of education and appointed by the State Board of Education. According to Section 1012.795, F. S., the EPC can suspend or revoke a teacher's certificate or take other appropriate action against a teacher, provided it can be shown that the teacher

- fraudulently obtained or attempted to obtain an educator certificate.
- knowingly failed to report actual or suspected child abuse or report alleged misconduct of school personnel that affects the health, safety, or welfare of a student as required by Florida law.
- is incompetent to perform his or her professional duties.
- is guilty of gross immorality or an act involving moral turpitude.
- has had an educator certificate revoked or suspended in another state.
- has been convicted of a felony or a misdemeanor other than a minor traffic violation.
- has been found guilty of personal conduct that seriously reduces the teacher's effectiveness.
- has breached a contract with a Florida school district.
- has violated the Principles of Professional Conduct for the Education Profession.
- has violated any law for which the penalty is revocation of the educator certificate.
- has violated any order of the EPC.
- is the subject of a court order directing the EPC to suspend the certificate due to delinquent child support obligation.
- is the subject of a court order requiring the surrender or relinquishment of the teacher's certificate.

The FLDOE Office of Professional Practices Services (PPS) investigates complaints of alleged ethical and conduct violations. The complaint/investigation process (in 2014) under Section 1012.796, through which suspension or revocation of a teacher's certificate for violations under Section 1012.79, F. S., is outlined on the PPS website at www.fldoe.org/edstandards/role_of_pps.asp. Here is a brief summary.

1. A complaint is filed with the PPS.

2. If warranted, a case is opened. The teacher and the district superintendent are notified that a complaint has been made. The teacher is informed of the substance of the complaint, unless to do so would compromise the investigation.

3. The PPS conducts an investigation and reports the findings to the commissioner of education.

4. The commissioner, after review of the findings by the FLDOE's general counsel, determines whether probable cause exists to further prosecute the complaint. Before the decision is made, the teacher must be granted upon request an opportunity for a conference with the commissioner. The commissioner makes the final decision concerning probable cause. If no probable cause is found, the commissioner dismisses the

complaint. If probable cause is found, the commissioner files a formal complaint to the EPC and proceeds with prosecuting the complaint under the provisions of Chapter 120, F. S., Administrative Procedure Act. The teacher is entitled to due process during the pursuit of actions against the teacher's certificate.

5. The teacher is notified of the formal complaint and has a limited time to respond with one of the following options:

   ■ Fail to respond, which is considered, by default, to be an admission of guilt.

   ■ Voluntarily surrender the certificate.

   ■ Reach a settlement agreement with the FLDOE.

   ■ Choose not to dispute the allegations, but request an informal hearing to personally appear before the EPC to present evidence and testimony in mitigation.

   ■ Request a formal hearing to dispute issues of material fact.

   (Source: Adapted from the Code of Ethics and Principles Awareness Training, FLDOE, 2007)

6. If the teacher requests a hearing, an administrative law judge hears the case and makes recommendations to a panel of members of the EPC. During the hearing, all interested parties have a right to be represented by legal counsel. They can present evidence and argument on the issues involved, can cross-examine witnesses, and may submit rebuttal evidence. The standard of proof for allegations of misconduct against the teacher is a persuasive and credible *preponderance of the evidence* (used in civil law), which is a lesser standard than *beyond a reasonable doubt* (used in criminal law). The teacher is entitled to a full or partial transcript of the proceedings at no more than actual cost (Section 120.57, F. S.).

7. The designated EPC panel issues a final order either dismissing the complaint or imposing one or more of the following penalties (Section 1012.796 (7), F. S.):

   ■ Revocation or suspension of the teacher's certificate

   ■ Placement of the teacher on probation for a specified time period

   ■ Imposition on the teacher of a fine up to $2,000 per offense

   ■ Restriction of the teacher's practice

   ■ Placement of a written letter of reprimand for unprofessional conduct in the teacher's certification file

   ■ Participation of the teacher in the recovery network program

When the penalty is suspension or revocation of the teacher's certificate, that teacher cannot be employed in any position involving direct conduct with students in a public school for the duration of the suspension or revocation (Section 1012.795 (1), F. S.).

When the complaint is an allegation of misconduct that affects the health, safety, or welfare of a student, the district school must immediately suspend the accused teacher from regularly assigned duties, with pay, and reassign that teacher to a position that does not require direct contact with students. The suspension shall continue until the completion of the complaint/investigation process (Section 1012.796 (5), F. S.).

Violation of a final order of the EPC can lead to further penalties or sanctions. The teacher has the right to appeal the decision made by the EPC to a higher legal authority, usually the state court system.

Checkpoint

Fill in the blank.

1. A school district can suspend or dismiss a teacher at _____ time during the school year for just cause.

2. In the case of incompetence, teachers are given an opportunity to _____ before charges of incompetence are filed.

3. The Education Practices Commission can suspend or revoke a teacher's certificate for conviction of a felony or a misdemeanor other than a _____ traffic violation.

4. The _____ makes the final decision concerning probable cause for action against a teacher's certificate.

Mark as true or false.

5. _____ (a) A teacher's activities that are not school-related can lead to charges of ethical conduct violations.

_____ (b) A teacher is entitled to due process when an action is taken against the teacher's certificate.

Checkpoint Answers

1. any

2. remediate

3. minor

4. commissioner

5. (a) true; (b) true

Avoiding Disciplinary Action

Teachers in Florida are role models for their students and their communities. Moreover, they have an ethical and a legal responsibility to adhere to a high moral standard. This responsibility is underscored by statements of the Florida 1st District Court of Appeals in the following two cases:

> "By virtue of their leadership capacity, teachers are traditionally held to a high moral standard in a community." *Adams v. State Professional Practices Council,* 406 So. 2nd 1170 (Fl. 1st DCA 1981)

> "A school teacher holds a position of great trust. We entrust the custody of our children to the teacher. We look to the teacher to educate and to prepare our children for their adult lives. To fulfill this trust, the teacher must be of good moral character; to require less would be to jeopardize the future lives of our children." *Tomerlin v. Dade School Board,* 381 So. 2nd 159 (Fl. 1st DCA 1975)

In the Code of Ethics and Principles Awareness Training, the FLDOE (2007) offered common-sense advice to teachers about how to avoid disciplinary action. A summary of their recommendations and those of other public school experts is presented here:

- Participate in ethics training, so that you know the Code of Ethics and Principles of Professional Conduct and its interpretation.

- Know federal and state law. Keep up to date on changes.

- Know your district and school policies. Read the handbooks from cover to cover.

- Make sure that you have clear grading criteria that are in writing and distributed to parents.

- Make sure that you have a written discipline policy that is distributed to students and parents.

- Keep your classroom door open when conferencing with a student.

- Do not use school property (for example, computers, copiers, fax machines, and e-mail) for personal use.

- Obey the federal copyright law (see the section "Important Legislation and Court Cases" later in this chapter for a description of PL 94-553 Copyright Law).

- Follow district and school policy regarding school trips, including arranging for transportation.

- Do not leave your students unattended.

- Keep a professional relationship with your students. Don't be a buddy or a pal.

- Do not give special privileges to a few students.

- Do not have a "teacher's pet."

- Do not flirt with a student.

- Do not establish an intimate relationship with a student, even if the student is over 18 or the student's parents approve.
- Do not make fun of a student, even jokingly.
- Do not harass, humiliate, or disparage a student.
- Do not make verbally abusive comments to students.
- Do not bully or intimidate students.
- Do not try to force your point of view on students.
- Do not discuss other students with a student.
- Do not ask your students to keep secrets.
- Avoid physically touching your students, especially students in the upper grades. Use verbal and nonverbal reinforcement instead.
- Do not discuss your personal life with students, even outside the classroom.
- Refer students to the school counselor when they need to talk about personal matters unrelated to your class.
- Do not "party" with your students.
- Do not drink alcoholic beverages in front of your students.
- Do not invite students to your home.
- Do not give a student a ride in your vehicle.
- Do not offer money to a student for favors.
- Do not make phone calls, write e-mails or text messages, or send notes of a personal nature to students.
- Do not post personal messages to students on social networking sites.
- Do not bring up controversial topics in your classroom unless the topic is clearly and defensibly related to a lesson objective *and* you have obtained prior approval from school administrators.
- Avoid vulgarity-centered assignments, even if your intent is to deter usage of vulgar language by students.
- Do not discuss religion with your students.
- Avoid stereotypical language.
- Do not talk about students with other teachers in the halls or other open places in the school.
- Do not talk about your students or the school in public places in the community.
- Dress and behave professionally in school and when attending public functions.
- Maintain ethical and decent standards in your personal life. You can be subject to disciplinary action for inappropriate behavior in your private life.
- If you are unsure whether a behavior is inappropriate, err on the side of caution and don't do it.

Checkpoint

Fill in the blank.

1. Teachers in Florida have an ethical and a legal responsibility to adhere to a high _____ standard.

2. Teachers should not use school property for _____ use.

3. Unethical or illegal conduct in a teacher's private life is grounds for _____ action.

Mark as true or false.

4. _____ (a) It is generally held acceptable for teachers to drink alcoholic beverages socially with their students who are 18 years of age or older.

_____ (b) It is acceptable for a teacher to tease a student about the student's sexual orientation as long as the student is not offended.

Checkpoint Answers

1. moral

2. personal

3. disciplinary

4. (a) false; (b) false

Professional Responsibility as Advocate for Students

Good teachers understand that various external factors can affect students' behavior and performance in school. As advocates for students and their health and safety, teachers need to be alert to signs of emotional distress, suicidal tendencies, substance abuse, child abuse or neglect, or eating disorders.

Emotional distress in students can stem from various sources (for example, dysfunctional family situations, conflict within peer relationships, victimization by others, or the intrusion of a new culture—"culture shock"). **Signs of emotional distress** include sudden changes in personality, behavior, or academic performance; nervousness/anxiety; frequent mood swings, sadness, or depression; irritability; lack of concentration; overreactions; withdrawal from relationships; frequent illness; tiredness; and sudden weight loss or gain. As an immediate measure to ease emotional distress, teachers should provide a predictable and routine environment where the student feels safe and accepted.

Students can become so distressed that they may begin to contemplate suicide. **Warning signs of suicide** include changes in sleep or eating patterns; neglect of personal appearance; depression, sadness, anger, or aggressiveness; alcohol or drug abuse; self-mutilation (for example, cutting oneself); isolation (withdrawing from family or friends); loss of interest in activities/hobbies; trouble with school or work; and perfectionism or being overly self-critical. **Urgent danger signs** are hopelessness or helplessness; talking, writing, or hinting about suicide; lethargy, apathy, or sadness; extreme changes in behavior; putting affairs in order (for example, giving away possessions); experiencing a relationship breakup; buying a gun or weapon or stockpiling drugs; or suddenly being happier and calmer—giving the impression that things have improved (Florida Suicide Prevention Coalition, 2011–15). With any indication of suicidal tendencies in a student, teachers should act immediately by referring the student to a school counselor or school psychologist.

According to the National Institute on Drug Abuse (NIDA) (2014), adolescent substance abuse is a major public health problem. The following behaviors, when sudden, extreme, or lasting for an extended period, are **signs of alcohol or drug abuse:** unexplained changes in personality; loss of interest in once-favorite pastimes; loss of interest in family activities previously enjoyed; decline in school or work performance or attendance; chronic tardiness; skipping school; changes in friends and reluctance or unwillingness to discuss new friends; difficulty in paying attention; forgetfulness; noticeable mood swings; aggressive behavior; edginess, irritability, nervousness, or giddiness; hypersensitivity or temper tantrums; an "I don't care" attitude; deterioration of personal grooming habits; changes in eating or sleeping habits; unexplained weight loss or gain; red or watery eyes; shaking of the hands, feet, or legs; frequent nausea or vomiting; excessive sweating; slurred speech; dilated pupils; excessive need for privacy or secrecy; an unexplained need for money or even stealing money; or a heightened sensitivity to inquiry. **Signs of performance-enhancing drugs** (for example, anabolic steroids, ephedrine, or diuretics) include an unusual gain in muscle mass; aggressive behavior or rage; deeper voice (especially in females); severe acne; complaints of stomach pain or nausea; or signs of kidney, liver, or heart damage. Having a reasonable suspicion is sufficient cause for a teacher to initiate a private conversation with the student to discuss the specific behaviors the teacher has observed. If substance abuse is clearly a problem, the teacher should take immediate action by contacting a school counselor, school psychologist, school social worker, or a professional from the FLDOE Student Support Services (www.fldoe.org/ese/StudentSupport.asp) for assistance.

Teachers in Florida have a legal obligation to report all actual or suspected cases of child abuse, harm, abandonment, or neglect to the Florida Abuse Hotline (Section 1006.061 (1), F. S.). They are not expected to, and should not, investigate the situation prior to making a report. The identity of the teacher making a report is kept confidential, and he or she is immune from liability unless the report is knowingly or intentionally false. Failure to report is a third-degree felony and can result in a fine and criminal prosecution (Section 39.205 (1), F. S.).

According to Florida law, **abuse** is any willful act that results in physical, mental, or sexual injury or harm to a child; **harm** is infliction of physical, mental, or emotional injury upon a child; **abandonment** is a willful rejection of parental obligation with no provisions for the child's support and no effort to communicate with the child; and **neglect** is failure to supply or make provisions for adequate food, clothing, shelter, or health care for a child, although financially able to do so or although offered financial or other means to do so (Section 39.01, F. S.). The following chart from *Recognizing Child Abuse and Neglect: Signs and Symptoms* (Child Welfare Information Gateway, 2007) summarizes signs and symptoms of child abuse, physical abuse, neglect, sexual abuse, and emotional maltreatment or harm.

Signs and Symptoms of Child Abuse and Neglect		
Type of Abuse	**The Child**	**The Parent**
Child abuse (general)	Shows sudden changes in behavior or school performance. Has not received help for physical or medical problems brought to the parents' attention. Has learning problems (or difficulty concentrating) that cannot be attributed to specific physical or psychological causes. Is always watchful, as though preparing for something bad to happen. Lacks adult supervision. Is overly compliant, passive, or withdrawn. Comes to school or other activities early, stays late, and does not want to go home. Is frequently absent from school.	Shows little concern for the child. Denies the existence of, or blames the child for, the child's problems in school or at home. Asks teachers or other caretakers to use harsh physical discipline if the child misbehaves. Sees the child as entirely bad, worthless, or burdensome. Demands a level of physical or academic performance the child cannot achieve. Looks primarily to the child for care, attention, and satisfaction of emotional needs.
Physical abuse	Has unexplained welts, burns, bites, bruises, broken bones, or black eyes. Has repeated occurrences of injuries, even when explanations are offered. Has fading bruises or other marks noticeable after an absence from school. Seems frightened of the parents and protests or cries when it is time to go home. Shows extremes in behavior such as being passive-aggressive. Shrinks at the approach of adults. Reports injury by a parent or another adult caregiver.	Offers conflicting, unconvincing, or no explanation for the child's injury. Describes the child as "evil" or in some other very negative way. Uses harsh physical discipline with the child. Has a history of abuse as a child.

Signs and Symptoms of Child Abuse and Neglect (*continued*)		
Type of Abuse	**The Child**	**The Parent**
Neglect	Is frequently absent from school. Begs or steals food or money. Lacks needed medical or dental care, immunizations, or glasses. Has noticeable below-average body weight and height. Is consistently dirty and has severe body odor. Lacks sufficient clothing for the weather. Abuses alcohol or other drugs. States that there is no one at home to provide care.	Appears to be indifferent to the child. Seems apathetic or depressed. Behaves irrationally or in a bizarre manner. Is abusing alcohol or other drugs.
Sexual abuse	Has difficulty walking or sitting. Suddenly refuses to change for gym or to participate in physical activities. Reports nightmares or bed-wetting. Experiences a sudden change in appetite. Demonstrates bizarre, sophisticated, or unusual sexual knowledge or behavior. Becomes pregnant or contracts a venereal disease, particularly if under age 14. Writes about sexual abuse in notes, journals, or other written assignments. Runs away. Reports sexual abuse by a parent or another adult caregiver.	Is unduly protective of the child or severely limits the child's contact with other children, especially of the opposite sex. Is secretive and isolated. Is jealous or controlling with family members.
Emotional maltreatment/harm	Shows extremes in behavior, such as overly compliant or demanding behavior, extreme passivity, or aggression. Is either inappropriately adult (parenting other children or younger siblings, for example) or inappropriately infantile (frequently rocking or head-banging, for example). Is delayed in physical or emotional development. Has poor self-concept. Has attempted suicide. Reports a lack of attachment to the parent.	Constantly blames, belittles, or berates the child. Is unconcerned about the child and refuses to consider offers of help for the child's problems. Overtly rejects the child.

Teachers should also be on the alert for eating disorders in young people. Eating disorders include **anorexia nervosa** (self-starvation, eating very little even to the point of death by starvation), **bulimia** (eating and then engaging in self-induced vomiting, taking laxatives, or over-exercising), and **binge eating** (frequent episodes of overeating). Eating disorders have both mental and physical consequences that can be difficult to overcome. Most cases occur in girls and young women, but boys also can fall victim. Some researchers suggest that individuals restrict food intake as a way to gain a sense of control over some aspect of their lives, while those who overeat do so as a way to cope with stress and relieve anxiety. Compounding the problem is popular culture's seeming adulation of thinness, which reinforces a preoccupation with diet. Signs of eating disorders are losing or gaining weight in a short period of time, complaining of abdominal pain, full or bloated feeling, faintness, or dizziness; showing tiredness or fatigue; having dry skin or hair; having tooth decay; dieting or having irregular food habits; pretending to eat and then throwing away food; over-exercising; wearing baggy clothes; going to the bathroom frequently; complaining about appearance, particularly about being or feeling fat; expressing helplessness; showing sadness, depression, or moodiness; or being a perfectionist or overly self-critical. Having a concern is reason enough for a teacher to initiate a private conversation with the student to discuss the specific behaviors he or she has observed. If the student's health is clearly at high risk, the teacher should take immediate action by contacting a school counselor or school psychologist for assistance (U.S. Department of Health and Human Services, 2005).

Another growing health issue for children in the United States is obesity. **Obesity** means having an abnormally high proportion of body fat. Obesity increases the risk of high blood pressure, stroke, cardiovascular disease, gallbladder disease, diabetes, respiratory problems, arthritis, cancer, and emotional problems such as depression and anxiety. Teachers can promote healthful eating habits in children by being positive role models of healthful living (www.womenshealth.gov/archive/bodyimage/kids/bodywise/bp/bodywise.pdf, 2005).

Teachers cannot supply everything their students need, but their professional advocacy is valuable to the students in their care. Teachers are in a unique position to detect behaviors or situations that pose threats to students' safety or health, so it is important for teachers to become familiar with the signs and symptoms of risky or harmful activities or conditions and act, when necessary. In addition, teachers can model coping skills and healthful behaviors and be warm, caring, and supportive toward their students. For some students, a trusted teacher is a lifeline to a better existence.

Checkpoint

Fill in the blank.

1. Substance abuse is a major public _____ problem.

2. Teachers _____ (should, should not) investigate before making a child abuse report.

3. Over-exercising is a sign of a(n) _____ disorder.

Mark as true or false.

4. _____ (a) The identity of the person making a child abuse report must be, by law, reported to the parents of the child.

   _____ (b) Only girls develop eating disorders.

Checkpoint Answers

1. health

2. should not

3. eating

4. (a) false; (b) false

Professional Conduct with ESE Students

In Florida, students who have special learning needs are **Exceptional Student Education (ESE) students. ESE students** include students with disabilities and gifted students. Working with ESE students and their families in a way that meets the students' special needs and that follows legal requirements is an important part of the classroom teacher's role.

According to the Individuals with Disabilities Education Act (IDEA, 2004) a **child with a disability** in general is a child who has one (or more) of the following disabilities and who, because of that disability, needs special education and related services: mentally handicapped, deaf or hard of hearing, speech or language impairments, visual impairments (including blindness), emotional disturbance, orthopedic impairments, autism, traumatic brain injury, other health impairments, or specific learning disabilities. In addition, for a child ages 3 through 9, the term **child with a disability** may be (at the discretion of the state and the local educational agency and as measured by appropriate diagnostic instruments and procedures) a child who is experiencing developmental delays in one or more of the following areas: physical development, cognitive development, communication development, social or emotional development, or adaptive development, and who, for that reason, needs special education and related services. However, if a child has a lack of instruction in math or reading or has limited English proficiency, he or she must not be identified as being a child with a disability, if any one of these is the reason for determining the child has a disability. Under IDEA, each student identified as a child with a disability must have an **Individualized Education Program** (in Florida, **Individual Educational Plan) (IEP)** and an **IEP team** in place (see the section "Role on Collaborative Teams" in Chapter 5 for a discussion of IEPs and IEP teams).

IDEA requires that states provide a **free appropriate public education (FAPE),** which must include specially designed instruction and related services to children with disabilities, ages 3 through 21, in the **least restrictive environment (LRE)** that is appropriate for the student. In Florida, Section 1003.57, F. S., sets forth the state law for Exceptional Student Education that parallels the federal law. Both federal and state law indicate a preference for educating students with disabilities in the regular education classroom. The following language in the Florida Statute clearly suggests that the regular classroom should be the first placement option for special education services to be considered: "In providing for the education of exceptional students, the district school superintendent, principals, and teachers shall utilize the regular school facilities and adapt them to the needs of exceptional students to the maximum extent appropriate. Segregation of exceptional students shall occur only if the nature or severity of the exceptionality is such that education in regular classes with the use of supplementary aids and services cannot be achieved satisfactorily" (Section 1003.57 (1)(a), F. S.). This mandate is in accord with the concept of *inclusion.*

Inclusion refers to the commitment to educate each child, to the maximum extent appropriate, in the regular education setting by bringing the support services to the child (Section 1003.57 (1)(a), F. S.). It requires only that the child will benefit from being in regular education class, instead of having to keep up with other students. In the spirit of inclusion, it is important that ESE students who are placed in regular education classrooms are an integral part of the class and participate to the greatest extent possible in all classroom activities. They should feel welcomed and accepted by the teacher and other students, and should not be made to feel singled out or stigmatized because of their disability. In general, they should not be isolated from their classmates, and they should be given frequent opportunities to interact and work closely with them.

Chapter 6A-6, Florida Administrative Code (FAC), operationally defines Section 1003.57, F. S, and provides the rules and regulations for ESE services, including those for students identified as gifted. This document defines a **gifted student** as "one who has superior intellectual development and is capable of high performance" (Rule 6A-6.03019 (1), FAC). Florida Plan for K-12 Gifted Education (FLDOE, 2013) requires an **Educational Plan (EP)** and an **EP team** for each student identified solely as gifted. When working with gifted students, teachers should recognize that high-ability students are ready for fast-paced, very abstract, and challenging instruction, and learn better in environments in which they are given opportunities to manage their own learning. They benefit from working with their classmates, but also need time to work alone and with other gifted students.

The FAC provides well-defined procedural safeguards for parents of ESE students. **Procedural safeguards** are the rights of parents and students relating to notice, consent, independent education evaluation, records, hearings, and appeals in accordance with federal and state law. Procedural safeguards are needed to ensure that parents have the opportunity to be partners in the decisions regarding their child (Rule 6A-6.03311, FAC). Informed parental consent for both initial evaluation and reevaluation of a child is required. The school must send written notice of the purpose, time, and place for IEP and EP team meetings to the parents. Parents are full participants as members of these teams, their input must be solicited during the evaluation process, and they are entitled to participate in making the decision regarding their child's educational placement. A parent may be accompanied to the IEP or EP team meeting by anyone the parent deems as having knowledge or special expertise regarding the student, including an attorney. If the parents are hearing impaired or have a home language other than English, the school must provide an interpreter at the meeting. Parents have the right to sign the IEP or EP and to indicate on the document whether they agree or disagree with the decisions made by the team; they also have the right to challenge or appeal any decision related to the identification, evaluation, or educational placement of their child. Parents have the right to inspect and review any educational records relating to their child that the school collects, maintains, or uses. In addition, they have the right to inspect and review all educational records with respect to identification, evaluation, and educational placement of the child. Parents have the right to obtain an independent educational evaluation of their child at public expense if the parent disagrees with an evaluation obtained by the school.

In order for ESE students to achieve their educational goals, teachers might need to adjust their instructional strategies, make changes in the learning environment, or make other accommodations. (See the section "Accommodations for Students with Disabilities" in Chapter 1 for discussion on this topic.) In addition, teachers should be knowledgeable of the procedural safeguards for parents of ESE students to ensure that the teachers do not unknowingly violate the parents' rights or misinform them concerning their rights.

Checkpoint

Fill in the blank.

1. In Florida, ESE services are provided to students with disabilities and to students identified as _____ students.

2. IDEA requires that states provide a free appropriate public education to children with disabilities in the _____ restrictive environment.

3. Both federal and state law indicate a preference for educating students with disabilities in the _____ education classroom.

Mark as true or false.

4. _____ (a) Under IDEA, limited English proficiency can be the sole reason for classification of a student as a student with a disability.

_____ (b) Procedural safeguards with regard to ESE services in Florida are the rights of ESE students and their parents under federal and state laws.

Checkpoint Answers

1. gifted

2. least

3. regular

4. (a) false; (b) true

Professional Responsibility Regarding Internet Safety

Internet safety for students is a great concern in Florida. The following recommendations for Internet safety are gathered and summarized from materials from the FLDOE, the U.S. Department of Education, the FBI, and Florida Center for Instructional Technology's Tech-Ease website (etc.usf.edu/techease/win/internet):

- Make sure that a firewall is in place. A **firewall** is software that prevents unauthorized access to the computer.
- Use a **virus scanner** to locate and remove infected files from the hard drive.
- Employ a **password policy** (e.g., password must be a minimum of eight characters long) to guard against unauthorized access to computers.
- Employ a **filtering** system to guard against student access to inappropriate Internet sites.
- Teach students that **surfing** the Internet (moving from site to site on the Internet in a random way) on school computers is an inappropriate activity.
- Teach students to never give out identifying information such as their name, home address, school name, or telephone number; to never post pictures of themselves on the Internet or give pictures to people they do not personally know; to never arrange a face-to-face meeting with someone they meet online; to never respond to messages or bulletin board postings that are suggestive, obscene, belligerent, or harassing; to never download pictures from an unknown source (as there is a good chance there could be sexually explicit images); and that whatever they are told online might or might not be true (Source: *A Parent's Guide to Internet Safety*, U.S. Department of Justice, FBI, Cyber Division, 2007).
- Teach students to report to appropriate authorities any suspicious or dangerous contact that makes the students feel uncomfortable.
- Teach students to document and report incidences of cyberbullying to an adult. **Cyberbullying** means bullying through the use of technology or any electronic communication and is expressly prohibited by Florida law (Section 1006.147, F. S.).
- Make sure teachers are vigilant in their monitoring of students' Internet activity and behavior online. The best way teachers can make sure students are not accessing inappropriate sites and/or engaging in inappropriate online activity is to circulate around the room and check on their online activity.
- Have a written **Acceptable Use Policy (AUP)** in place. The purpose of an AUP is to be certain that everyone understands that along with the privilege of Internet usage comes the responsibility of appropriate usage. It is of critical importance that students have specific written approval of a parent for school-based Internet access. The AUP for a school or district applies to all users who might access the Internet, including administrators, teachers, students, parents, staff members, and other members of the community who might be given access. An AUP should include the following:
  - Notice of the rights and responsibilities of computer and network users
  - Notice of legal issues, such as copyright and privacy
  - Notice of acceptable content and conduct on the network
  - Description of behaviors that could result in disciplinary action
  - Description of the range of disciplinary options, including the removal of access privileges

Source: *Weaving a Secure Web Around Education: A Guide to Technology Standards and Security,* a publication of the U.S. Department of Education (2003)

Checkpoint

Fill in the blank.

1. Schools should employ a _____ system to guard against student access to inappropriate Internet sites.

2. Teach students to never give out identifying information to someone they meet _____.

3. Teachers should be vigilant in _____ students' Internet activity and behavior online.

Mark as true or false.

4. _____ (a) Internet safety is the responsibility of the parents, not the school.

_____ (b) A benefit of an Acceptable Use Policy is the promotion of student responsibility for ethical online behavior.

Checkpoint Answers

1. filtering

2. online

3. monitoring

4. (a) false; (b) true

Florida Statutes Relevant to Teachers

Following are summaries of several Florida Statutes (current in 2014) that are relevant to teachers:

Section 1008.31 (2)(a)—The mission of Florida's K-20 education system is to increase the proficiency of all students within one seamless, efficient system, by allowing them the opportunity to expand their knowledge and skills through learning opportunities and research valued by students, parents, and communities.

Section 1001.33—Schools are under the direction and control of the district school board with the district school superintendent as executive officer.

Section 1012.53 (1)—The primary duty of instructional personnel is to work diligently and faithfully to help students meet or exceed annual learning goals, to meet state and local achievement requirements, and to master the skills required to graduate from high school prepared for postsecondary education and work.

Section 1003.21—Children must attain the age of 5 years on or before September 1 of the school year to be eligible for admission to public kindergarten. Those who have attained the age of 6 years on or before September 1 and have completed requirements for kindergarten may progress according to the district's student progression plan.

Section 1000.21 (5)—For purposes of Florida school law, a *parent* is either or both parents, a guardian, or any person in a parental relationship to a student or who has charge over a student in place of the parent.

Section 1002.20 (13)(a)—Parents have rights regarding the student records of their children, including right of access, right of waiver of access, right to challenge and hearing, and right of privacy in accordance with the Family Educational Rights and Privacy Act (FERPA), 20 U.S.C. § 1232g.

Section 1002.20 (21)(a)—Parents may invite another adult of their choice to any meeting with school district personnel (including parent-teacher conferences, IEP team meetings, EP team meetings, and so on).

Section 1002.20 (13)(b)—Students cannot be required to provide Social Security numbers as a condition for enrollment or graduation.

Section 1002.20 (12)—A student does not have to recite the Pledge of Allegiance if the student's parents have requested in writing that the student be excused from doing so.

Section 1003.31 (4)(a–g)—Each student may be required to take the following school child's daily conduct pledge: I will be respectful at all times and obedient unless asked to do wrong. I will not hurt another person with my words or my acts, because it is wrong to hurt others. I will tell the truth, because it is wrong to tell a lie. I will not steal, because it is wrong to take someone else's property. I will respect my body and not take drugs. I will show strength and courage and not do something wrong just because others are doing it. I pledge to be nonviolent and to respect my teachers and fellow classmates.

Section 1003.42 (3)—A student can be exempted from the teaching of reproductive health or any disease, including HIV/AIDS, upon written request of the parent.

Section 1003.33 (1)(a–c)—Report cards for students in grades 1–12 must clearly depict and grade (a) the student's academic performance, which must be based upon examinations as well as written papers, class participation, and other academic performance criteria, and must include the student's performance or nonperformance at his or her grade level; (b) the student's conduct and behavior; (c) the student's attendance, including absences and tardiness.

Section 1003.437 (1–6)—For students in grades 6–12, the grading system and interpretation of letter grades is as follows: (1) 90 percent through 100 percent equals grade A, has a grade point average value of 4, and is defined as "outstanding progress"; (2) 80 percent through 89 percent equals grade B, has a grade point average value of 3, and is defined as "above average progress"; (3) 70 percent through 79 percent equals grade C, has a grade point average value of 2, and is defined as "average progress"; (4) 60 percent through 69 percent equals grade D, has a grade point average value of 1, and is defined as "lowest acceptable progress"; (5) 0 percent through 59 percent equals F, has a grade point average value of 0, and is defined as "failure"; (6) 0 percent equals grade I, has a grade point average value of 0, and is defined as "incomplete."

Section 1002.20—Parents must receive accurate and timely information regarding their child's academic progress and must be informed of ways they can help their child to succeed in school.

Section 1002.20 (14)—Students and their parents must receive student report cards on a regular basis that clearly depict and grade the student's academic performance in each class or course, the student's conduct, and the student's attendance.

Section 1008.25 (4)(a)—Each student must participate in the statewide assessment tests.

Section 1008.25 (4)(b)—For each student who does not meet specific levels of performance as determined by the district school board on statewide assessments in reading, writing, science, and mathematics for each grade level, or who scores below Level 3 in reading or mathematics, a school must develop (in consultation with the parent) and implement a Progress Monitoring Plan. A student who is not meeting the school district or state requirements for proficiency in reading and math shall be covered by one of the following plans to target instruction and identify ways to improve his or her academic achievement: a federally required student plan such as an Individual Education Plan, a school-wide system of progress monitoring for all students, or an individualized Progress Monitoring Plan.

Section 1008.24 (1)—Teachers must follow test security rules adopted by the State Board of Education for mandatory tests. It is unlawful for teachers to (a) give students access to test questions prior to testing; (b) copy, reproduce, or use in any manner inconsistent with test security rules all or any portion of any secure test booklet; (c) coach students during testing or alter or interfere with their responses in any way; (d) make answer keys available to students; (e) fail to follow security rules for distribution and return of secure test as directed, or fail to account for all secure test materials before, during, and after testing; (f) fail to follow test administration directions specified in the test administration manuals (for example, test administration manuals specify that teachers are prohibited from debriefing students over test items after testing is completed); or (g) participate in, direct, aid, counsel, assist in, or encourage any of the acts prohibited in this section. *Note:* Violation of this section is a misdemeanor of the first degree, punishable according to Florida law.

Section 1008.25 (6)(a)—No student may be assigned to a grade level based solely on age or other factors that constitute social promotion.

Section 1002.20 (2)(a)—The compulsory school attendance laws apply to all children between the ages of 6 and 16 years.

Section 1001.42 (4)(f)—The opening date for schools in Florida may not be earlier than 14 days before Labor Day each year.

Section 1003.42 (2)(a–t)—Instruction in Florida's public schools must include the following:

- The history and content of the Declaration of Independence.
- The history and effect of the provisions of the Constitution of the United States and amendments thereto, with emphasis on each of the 10 amendments that make up the Bill of Rights and how the Constitution provides the structure of our government.
- The arguments in support of adopting our republican form of government.
- Flag education, including proper flag display and flag salute.
- The elements of civil government.
- The history of the United States with American history viewed as factual, not constructed; as knowable, teachable, and testable; and defined as the creation of a new nation based largely on the universal principles stated in the Declaration of Independence.
- The history of the Holocaust (1933–1945), to be taught in a manner that leads to an investigation of human behavior; an understanding of the ramifications of prejudice, racism, and stereotyping; and an examination of what it means to be a responsible and respectful person—for the purposes of encouraging tolerance of diversity in a pluralistic society and for nurturing and protecting democratic values and institutions.
- The history of African Americans, including the contributions of African Americans to American society.
- The study of Hispanic contributions to the United States.
- The study of women's contributions to the United States.
- The nature and importance of free enterprise to the United States economy.
- The history of the state.
- The elementary principles of agriculture.
- The conservation of natural resources.
- Consumer health and environmental health.
- Comprehensive health education that addresses concepts of community health.
- Nutrition and personal health.
- Substance use and abuse.
- The true effects of all alcoholic and intoxicating liquors and beverages and narcotics upon the human body and mind.
- Mental and emotional health.
- Injury prevention and safety.
- Disease prevention and control.
- Family life, including an awareness of the benefits of sexual abstinence as the expected standard and the consequences of teenage pregnancy.
- Kindness to animals.
- A character-development program that stresses the qualities of patriotism, responsibility, citizenship, and kindness; respect for authority, life, liberty, and personal property; honesty, charity, and self-control; racial, ethnic, and religious tolerance; and cooperation.

Section 1003.428 (2)—Students must complete at least one course within the 24 credits required for graduation through online learning.

Section 1012.22 (1)(c)—School boards must adopt a performance salary schedule that provides annual salary adjustments for instructional personnel and school administrators based upon performance evaluations.

Section 1012.22 (1)(h)—Teachers must have time for lunch, professional planning, and professional learning when they will not be directly responsible for students if some adult supervision is furnished for the students during such periods.

Section 1012.31 (1)(a–b)—No derogatory materials relating to a teacher's conduct, service, character, or personality shall be placed in the teacher's personnel file, except for materials pertaining to work performance or such other matters that may be cause for discipline, suspension, or dismissal; and no anonymous letters or other anonymous materials shall be placed in the personnel file.

Section 1012.42 (2)—When a teacher is teaching out-of-field, the parents of all students in the class must be notified in writing of such assignment.

Section 1012.61 (2)(a)(1)—Full-time teachers are entitled to 4 days of sick leave as of the first day of employment of each contract year and thereafter earn 1 day of sick leave for each month of employment.

Section 1012.561—Each certified educator or applicant for certification is solely responsible for maintaining his or her current address with the Florida Department of Education and for notifying the department in writing of a change of address.

Section 1012.98 (12)—The department shall require teachers in grades 1–12 to participate in continuing education training provided by the Department of Children and Family Services on identifying and reporting child abuse and neglect.

Section 1002.31 (2)—Florida Statutes (Public school parental choice) requires each school district to develop a controlled open enrollment plan and submit the plan to the Commissioner of Education. Controlled open enrollment is the system by which school districts make student school assignments based on parents' preferential school choice as a significant factor. The controlled open enrollment program must be offered in addition to the existing choice programs such as magnet schools, alternative schools, special programs, advanced placement, and dual enrollment.

Section 1003.57—Each local education agency (LEA) is responsible for providing an appropriate program of special instruction, facilities, and services for all exceptional students (1)(b). (1)(e) specifies "Segregation of exceptional students shall occur only if the nature or severity of the exceptionality is such that education in regular classes with the use of supplementary aids and services cannot be achieved satisfactorily."

Checkpoint

Fill in the blank.

1. A student does not have to recite the Pledge of Allegiance if the student's parents have requested in _____ that the student be excused from doing so.

2. The compulsory school attendance laws apply to all children between the ages of 6 and _____ years.

3. Report cards must clearly depict and grade the student's academic performance in each class or course, the student's _____, and the student's attendance.

Mark as true or false.

4. _____ (a) Every student must have a Social Security number in order to enroll in school.

   _____ (b) Anonymous letters are placed in a teacher's personnel file.

Checkpoint Answers

1. writing

2. 16

3. conduct

4. (a) false; (b) false

Important Legislation and Court Cases

Historically, education has undergone a series of changes prompted by legislation and decisions in court cases. Following is a listing of important legislation and court cases at the state and federal levels that teachers should know:

West Virginia State Board of Education v. Barnette (1943)—prohibited schools from requiring that students participate in flag salutes or other patriotic ceremonies as a part of the school curriculum.

Brown v. Board of Education (1954)—banned the practice of racial segregation in schools, striking down the notion of "separate but equal" schooling.

Engel v. Vitale (1962)—found that school-created prayer in school, even when students pray voluntarily, is unconstitutional.

Chapter 1 (formerly Title 1) of the Elementary and Secondary Education Act of 1965 (ESEA)—provided a comprehensive plan for addressing the inequality of educational opportunity for economically disadvantaged children.

Epperson v. Arkansas (1968)—found prohibition of teaching evolution to be unconstitutional.

Pickering v. Board of Education (1968)—provided that teachers have the right of free speech on matters of public concern.

Tinker v. Des Moines Independent Community School District (1969)—supported students' right to free expression, ruling that students "do not shed their constitutional rights . . . at the schoolhouse gate."

Title IX of the Education Amendments of 1972—prohibited sex discrimination in any public school; also, protected students (both male and female) from sexual harassment in all of a school's programs or activities, whether they take place at school, on the bus, or at a function sponsored by the school that takes place off-campus.

Section 504 of the Rehabilitation Act of 1973—prohibits schools (and other institutions receiving federal funds) from discriminating against students with disabilities.

The Family Educational Rights and Privacy Act of 1974 (FERPA)—protects the privacy of student education records. Generally, schools must have written permission from the parent or eligible student in order to release any information from a student's education record. However, FERPA allows schools to disclose those records, without consent, to school officials with "legitimate educational interest" in the child. Parents or eligible students have the right to request that a school correct records that they believe to be inaccurate or misleading. If the school decides not to amend the record, the parent or eligible student then has the right to a formal hearing. After the hearing, if the school still decides not to amend the record, the parent or eligible student has the right to place a statement with the record setting forth his or her view about the contested information. *Note:* Divorced or noncustodial parents have the same rights as custodial parents with respect to their child's school records unless a state law, court order, or binding custody agreement declares otherwise.

Tomerlin v. Dade School Board, **381 So. 2nd 159 (Fl. 1st DCA 1975)**—decided that teachers in Florida are held to a high moral standard by virtue of their positions.

PL 94-142 Education of All Handicapped Children Act (1975)—mandated that children with disabilities are entitled to a free appropriate public education in the least restrictive environment.

PL 94-553 Copyright Law (1978)—restricted copying of copyrighted material including text, audio, video, graphics, computer software, and so on; under **"Fair Use,"** teachers can do limited copying, but the amount needs to be brief and the use must not be long term.

Adams v. State Professional Practices Council, **406 So. 2nd 1170 (Fl. 1st DCA 1981)**—confirmed that teachers in Florida are held to a high moral standard.

Anderson v. Evans (1981)—limited teachers' free speech rights by indicating that "a balance must be struck between the interest of the employee as an individual and the public interest served by the employer."

Castañeda v. Pickard (1981)—established the **"Castañeda Test"** for programs that serve Limited English Proficient (LEP) students, which includes the following criteria: (1) Theory: The school must pursue a program based on sound educational theory or, at least, as a legitimate experimental strategy; (2) Practice: The school must actually implement the program in the manner necessary to transfer theory into reality; (3) Results: The school cannot continue a program that fails to produce positive results.

Plyler v. Doe (1982)—decided that a state's statute denying school enrollment to children of illegal immigrants "violates the Equal Protection Clause of the Fourteenth Amendment."

Florida Educational Equity Act (FEEA) of 1984—prohibited discrimination against students and employees in the Florida K-20 public education system on the basis of race, ethnicity, national origin, gender, disability, or marital status. It specifies that no person shall be excluded from participation in, be denied the benefits of, or be subjected to discrimination under any K-20 public education program or activity.

New Jersey v. T. L. O. (1985)—permitted a school to search students and their property without a search warrant if the school has a "reasonable suspicion" of wrongdoing.

Bethel School District v. Fraser (1986)—permitted schools to punish students for lewd/obscene speech.

Hazelwood School District v. Kuhlmeier (1988)—gave schools the right to censor student speech in circumstances where the speech is contrary to the schools' "basic educational mission."

Virgil v. School Board of Columbia County (1989)—permitted a school board to remove an offensive book from the curriculum.

Americans with Disabilities Act of 1990—prohibited discrimination against any person with disabilities.

League of United Latin American Citizens (LULAC) et al. v. Florida Board of Education (1990)—resulted in the Florida Consent Decree, which mandates equal access to program subject matter, content, and benefits to English for Speakers of Other Languages (ESOL) students in Florida public schools.

Lee v. Weisman (1992)—prohibited clergy from offering prayer at public school ceremonies.

Individuals with Disabilities Education (Improvement) Act (IDEA, 1997 and 2004, formerly PL 94–142)—provided updated mandates regarding students with disabilities and the rights of their parents.

No Child Left Behind Act of 2001—provided "stronger accountability for results, more freedom for states and communities, proven education methods, and more choices for parents" (www.ed.gov/).

McKinney-Vento Act (reauthorized 2001, 2003)—required districts to provide access to a free and appropriate education for homeless children, prohibited the segregation of homeless students (specifically stating that "districts must ensure that homeless children are not segregated or stigmatized due to their homelessness"), and protected other rights of homeless children and their families (www.ed.gov/).

Relevant Amendments to the U.S. Constitution include the following:

- **Amendment I:** Requires separation of church and state.
- **Amendment IV:** Protects against unreasonable search and seizure.
- **Amendment X:** Puts the responsibility of education at the state and local levels by the failure of the U.S. Constitution to mention education as a duty of the federal government.
- **Amendment XIV:** Provides that no state shall deprive a person of life, liberty, or property without "due process" of law. The core element of due process is fairness and includes the right to a hearing, to be

represented by legal counsel, to present evidence (including witnesses), to confront the accuser, to cross-examine witnesses and challenge evidence, to have a written transcript of the proceedings of a hearing, and to appeal an adverse ruling of a hearing to a higher legal authority.

Checkpoint

Fill in the blank.

1. By case law, schools cannot require that students participate in _____ salutes or other patriotic ceremonies as a part of the school curriculum.

2. Divorced or noncustodial parents have the _____ rights as custodial parents with respect to their child's school records.

3. The McKinney-Vento Act prohibits segregation in schools of _____ children.

Mark as true or false.

4. _____ (a) By case law, teachers lose the right to make public statements of any kind when they become employed by a school district.

   _____ (b) By case law, teachers in Florida are held to a high moral standard.

Checkpoint Answers

1. flag

2. same

3. homeless

4. (a) false; (b) true

Summary

In summary, teachers in Florida must know and apply the Code of Ethics and Principles of Professional Conduct for the Education Profession in Florida. Effective teachers know their roles and responsibilities as professionals. They work collaboratively and cooperatively within the Florida system of education to accomplish learning goals for students.

Sample Questions

1. Which of the following would constitute a violation of the Code of Ethics and Principles of Professional Conduct for the Education Profession in Florida?

   A. A teacher writes nonspecific praise comments (for example, "Good job!") on students' papers.
   B. A teacher encourages students to consider views opposite their own.
   C. A teacher intentionally embarrasses a student about the student's behavior.
   D. A teacher makes an unintentional error when grading a unit test.

2. Which of the following is NOT acceptable use of school property by a teacher?

   A. using a school computer to create worksheets for after-school tutorials
   B. using a school copier to make invitations to a surprise celebration for the principal
   C. using a school fax machine to fax copies of assignments to a parent
   D. using a school e-mail account to send a copy of a lesson plan to a colleague

3. Students in a social studies class have been researching the history of the U.S. flag and the Pledge of Allegiance. One student comments, "My father said that the school can't make us say the Pledge of Allegiance if we don't want to." The student's parent is

   A. correct, based on a Supreme Court decision stating that no student can be compelled to salute the flag.
   B. correct, because the student is protected under the Family Rights and Privacy Act.
   C. incorrect, because the school may require all students to salute the flag.
   D. incorrect, because, by refusing, the student would be disrupting the educational process at school.

Answer Explanations for Sample Questions

1. **C.** Eliminate **A** because even though teachers should use specific praise comments, it is not a violation of the Code of Ethics and Principles of Professional Conduct for a teacher to use nonspecific praise comments. Eliminate **B** because this behavior is consistent with the Code of Ethics and Principles of Professional Conduct. Eliminate **D** because the teacher made the error unintentionally. Teachers should know that embarrassing students is not acceptable professional conduct. Thus, **C** is the correct response.

2. **B.** Eliminate **A, C,** and **D** because these uses of school property are acceptable. Using a school copier to make invitations for a celebration that is not an *official* school function falls under personal use of school property, so it is unacceptable. Thus, **B** is the correct response.

3. **A.** This question takes up the issue of a student's right to refuse to salute the flag. The Supreme Court has ruled that no student may be required to take part in a flag salute ceremony as a condition of attendance, making **A** the correct response. Choice **B** correctly says that the student has the right to refuse to salute the flag, but gives the wrong reason; the Family Rights and Privacy Act of 1974 does not apply to this situation. Eliminate **C** and **D** because these responses directly contradict the Supreme Court decision. Furthermore, in regard to **D**, no evidence in the question stem indicates that a student's refusal to say the Pledge will be disruptive. Teachers should handle such situations carefully and professionally, so that disruptions do not occur.

Chapter 7

Competency 7: Teaching English Language Learners (ELLs)

Competency Description and Key Indicators

According to the *Competencies and Skills Required for Teacher Certification in Florida,* 20th Edition (available at www.fldoe.org/asp/ftce/pdf/ftce20edition.pdf), **Competency 7** of the FTCE PEd Test addresses **Teaching English Language Learners (ELLs)** as follows:

> *Knowledge of research-based practices appropriate for teaching English Language Learners (ELLs)*

Key indicators:

- Relate the nature and role of culture, cultural groups, and individual cultural identities into learning experiences for all students.
- Analyze student developmental characteristics in relation to first and second language literacy acquisition stages to design instruction for students.
- Interpret the Consent Decree to integrate teaching approaches, methods, strategies, and communication with stakeholders in order to improve learning for ELLs.
- Evaluate and differentiate standards-based curriculum, materials, resources, and technology for ELLs based on multicultural, multilevel learning environments.
- Analyze assessment issues as they affect ELLs and determine appropriate accommodations according to ELLs' varying English proficiency levels and academic levels.

Overview

Teaching English Language Learners is a term that describes research-based practices and strategies that teachers use with English Language Learners (ELLs). Teachers in Florida are expected to be aware of the strict state mandate for meeting the needs of ELLs in Florida's public schools. In compliance with the Florida Consent Decree, they are expected to know and understand ELL terminology and teaching strategies and to use this knowledge to plan and implement appropriate and effective instruction. Teachers are responsible for ensuring that ELLs understand the instruction being provided.

This chapter provides a general review of Teaching ELLs with sample questions and explanations at the end of the chapter. Checkpoint exercises are found throughout the review material. These exercises give you an opportunity to practice what you just learned. The answers to the Checkpoint exercises are found immediately following the set of exercises. When doing the Checkpoint exercises, you should cover up the answers. Then check your answers when you've finished the exercises. The sample questions at the end of the chapter are multiple-choice questions that are similar to what you might expect to see on the FTCE PEd Test. The answer explanations for the sample questions are provided immediately after the questions.

Acronyms and Abbreviations to Know

Following is a list of acronyms and abbreviations that you might encounter on the FTCE PEd Test:

AMAOs: Annual Measurable Achievement Objectives

BICS: Basic Interpersonal Communication Skills

CALLA: Cognitive Academic Language Learning Approach

CALP: Cognitive Academic Language Proficiency

CELLA: Comprehensive English Language Learning Assessment

CI: Comprehensible Input

EDL: English Language Development

EFL: English as a Foreign Language

ELL: English Language Learner

ESE: Exceptional Student Education

ESL: English as a Second Language

ESOL: English for Speakers of Other Languages

FEP: Fluent English Proficient in listening, speaking, reading, and writing

FES: Fluent English Speaker

L1: The student's home/native language

L2: The language the student is in the process of learning (usually English)

LEP: Limited English Proficient (or Language Enriched Pupil)

LER: Limited English Reader

LES: Limited English Speaker

LULAC: League of United Latin American Citizens

MBE: Maintenance Bilingual Education

META: Multicultural Education, Training, and Advocacy, Inc.

NEP: Non-English Proficient

NER: Non-English Reader

NES: Non-English Speaker

NNS: Non-Native Speaker

TESOL: Teachers of English to Speakers of Other Languages

PEP: Partially English Proficient

SALA: Bureau of Student Achievement through Language Acquisition

SLA: Second Language Acquisition

TPR: Total Physical Response

The Florida Department of Education (FLDOE) currently codes ELLs into the following categories (Source: www.fldoe.org/aala/9596data.asp):

LY: K-12 grade ELL enrolled in classes specifically designed for ELLs

LP: 4-12 grade ELL who is aural/oral full English proficient based on testing, but for whom the reading/writing test is pending

LF: K-12 grade former ELL who is followed for a 2-year period after having exited from the ESOL program

LZ: K-12 grade former ELL who exited the program more than 2 years ago

ZZ: K-12 grade non-ELL

Checkpoint

Fill in the blank.

1. In Florida, the code used for a non-ELL is _____.

2. In Florida, the code used for a student who is currently enrolled in classes designed for ELLs is _____.

Mark as true or false.

3. _____ (a) The acronym ELL stands for English Language Learner.

_____ (b) The acronym ESOL stands for English as a Second Other Language.

_____ (c) The acronym BICS stands for Basic Interpersonal Communication Skills.

Checkpoint Answers

1. ZZ

2. LY

3. (a) true; (b) false; (c) true

The Florida Consent Decree

Prior to 1990, there was no state policy for ESOL programs, and, regrettably, few ESOL accommodations were implemented in Florida schools. The **Florida Consent Decree (Decree)** dramatically changed this situation. The **Decree** is a settlement agreement reached in 1990, as a result of the lawsuit *LULAC et al. v. Florida Board of Education et al.,* between the state of Florida and a coalition of eight groups (led by LULAC) who were advocating for the rights of ELLs (referred to as LEP students at the time of the Decree) in Florida. The Decree contains six sections:

- **Section I:** Identification and Assessment
- **Section II:** Equal Access to Appropriate Programming
- **Section III:** Equal Access to Appropriate Categorical and Other Programs for LEP Students
- **Section IV:** Personnel
- **Section V:** Monitoring Issues
- **Section VI:** Outcome Measures

The following terminology and information are taken from the Decree and/or from Rules 6A-6.0900 though 6A-6.0909, FAC:

- **ELL (or LEP student)** means "(a) individuals who were not born in the United States and whose native language is a language other than English; or (b) individuals who come from home environments where a language other than English is spoken in the home; or (c) individuals who are American Indian or Alaskan natives and who come from environments where a language other than English has had a significant impact on their level of English language proficiency; and (d) individuals who, by reason thereof, have sufficient difficulty speaking, reading, writing, or listening to the English language to deny such individuals the opportunity to learn successfully in classrooms where the language of instruction is English."

- The term **home** or **native language** means the language normally used by an ELL student or the student's parents*.

*Note: By Florida school law, a *parent* is either or both parents, a guardian, or any person in a parental relationship to a student or who has charge over a student in place of the parent.

- The **home language survey** refers to the survey that is given to all Florida students at the time of enrollment. The home language survey must include the following questions: (a) Is a language other than English used in the home? (b) Did the student have a first language other than English? and (c) Does the student most frequently speak a language other than English? A student who responds "yes" to one or more of these questions is assessed to determine whether the student is an ELL. If the student's "yes" response is to question (b) or (c), or both, the student is placed in an English for speakers of other languages (ESOL) program and coded LY, pending assessment to determine if the student is an ELL. A student who responds "yes" to question (a) only does not need to be placed in an ESOL program pending assessment.

171

- The **assessment procedure** varies according to grade level. Within 20 school days of registration, potential ELLs are given an age-appropriate English language aural/oral proficiency test to assess English language speaking and listening. If a student's test results do not indicate proficiency, the student (K-12) is classified as an ELL and remains in the ESOL program with the code LY. If the aural/oral test determines that a student in grades K-3 is full English proficient, then the student is placed in the regular education program, and the student's code is changed from LY to ZZ. If the aural/oral test determines that a student in grade 4 or above is full English proficient, then the student remains in the ESOL program with the code LY, pending completion of a norm-referenced reading/writing assessment. If the student scores at or above the 33rd percentile on the reading and writing sub-parts of the test, then the student is placed in the regular education program, and the student's code is changed from LY to ZZ. If the student scores at or below the 32nd percentile on the reading and writing sub-parts of the test, the student is classified as an ELL and remains in the ESOL program with the code LY. During the assessment process, a parent or teacher may request that the student be referred to an ELL committee. Furthermore, students in grade 4 who scored English language proficient on the aural/oral assessment but who have not been given a reading/writing assessment must be referred to an ELL committee if the student is not receiving ESOL services. The ELL committee determines the eligibility of a student for an ESOL program.

- **ELL (or LEP) Committee** means a committee composed of the ESOL teacher(s), the home language teacher (if any), an administrator (or designee), plus a guidance counselor(s), social worker, school psychologist, or other educators appropriate for the situation. The parents are also invited to serve on their child's ELL Committee and/or attend any committee meetings. An ELL's teacher, parent, or other school personnel may request an ELL Committee meeting at any time after the end of the student's first semester in the program (6A-6.0904 (2)(e), FAC).

- **Basic subject areas** means reading, mathematics, science, social studies, and computer literacy instruction (Section 1003.56 (3)(d), F. S.). School districts must provide appropriate ESOL content instruction or home language instruction or a combination of the two in basic subject areas in addition to basic ESOL instruction (6A-6.0904 (3)(a), FAC). Basic subject areas instruction to ELLs through ESOL or through home language strategies must be taught by qualified personnel and appropriate materials must be available to such personnel. The focus of instruction in basic subject areas must be substantive subject matter knowledge that is consistent with state-required curriculum frameworks and student performance standards. Program goals and objectives must be the same as those for all students. The instruction must be equal and comparable in amount, scope, sequence, and quality to that provided to non-ELLs.

- **Basic ESOL** means the teaching of English to students whose native language is other than English using the English language as the medium of instruction (6A-6.0901 (7), FAC). Basic ESOL programs must include instruction to develop skills in speaking, listening, reading, and writing English to enable the student to be English proficient (6A-6.0904 (2)(a), FAC). ELLs should not receive less than the total amount of instruction received by an English proficient student at the same grade (6A-6.0904 (2)(c), FAC).

- **Other subject areas** refers to areas of instruction other than basic ESOL or basic subject areas.

- **ELL student plan** means a written document or electronic file that identifies student name, plan date, instruction by program (including programs other than ESOL provided), amount of instructional time or schedule, date of ELL identification, assessment data used to classify or reclassify as ELL, date of exit, and assessment data used to exit student from the ESOL program. Every ELL student must have an ELL student plan on file.

- **Student supportive services** means services provided by guidance counselors, psychologists, social workers, visiting teachers, occupational placement specialists, health service providers, school administrators, district level program coordinators, teachers as advisors, or parents.

- **District ELL plan** means the written state-approved plan prepared by the district that describes the district's proposed procedures and methodologies for serving ELLs. The district's plan must rely upon and incorporate home language instruction in basic subject areas in addition to basic ESOL instruction.

A district's ELL plan must be updated and resubmitted every three years. Councils representing parents of ELLs shall be consulted prior to submission of ELL district plans to the state.

- **Parent Leadership Council** means a group that provides parents an opportunity to be involved in and participate in their students' educational programming. A majority of the parents on the Parent Leadership Council must be parents of ELLs. This council must be consulted prior to submission of the ELL district plan to the state for approval.

The Decree specifies that each ELL is entitled to "equal access to programming which is appropriate to his or her level of English proficiency, academic achievement and special needs [such as remedial or ESE education]" and that the main goal of the ESOL program is to develop the student's English proficiency and academic potential, efficiently and effectively. Students are entitled to "intense English language instruction" while receiving comprehensible instruction in basic subject matter areas. The ESOL program must also "provide positive reinforcement of the self-image and esteem of participating pupils, promote cross-cultural understanding, and provide equal educational opportunities." Schools are prohibited from eliciting, compiling, or recording any information regarding a student's immigration status.

Under the No Child Left Behind Act of 2001 (NCLB), parents have the right to remove their children from ESOL programs, but such students will continue to be classified as ELL and to receive instruction by a qualified ESOL-endorsed and certified teacher until being reclassified as English proficient. Communication with parents who are not proficient in the English language must be in the language or other mode of communication commonly used by the parents unless such communication is clearly not feasible.

The Decree mandates regular review of program effectiveness and district compliance with federal and state law. Under NCLB, states must annually assess the English language proficiency of ELLs in grades K-12. Districts in Florida administer the CELLA to measure the English proficiency in listening, speaking, reading, and writing of Florida's ELLs.

Checkpoint

Fill in the blank.

1. The Florida Consent Decree came about as a result of a _____ against the Florida Board of Education and others.

2. The Florida Consent Decree specifies that every ELL is entitled to _____ access to appropriate programming.

3. The Florida Consent Decree specifies that the main goal of the ESOL program is to develop the student's _____ in English and academic potential.

Mark as true or false.

4. _____ (a) A student must respond "yes" to all three questions on the home language survey in order to be assessed to determine whether the student is an ELL.

   _____ (b) A majority of the parents on the Parent Leadership Council must be parents of non-ELL students.

Checkpoint Answers

1. lawsuit
2. equal
3. proficiency
4. (a) false; (b) false

CELLA

The Comprehensive English Language Learning Assessment (CELLA) is the state-approved assessment for English language proficiency. Florida uses the CELLA to measure ELLs' progress toward attaining English language proficiency in *oral language skills* (listening and speaking) and *literacy skills* (reading and writing). These four skills are included in each of the four test levels: Level A (grades K-2), Level B (grades 3-5), Level C (grades 6-8), and Level D (grades 9-12). By Florida law, ELLs take the CELLA annually until they are reclassified as English proficient (Rule 6A-6.09021 (1), FAC).

The English language proficiency levels and descriptors (as given in the *CELLA Interpretive Guide* available at www.fldoe.org/aala/pdf/IGEnglish13.pdf) are as follows:

Listening and Speaking Skills

Proficiency Level	Descriptor
Beginning	Speaks and understands below grade level spoken English
Low Intermediate	Speaks and understands at or below grade level spoken English
High Intermediate	Speaks and understands at grade level spoken English with minimal support
Proficient	Speaks and understands at grade level spoken English in a manner similar to non-ELLs

Reading

Proficiency Level	Descriptor
Beginning	Reads in English below grade level text
Low Intermediate	Reads in English at or below grade level text
High Intermediate	Reads in English at grade level text with minimal support
Proficient	Reads in English at grade level text in a manner similar to non-ELLs

Writing

Proficiency Level	Descriptor
Beginning	Writes in English below grade level and requires continuous support
Low Intermediate	Writes in English at or below grade level and requires some support
High Intermediate	Writes in English at grade level with minimal support
Proficient	Writes in English at grade level in a manner similar to non-ELLs

Checkpoint

Fill in the blank.

1. CELLA is the state-approved assessment for English language _____.

2. CELLA measures two oral language skills: _____ and _____.

3. CELLA measures two literacy skills: _____ and _____.

Mark as true or false.

4. _____ (a) An ELL whose speaking and listening skills are low intermediate should be able to participate, without support, in a class discussion about a book the teacher has read aloud.

_____ (b) An ELL whose writing skills are low intermediate should be able write a story, without support, about the way his or her own family celebrates a special holiday.

Checkpoint Answers

1. proficiency

2. listening; speaking

3. reading; writing

4. (a) true; (b) false

Second Language Development

According to Krashen and Terrell (in Nutta, 2006), when acquiring a new language, all students progress through predictable stages or levels; however, the length of time each student spends before moving to the next level can be expected to vary greatly. The following chart is an adaptation of Krashen and Terrell's stages. It contains a brief description of each level of language acquisition, some characteristic milestones of each level, and suggestions for teachers.

Level of Development	Description	Characteristic Milestones of Student	Suggestions for Teachers
Level 1: Pre-Production	This is the silent period in which students are listening to the new language, but rarely speaking it, while acquiring a receptive vocabulary of about 500 words. It might last up to 6 months.	Shy, but listens attentively; will respond nonverbally; can copy words from board or overhead; can watch, pay attention, and listen; responds to visuals/graphics; understands gestures; can show understanding by gesturing, miming, pointing, or drawing.	Focus on listening skills and acquisition of receptive vocabulary; use frequent repetition; use visuals to support verbal speech; use modeling, pictures, props, and realia (real objects); use gestures, body language, facial expressions, and miming to support verbal communication; do not force student to talk; accept nonverbal responses.
Level 2: Early Production	During this stage, students begin to use one word or short phrases to communicate, while acquiring a receptive and active vocabulary of about 1,000 words. It might last up to 6 months.	Can show understanding by responding with one- or two-word answers; has limited comprehension; can use short phrases that have been memorized to communicate; can use simple communication with classmates in pairs or small groups.	Focus on providing opportunities for language development along with the same types of supports used in Level 1; ask questions that have one-word responses (for example, yes/no, either/or); use simple, high-frequency words; use fewer pronouns; avoid contractions; explain idioms and limit their use; use fewer multi-syllabic words; use a simplified sentence structure; paraphrase content into simpler language; preteach difficult or technical vocabulary before an assignment; use concrete examples when explaining concepts; accept one-word or short responses from student; provide opportunities for student to work in pairs or small groups with other students to practice speaking and negotiating meaning.

(continued)

Level of Development	Description	Characteristic Milestones of Student	Suggestions for Teachers
Level 3: Speech Emergence	During this stage, students use phrases and short sentences to express complete thoughts, while acquiring an expressive vocabulary of about 3,000 words along with a receptive vocabulary of about 7,000 words. This stage takes from 1 to 3 years to reach.	Can show understanding by using phrases and short sentences; has increased comprehension; will initiate and engage in simple discourse; can ask simple questions; can understand simple stories read aloud; can follow simple directions; can read simplified text; can do fill-in-the-blank when provided a word bank; can match vocabulary to definitions; can understand charts and graphs; can write original materials, but writing will have many mechanical errors; can create original stories based on personal experience.	Continue to use supportive strategies such as frequent repetition of key terms, modeling, gesturing, using models and visual representations, and preteaching vocabulary; use simple, predictable books for reading; use graphic organizers, charts, and graphs; provide word banks for assignments such as filling in a graphic organizer or labeling a diagram; provide an outline or template for writing assignments; continue to provide opportunities for interactions with peers.
Level 4: Intermediate Fluency	During this stage, students use BICS, the social skills of language, without difficulty and are beginning to develop CALP, academic language skills (see the section "BICS and CALP" later in this chapter for a discussion of these topics). They are beginning to use more complex sentences and to engage in extended discourse, while acquiring an expressive vocabulary of about 6,000 words along with a receptive vocabulary of about 12,000 words. This stage takes from 3 to 4 years to reach.	Can speak in sentences and phrases and produce connected narrative; can show understanding by speaking or writing to give opinions, defend, debate, justify, examine, predict, hypothesize, analyze, synthesize, or evaluate; has very good comprehension; will ask questions for clarification; can answer complex questions; can write essays and other creative works; solve complex problems; engage in research; critique literature.	Focus on learning strategies; provide contextual support and scaffolding for academic tasks; check for prior understanding and use task analyses to make sure learning experiences are appropriate.
Level 5: Advanced Fluency	In this stage, students have achieved CALP and have likely exited the ESOL program; receptive and expressive vocabulary continues to expand, particularly with regard to content vocabulary. This stage takes from 5 to 7 years to reach.	Can perform listening, speaking, reading, and writing comparable to native speakers in social and academic situations; has very good comprehension; understands complex language.	Continue to provide scaffolding and other supports that enhance understanding for all students.

Some general tips from Badía (1996), Reiss (2001), and other experts for working with ELLs at all levels of second language development are the following:

- Learn each student's name and how to pronounce it.
- Use seating that maximizes student participation.
- Make sure that new students are oriented to the school setting and classroom rules and procedures.
- Use trained peer tutors for struggling students.
- Provide frequent opportunities for students to work in pairs or small groups to practice language skills and negotiate meaning with peers.
- Use knowledge of cultural characteristics to promote understanding.
- Use concrete models and hands-on activities.
- Use graphic organizers, graphs, charts, maps, diagrams, sketches, photos, sequenced pictures, and other visual supports of content.
- Use explicit strategies to activate prior knowledge so that learners can relate new material to existing knowledge.
- Preteach the meaning of difficult or technical vocabulary using ESOL strategies such as pointing out cognates, which are words that come from the same root word (for example, *liberty* and *libertad*), and providing examples and nonexamples.
- Use a variety of instructional strategies to make instruction relevant and meaningful to students.
- Use lessons that encourage students to use creative and critical thinking and metacognitive and study skills.
- Use lessons that require active student engagement.
- Use technology to enhance instruction.
- Give frequent, constructive feedback.
- Speak naturally, but at a slower pace, and enunciate clearly.
- Use gestures, facial expressions, pantomime, and so on to enhance your words.
- Give clear oral directions, which are supported with written directions that can be reviewed as needed.
- Restate, repeat, and paraphrase frequently.
- Monitor for understanding by watching facial expressions and other body language.
- Model acceptance of the student's culture and home language.
- Allow adequate wait time for students' responses. Do not give up on a student.
- Extend students' responses to encourage students to go beyond their original responses.
- Avoid correcting student's language attempts. Accept the student's effort and model the response correctly without comment.
- Allow students to negotiate meaning through their home language.
- Provide frequent opportunities for ELLs to have meaningful interactions in a variety of situations with native English-speaking students.
- Provide opportunities for students to learn the language in real-life, experiential settings such as the grocery store, library, community park or playground, restaurant, and public transportation.
- Don't assume that a student who has acquired proficiency in social language skills has acquired academic language skills as well.
- Use a variety of assessment methods that allow students multiple ways (for example, through speaking, writing, or performing) to demonstrate what they have learned, while minimizing the potential effect of limited English proficiency on assessment results.
- When scoring oral presentations, do not penalize students for dialect features, accents, and pronunciation.
- Treat students as individuals with their own unique needs and interests.
- Create a classroom environment that promotes learning and self-esteem for all students. Do not make ELLs feel singled out or stigmatized.

- Set high but reasonable expectations and provide ongoing instructional support.
- Differentiate instruction based on English language proficiency and/or academic need. Instruction and interventions must consider ELLs' native language proficiency and cultural background/experiences. (See the section "MTSS PS/RtI" in Chapter 1 for additional discussion on differentiating instruction.)

Checkpoint

Fill in the blank.

1. During the pre-production stage, students are _____ to the new language, but rarely speaking it.
2. Students begin to use one word or short phrases to communicate during the _____ production stage.
3. During the intermediate fluency stage, teachers should focus on _____ strategies.

Mark as true or false.

4. _____ (a) Reaching advanced fluency usually takes from 5 to 7 years.

   _____ (b) Although the stages of language development are predictable, the length of time students remain in any given stage varies greatly.

Checkpoint Answers

1. listening
2. early
3. learning
4. (a) true; (b) true

Krashen's Theory of Second Language Acquisition

Five hypotheses are central to Stephen Krashen's (in Schütz, 2005; in Badía, 1996) theory of second language acquisition:

- **The Acquisition-Learning hypothesis:** An adult's second language ability is acquired through two interrelated systems: subconscious language **acquisition** and conscious language **learning.** Subconscious acquisition requires meaningful interaction and natural communication in the second language. Conscious language learning occurs through formal instruction and is characterized by error correction and explicit teaching of rules.
- **The Monitor hypothesis:** The crux of this hypothesis is that conscious learning can be used only as a monitor for the language attempts of the acquisition system. Language that is acquired through natural means is edited, either before or after production, for correctness and accuracy by the conscious learning system. Krashen pointed out that language learners can underuse, overuse, or optimally use the monitor function. Extroverts tend to be underusers, while introverts, perfectionists, and self-conscious individuals are overusers.
- **The Natural Order hypothesis:** The grammatical rules and structures of a language are acquired in a predictable order.
- **The Input hypothesis:** Acquiring second language ability requires that learners receive comprehensible input that slightly exceeds their current level of ability. Comprehensible input is advanced by the use of visuals, graphics, gestures, and actions along with multiple and frequent exposure to the words and concepts.
- **The Affective Filter hypothesis:** Affective factors such as emotions, feelings, and dispositions can impact second language acquisition. Negative affective factors can create a "mental block" or imaginary filter in the brain that makes input unavailable for acquisition. The affective filter is said to be "up" when this occurs. The affective filter is said to be "down" when positive affective factors are predominant. According

to Krashen (in Badía, 1996), the optimal affective conditions are the following: The language learner is motivated, has self-confidence and a good self-image, and has a low-level of anxiety.

Checkpoint

Fill in the blank.

1. According to Krashen, subconscious language acquisition requires meaningful interaction and _____ communication in the second language.

2. According to Krashen, the grammatical rules and structures of a language are acquired in a _____ order.

3. According to Krashen, acquiring second language ability requires that the learner receives comprehensible input that slightly _____ the learner's current level of ability.

Mark as true or false.

4. _____ (a) Extroverts tend to be overusers of the monitor function.

 _____ (b) Being nervous likely would cause the affective filter to be up.

Checkpoint Answers

1. natural

2. predictable

3. exceeds

4. (a) false; (b) true

BICS and CALP

The language skills required for everyday activities are called **Basic Interpersonal Communication Skills (BICS).** These are the language skills that are used to communicate with others in a social environment. For example, children acquire BICS in a natural way from their friends, the media, and day-to-day experiences. After initial exposure to the second language, it takes only from 6 months to 2 years to acquire BICS (Jim Cummins in Shoebottom, 1996–2014).

In contrast, **Cognitive Academic Language Proficiency (CALP),** the language skills required for academic achievement, are seldom acquired as easily as BICS. The cognitive demands of the language of the classroom are usually much higher than those of social situations. In addition, the contextual support that is often found in social situations (for example, gestures, facial expressions, and so on) cannot be counted on for academic tasks. According to Cummins, it takes from 5 to 7 years for students to acquire CALP after initial exposure to the second language.

Cummins conceptualized language difficulty for given situations as depending on a combination of the cognitive challenge and the contextual support available. He identified four levels of increasing language difficulty, as shown in the following chart.

Level of Difficulty	Examples
Level 1: Cognitively Undemanding + Context-Embedded	Having a conversation with friends; ordering food at a cafeteria; playing sports; talking at parties
Level II: Cognitively Undemanding + Context-Reduced	Ordering food over the telephone; following instructions given on a tape-recorded message; reading a letter from a friend

Level of Difficulty	Examples
Level III: Cognitively Demanding + Context-Embedded	Solving math problems using graphs, charts, figures, diagrams, or manipulatives; doing a hands-on science experiment; playing an interactive computer simulation game
Level IV: Cognitively Demanding + Context-Reduced	Proving math theorems; writing a research report; listening to a presentation on an unfamiliar topic

As students progress through the grades, cognitive demand increases and contextual support tends to decrease for academic tasks. Reiss (2001) asserted that, in the upper grades, class work and homework are usually cognitively demanding and context-reduced. ELLs who have not yet developed CALP will experience limited success with this type of schoolwork. Content teachers of basic subject areas assigned to instruct ELLs need to have an understanding of the complexity of academic tasks in order to plan and use appropriate ESOL strategies in their classrooms. Particularly, when academic tasks are cognitively demanding, teachers should make efforts to provide adequate contextual support such as concrete examples, demonstrations, pictures, graphs, charts, and tables to decrease the language difficulty level of the task.

Checkpoint

Fill in the blank.

1. It takes from 6 months to _____ years to acquire BICS after initial exposure to the second language.

2. It takes from 5 years to _____ years to acquire CALP after initial exposure to the second language.

3. In the upper grades, class work and homework are usually cognitively _____ (demanding, undemanding) and context-_____ (embedded, reduced).

Mark as true or false.

4. _____ (a) The cognitive demands of the language of the classroom are usually much higher than those of social situations.

   _____ (b) Providing contextual support can reduce the language difficulty level of an academic task.

Checkpoint Answers

1. 2
2. 7
3. demanding; reduced
4. (a) true; (b) true

ELL Instruction

By law, ELLs should receive basic ESOL or Language Arts/English instruction through ESOL methods and math, science, social studies, and computer literacy instruction using ESOL content instruction or home language instruction or a combination of the two. Allowable models include the following:

- **ESOL Sheltered-Instruction/Structured Submersion:** An approach used to make academic content comprehensible to ELLs using ESOL strategies. The students are "sheltered" since their classes include only ELLs. Students can share the same home language or have different home languages. Students may use their home language in class. However, English is the teacher's language of instruction and is adapted to the students' proficiency levels and contextually supported with gestures, models (including manipulatives and concrete representations), and visuals.

- **ESOL Mainstream/Inclusion Instruction:** ELLs are instructed in regular education classes with fluent English speakers where they are taught by a subject area qualified ESOL-endorsed and certified teacher, along with additional instructional supports and services as needed to make inclusion successful for the ELLs. Teachers use ESOL strategies to make academic content comprehensible to ELLs. English is the language of instruction and is adapted to the students' proficiency levels and contextually supported with gestures, models (including manipulatives and concrete representations), and visuals.

- **Home Language/Maintenance (or Developmental) Bilingual Education (MBE):** ELLs are taught basic subject areas by a bilingual teacher in their native language in classes composed of only ELLs. The aim is to preserve and build on ELLs' native language skills as they learn English.

- **Dual Language (Two-way Developmental Bilingual Education):** Classrooms are composed of both ELLs and native English speakers. Instruction in all subject areas is in English and in the ELLs' native language, so both groups of students become proficient in both languages.

Within these delivery models, student placement might be according to English language proficiency and/or academic needs. Two popular ways of *clustering* are the following: (1) ELLs are grouped by English language ability and previous academic experiences in a "school-within-a-school" and instruction is differentiated by English language proficiency and/or academic need; or (2) ELLs at a particular grade level are assigned to the same classroom or ELLs are assigned to self-contained classrooms after careful consideration of teacher expertise, certification, and proven success in teaching ELLs and sheltered instruction is differentiated by English language proficiency and/or academic need. Clustering must not shortchange ELL students or result in their isolation from regular school life (Bureau of Student Achievement through Language Acquisition, 2013–14).

Additionally, schools with at least 15 students speaking the same home language must provide at least one aide or teacher proficient in the same language and trained to assist in ESOL basic subject area instruction **(Decree).** The teachers should instruct in English and provide assistance in the native language as needed. Paraprofessionals, usually working with small groups or individuals, help students comprehend test questions, homework assignments, textbooks, and other classwork.

The Decree does not mandate a specific instructional methodology. Therefore, school districts may provide ESOL services by using a range of instructional delivery strategies in a variety of combinations. Following are some common ESOL instructional strategies:

- **The Cognitive Academic Language Learning Approach (CALLA):** A content-based approach to language acquisition that makes content and learning strategies the main focus of instruction, while language skills are acquired in context as needed.

- **Language Experience Approach:** An approach based on the idea that students can produce language from firsthand experiences, and that this then can be turned into written material for reading. It consists of eight steps: providing an experience that stimulates students' thinking and language production, facilitating language production, having the students graphically depict the experience, involving students in group sharing about the experience, writing and organizing students' statements into a story about the experience, reading the story, having the students copy the story (appropriate for older learners), and engaging students in follow-up activities such as creating a class book of student-created stories. For younger learners, an appropriate writing activity is having them write one sentence about the story/experience using self-generated sentence structure and invented spelling (phonetic spelling). The writing/spelling of all students develops over time with good modeling. The most important outcome, however, is that they can *read* what they write.

- **The Natural Approach:** An approach based on Krashen's stages of language acquisition designed to develop communicative language skills, both oral and written, through experiences with words in accordance with the way children acquire language naturally.

- **Total Physical Response (TPR):** An approach developed by James Asher that uses commands and physical activity to increase language retention and understanding. This approach has been shown to be effective with initial language instruction. Students demonstrate understanding through physical responses and are not pressured to respond orally (Badía, 1996). For example, the teacher may say "stand up" as he or she

181

demonstrates standing up from a seated position. The teacher then would gesture for students to engage in this activity as he or she again says "stand up."

- **Whole-Language Approach:** Teaching literacy through the integration of listening, speaking, reading, and writing.
- **Integrated Language Teaching:** Language learning is interwoven with instruction in the content area, rather than treated as an isolated topic in which instruction concentrates on grammar rules and verb conjugations. Students build literacy skills while learning academic subject matter.
- **Storytelling/Retelling:** Telling or reading highly predictable or familiar stories that make regular use of patterns and that can be easily pantomimed or dramatized.

Checkpoint

Fill in the blank.

1. In the inclusion approach, ESOL students are instructed in a _____ education classroom.
2. In the sheltered approach, the language of instruction is _____.
3. The total physical response approach has been shown to be effective with _____ language instruction.

Mark as true or false.

4. _____ (a) Clustering is another name for inclusion.

   _____ (b) In the whole-language approach, language skills are integrated.

Checkpoint Answers

1. regular
2. English
3. initial
4. (a) false; (b) true

Multiculturalism: Celebrating Diversity

Multiculturalism has been defined in various ways. In Florida, **multiculturalism** is probably best defined as celebrating diversity. Embracing multiculturalism calls into question **ethnocentrism,** which is the natural tendency to view one's own cultural or familial ways of doing things as best and most acceptable. Ethnocentrism can be divisive because it is exclusive, rather than inclusive like multiculturalism.

Teachers should be careful not to view students whose behaviors are different from those of the predominant social or cultural group as less worthy or less capable. The first step teachers need to take is to examine their own views and feelings about cultural differences. Having biases is common, so it takes a concentrated effort to avoid stereotypical expectations. To meet this challenge, teachers can begin by developing good teacher-student relationships. Teachers need to develop an awareness of practices common in various cultures so that when children behave in a manner consistent with their culture, the behavior will not be misinterpreted. For instance, in some cultures a person in a subordinate position would not make eye contact with a superior because doing so would be disrespectful. Therefore, a student may avoid making eye contact with a teacher for this reason. However, the teacher may view this student's actions as disrespectful if he or she is unfamiliar with the cultural expectation that has influenced the student's behavior. Nevertheless, teachers should discuss with students that some behaviors that are acceptable at home are not acceptable at school.

Teachers must realize that they themselves are the essential factor in creating a multicultural environment because they set the climate for learning. It is of paramount importance for teachers to embrace the attitude that if the materials are suitable and presented on the appropriate level, all students can learn. Whether children achieve is contingent on whether they have self-esteem and are confident in their own abilities and on whether their teachers believe they can succeed. Creating an environment that respects and confirms the dignity of students as human beings is essential in meeting the needs of diverse students. Teachers must be aware of cultural and sexual stereotypes and should avoid behavior that pigeonholes students. Rather, teachers must promote learning for all students. In her review of the research, Kathleen Cotton (1993) found that effective teachers of culturally diverse classes

- reflect on their own values, stereotypes, and prejudices and how these might be affecting their interactions with children and parents.
- engage in staff development activities that can expose and reduce biases and increase skill in working with diverse populations.
- arrange their classrooms for movement and active learning.
- interact one-on-one with each child at least once daily.
- communicate high expectations for the performance of all students.
- give praise and encouragement.
- communicate affection for and closeness with students through verbal and nonverbal means, such as humor, soliciting student opinion, self-disclosure, eye contact, close proximity, and smiling.
- avoid public charting of achievement data.
- give children responsibility for taking care of materials, decorating, greeting visitors, and so on.
- treat all students equitably and fairly.
- have classrooms that reflect the ethnic heritage and background of all the children in the classroom.
- form flexible reading groups.
- make use of cooperative learning groups that are culturally heterogeneous and teach students skills for working in these groups.
- offer learning activities congruent with the cultural and individual learning styles and strengths of students.
- explicitly teach students social skills related to getting along well together.
- conduct many learning activities that are not graded.
- include student-selected activities.
- provide accurate information about cultural groups through straightforward discussions of race, ethnicity, and other cultural differences.
- teach about both cross-cultural similarities and cross-cultural differences.
- learn a few words of the language and general information about the backgrounds, customs, traditions, holidays, festivals, practices, and so on of students and incorporate this information into learning experiences for them.
- use a variety of materials rather than relying only on the information in textbooks.
- review materials for cultural biases and stereotypes and remove biased items from the curriculum.
- take issue with culturally demeaning statements, jokes, graffiti, and so on.
- use gender, racial, or other intercultural conflicts as a springboard for providing information and skills to avoid such incidents.
- encourage parent involvement.
- demonstrate interest in and respect for the family's culture when interacting with parents.
- find out as much as they can about each child's experiences and family situation to help them to understand and meet the child's needs.

Some suggestions for teachers are the following:

- Remember that cultural diversity in our schools and society can be recognized and appreciated without denunciation of Western values and cultural traditions.

- Be prepared to expect differences within a group as well as between groups.
- Remember there is a positive correlation between teacher expectations and student success.
- Remember to hold high expectations for all students, regardless of ethnicity, gender, or other student characteristic.
- Remember that self-esteem and academic achievement are closely linked.
- Remember there is no one best approach to meeting the educational needs of all children in a multicultural classroom.
- Remember multiculturalism is a joint venture, not a minority agenda (McCune, Lowe, and Stephens, 1999).

Furthermore, numerous research studies consistently support the idea that each student learns differently. When each student is taught through the method that he or she prefers, students do better. Teachers should be aware of student differences and be willing to examine their own teaching styles in order to modify classroom practices and procedures to optimize the learning situation for all students. Considering the diverse demographic characteristics of the students in most Florida classrooms, this recommended strategy might be particularly useful in spotting learning problems and enhancing the overall performance of Florida schoolchildren. Teachers should respond flexibly and creatively to students' needs. They should provide varied environments within the classroom and use multisensory resources in the delivery of instruction.

Checkpoint

Fill in the blank.

1. Teachers must embrace the attitude that _____ students can learn.

2. In diverse classrooms, teachers should explicitly teach students _____ skills related to getting along well together.

3. Teachers should be prepared to expect differences _____ a group as well as between groups.

Mark as true or false.

4. _____ (a) Multiculturalism and ethnocentrism are interchangeable ideas.

   _____ (b) Teachers are the essential factor in creating a multicultural classroom.

Checkpoint Answers

1. all

2. social

3. within

4. (a) false; (b) true

Florida English Language Development/Proficiency Standards

The Florida English Language Development/Proficiency (ELD) standards are a revision of Florida's English Language Proficiency standards to assure their alignment with the Language Arts Florida Standards (LAFS), which were approved by the Florida State Board of Education in February 2014 (available at www.fldoe.org/pdf/lafs.pdf). The Florida ELD standards are intended to make transparent the intrinsic language demands of each of the LAFS. By doing so, the ELD standards provide essential information to support teachers' planning, instructional delivery, and assessment decisions for ELLs.

The ELD standards cover six domains: reading literature, reading informational text, foundational skills, writing, speaking and listening, and language. The standards are presented by grade level and language domain at four levels of language development. Levels 1 through 3 represent stages of ELD that ELLs are expected to progress through as they gain increasing proficiency in English. When ELLs reach level 4, they are fully English proficient in listening, speaking, reading, and writing, both academically and socially, in a manner on par with their native English speaking peers. Students at levels 1 through 3 receive ESOL instruction and language support. Level 4 students exit the ESOL program, but are monitored for a period of time to ensure continued academic achievement.

Checkpoint

Fill in the blank.

1. The Florida ELD standards are intended to _____ (align with, replace) the Language Arts Florida Standards.

2. The ELD standards cover _____ domains.

3. The standards are presented at _____ levels of language development.

Mark as true or false.

4. _____ (a) ELLs at ELD standards proficiency levels 1 through 3 receive ESOL instruction.

   _____ (b) Students at ELD standards proficiency level 4 often experience a "silent period" where they do not speak English.

Checkpoint Answers

1. align with

2. six

3. four

4. (a) true; (b) false

Additional ESOL Terms to Know

Here are some additional ESOL terms to know for the FTCE PEd Test:

code-switching: The alternate use of two languages interchangeably within a language utterance; for example, "Good, *hijo* (son)."

cognates: Words that are related in meaning and form to words in another language; for example, *animal* in English and *animal* in Spanish are cognates.

dialect: A variation of a language used by a particular group of people.

expressive language skills: Speaking and writing; also called **productive language skills.**

false cognates: A pair of words in two different languages that are the same or similar in appearance but differ in meaning; for example, *boot* (boat in German) and *boot* (footwear in English).

function: The intended use of language; for example, to satisfy wants and needs **(instrumental function);** to control the behavior of others **(regulatory function);** to exchange information with others **(interactional function);** to maintain contact with others **(personal function);** to assert identity, make choices, and take responsibility **(heuristic function);** to pretend and create images **(imaginative function);** and/or to inform **(informative function)** (Halliday in Badía, 1996).

idioms or **idiomatic expressions:** Expressions, peculiar or characteristic of a given language, that are difficult to understand when translated literally.

jargon: The technical language of a discipline or profession.

lexicon: The vocabulary used in a particular profession, subject area, or social group.

linguistics: The structural aspects of a language.

literacy: The ability to read and write.

morpheme: The smallest unit of meaning; for example, the word *dogs* has two morphemes: the root *dog* and the *s* that indicates plural.

morphology: The study and description of word patterns and how words are formed.

overcorrection: Overdoing a grammatical rule by applying it unnecessarily, such as adding *–s* to a plural form of a noun; for example, *peoples* instead of *people*.

overgeneralization: Extending a grammatical rule inappropriately, such as adding *–ed* to the end of irregular verbs; for example, *goed* instead of *went*.

phoneme: The smallest unit of meaningful sound.

phonology: The study of speech sounds.

pragmatics: The use of language in social contexts.

receptive language skills: Listening and reading.

register: An appropriate form of language determined by the setting and the relationship to the person or persons to whom the speaker is speaking.

semantics: The study of the meaning of words.

submersion: Placing ELLs in regular, English-only classrooms with little or no support.

syntax: The systematic arrangement of words in a sentence.

target language: The second language being learned.

Checkpoint

Fill in the blank.

1. "Adios, my friend" is an example of _____.
2. "The boy runned home" is an example of _____.
3. Two words from different languages that look alike and have similar meanings are _____.

Mark as true or false.

4. _____ (a) When giving a speech at a graduation ceremony, a student likely would use a formal register.

   _____ (b) When talking with a friend on the telephone, a student likely would use a casual register.

Checkpoint Answers

1. code-switching
2. overgeneralization
3. cognates
4. (a) true; (b) true

Summary

In summary, ELLs come to Florida schools with a diversity of cognitive development, cultural and linguistic background, socioeconomic status, experience with formal schooling, native language proficiency and English literacy, and migrant status, as well as a variety of other home, school, and community experiences. All of these factors impact ELLs' ability to achieve school success. Teachers in Florida, even teachers of basic subject areas, must have knowledge of specific ESOL approaches, methods, and strategies for working with ELLs. Since 1990, the year the Florida Consent Decree was implemented, meeting the needs of ELLs in Florida has been highly regulated. Classroom teachers need to be aware of their responsibilities toward ELLs, so that all students in Florida will have opportunities to achieve success.

Sample Questions

1. A K-12 grade English Language Learner (ELL) who is currently enrolled in classes specifically designed for ELLs is coded as

   A. LY.
   B. LP.
   C. LF.
   D. ZZ.

2. Which of the following questions is NOT part of the home language survey?

   A. What is the student's immigration status?
   B. Is a language other than English used in the home?
   C. Did the student have a first language other than English?
   D. Does the student most frequently speak a language other than English?

3. Which of the following provides contextual support for oral language?

   A. repetition
   B. paraphrasing
   C. facial expressions
   D. summarizing

4. A high school teacher assigns students to work with a partner to do a hands-on science experiment. According to Cummins, the teacher's assignment is

   A. cognitively undemanding and context-embedded.
   B. cognitively undemanding and context-reduced.
   C. cognitively demanding and context-embedded.
   D. cognitively demanding and context-reduced.

Answer Explanations for Sample Questions

1. **A.** For purposes of data collection, the State of Florida uses a coding system for ELLs and non-ELLs (Bureau of Student Achievement Through Language Acquisition, www.fldoe.org/aala/9596data.asp). Choice **A** is the correct response. A K-12 grade ELL enrolled in classes specifically designed for ELLs is coded LY. Eliminate **B** because the code LP designates a 4-12 grade ELL who is aural/oral full English proficient based on testing, but for whom the reading/writing test is pending. Eliminate **C** because the code LF designates a former K-12 grade ELL who exited the program within the last 2 years. Eliminate **D** because the code ZZ designates a K-12 grade non-ELL.

2. **A.** Choice **A** is the correct response. This question does not appear on the home language survey. Schools are prohibited from eliciting, compiling, or recording any information regarding a student's immigration status. Eliminate **B, C,** and **D** because these questions do appear on the home language survey.

3. **C.** Adding visual cues such as facial expressions provides contextual support to oral language. Choice **C** is the correct response. The strategies given in the other answer choices reinforce content but do not add context.

4. **C.** Eliminate **A** and **B** because a science experiment in high school is cognitively demanding. Eliminate **D** because the experiment is contextually supported by being hands-on. Thus, **C** is the correct response.

Competency 8: Literacy Strategies

Competency Description and Key Indicators

According to the *Competencies and Skills Required for Teacher Certification in Florida,* 20th Edition (available at www.fldoe.org/asp/ftce/pdf/ftce20edition.pdf), **Competency 8** for the PEd Test addresses **Literacy Strategies** as follows:

> *Knowledge of effective literacy strategies that can be applied across the curriculum to impact student learning*

Key indicators:

- Apply effective instructional practices to develop text reading skills in the appropriate content area.
- Select instructional practices for developing and using content area vocabulary.
- Determine instructional practices to facilitate students' reading comprehension through content areas.
- Apply appropriate literacy strategies for developing higher-order critical thinking skills.
- Select appropriate resources for the subject matter and students' literacy levels.
- Differentiate instructional practices based on literacy data for all students.

Overview

Literacy Strategies are the systematic approaches good readers use to extract meaning from text. Reading proficiency is a high priority in the state of Florida. It is a primary focus of the pre-K through 12th-grade curriculum. Resources are provided to identify and provide specialized instruction for students with reading deficiencies. Reading, writing, and spelling instruction is integrated into content area instruction. The curriculum and instructional strategies for reading are consistent with the Next Generation Sunshine State Standards and grounded in scientifically based reading research.

This chapter provides a general review of Literacy Strategies with sample questions and explanations at the end of the chapter. Checkpoint exercises are found throughout the review material. These exercises give you an opportunity to practice what you just learned. The answers to the Checkpoint exercises are found immediately following the set of exercises. When doing the Checkpoint exercises, you should cover up the answers. Then check your answers when you've finished the exercises. The sample questions at the end of the chapter are multiple-choice questions that are similar to what you might expect to see on the FTCE PEd Test. The answer explanations for the sample questions are provided immediately after the questions.

Florida's K-12 Comprehensive Research-Based Reading Plan

Rule 6A-6.053, FAC, details Florida's K-12 Comprehensive Research-Based Reading Plan. Selected elements of the plan are summarized here:

- Each district annually must submit a **K-12 Comprehensive Reading Plan (Plan)** that must be approved by the FLDOE Just Read, Florida! Office.
- Principals must form and maintain **Reading Leadership Teams (RLTs).** RLTs work with the principal to ensure effective implementation of the district Plan.

- Districts must allocate resources to hire reading/literacy coaches for schools determined to have the greatest need (see the section "Reading/Literacy Coaches" later in this chapter for further discussion of this topic).
- Principals must identify mentor teachers and establish model classrooms within the school.
- Districts must monitor implementation of the Plan to ensure that
  - all reading instruction is based on data, is systematic and explicit, and follows a research-based sequence of reading instruction and strategies to meet students' needs.
  - content area teachers incorporate reading and literacy instruction into their subject areas.
- Elementary schools must provide daily core reading instruction to all students in a dedicated, uninterrupted block of time of at least 90 minutes in duration. The reading block must include whole-group instruction and differentiated small-group instruction.
- Reading must be taught using a **Comprehensive Core Reading Program (CCRP).** A CCRP is a research-based reading program featuring developmentally appropriate sequenced instruction, materials, activities, and assignments.
- K-12 reading instruction must align with **Florida's Formula for Success, 6 + 4 + ii + iii.** This formula includes six (**6**) essential components of reading: oral language, phonological awareness, phonics, fluency, vocabulary, and comprehension; four (**4**) assessment types: screening, diagnostic, progress monitoring, and outcome measures; initial instruction (**ii**) that is print-rich, explicit, systematic, scaffolded, and differentiated and includes considerations for background knowledge and motivation and the reading/writing connection; and immediate, intensive intervention (**iii**) that is targeted, systematic, and explicit and includes extended time, smaller group size, and more frequent progress monitoring.

In the elementary school, initial instruction (ii) is delivered through a CCRP. The CCRP guides teachers through developmentally appropriate, systematic, explicit instruction and assessment directed toward student competency in oral language, phonemic awareness, phonics, fluency, vocabulary, and comprehension. Students are actively engaged in a variety of research-based reading activities. Instructional grouping is in place, including whole-group and small-group instruction as appropriate, to meet students' needs. Grouping is flexible, not static, and based on progress-monitoring assessments. Group membership is based on students' instructional needs and abilities and regrouping occurs as instructional needs change.

Immediate, intensive intervention (iii) must be provided daily to students identified as having a reading deficiency in addition to or as an extension of the 90-minute reading block. Depending on the level of intensity needed, intervention can be provided to small groups (three to five students) or one-on-one by the classroom teacher, a well-trained and supervised paraprofessional, or another qualified educator, and can take place within or outside the regular classroom. Important characteristics of effective interventions for students who are at risk for reading difficulties include the following:

- Interventions should be offered as soon as it is clear the student is lagging behind in the development of skills or knowledge critical to reading growth.
- Interventions must significantly increase the intensity of instruction and practice, which is accomplished primarily by increasing instructional time or reducing size of the instructional group, or doing both.
- Interventions must provide the opportunity for explicit (direct) and systematic instruction and practice along with cumulative review to ensure mastery.
- Interventions must provide skillful instruction, including good error correction procedures, along with many opportunities for immediate positive feedback and reward.
- Interventions must be guided by, and responsive to, data on student progress.
- Interventions must be motivating, engaging, and supportive—a positive atmosphere is essential.

Source: *Torgeson, J. (2005). A Principal's Guide to Intensive Reading Interventions for Struggling Readers in Reading First Schools (available at www2.ed.gov/programs/readingfirst/support/principal.pdf)*

See the section "Florida's K-12 Student Reading Intervention Requirements" that follows for additional discussion of reading interventions.

Checkpoint

Fill in the blank.

1. In Florida's public schools, all reading instruction must be systematic and explicit and follow a research-based _____ of reading instruction and strategies to meet students' needs.

2. Florida content area teachers must incorporate _____ and literacy instruction into their subject areas.

3. In Florida's Formula for Success, the four types of assessments are _____, _____, _____, and _____ measures.

4. In Florida's Formula for Success, 6 + 4 + ii + iii, "iii" stands for _____, intensive intervention.

5. Interventions must provide skillful instruction, including good _____ correction procedures.

Checkpoint Answers

1. sequence

2. reading

3. screening; diagnostic; progress monitoring; outcome

4. immediate

5. error

Florida's K-12 Student Reading Intervention Requirements

By rule 6A-6.054 (1), FAC, elementary students identified as having reading deficiencies based on statewide or district assessments or through teacher observations must be given intensive reading intervention immediately following the identification of the reading deficiency. For students eligible to participate in the statewide, standardized assessment program, a substantial deficiency in reading is defined as scoring below Level 3 on the statewide reading assessment. (For other students, a substantial deficiency in reading is defined by the district school board.) Students so identified must be given additional diagnostic assessments to determine the nature of their reading difficulties, the areas of academic need, and strategies for appropriate intervention and instruction.

Immediate, intensive intervention must be provided daily, in a smaller group size setting or one-on-one, to all elementary students who have been identified as having a reading deficiency. This intervention must be in addition to or as an extension of the 90-minute reading block. It must be provided until the reading deficiency is remedied. Schools must progress-monitor students with a reading deficiency at least three times per year including a baseline, midyear, and end-of-year assessment.

By Section 1008.25 (5), F. S., any kindergarten or grade 1, grade 2, or grade 3 student who is given intensive reading instruction must be reassessed by locally determined assessments or through teacher observations at the beginning of the grade following the intensive reading instruction. The student must continue to be provided with intensive reading instruction until the reading deficiency is remedied. If a student's reading deficiency is not remedied by the end of grade 3, as demonstrated by scoring Level 2 or higher on the statewide, standardized grade 3 reading assessment, the student must be retained (unless the student is exempt from mandatory retention for good cause as defined in Section 1008.25 (6)(b), F. S.). The parents* of a student who exhibits a substantial deficiency in reading must be notified in writing that their child has been identified as having a substantial deficiency in reading and if the child's reading deficiency is not remediated by the end of grade 3, the child must be retained unless he or she is exempt from mandatory retention for good cause. The parents are provided other relevant information as well, such as strategies for helping their child succeed in reading proficiency.

*Note: By Florida school law, a *parent* is either or both parents, a guardian, or any person in a parental relationship to a student or who has charge over a student in place of the parent.

By rule 6A-6.054 (2-3), FAC, middle school or high school students who score Level 1 on the statewide English Language Arts (ELA) assessment are required to complete an intensive reading course. Those who score Level 2 must be placed in an intensive reading course or a content area reading intervention course. Intervention courses must be taught by qualified, successful teachers. The courses should include the following on a daily basis: whole-group explicit instruction, small-group differentiated instruction, independent reading practice, integration of NGSSS benchmarks specific to the subject area (if a content area reading intervention course), a focus on informational text at a ratio matching the statewide assessment, and opportunities for accelerated achievement.

Districts must diagnose specific reading deficiencies of middle school or high school students scoring below Level 3 on the statewide ELA assessment. Students who have intervention needs in the areas of decoding and/or text reading efficiency must have extended time for reading intervention. Extended time might include, for example, students reading on a regular basis before and after school under the guidance and support of a teacher. Schools must progress-monitor students with a reading deficiency at least three times per year, including a baseline, mid-year, and end-of-year assessment. End-of-year assessments must be used to determine specific areas of student reading difficulty and reading intervention placement.

Checkpoint

Fill in the blank.

1. For students eligible to participate in the statewide, standardized assessment program, a substantial deficiency in reading is defined as scoring below Level _____ on the statewide reading assessment.

2. Immediate, intensive intervention must be provided _____ (daily, weekly) to all elementary students who have been identified as having a reading deficiency.

3. If a student's reading deficiency is not remedied by the end of grade 3, the student must be_____.

4. Middle school or high school students who score Level _____ on the statewide English Language Arts (ELA) assessment are required to complete an intensive reading course.

5. Schools must progress-monitor students with a reading deficiency at least _____ times per year.

Checkpoint Answers

1. 3
2. daily
3. retained
4. 1
5. three

Just Read, Florida!

Just Read, Florida! is a statewide reading initiative. Section 1001.215 (2-3) authorized creation of the Just Read, Florida! Office (www.justreadflorida.com/). The duties of this office include

- training highly effective reading coaches (see the section "Reading/Literacy Coaches" that follows for a discussion of reading coaches).
- creating multiple designations of effective reading instruction that encourage all teachers to integrate reading instruction into their content areas.

- training K-12 teachers and school principals on effective content area–specific reading strategies. For secondary teachers, emphasis is on technical text.

- providing parents with information and strategies for assisting their children in reading in the content areas.

- providing technical assistance to school districts in the development and implementation of district reading plans and annually reviewing and approving such plans.

- working with the Florida Center for Reading Research (FCRR) to provide information on research-based reading programs and effective reading in the content area strategies.

- periodically reviewing the NGSSS English Language Arts standards at all grade levels.

- periodically reviewing teacher certification examinations to ascertain whether the examinations measure the skills needed for research-based reading instruction and instructional strategies for teaching reading in the content areas.

- working with teacher preparation programs to integrate research-based reading instructional strategies and reading in the content area instructional strategies into teacher preparation programs.

- administering grants and performing other functions as necessary to meet the goal that all students read at grade level.

Section 1004.645, F. S. authorized the creation of the **Florida Center for Reading Research (FCRR).** Its four-part mission as stated on its website (www.fcrr.org/) is to

- conduct basic research on reading, reading growth, reading assessment, and reading instruction that will contribute to the scientific knowledge of reading and benefit students in Florida and throughout the nation.

- disseminate information about research-based practices related to literacy instruction and assessment for children in pre-K through 12th grade.

- conduct applied research that will have an immediate impact on policy and practices related to literacy instruction in Florida.

- provide technical assistance to Florida's schools and to the FLDOE for the improvement of literacy outcomes in students from pre-K through 12th grade.

The Just Read, Florida! Office and the FCRR collaborated in the development of the Florida Assessments for Instruction in Reading (FAIR). **FAIR** is a statewide reading assessment system that provides statewide K-12 screening, diagnostic, and progress-monitoring data. It is managed and administered by the Just Read, Florida! Office. FAIR is given three times a year and is offered free of charge to Florida school districts.

The FCRR in conjunction with the Just Read, Florida! Office developed and maintains the Progress Monitoring and Reporting Network (PMRN). The **PMRN** is a web-based data management system that records and reports student data from the FAIR. Through the PMRN, demographic and assessment data are easily accessible to Florida educators. Teachers can use PMRN reports to monitor their students' progress in acquiring reading proficiency and to plan classroom instruction and interventions as indicated.

Checkpoint

Fill in the blank.

1. The Just Read, Florida! Office is charged with training highly _____ reading coaches.

2. The Just Read, Florida! Office provides parents with information and strategies for assisting their children in reading in the _____ areas.

3. The FCRR disseminates information about _____ practices related to literacy instruction and assessment for children in pre-K through 12th grade.

4. The PMRN is a web-based _____ management system.

5. The FAIR is administered _____ times per year.

Checkpoint Answers

1. effective
2. content
3. research-based
4. data
5. three

Reading/Literacy Coaches

Reading/literacy coaches are reading experts hired by districts and assigned to schools, based on greatest need, with the goal of improving reading achievement in the assigned school. According to the Just Read, Florida! reading/literacy coach model (mandated under Rule 6A-6.053, FAC), reading/literacy coaches

- serve as resources for professional development to generate improvement in reading and literacy instruction and student achievement.
- model effective instructional strategies for teachers.
- facilitate study groups.
- train teachers in performing data analysis and using data to differentiate instruction.
- coach and mentor colleagues.
- provide daily support to classroom teachers.
- work with teachers to ensure that research-based reading programs are implemented with fidelity.
- help to increase instructional density to meet the needs of all students.
- help lead and support reading leadership teams at their schools.
- continue to increase their knowledge base in best practices in reading instruction, intervention, and instructional reading strategies.
- report their time to PMRN on a biweekly basis.
- work with all teachers in the schools they serve, prioritizing their time to those teachers, activities, and roles that will have the greatest impact on student achievement, namely coaching and mentoring in classrooms.
- work frequently with students in whole- and small-group instruction in the context of modeling and coaching in other teachers' classrooms.

Reading/literacy coaches will not be asked to perform administrative functions that will confuse their role for teachers, and should spend limited time administering or coordinating assessments. They must not be assigned a regular classroom teaching assignment. However, they are expected to work frequently with students in whole- and small-group instruction in the context of modeling and coaching in other teachers' classrooms.

Checkpoint

Fill in the blank.

1. Reading/literacy coaches are hired by districts and assigned to schools with the goal of improving reading _____ in the assigned school.

2. Reading/literacy coaches train teachers in performing data analysis and using data to _____ instruction.

3. Reading/literacy coaches make coaching and mentoring in _____ a priority.

Mark as true or false.

4. _____ (a) Reading/literacy coaches regularly perform administrative functions.

_____ (b) Reading/literacy coaches work as full-time teachers in regular classrooms.

Checkpoint Answers

1. achievement

2. differentiate

3. classrooms

4. (a) false; (b) false

Emergent Literacy

Emergent literacy describes the skills, knowledge, and attitudes that are developmental precursors to conventional forms of reading and writing. Emergent literacy provides the foundation for learning to read and write. Research indicates that the most important emergent literacy skills for the development of reading are *oral language, concepts of print and letter knowledge*, and *phonological sensitivity* (Lonigan et al., 2008).

Oral language is the ability to speak and listen. Oral language skills are the building blocks for understanding what words mean and how words combine to make sentences and for developing listening comprehension. Extensive oral language experiences such as classroom discussions, songs, poems, chants, vocabulary-building games, and listening activities should be a central component of early reading instruction.

Concepts of print include knowing the difference between the covers and the pages of a book and the difference between pictures and print on a page; knowing that print carries a message, that print in a book is read left-to-right and top-to-bottom, and that print progresses from front to back across pages; and knowing the uses of upper- and lowercase letters and punctuation, including spaces between words.

Letter (alphabetic) knowledge is the ability to recognize and name upper- and lowercase letters. Letter naming fluency is a strong predictor of future success in reading and writing (National Institute for Literacy, 2008).

Phonological sensitivity is the ability to detect and manipulate rhymes, syllables, or phonemes (see the section "Phonemic Awareness and Phonics" that follows for a discussion of the term *phoneme*). The sequence of phonological sensitivity usually begins with larger units of speech sounds (words) and progresses to smaller (syllables) and smaller units of sound (phonemes). Activities to enhance phonological sensitivity include recognizing and making rhymes, moving blocks to count words, clapping to count syllables, blending **onsets** and **rimes** (for example, in *m-at*, *m* is the onset and *at* is the rime), and identifying beginning, final, and middle sounds in **CVC** (consonant-vowel-consonant) words.

Children's awareness of the sounds of spoken language and their knowledge of letter names prepares them to understand the **alphabetic principle,** the concept that letters and letter patterns represent the sounds of spoken language.

Parents can have a powerful impact on their child's literacy development through reading aloud (that is, doing **shared reading,** in which the parent reads a story while the child looks at the text being read and follows along), providing print materials, and serving as role models for positive attitudes toward reading.

Checkpoint

Fill in the blank.

1. Emergent literacy describes the skills, knowledge, and attitudes that are developmental _____ to conventional forms of reading and writing.

2. Oral language is the ability to _____ and _____.

3. Letter naming fluency is a strong predictor of future success in _____ and writing.

4. The concept that letters and letter patterns represent the sounds of spoken language is known as the _____ principle.

Checkpoint Answers

1. precursors

2. speak; listen

3. reading

4. alphabetic

Phonemic Awareness and Phonics

Phonemic awareness is the ability to recognize, think about, and work with the individual sounds in spoken words. Before students learn to read print, they need to become aware of how the sounds in words work. **Phonemes** are the smallest parts of sound in a spoken word. For example, the first phoneme of the word *bat* is the sound that the *b* makes. Students can show that they are phonemically aware in various ways. For instance, they can

- recognize which words in a set of words begin with the same sound.
- isolate and say the first or last sound in a word.
- combine and blend separate sounds in a word.
- break or segment a word into its separate sounds.

Phonemic awareness is important because it improves students' word reading and reading comprehension. It can be developed through a number of activities, including asking students to do the following:

- Identify phonemes.
- Categorize phonemes.
- Blend phonemes to form words.
- Segment words into phonemes.
- Delete or add phonemes to form new words.
- Substitute phonemes to make new words.

Phonics instruction teaches students the relationship between the letters **(graphemes)** of written language and the individual sounds **(phonemes)** of spoken language. Students can then use this knowledge in reading and in spelling words for writing. Systematic, explicit, and sequenced phonics instruction benefits all students. This direct instruction approach provides students with strategies for independently **decoding** (sounding out) new words. In contrast, using a rote learning approach to word recognition is inefficient and gives poor results.

Because phonics instruction helps students learn to identify words, it increases their ability to comprehend what they read. Strong decoding skills are essential to reading comprehension. Reading words accurately and automatically enables students to focus on the meaning of the text. Knowledge of phonics gives students ample opportunities to apply what they are learning about letters and sounds to the reading of words, sentences, and stories.

Checkpoint

Fill in the blank.

1. The ability to hear individual sounds in spoken words is _____ (two words).

2. _____ instruction helps students learn the relationship between the letters of written language and the sounds of spoken language.

3. The smallest part of sound in a spoken word is a _____.

4. A direct instruction approach to teaching phonics provides students with strategies for _____ decoding new words.

Checkpoint Answers

1. phonemic awareness

2. Phonics

3. phoneme

4. independently

Fluency

Fluency is the ability to read a text accurately, quickly, and expressively. It includes *rate* (words per minute), *automaticity* (fluent processing of information), and *prosody* (pitch, phrasing, intonation, and expression). Fluency is a critical factor in reading development because it builds a bridge between word recognition and comprehension. Because fluent readers do not have to concentrate on decoding the words in a text selection, they can focus their attention on the meaning of the text selection.

There are two major instructional approaches related to fluency:

- Repeated and monitored oral reading in familiar texts (commonly called *repeated reading*).
- Independent silent reading in an easy text that is at or near the student's independent reading level (word recognition 95 percent or better).

In **repeated reading,** students read passages aloud three to four times and receive guidance and feedback from the teacher. In **independent silent reading,** students are encouraged to read and reread familiar text extensively on their own. Students can practice orally rereading text in several ways, including the following:

- **Student-adult reading:** The student reads one-on-one with an adult. The adult reads the text aloud first, providing the student with a model of fluent reading. Then the student reads the same passage aloud to the adult with the adult providing assistance and support. The student rereads the passage until he or she reads it fluently.
- **Choral reading:** Students read (aloud) as a group along with the teacher or another fluent adult reader. Students must be able to see the same text that the reader is reading. They may follow along with a big book or have their own copies. The book chosen should be at or near the independent reading level of most of the students in the group.
- **Tape-assisted reading:** A student reads (aloud) along with a fluent reader reading a book on audiotape. The book should be at or near the student's independent reading level.
- **Partner reading:** Students take turns reading aloud to each other. For partner reading, more fluent readers can be paired with less fluent readers. The stronger reader reads first. Then the less fluent reader reads the same text aloud. The stronger reader gives help with word recognition and encourages the less fluent reader.

- **Readers' theater:** Students develop a script and dramatize a reading selection or book. No sets, props, or costumes are used. Students make the story more interesting by using voice inflection, gestures, facial expressions, and so on.

To meet grade-level expectations for reading fluency, students must maintain high levels of engagement in reading and expand their store of sight words year after year; otherwise, they can fall behind. Reading fluency and vocabulary development go hand-in-hand. For reading practice to make a difference in reading fluency, students must, with reasonable accuracy, identify unknown words they encounter in text (see the section "Vocabulary" that follows for a discussion on this topic).

Checkpoint

Fill in the blank.

1. Fluency is the ability to read a text _____, quickly, and expressively.

2. Prosody refers to the pitch, phrasing, intonation, and _____ of reading.

3. In _____ reading, students read along as a group with the teacher or another fluent adult reader.

4. Repeated and monitored oral reading improves reading _____ and overall reading achievement.

Checkpoint Answers

1. accurately

2. expression

3. choral

4. fluency

Vocabulary

Vocabulary refers to the words that one knows and understands. When reading comprehension is preventing the mastery of subject matter, teachers customarily assess students' vocabulary development. A reader's background knowledge is very important in determining how much of the vocabulary the reader will understand and absorb. Students with a broad background and understanding of the world will have an easier time learning vocabulary because of their greater experience. Explicit and systematic instruction that builds vocabulary through listening and discussion activities is important for those students with relatively small vocabularies. Providing rich and varied language experiences is important as well, because most words are learned indirectly. The three main ways children acquire the majority of their vocabulary are through talking with adults, listening to adults read to them, and reading on their own. Indeed, children cannot build rich and powerful vocabularies without reading a great deal.

Teachers must find ways to help students to establish a conceptual base of understanding—an underlying knowledge of the subject matter—with which to grow in knowledge of vocabulary. Explicit and systematic instruction of vocabulary is essential for increasing the base of knowledge in any phase of a lesson.

Students need preparation in vocabulary before reading text. They need assistance with vocabulary during or immediately after the reading as well, and on occasion, students need longer periods of reflection on vocabulary to understand how terms convey meaning and relationships. Vocabulary development can be effective when taught at any of these stages—before, during, or after the reading assignment. The teacher should explicitly teach critical concept words whose meanings students might not easily understand.

Before reading, teachers should facilitate meaningful dialogue with a new vocabulary word when students have no frame of reference with which the word is associated. For instance, **context word mapping** is a vocabulary development activity whereby students enhance their understanding of key words by graphically mapping them. The map is a graphic array using such figures as boxes and circles to house the words. The figures are arranged and linked in ways to show the relationship of the whole to its parts and the parts to the whole. For example, the teacher writes the word *photosynthesis* on the whiteboard/SMART Board and draws a circle around the word. Students are asked to tell what they know about the word. As students contribute the subconcepts, the teacher links those attribute words to the concept word. Thus, the context word embraces all of its many parts.

Explicitly teaching **word learning strategies** is extremely important in vocabulary development. Teachers use modeling, think-alouds, and guided practice to assist students in learning the strategies. Effective strategies that teachers can model and teach students to help them become increasingly competent at learning words on their own are

- Searching for context clues
- Looking at word parts
- Using reference materials

Searching for context clues is important because most words are learned from **context,** meaning the elements surrounding the words. Therefore, it is important to provide students with in-depth and sustained instruction in context clues. To help students develop the ability to use context to discover the meaning of an unfamiliar word, teachers directly teach specific clues that students should look for in the text. Some of those context clues are as follows:

- **Mood and tone:** Students often can infer the meaning of an unfamiliar word from the mood and tone of the selection. In this case, meaning must be deduced through a combination of the author's mood, tone, and imagery and the reader's background knowledge and experience. The author paints a picture of meaning instead of concretely defining or explaining the word within the text.
- **Definitions:** Words often are defined within the sentence in which the word appears. This technique is used frequently in textbooks when the author is introducing terminology.
- **Signal words:** When a word or a term is about to be explained, certain words or phrases might be used to signal the reader. Some frequently used signal words are the following:
  - Such, such as
  - Like
  - For example, for instance
  - This way, in the way that, in a way that
  - Especially
  - These
- **Explanations:** Sometimes when a term is being introduced, an author might provide an explanation of the unfamiliar term. In difficult technical writing, authors will many times provide a direct explanation.
- **Similar words:** Although there are subtleties in definition from one word to the next, some words do have the same meaning. They are **synonyms.** A complex term might be followed by a simpler, more commonly understood word, even though the words might not be exact synonyms.
- **Opposites:** An author might define or explain a term by contrasting it with **antonyms,** words of opposite meaning. The use of antonyms is helpful in determining unfamiliar words.
- **Picture clues:** Students in early grades often use the illustrations in the book to help identify unfamiliar words. These picture clues aid in making connections between the illustration and text.

Looking at word parts is another important word learning strategy. Once students are competent at using letter-sound relationships to decode words, they begin to recognize meaningful units of words, such as graphemic bases (*–an, –ain*), affixes (*–ed, re–*), or syllables (*be • cause, to • geth • er*). Structural elements of words follow predictable patterns. All students, even those who read with ease, spell more accurately as cognizance of **orthographic** (spelling) features advances.

Morphology is the study of how morphemes are combined to make words. A **morpheme** is the smallest unit of meaning in the language. The curriculum must include direct instruction of base words, roots, and affixes. The morphological approach to vocabulary development is a way to scaffold prior and new knowledge. The use of affixes and roots strongly promotes vocabulary growth, since literally thousands of English words can be quickly recognized and understood if the reader knows only a relatively few base word parts. Readers who learn to use affixes and roots proficiently are more fluent and successful readers than those lacking this skill. Teachers can use the morphemic analysis strategy to teach students how to identify and define each morpheme within a word.

Using reference materials is advantageous to student success in self-monitoring their reading. Students need to know where to find information in textbooks, dictionaries, encyclopedias, thesauruses, and other reference resources. It is important that students become efficient and effective in using these tools.

Direct instruction in using a dictionary in a meaningful way should begin as soon as reading instruction starts. Picture dictionaries can provide an introduction to this reference skill. Younger students can create handmade picture dictionaries with words and pictures that match to each other. They can create these ongoing dictionaries from file cards of words, including unfamiliar words, encountered in their reading. As children mature, they can be taught how to file pictures and materials alphabetically according to key index words. Student-made dictionaries (word journals) are helpful in all grades and can be created in a notebook or electronically on the computer. The document is divided into alphabetical sections to which students add words from all content areas—troublesome words, new words, interesting words, subject matter words, and so forth. Teachers should avoid having students look up words and copy definitions because research shows this approach produces poor results.

To help students become efficient and effective dictionary users, it is imperative that the dictionaries provided to them are at a level appropriate for their ages. Students should learn the general approach to using a dictionary and some things about the particular dictionary they use—what the entries for individual words contain and how they are arranged, what aids the dictionary provides (such as guide words on the top of each page), and what features beyond the basic word list the dictionary includes (such as providing the part of speech for a word). Also, because many young children are acquainted with computer technology, they should be shown how to use electronic dictionaries and encyclopedias.

Students also need instruction in using a thesaurus. Because a thesaurus is used for a somewhat different purpose from a dictionary, specific attention is needed. Getting students in the habit of using a thesaurus is a step toward getting them to enlarge their active vocabularies as well as a step toward getting them interested in words.

Checkpoint

Fill in the blank.

1. Explicitly teaching word learning strategies is extremely important in _____ development.
2. Information from the immediate textual setting that helps identify a word from the surrounding context is a _____ (two words).
3. An affix attached before a base or root word is a _____. An affix attached to the end of a base, root, or stem that changes the meaning or grammatical function of the word is a _____.
4. _____ analysis involves the identification of roots and affixes.

Mark as true or false.

5. _____ (a) Most words are learned indirectly.

   _____ (b) Teachers should avoid having students look up words and copy definitions because research shows this approach produces poor results.

Checkpoint Answers

1. vocabulary
2. context clue
3. prefix; suffix
4. Structural
5. (a) true; (b) true

Comprehension

Comprehension is an active process to derive or construct meaning from a text selection. It depends at least in part on the purpose of the task and on the reader's **prior knowledge,** which is information the reader already knows about a topic or reading assignment. Prior knowledge is the reader's frame of reference. Such knowledge influences a reader's comprehension and the knowledge structures brought to learning. Proficient readers use comprehension strategies as they read. They self-evaluate and self-monitor how well they understand while they read. If comprehension is not proceeding well, they have strategies for going back and repairing their comprehension.

New interest in how to teach reading comprehension has been generated by the recognition that comprehension is not a passive, receptive pursuit but an active, constructive, reader-based process that can be enhanced through systematic and explicit teaching strategies. Comprehension is the ultimate goal of reading, so it is critical that Florida teachers become knowledgeable about strategies for teaching reading comprehension.

A **comprehension strategy** is a systematic approach used by readers for learning. It involves flexible, adaptable, and conscious use of knowledge, reading, and learning to *predict* (anticipate the outcome of a situation), confirm, and integrate as they read. There are two broad categories of reading strategies: "in-the-head" and "on paper." Examples of "in-the-head" reading strategies are making predictions, visualizing, monitoring, inferring, and using background knowledge. Examples of "on paper" strategies are taking notes, using a highlighter, underlining, and using graphs and diagrams. Both "in-the-head" and "on paper" strategies are used by students as they read to make meaning of the text. There should be a clear relationship between the strategy selected, the task, and the text. The challenge for the reader and teacher is to choose the appropriate strategy for the task. Certain reading strategies are appropriate to use before reading, such as making predictions and generating questions. Strategies used during reading can include visualizing, inferring, and monitoring. After-reading strategies include providing opportunities for students to summarize, review, and paraphrase.

Direct instruction of comprehension strategies is an important way for teachers to involve students in their own learning. In direct instruction, the teacher explicitly informs students as to the nature of a reading strategy, how it works, why it should be used, and where and when to use it. Through the teaching of strategies, teachers foster the development of the awareness and understanding of the students' own cognitive processes. An effective teacher can model or guide the students through actions that they can take to enhance the comprehension process used before, during, and after reading. Students practice those strategies with the teacher's assistance until they achieve mastery of the process. Direct instruction is provided within each of three instructional stages: *pre-reading, during reading,* and *after reading.* Teachers systematically and explicitly involve students in a series of activities as they guide, support, and scaffold students' construction of meaning during these three stages of reading.

The **pre-reading stage** is the first stage of instruction; this stage is also known as **before reading.** The reading process does not begin as readers open a book and read the first sentence. The first stage is preparing to read. As readers prepare to read, they activate background knowledge (schemata), set purposes, and plan for reading. Students make predictions about the content of the text and preview the reading selection during the pre-reading stage. Pre-reading exercises include the following: structural analysis of content area words, morphological approach to vocabulary development, explicit and systematic instruction of content area vocabulary, content area word mapping, and meaningful dialogue and writing with new content area vocabulary. (See the section "Vocabulary" earlier in this chapter for a discussion of these strategies.)

In the **during-reading stage,** students use their knowledge of decoding and word identification, high-frequency words, strategies, and skills to understand what they are reading. Teachers choose the amount of scaffolding needed according to the purpose for reading and students' reading levels. Teachers observe students as they read and take note of strategies that are mastered and those that should be introduced, reinforced, and/or practiced. The following is a sample of activities teachers use during reading:

- **Monitoring comprehension:** Becoming aware of their own cognitive processes requires students to become self-regulated learners. They must self-monitor their reading. This process of self-monitoring is **metacognition.** A think-aloud is an effective way to teach the skill of comprehension monitoring. Using a difficult text, the teacher talks it through aloud while students follow the text silently. This training helps poor readers realize that text should make sense and that good readers use both information from the text and prior knowledge to construct meaning. Students can be taught to ask themselves questions as they read to monitor their comprehension. For example, a reader might ask

- Does this make sense to me?
- What did the author just tell me?
- What is going to happen next?

Note: This questioning is a student behavior ("reading strategy")—therefore, it is different from the "question answering" discussed next, which is a teacher behavior (teaching strategy) since the teacher is doing the asking/answering.

- **Question answering:** Asking and answering questions about the text selection is a straightforward procedure, easily implemented, quickly beneficial to students, and useful at any grade level and in any content area. This procedure is known to increase students' comprehension, especially their inferential comprehension (National Reading Panel, 2000). The best way to introduce question answering is with a visual aid showing the question-answer relationships. This is a four-level taxonomy: (1) right there, (2) think and search, (3) the author and you, and (4) on your own. The teacher uses a short passage to demonstrate how question answering is applied. The teacher provides labels and models the process by answering at least one question at each level. The teacher then moves gradually to having students answer.

- **Reciprocal teaching:** Using a teaching strategy in which students are involved in the cognitive strategies of summarizing, questioning, clarifying, and predicting as they read texts improves students' comprehension (Palincsar & Brown, 1984). With this strategy, both teacher and students share responsibility for the conduct of the discussion.

- **Identifying text structure:** Using explicit instruction in identifying the structure of narrative and expository text is helpful to students. Teachers use story maps, story grammar, and storyboarding to help students interpret the structure of children's literature. Unlike narrative text, expository text structure does not have a generic set of features; rather, expository text structure is characterized by a number of organizational patterns. These include cause/effect, compare/contrast, problem/solution, persuasion/argument, question/answer, definition/explanation, description, and sequence. By identifying the way in which ideas and concepts are logically arranged, students are better able to extract key information from the text material. Text structure is intentionally taught during reading comprehension instruction. At that time, understanding, particularly of the most important information, improves.

- **Multiple strategy instruction:** Assisting students in applying and practicing multiple strategies while reading is significant to students' self-monitoring systems. Each student needs a toolbox of strategies to use when reading for comprehension; however, teachers should encourage students to check one kind of strategy against another. When students can monitor their own reading and can search for and use multiple strategies, both their reading ability and academic achievement improve (National Reading Panel, 2000).

The **after-reading stage** is the time when the teacher interacts with both the student and text in meaningful dialogue. In order to further clarify students' understanding of the meaning of the text selection and help them synthesize the newly developed knowledge, alignment of both the content and process of the after-reading stage with that of the previous two stages is important. Students must be given additional opportunities to use what was introduced in the pre-reading and during-reading stages of the lesson. After-reading activities can include the following:

- **Summarizing:** Restating main ideas in one's own words is a way to enhance comprehension. When writing a summary, only the main idea and key supporting details in order of importance are presented. Because it omits minor supporting details, a summary is much shorter than the original on which is it based. A good rule of thumb is that a summary should be one-fourth of the length of the original. A good way to identify the key supporting details is to answer as many of the *who, what, when, where, why,* and *how* questions about the selection as apply.

- **Question generating:** Engaging in interactive questioning about the selection will help students clarify their thinking about the selection and allow the teacher to check understanding. Listed here are important considerations for constructing good questions for this purpose:

  - Simplify the question. Challenge within a range that allows students to succeed by identifying the purpose of the question, the type of response expected, and then, asking whether the question can elicit more than one reasonable response. Stating the question clearly and concisely is important.

- Share with the students the reason for the questions.
- Encourage students to ask questions about your questions and to ask their own questions.
- Provide ample practice in answering questions at different levels of comprehension.
- Allow discussions, which give students practice in asking and answering questions.
- Ask students the types of questions you know they are able to answer.

- **Using graphic and semantic organizers:** Creating visual depictions of concepts and their interrelationships after reading is effective for increasing comprehension for students at all grade levels. For instance, the use of concept maps shows promise in assisting students in relating prior knowledge more efficiently and, thus, expedites current learning. Furthermore, concept maps have a long history of helping students to absorb content at higher levels. Using graphic and semantic organizers in teaching might help students reach a level of understanding they would not reach without the organizers. Here are examples of graphic and semantic organizers commonly used in the after-reading stage:

  - Tables
  - Venn diagrams
  - Family trees
  - Pie graphs
  - Flowcharts
  - Continuum scales
  - Semantic feature maps
  - Timelines
  - Content outlines
  - Story maps
  - Story frames

  Note: See the section "Graphic Organizers" in Chapter 3 for additional discussion of graphic organizers.

- **Return to the text:** It is important for the teacher to allow students to literally "return to the text" in the after-reading stage. So many teachers want students to "close the book" and talk/interact from memory. Comprehension increases when students are allowed to return to the text to confirm thoughts and responses. It also allows students to prove/justify thoughts and encourages a higher level of thinking on Bloom's Taxonomy scale.

In reading comprehension, the skills progress in level of difficulty from **literal comprehension skills** (for example, identifying stated main ideas, recalling details), to **inferential comprehension skills** (for example, inferring cause-and-effect relationships, making predictions/inferences, summarizing information), to **evaluative comprehension skills** (for example, analyzing character development and use of language, determining the author's point of view, detecting faulty reasoning). The simplest skills are taught first, and the more complex skills are taught later.

Checkpoint

Fill in the blank.

1. Preparing a brief synopsis that contains the essential ideas of a longer passage or selection is _____.

2. _____ (two words) are used to visualize the organization of information.

3. _____ text is explanatory text.

4. A systematic plan to improve one's performance in learning is a _____.

Checkpoint Answers

1. summarizing

2. Graphic organizers

3. Expository

4. strategy

Critical Thinking Skills

Higher-level thinking involves the higher levels in Bloom's Taxonomy—analysis, synthesis, and evaluation. Higher-level thinking skills, also known as **critical thinking skills,** consist of the application of these three levels. To teach critical thinking, teachers must first develop an overall awareness—the need to focus on thinking in all classes at all times. Thinking must be taught across all subjects and all grade levels. Teachers must stress meaningfulness, but students must be taught how to understand and think. For example, the teacher might have the student ask one reflective question after they read a passage. Also, after the teacher has introduced a concept, the teacher could challenge the class to use process skills. By continuously reviewing thinking skills, the teacher establishes a base of knowledge and an attitude of inquiry.

A critical thinker must be ready to examine and question claims and assumptions. Critical thinking requires an open and questioning mind and a thoughtful, analytical mind-set. **Critical response journals** are valuable tools in encouraging students to read analytically. A series of questions to use in analyzing text and personal responses is helpful in the initial stages of critical response journaling. These questions help students to focus their thoughts and critically analyze what they are reading.

Effective research-based strategies for improving students' critical thinking include the following:

- Create conflict or perplexity by using paradoxes, dilemmas, or other situations to challenge concepts, beliefs, ideas, and attitudes.
- Focus on how to recognize and generate proof, logic, argument, and criteria for judgments.
- Include practice in detecting mistakes, false analogies, relevant vs. irrelevant issues, contradictions, discrepant events, and predictions.
- Provide practice in drawing inferences from observations and making predictions from limited information.
- Explain and provide practice in recognizing factors or biases that may influence choice and interpretations such as culture, experience, preferences, desires, interests, and passions, as well as systematic thinking.
- Require students to explain how they form new conclusions and how and why present conclusions may differ from previous ones (FLDOE, 2013–14, p. 21).

Note: See the section "Critical and Creative Thinking" in Chapter 3 for additional discussion of critical thinking.

Checkpoint

Fill in the blank.

1. _____ thinking involves the logical thought processes.

2. Analysis, synthesis, and _____ are higher-order thinking skills.

3. A critical thinker must be ready to examine and _____ claims and assumptions.

4. To improve students' critical thinking, teachers should provide practice in drawing _____ from observations and making _____ from limited information.

Checkpoint Answers

1. Critical

2. evaluation

3. question

4. inferences; predictions

Top Ten Research Findings in the Area of Reading

In *THE SOURCE: A Curriculum Guide for Reading Mentors* (available at www.justreadflorida.com/docs/manual.pdf), FLDOE lists the following as the top ten research findings in the area of reading:

1. **Phonics instruction can help all students learn to read.** All students, particularly students at risk for learning difficulties, can benefit from instruction in the most common sound-letter relationships and spelling patterns in English. Readers who are skilled at decoding usually comprehend text better than those who are poor decoders.

2. **Direct instruction is better than "discovery" methods.** The most effective approach to help students learn to read, especially students at risk for reading difficulties, is systematic and explicit direct instruction.

3. **Most poor readers have weak phonics skills and a strategy imbalance.** Poor readers tend to rely on just one reading strategy such as using context clues. They do not use other strategies that might be more appropriate. Younger and less skilled readers rely more on context than other, more effective strategies. Stronger readers don't need to rely on context clues because they can quickly and accurately decode words by sounding them out. To become skilled, fluent readers, children need to have a variety of strategies to figure out unfamiliar words and to know when to use them.

4. **Phonics knowledge has a powerful effect on decoding.** Word recognition speed in first grade was found to be a strong predictor of reading comprehension ability in second grade. Phonics instruction is one way to help students achieve automaticity in decoding words.

5. **Good readers rely less on context clues than poor readers.** Good readers don't have to rely on context clues as much because their decoding skills are so strong. Good readers rely on context clues only when they can't use their knowledge of sound-letter correspondence to figure out an unfamiliar word. In contrast, poor readers, who often have weak decoding skills, rely more heavily on context clues to try to make meaning of text. Use of context clues is a limited strategy because researchers estimate that only 25 percent of words can be predicted using context clues.

6. **The reading process relies on a reader's attention to each letter in a word.** Skilled readers attend to almost every word in a sentence and process the letters that make up each word. Poor readers do not fully analyze words; for example, some poor readers tend to rely on initial consonants only to decode.

7. **Phonemic awareness is necessary for phonics instruction to be effective.** Without the awareness that words are made up of a series of discrete sounds, phonics instruction will not make sense to children. Some students with weak phonemic awareness skills are able to make it through the first few years of reading instruction by memorizing words. This strategy breaks down when the number of unique words in text increases in grades 3 and up. Therefore, if weak phonemic awareness skills are not detected and corrected, these students may enter the intermediate grades with very serious reading deficits, and they will need intensive intervention.

8. **Phonics instruction improves spelling ability.** Good spellers are generally good readers because spelling and reading share an underlying knowledge base. Poor readers, however, are rarely good spellers. Phonics is a particularly powerful tool in improving spelling because it emphasizes spelling patterns, which become familiar from reading.

9. **A teacher's knowledge of phonics affects his or her ability to teach phonics.** Understanding phonics enables teachers to choose the best examples for instruction, provide focused instruction, and better understand and interpret students' reading and writing errors in relationship to their developing language skills.

10. **Knowledge of common syllable patterns and structural analysis improves the ability to read, spell, and learn the meanings of multisyllabic words.** Explicit instruction in common spelling patterns, the most common syllable types (e.g., CVC, CVCe, CVVC), prefixes, suffixes, roots, and word origins helps students recognize larger word chunks in multisyllabic words, thereby making decoding and figuring out meaning easier.

Checkpoint

Fill in the blank.

1. Readers who are skilled at decoding usually comprehend text _____ than those who are poor decoders.

2. The most effective approach to help students learn to read is systematic and explicit _____ instruction.

3. Poor readers rely more heavily on _____ clues to try to make meaning of text than do good readers.

4. Phonics is a particularly powerful tool in improving _____.

Checkpoint Answers

1. better

2. direct

3. context

4. spelling

Multidisciplinary Studies

Multidisciplinary studies is also referred to as *interdisciplinary, multisubject,* or *thematic instruction.* In this type of instructional design, although a central or controlling theme is also identified, there is a major issue or **theme.** This issue becomes the question around which teachers from various subject disciplines collaborate to develop a thematic unit. Although the theme acts as a central organizer, each subject discipline teacher contributes from his or her own content area. Students remain engaged in learning the knowledge and skills of the separate disciplines because a sense of meaningfulness or wholeness is generally a goal of the teachers. By relating content and skills from each of their separate disciplines to the central concept of the theme, the learning is more relevant, connected, and meaningful to the students.

Since this approach is rewarding to students and teachers alike, strategies should be in place to encourage multidisciplinary studies. The strategies to consider when implementing this approach are the following:

- Integrate information and activities from different subject domains.
- Use reading, writing, art, and mathematics across disciplines.
- Work collaboratively with other teachers to plan the unit.
- Implement the unit separately in each teacher's own classroom.

A thematic unit for 4th grade in New York State is the study of first inhabitants of the region (available at schools.nycenet.edu/offices/teachlearn/ss/41.pdf). In social studies, students read about the Algonquin and Iroquois nations that thrived in the region of New York State before the arrival of Europeans. In English language arts, students compare and contrast myths and legends generated from the two nations. Science connects protecting natural resources to the natives' lifestyles. Math, art, and technology are incorporated as well. Students engage in problem solving, and integration is achieved across academic subjects.

Checkpoint

Fill in the blank.

1. _____ studies involve integrating academic fields of study.

2. The organization of instruction around a central topic is called _____.

Mark as true or false.

3. _____ (a) In a multidisciplinary studies unit, mathematics is excluded.

   _____ (b) Problem solving is discouraged in multidisciplinary studies.

Checkpoint Answers

1. Multidisciplinary

2. thematic

3. (a) false; (b) false

Additional Literacy/Reading Terms to Know

academic literacy: The ability to construct meaning from content area texts and literature encountered in school.

active vocabulary: Words one uses frequently and comfortably in speaking and writing.

balanced reading program: A reading program that includes explicit, systematic phonics instruction in the context of meaningful connected reading of informative, engaging text.

blending: Quickly and smoothly combining sounds to accurately sound out a word.

book structure: Features such as table of contents, chapters, glossary, and index. Analyzing book structure is a good reading strategy in that it helps the brain know how the information is organized ahead of time. However, many students do not automatically see it as a helpful tool. Therefore, direct instruction/ modeling is often necessary for introducing students to this useful reading strategy; it improves comprehension by helping students gain new knowledge of how writers organize ideas and concepts.

cloze passage: A text with blanks inserted where a word or words need to be filled in. Cloze passages are used to promote comprehension through the use of context clues.

connected text: Words that are meaningfully linked as in sentences, phrases, and paragraphs as opposed to words in a list.

content area: An organized body of knowledge or discipline such as mathematics, social studies, or science.

decoding: Translating printed words into spoken language; that is, sounding out words in print.

Elkonin box: A series of connected boxes used to assist students in segmenting words into individual sounds. The number of boxes corresponds to the number of phonemes in the target word. The teacher or a student says the word very slowly. Students are given chips (or other small objects) to move onto the boxes as each sound is heard.

expressive language: Speaking and writing.

high-frequency words: A small group of from 300 to 500 words that are frequently encountered in text.

invented spelling: A child's attempt to spell a word based on what the child hears in the word (for example, *egul* for *eagle*).

modeling: Showing students how to do a task with the expectation that the students will then emulate the model. In reading, modeling often involves talking about how one thinks through a task. Thinking aloud through a task is referred to as a **think-aloud.** After modeling, teachers employ **guided practice,** a process in which the teacher works students through a new procedure or strategy, providing assistance when needed.

nonsense words: Pseudo-words that follow the spelling patterns of standard English.

onset and rimes: In a syllable, the **onset** is the initial consonant (or consonants), and the **rime** is the vowel and any other consonants that follow. In the word *bat,* the onset is *b* and the rime is *at.* In the word *shout,* the onset is *sh* and the rime is *out.*

orthographic knowledge: Knowledge of spelling patterns.

passive vocabulary: Words one recognizes when heard or read, but does not use frequently.

phonemic decoding: Using letter-sound correspondence and blending to sound out words.

reading levels: The **frustrational reading level** is the level at which a reader reads with less than 90 percent word recognition accuracy and has average comprehension of less than 50 percent. The **instructional reading level** is the level at which a reader can read text with 90 percent word recognition accuracy and has average comprehension of 75 percent or greater. The **independent reading level** is the level at which a reader can read text with 95 percent word recognition accuracy and has average comprehension of 90 percent or greater (FLDOE, 2003b).

receptive language: Listening and reading.

semantics: The study of the meanings of words and phrases.

sight words: Words that readers should immediately recognize.

syllabication principles: Rules for dividing words into syllables. For example, "Every syllable has only one vowel sound."

Text: Any type of written material.

Acronyms to Know

ISF: Initial sound fluency

LNF: Letter naming fluency

NWF: Nonsense word fluency

ORF: Oral reading fluency

PSF: Phoneme segmentation fluency

RTF: Retell fluency

Checkpoint

Fill in the blank.

1. A text with blanks inserted where a word or words need to be filled in is a _____ passage.

2. Knowledge of spelling patterns is _____ knowledge.

3. At the independent reading level, a reader can read text with _____ percent word recognition accuracy.

4. Every syllable has only one _____ sound.

Checkpoint Answers

1. cloze

2. orthographic

3. 90

4. vowel

Summary

In summary, all teachers, whatever the subject or grade level, are reading teachers in the sense that they should help their students read and understand text-based materials. Thus, and due to Florida's state reading initiative, it is critical that Florida teachers become knowledgeable of strategies for explicitly teaching students how to read and how to comprehend what they are reading. Literacy strategies must be applied across the curriculum to enhance students' knowledge and understanding of subject matter.

Sample Questions

1. Which of the following instructional methods is best for teaching reading?

   A. direct instruction
   B. inquiry-based learning
   C. discovery learning
   D. traditional lecture

2. Which of the following tasks requires a student to demonstrate phonemic awareness?

   A. asking a student to listen to the words *cat, rat, mat,* and *cot* and identity the non-rhyming word
   B. showing a student the letter *m,* and asking the student to respond orally with the letter's corresponding sound
   C. asking a student to listen to the word *umbrella* and determine its number of syllables
   D. asking a student to listen to the word *put* and identify its final sound

3. Suri, a third-grader, is having problems with fluency. In order to help her, the teacher should

   A. encourage Suri to monitor her own thinking while reading.
   B. tell Suri to try harder.
   C. have Suri practice rereading familiar text.
   D. explicitly work with Suri on word families.

4. Teaching text structures is essential to the student's comprehension of content area text because

   A. students are unable to access this information on their own.
   B. students learn how content area texts are organized, facilitating extraction of important information.
   C. it will assist the teacher in understanding the student's ability to decipher difficult vocabulary.
   D. students need access to ways in which authors attempt to check for understanding by misleading the reader.

5. A science teacher is teaching an integrated unit on *Hatchet* by Gary Paulsen. The teacher is integrating other subjects through this book by discussing edible plant life, single-engine aircrafts, and aspects of both survival skills and problem solving. Integration across disciplines like this is best described as part of what kind of instructional approach?

   A. intersected
   B. multifaceted
   C. multidisciplinary
   D. variety instruction

Answer Explanations for Sample Questions

1. **A.** Choice **A** is the correct response. Research consistently points to direct instruction as a highly effective instructional method for teaching reading. The methods in the other answer choices are not as effective.

2. **D.** Phonemic awareness is the ability to recognize the individual sounds in spoken words. Choice **D** is the correct response. Identifying the final sound in a word demonstrates phonemic awareness. Eliminate **A, B,** and **C** because these tasks can be performed without the ability to recognize the individual sounds in a spoken word.

3. **C.** Eliminate **A** and **D** because these measures do not explicitly address fluency. Eliminate **B** because telling a student to try harder is not an effective strategy. Choice **C** is the correct response. Fluency should be worked on every day under the direction of the classroom teacher. Having Suri practice fluency by rereading familiar texts should improve her reading fluency.

4. **B.** Eliminate **A** because it promotes a negative perception of student ability; although students need explicit instruction, this does not imply an innate lack of ability. Eliminate **C** because it focuses on vocabulary instruction rather than comprehension of content area texts. Eliminate **D** because authors of content area texts do not attempt to mislead students but write in organized ways to allow students to gather information and check for understanding. Teaching text structures helps students learn how content area texts are organized, facilitating extraction of important information. Thus, **B** is the correct response.

5. **C.** Choice **C** is the correct response because *multidisciplinary* is the correct term to describe integrating across disciples in instruction. Eliminate **A, B,** and **D** because the terms given in these answer choices do not accurately describe the instructional approach reflected by the use of an integrated unit.

Practice Test 1

Answer Sheet for Practice Test 1

1 Ⓐ Ⓑ Ⓒ Ⓓ	41 Ⓐ Ⓑ Ⓒ Ⓓ	81 Ⓐ Ⓑ Ⓒ Ⓓ
2 Ⓐ Ⓑ Ⓒ Ⓓ	42 Ⓐ Ⓑ Ⓒ Ⓓ	82 Ⓐ Ⓑ Ⓒ Ⓓ
3 Ⓐ Ⓑ Ⓒ Ⓓ	43 Ⓐ Ⓑ Ⓒ Ⓓ	83 Ⓐ Ⓑ Ⓒ Ⓓ
4 Ⓐ Ⓑ Ⓒ Ⓓ	44 Ⓐ Ⓑ Ⓒ Ⓓ	84 Ⓐ Ⓑ Ⓒ Ⓓ
5 Ⓐ Ⓑ Ⓒ Ⓓ	45 Ⓐ Ⓑ Ⓒ Ⓓ	85 Ⓐ Ⓑ Ⓒ Ⓓ
6 Ⓐ Ⓑ Ⓒ Ⓓ	46 Ⓐ Ⓑ Ⓒ Ⓓ	86 Ⓐ Ⓑ Ⓒ Ⓓ
7 Ⓐ Ⓑ Ⓒ Ⓓ	47 Ⓐ Ⓑ Ⓒ Ⓓ	87 Ⓐ Ⓑ Ⓒ Ⓓ
8 Ⓐ Ⓑ Ⓒ Ⓓ	48 Ⓐ Ⓑ Ⓒ Ⓓ	88 Ⓐ Ⓑ Ⓒ Ⓓ
9 Ⓐ Ⓑ Ⓒ Ⓓ	49 Ⓐ Ⓑ Ⓒ Ⓓ	89 Ⓐ Ⓑ Ⓒ Ⓓ
10 Ⓐ Ⓑ Ⓒ Ⓓ	50 Ⓐ Ⓑ Ⓒ Ⓓ	90 Ⓐ Ⓑ Ⓒ Ⓓ
11 Ⓐ Ⓑ Ⓒ Ⓓ	51 Ⓐ Ⓑ Ⓒ Ⓓ	91 Ⓐ Ⓑ Ⓒ Ⓓ
12 Ⓐ Ⓑ Ⓒ Ⓓ	52 Ⓐ Ⓑ Ⓒ Ⓓ	92 Ⓐ Ⓑ Ⓒ Ⓓ
13 Ⓐ Ⓑ Ⓒ Ⓓ	53 Ⓐ Ⓑ Ⓒ Ⓓ	93 Ⓐ Ⓑ Ⓒ Ⓓ
14 Ⓐ Ⓑ Ⓒ Ⓓ	54 Ⓐ Ⓑ Ⓒ Ⓓ	94 Ⓐ Ⓑ Ⓒ Ⓓ
15 Ⓐ Ⓑ Ⓒ Ⓓ	55 Ⓐ Ⓑ Ⓒ Ⓓ	95 Ⓐ Ⓑ Ⓒ Ⓓ
16 Ⓐ Ⓑ Ⓒ Ⓓ	56 Ⓐ Ⓑ Ⓒ Ⓓ	96 Ⓐ Ⓑ Ⓒ Ⓓ
17 Ⓐ Ⓑ Ⓒ Ⓓ	57 Ⓐ Ⓑ Ⓒ Ⓓ	97 Ⓐ Ⓑ Ⓒ Ⓓ
18 Ⓐ Ⓑ Ⓒ Ⓓ	58 Ⓐ Ⓑ Ⓒ Ⓓ	98 Ⓐ Ⓑ Ⓒ Ⓓ
19 Ⓐ Ⓑ Ⓒ Ⓓ	59 Ⓐ Ⓑ Ⓒ Ⓓ	99 Ⓐ Ⓑ Ⓒ Ⓓ
20 Ⓐ Ⓑ Ⓒ Ⓓ	60 Ⓐ Ⓑ Ⓒ Ⓓ	100 Ⓐ Ⓑ Ⓒ Ⓓ
21 Ⓐ Ⓑ Ⓒ Ⓓ	61 Ⓐ Ⓑ Ⓒ Ⓓ	101 Ⓐ Ⓑ Ⓒ Ⓓ
22 Ⓐ Ⓑ Ⓒ Ⓓ	62 Ⓐ Ⓑ Ⓒ Ⓓ	102 Ⓐ Ⓑ Ⓒ Ⓓ
23 Ⓐ Ⓑ Ⓒ Ⓓ	63 Ⓐ Ⓑ Ⓒ Ⓓ	103 Ⓐ Ⓑ Ⓒ Ⓓ
24 Ⓐ Ⓑ Ⓒ Ⓓ	64 Ⓐ Ⓑ Ⓒ Ⓓ	104 Ⓐ Ⓑ Ⓒ Ⓓ
25 Ⓐ Ⓑ Ⓒ Ⓓ	65 Ⓐ Ⓑ Ⓒ Ⓓ	105 Ⓐ Ⓑ Ⓒ Ⓓ
26 Ⓐ Ⓑ Ⓒ Ⓓ	66 Ⓐ Ⓑ Ⓒ Ⓓ	106 Ⓐ Ⓑ Ⓒ Ⓓ
27 Ⓐ Ⓑ Ⓒ Ⓓ	67 Ⓐ Ⓑ Ⓒ Ⓓ	107 Ⓐ Ⓑ Ⓒ Ⓓ
28 Ⓐ Ⓑ Ⓒ Ⓓ	68 Ⓐ Ⓑ Ⓒ Ⓓ	108 Ⓐ Ⓑ Ⓒ Ⓓ
29 Ⓐ Ⓑ Ⓒ Ⓓ	69 Ⓐ Ⓑ Ⓒ Ⓓ	109 Ⓐ Ⓑ Ⓒ Ⓓ
30 Ⓐ Ⓑ Ⓒ Ⓓ	70 Ⓐ Ⓑ Ⓒ Ⓓ	110 Ⓐ Ⓑ Ⓒ Ⓓ
31 Ⓐ Ⓑ Ⓒ Ⓓ	71 Ⓐ Ⓑ Ⓒ Ⓓ	111 Ⓐ Ⓑ Ⓒ Ⓓ
32 Ⓐ Ⓑ Ⓒ Ⓓ	72 Ⓐ Ⓑ Ⓒ Ⓓ	112 Ⓐ Ⓑ Ⓒ Ⓓ
33 Ⓐ Ⓑ Ⓒ Ⓓ	73 Ⓐ Ⓑ Ⓒ Ⓓ	113 Ⓐ Ⓑ Ⓒ Ⓓ
34 Ⓐ Ⓑ Ⓒ Ⓓ	74 Ⓐ Ⓑ Ⓒ Ⓓ	114 Ⓐ Ⓑ Ⓒ Ⓓ
35 Ⓐ Ⓑ Ⓒ Ⓓ	75 Ⓐ Ⓑ Ⓒ Ⓓ	115 Ⓐ Ⓑ Ⓒ Ⓓ
36 Ⓐ Ⓑ Ⓒ Ⓓ	76 Ⓐ Ⓑ Ⓒ Ⓓ	116 Ⓐ Ⓑ Ⓒ Ⓓ
37 Ⓐ Ⓑ Ⓒ Ⓓ	77 Ⓐ Ⓑ Ⓒ Ⓓ	117 Ⓐ Ⓑ Ⓒ Ⓓ
38 Ⓐ Ⓑ Ⓒ Ⓓ	78 Ⓐ Ⓑ Ⓒ Ⓓ	118 Ⓐ Ⓑ Ⓒ Ⓓ
39 Ⓐ Ⓑ Ⓒ Ⓓ	79 Ⓐ Ⓑ Ⓒ Ⓓ	119 Ⓐ Ⓑ Ⓒ Ⓓ
40 Ⓐ Ⓑ Ⓒ Ⓓ	80 Ⓐ Ⓑ Ⓒ Ⓓ	120 Ⓐ Ⓑ Ⓒ Ⓓ

CUT HERE

Practice Test 1

2½ Hours
120 Questions

Directions: Read each item and select the best response.

1. A social studies teacher asks the students in the class how they could use the word HOMES to help them remember the names of the Great Lakes: Huron, Ontario, Michigan, Erie, and Superior. The students quickly recognize that the first letters of the names of the lakes can be arranged to spell HOMES. This approach to memorizing information best exemplifies using

   A. an acronym.
   B. chunking.
   C. rehearsal.
   D. rote.

2. During a class discussion, for which of the following purposes would it be appropriate for a teacher to ask a closed-ended question?

   A. to check for agreement among students
   B. to encourage brainstorming
   C. to probe for more information
   D. to foster creativity

3. After reading essays students have written, a sixth-grade language arts teacher consults a colleague about how to improve the quality of students' writing assignments. The teacher's decision to ask a colleague for help illustrates which of the following principles?

   A. Teachers need to understand the importance of being reflective practitioners.
   B. Teachers should actively engage in group processes to make decisions.
   C. Teachers should know how to encourage student achievement of desired outcomes.
   D. Teachers need to stay abreast of current knowledge and practices.

4. Which of the following actions should the teacher take at the end of a computer simulation activity to promote students' evaluation-level thinking?

   A. Give a short quiz over the vocabulary encountered during the simulation activity.
   B. Have a whole-class discussion in which students are asked to tell why they did or did not like the simulation activity.
   C. Have students write a paragraph explaining how they participated in the simulation activity.
   D. Have students work in groups to make a list of concepts they learned from the simulation activity.

5. Students in a fourth-grade class are making drawings to illustrate their writing projects. The teacher observes a few students who are artistically talented making rude comments about the drawings of their classmates who are less artistically inclined. The teacher immediately lets the rude students know that such behavior will not be tolerated. The best follow-up response from the teacher to this situation is to

   A. allow students the option of downloading free clip art from the Internet to illustrate their writing projects.
   B. assign the rude students to work one-on-one with their classmates who are less artistically inclined to help them create better drawings.
   C. have students who make rude comments stay after class and talk with them about respecting others.
   D. hold a class meeting to establish consequences for rude behavior and enforce the consequences consistently.

GO ON TO THE NEXT PAGE

6. Which of the following would constitute a violation of the Florida Code of Ethics and Principles of Professional Conduct?

   A. disagreeing with the principal about a discipline issue concerning a student

   B. presenting diverse points of view about a topic to students

   C. representing one's personal views as those of the school district

   D. dating a colleague who teaches in the same school

7. In recent years, the Florida Legislature passed legislation that focuses on using reading as the foundation to improve student achievement in all subject areas. In general, which of the following ways would be best for promoting struggling middle school readers' growth as effective and competent readers of expository text?

   A. regularly require struggling readers to do academically challenging assignments that are reading-intensive

   B. provide instruction to help struggling readers learn when and how to use different comprehension strategies and to repair comprehension problems

   C. explicitly teach struggling readers to make a regular practice of skimming through every text that they plan to read before actually reading it

   D. base struggling readers' grades on research assignments in the content areas as much on their adherence to specific processes as on the content of the final product

8. A teacher is concerned about appropriate assessment of content area learning for students in the class who have histories of limited academic success. To ensure fair and accurate assessment of these students, it would be most appropriate for the teacher to

   A. develop separate, more lenient criteria for assessing their progress.

   B. modify their assignments to reflect less-challenging expectations.

   C. use a variety of formal and informal assessment measures, such as observations, interviews, test scores, and samples of daily work.

   D. rely mainly on the use of students' self-assessment procedures in assessing their acquisition of knowledge and skills.

9. After giving an assignment, a teacher notices that a student, Carl, is frowning. The teacher walks over to Carl's desk and the following exchange occurs:

   Teacher: Do you have a question about the assignment?

   Carl: This is a stupid assignment.

   Teacher: You sound upset. Would you like to talk about it?

   In her interaction with Carl, which of the following elements of effective communication did the teacher exhibit?

   A. being sensitive to nonverbal cues and paraphrasing

   B. being sensitive to nonverbal cues and being a reflective listener

   C. being a thoughtful questioner and paraphrasing

   D. redirecting and paraphrasing

10. A high school calculus teacher decides to attend a workshop on a sophisticated mathematical software program at a state conference. The teacher's probable purpose for attending the workshop is to

   A. be a risk-taker and innovator.

   B. participate in collaborative decision making.

   C. demonstrate that the teacher has clearly defined goals.

   D. enhance the teacher's own professional skills and knowledge.

11. An interdisciplinary team of middle school teachers wants to develop lessons that promote students' higher-order thinking skills. Which of the following is most likely to promote the higher-order thinking skills of middle school students?

   A. in math, filling in the missing components of a pattern

   B. in social studies, creating a timeline showing significant events of a historical period

   C. in science, graphing data from an experiment

   D. in language arts, memorizing a favorite poem

12. A first-year third-grade teacher has received her class roster for the upcoming school year. She notes that the 19 students in her class are culturally diverse and that two students are receiving Exceptional Student Education (ESE) services—one is visually impaired, and the other has mild hearing loss. In planning her classroom layout, it is most important for the teacher to consider the

A. materials and resources available in her classroom.

B. availability of assistive technology equipment in the school.

C. potential discipline problems she might encounter with such a varied group of students.

D. instructional approaches she is planning to use in her classroom.

13. Ms. Kim, a middle school teacher, overhears two students, Jimmy and Curtis, talking about drugs. The teacher confronts the students to discuss what she heard. Following is an excerpt from their discussion:

Ms. Kim: Jimmy, I want to talk to you about what you said to Curtis about needing some drugs.

Jimmy: Ms. Kim, you got it all wrong. I was just kiddin' around. I don't do drugs.

Curtis: That's right, Ms. Kim. Jimmy doesn't mess with drugs.

Ms. Kim: I'm not so sure. Some of your other teachers have told me that your grades have dropped a lot since school started, Jimmy. Aren't you failing math and English?

Jimmy: Well, I'm not doing real good in school right now, but it's not because of drugs. You gotta believe me, Ms. Kim.

Ms. Kim: Well, you two go on to your next class. I'll talk to you about this later.

When Ms. Kim discussed Jimmy's grades in front of Curtis, her actions were

A. inappropriate, because the suspected drug abuse was a more important issue.

B. inappropriate, because she publicly disparaged Jimmy.

C. appropriate, because Jimmy's behavior will likely change as a result.

D. appropriate, because peer pressure from Curtis toward Jimmy to do better will likely result.

14. Which of the following strategies would be best for developing a fourth-grade student's reading fluency?

A. Encourage the student to reread books written at the student's independent reading level.

B. Encourage the student to memorize common phonics rules to improve decoding skills.

C. Have a peer give constructive feedback after listening to the student read aloud.

D. Have the student practice blending onsets and rimes for word families quickly and accurately.

15. After a cooperative learning activity in language arts, the teacher asks students to determine whether the activity was successful and to reflect on their roles and participation. Which of the following is a benefit of having students do this assignment?

A. It will allow the teacher to assess students' mastery of the language arts objective for the cooperative learning activity.

B. It will promote self-reflection and self-assessment on the part of the student.

C. It will promote a healthy, competitive spirit among students.

D. It will allow the teacher to identify those students who exhibited leadership skills.

16. A social studies teacher uses a town controversy over whether a large oil company should be permitted to drill on the site of a historic landmark as the basis for a discussion in class. The teacher poses the following question to the class: "Should preservation of historic landmarks stand in the way of economic development? Why or why not?" The teacher's questions are probably posed for the purpose of

A. encouraging students to recall factual information.

B. providing students with clues to the teacher's personal opinion about the controversy.

C. checking students' understanding of the nature of the controversy.

D. providing a framework for engaging students in critical thinking about the controversy.

GO ON TO THE NEXT PAGE

17. The computer science teacher volunteers to conduct a professional learning workshop for the other teachers at school on using a popular spreadsheet software program. Conducting the workshop best illustrates that the teacher knows how to

    A. use technology to enhance the mission of the school.

    B. actively share ideas with colleagues to contribute to a successful learning community.

    C. use community resources to promote professional growth.

    D. use group processes to make decisions and solve problems.

18. Students in a high school history class are debating a controversial historical issue. The teacher's main purpose for having the class debate is to

    A. provide a means for students to practice public speaking skills.

    B. give students an opportunity to engage in collaborative problem solving.

    C. engage students in higher-order thinking in an authentic context.

    D. minimize the negative effects of historical controversies on student performance.

19. A science teacher observes that most of her students seem to think of scientists as men. Which of the following would be the most effective way for the teacher to counter gender stereotyping?

    A. Have the students do research papers on female scientists.

    B. Show a video about famous female scientists.

    C. Have a day in which the class learns about and celebrates women in science.

    D. Invite a variety of male and female guests who have science-related careers to visit the class throughout the year.

20. Parents of a student ask Mr. Mann, their child's teacher, to show them their child's grades and also the grades of the child's classmates. Which of the following actions would be appropriate for Mr. Mann to take in response to the parents' request?

    A. Tell the parents that he cannot legally show them other students' grades.

    B. Show the parents the grades of the other students, but caution that they must keep them confidential.

    C. Explain to the parents that there is no point in their seeing the grades because teachers have the sole right to assign grades.

    D. Tell the parents that their request must go through the principal's office first.

21. An effective strategy for promoting fifth graders' vocabulary development is to have the students

    A. look up new words in the dictionary and use information from the definitions they find to write sentences containing the new words.

    B. discuss the unfamiliar words in a story that was read aloud by the teacher.

    C. make a list of high-frequency words in a word journal.

    D. memorize definitions of unfamiliar words encountered in stories read in the reading center.

22. At midyear, a high school teacher asks the students to respond to the following three prompts:

What I like best about this class

What I like least about this class

What I would change to make this class better

This type of assessment is called a

    A. criterion-referenced assessment.

    B. formative assessment.

    C. needs assessment.

    D. norm-referenced assessment.

23. Florida law explicitly states that immediate intensive intervention for an elementary school student who has been identified with a reading deficiency must be provided

- **A.** daily.
- **B.** twice a week.
- **C.** three times a week.
- **D.** every two weeks.

24. A first-year third-grade teacher asks a counselor for professional advice on how best to help a student who has an individualized Progress Monitoring Plan (PMP) meet state and district standards for proficiency in reading. The teacher's decision to consult the counselor is most in accord with which of the following principles?

- **A.** Teachers should understand that different students learn in different ways and can apply this understanding to promote learning.
- **B.** Teachers should know how to design outcome-oriented learning experiences that enhance academic success for all students.
- **C.** Teachers should be reflective practitioners who know how to work within a learning community to enhance students' academic performance.
- **D.** Teachers should use effective communication to shape the classroom into a community of learners.

25. Students in a second-grade class have finished reading a version of the classic tale, "Jack and the Beanstalk." The story tells about a boy named Jack who climbs a beanstalk and meets an unfriendly giant. At the end of the story, Jack deposes the giant. Which of the following questions about the story would likely be most effective for assessing students' creative thinking skills?

- **A.** Why did Jack climb the beanstalk?
- **B.** Why do you think Jack kept returning to the giant's castle even though he was scared of the giant?
- **C.** What did Jack do that made his mother angry?
- **D.** What would have happened if the giant and Jack had become good friends?

26. To promote all students' understanding and appreciation of diversity, it would be most beneficial for a teacher to

- **A.** decorate the classroom with students' drawings based on readings of stories from students' home cultures.
- **B.** make a presentation about the holiday traditions of people from a variety of cultures.
- **C.** teach students numbers and other vocabulary from a variety of languages spoken in the community.
- **D.** invite visitors from the different cultural backgrounds represented in the class to lead and participate in a variety of activities.

27. Which of the following is NOT one of the Principles of Professional Conduct for the Education Profession in Florida?

- **A.** Obligation to the student requires that the individual shall not unreasonably deny a student access to diverse points of view.
- **B.** Obligation to the parents requires that the individual shall maintain a classroom climate that promotes the lifelong pursuit of learning.
- **C.** Obligation to the profession of education requires that the individual shall maintain honesty in all professional dealings.
- **D.** Obligation to the public requires that the individual shall not use institutional privileges for personal gain or advantage.

28. Before students begin a reading assignment on the hydrologic cycle, a seventh-grade science teacher could best prepare students to understand the reading assignment by

- **A.** giving the students articles about the hydrologic cycle to scan through.
- **B.** explicitly teaching the technical vocabulary the students will encounter in the reading assignment.
- **C.** reminding the students to read the assignment slowly and carefully.
- **D.** encouraging students to look up unfamiliar words in a dictionary as they do the reading assignment.

GO ON TO THE NEXT PAGE

29. To obtain information about a high school student's strengths and weaknesses in a subject area, which of the following types of assessment would be best to use?

    A. diagnostic
    B. outcome measure
    C. progress monitoring
    D. screening

30. A language arts teacher wants to help students develop their critical thinking skills, so the teacher asks many questions during each class. Typically, his questions are similar to the following:

    Who is the author of *Beowulf?*

    What is the subject of this sentence?

    What is the main idea of the first paragraph?

    To improve his questioning techniques, the teacher should do which of the following?

    A. Ask more divergent questions.
    B. Ask more questions that have only "yes" or "no" answers.
    C. Ask more convergent questions.
    D. Ask more focusing questions.

31. Ms. Carter, a first-year teacher, is having trouble dealing with a student who is very disruptive in her class. Ms. Carter wants to ask a colleague for advice about what she should do to discourage the student's misbehavior, but she is reluctant to discuss the problem when the opportunity arises. The most likely basis for Ms. Carter's reluctance to ask for assistance from her colleague is that she believes that

    A. she will be perceived as ill-prepared or incompetent.
    B. the best way to learn is to work through problems by herself.
    C. experienced teachers do not have time to give beginning teachers assistance after school starts.
    D. most strategies used by experienced teachers are too difficult for a beginning teacher to use.

32. In keeping with a desire to foster higher-order thinking and enhance problem-solving skills, which of the following strategies would be LEAST desirable for an algebra teacher to use?

    A. Establish a highly managed classroom environment that focuses on procedural knowledge.
    B. Encourage students to take time to think before deciding on a solution strategy when they are initially given a word problem.
    C. Spend more class time on problems requiring analytical skills than on basic algebraic manipulation problems.
    D. Provide opportunities for students to correct their errors rather than expecting them to rely on the teacher to determine whether their work is mathematically correct.

33. Which of the following practices would best promote social harmony among diverse students in a middle school social studies class?

    A. Avoid discussing racial or ethnic relations with the class.
    B. Use competitive games and contests.
    C. Display artifacts in the classroom that reflect students' varied cultural backgrounds.
    D. Encourage students to share ideas relevant to their cultural backgrounds during class discussions.

34. Ms. Alford is a veteran teacher with 20 years' experience. After school one day, she walks across the hall to Mr. Pennywell's room and criticizes him for allowing his students to play a game in class. Mr. Pennywell does not want to be argumentative with Ms. Alford, so he explains calmly and politely why he feels the game was a worthwhile activity for his students. The next day, the principal tells Mr. Pennywell that Ms. Alford has complained to the principal that Mr. Pennywell used profanity toward her and behaved unprofessionally during their conversation the day before. Ms. Alford's behavior is unethical because, according to the Code of Ethics and Principles of Professional Conduct for the Education Profession in Florida, a teacher should NOT

A. use coercive means to influence professional judgments of colleagues.

B. engage in harassment that unreasonably interferes with an individual's performance of professional work.

C. interfere with a colleague's exercise of civil rights and responsibilities.

D. make intentionally false statements about a colleague.

35. Before students begin reading a passage from their social studies textbook, the teacher gives the students a list of statements related to the topic of the passage. The teacher asks the students to mark whether they agree or disagree with each of the statements. After the students mark their responses, the teacher encourages students to discuss their responses and defend their positions. This practice best represents an application of which of the following strategies for increasing students' comprehension of content area reading?

A. previewing and making predictions about the passage to be read

B. generating questions the students would like answered about the topic of the passage

C. participating in self-questioning activities that require them to clarify and monitor their comprehension as they proceed through the passage

D. setting a purpose for reading the passage

36. Which of the following is NOT a recommended practice in regard to homework for middle school students?

A. limiting homework assignments to 15 minutes per day

B. giving prompt comments and criticism when work is completed

C. coordinating homework assignments with other teachers to avoid homework overload

D. giving homework assignments that are appropriate to students' levels of achievement and individual differences in ability

37. To improve participation in and the quality of whole-class discussions, a teacher should

A. use *who, what, where,* and *when* questions only.

B. recognize only those students with hands raised.

C. ask more knowledge-level and comprehension questions.

D. ask the question before calling on a student by name.

38. A sixth-grade social studies teacher designs a unit test, being careful to ensure that the test is aligned with the instructional content that was addressed in class. Upon administering and grading the test, the teacher finds that each of the students earned a score of 90 percent or better. When reflecting upon these test results, the most appropriate conclusion for the teacher to draw about her teaching practices is that she

A. needs to move at an accelerated pace of instruction for the next unit.

B. made the test too easy and, thus, failed to differentiate adequately among the students.

C. is an effective teacher because the students have mastered the unit content.

D. is targeting instruction at a level that is too low for the students in the class.

39. In giving students problems in which they must draw a general conclusion based on a number of examples, a mathematics teacher is most likely promoting students' use of

A. deductive reasoning.
B. differential reasoning.
C. evaluative reasoning.
D. inductive reasoning.

40. With regard to gender differences, a teacher should plan to

A. make allowances for gender differences by giving students freedom to pursue their own interests.
B. use more masculine-oriented modeling to increase female students' assertiveness.
C. treat male and female students similarly whenever appropriate.
D. have more activities where boys and girls are grouped separately.

41. At the beginning of the school year, a school's fourth-grade students are administered a screening assessment. A fourth-grade teacher examines the results of the school-wide screening assessment and determines that two students in his class performed slightly below grade level in writing. To collect additional data for developing effective interventions, the teacher should

A. analyze writing samples in the students' language arts portfolios for an initial time period.
B. ask the reading coach to review the screening assessment data with the teacher.
C. assign peer tutors to each of the two students.
D. monitor the students' engagement during in-class writing assignments.

42. A third-grade teacher informally assesses a student's reading comprehension by having the student silently read the following paragraph about Kendra, a young girl who moves from Florida to a new state:

Kendra woke up early. She could hear her parents talking downstairs in the kitchen. Quickly, she began to get dressed. She wanted to explore her new neighborhood. She put on jeans, a sweater, and a coat. Then she looked for her gloves and wool scarf. She was glad her mom had taken her shopping yesterday to buy the gloves and scarf. Kendra knew she would need them often in this new place.

The teacher could best test the student's literal comprehension of the paragraph by asking which of the following questions?

A. Why did Kendra's family move from Florida?
B. Where were Kendra's parents when she woke up?
C. Did Kendra like her new home?
D. Why did Kendra's mom buy Kendra the gloves and scarf?

43. A language arts teacher makes the following list of tentative test items over the novel *Huckleberry Finn,* by Mark Twain:

1. Tom Sawyer's aunt is named Aunt _____.
2. True or false: Mark Twain was the pen name for Samuel Coleridge.
3. Who is Widow Douglas?
4. Discuss the role of superstition in the novel *Huckleberry Finn,* by Mark Twain.

On which item does guessing have the most effect?

A. Item 1
B. Item 2
C. Item 3
D. Item 4

44. Which of the following would NOT be an effective way to communicate high expectations to at-risk students?

- **A.** accepting and praising all work
- **B.** supporting their efforts to give oral responses
- **C.** allowing sufficient wait time for student responses to questions
- **D.** expressing expectations clearly and directly

45. When teachers challenge students to reason from basic assumptions to reach a logical conclusion, they are most likely promoting students' use of

- **A.** creative thinking.
- **B.** deductive reasoning.
- **C.** imaginative thinking.
- **D.** inductive reasoning.

46. A high school teacher is creating a lesson plan in which students will investigate their own learning styles. Learning style experts generally agree that learning style is

- **A.** an indication of one's intelligence.
- **B.** fixed and unchangeable for a particular individual.
- **C.** different from person to person.
- **D.** strictly a result of biological factors.

47. A school district wants to develop a benchmark test to see how well students are progressing toward the academic goals of the district. What type of test would be best for this purpose?

- **A.** aptitude
- **B.** criterion-referenced
- **C.** norm-referenced
- **D.** psychomotor

48. A teacher asks a question, calls on Sabrina to respond, and then waits patiently for Sabrina's answer even though Sabrina is one of the lower-achieving students. When Sabrina does not respond, the teacher rephrases the question and then continues to wait. How would you evaluate this teacher's approach to Sabrina at this point?

- **A.** ineffective, because it places Sabrina and the teacher in a power struggle
- **B.** ineffective, because it communicates a negative impression about Sabrina to the class
- **C.** effective, because it communicates positive expectations to Sabrina
- **D.** effective, because it establishes the teacher's authority in the classroom

49. A high school algebra teacher gives students the following task:

> Use what you know about adding two fractions in arithmetic to write out a plan for adding two algebraic fractions.

In giving the students this task, the teacher is most likely promoting students' use of

- **A.** creativity.
- **B.** discrimination.
- **C.** generalization.
- **D.** overlearning.

50. A language arts teacher is planning to implement a more culturally diverse approach to the study of literature in her class. An effective first step to enhance teaching by appreciating cultural diversity is for the teacher to

- **A.** persuade the principal to hold a campus-wide diversity awareness week.
- **B.** spend some time in self-reflection to examine her own attitudes and beliefs about cultural groups.
- **C.** examine the books she is currently using for bias or stereotyping of cultural groups.
- **D.** use literature that depicts main characters striving to develop bicultural identities.

GO ON TO THE NEXT PAGE

51. Which of the following assessment methods is considered an authentic way to assess kindergarten children's learning in learning centers?

    A. informal teacher observation

    B. multiple-choice testing

    C. peer assessment

    D. standardized assessment

52. A teacher notices that Katlin, one of his high-achieving students, is very inattentive in class. When he has a chance to talk with Katlin privately, she begins to tell him about a problem she is having with a group of girls that are bullying her. To encourage Katlin to continue telling him about the situation, the teacher should

    A. immediately advise Katlin that she needs to stand up to the bullies.

    B. listen with a concerned look and limit interruptions.

    C. empathize with Katlin by telling her about experiences he had with bullies when he was in school.

    D. try not to maintain eye contact with Katlin because it might make her feel uncomfortable.

53. A social studies teacher assigns students to read an overview of the three branches of government and their functions. Next, the teacher displays the following transparency on the overhead projector:

> **BALANCE OF POWER**
>
> Explain in your own words what you think this term means.

This activity will benefit students most by

    A. accommodating their various learning styles.

    B. involving them in thinking about topics that are important to them.

    C. encouraging them to memorize key terminology.

    D. engaging them in higher-order thinking.

54. A history teacher is concerned about her students' low grades. She feels the low grades are mainly due to the students' lack of interest and enthusiasm in history class. Which of the following measures related to assessment would be best for motivating students to earn better grades in history?

    A. reducing the number of tests, quizzes, and homework assignments given

    B. including comments related to improvement in reports to students and parents

    C. giving feedback several weeks after administering a test

    D. using a lower standard for grading

55. During class discussions, teachers often find it difficult to apply the recommended 3-second wait time for students' responses to questions. According to experts, which of the following is the main reason for this difficulty?

    A. Teachers fear that silence might disturb the momentum of their lessons.

    B. Teachers are subject to the strong norm in American culture to avoid empty silence.

    C. Teachers believe that silence might lead to student misbehavior.

    D. Teachers are concerned that student achievement will suffer.

56. Which of the following teacher behaviors would LEAST likely promote students' critical thinking skills?

    A. teaching for deeper understanding of concepts

    B. focusing on making students memorize significant facts and formulas.

    C. requiring students to justify the reasoning behind their conclusions

    D. giving explicit instruction in critical thinking.

57. In high school, students should be given homework primarily to

    A. improve their academic achievement.

    B. help them develop good study habits.

    C. foster in them positive attitudes toward school.

    D. enhance their self-discipline.

58. Students in a high school geography class are learning about interrelationships between people and their environment. On an outside tour around their school, the students are dismayed about how much trash they see. When they return to class, a discussion about trash disposal ensues. "Is there going to be room for us with all this trash in the world?" asks Maria. The teacher responds to the whole class, "What do you think about Maria's concern?" This question to the whole class in response to Maria's question is an example of

   A. using a student's contribution to make a point.
   B. paraphrasing a student's contribution.
   C. using a student's contribution as an example.
   D. using a student's contribution to stimulate additional discussion.

59. A second-grade teacher is using a computer simulation activity to help students learn social studies concepts. A major advantage of using a computer simulation activity in social studies is that it

   A. provides an efficient means for recording and analyzing data.
   B. enhances students' mapping skills.
   C. allows students to make decisions in a safe environment.
   D. promotes low-achieving students' mastery of basic skills.

60. Ms. Curl, a new third-grade teacher, is enthusiastic about her first year. She looks forward to meeting her students and has many plans for them. The first day of class, Ms. Curl introduces herself and shares with the students some of her ideas for the classroom. As a new teacher, Ms. Curl needs to be aware of which of the following?

   A. During the first few days of school, teachers need to teach students specific procedures for how to move from group to group, how to ask for help, how to obtain needed materials, and so forth.
   B. To avoid problems later on in the year, teachers need to establish a disciplined climate in their classrooms by using frequent timeouts during the first few days of school.
   C. During the first few days of school, classroom management will be easier if the teacher works with individual students to explain classroom rules and procedures.
   D. Early on, teachers need to establish a warm and caring environment by ignoring misbehavior unless it disrupts the flow of the lesson.

61. A high school humanities teacher has observed a difference in the achievement of students of low socioeconomic backgrounds and that of middle-class students in her class. The teacher's observation is related to the finding of studies that show that students from low socioeconomic backgrounds usually

   A. do better in school than children from middle-class backgrounds.
   B. do about as well as children from middle-class backgrounds.
   C. do more poorly in school than children from middle-class backgrounds.
   D. enter school behind children from middle-class backgrounds but eventually close the gap in high school.

GO ON TO THE NEXT PAGE

62. During a class discussion, a teacher calls only on students who raise their hands to respond. This teacher's method of recognizing students for responses is

    A. positive, because it avoids having to call on shy students who do not know the answer and might be embarrassed in front of the whole class.

    B. positive, because it is more effective than calling on students using a random process.

    C. limited, because students who don't volunteer might miss an opportunity to be actively engaged in the lesson.

    D. positive, because volunteers give a higher proportion of correct responses from which all might benefit.

63. A teacher is excited about implementing cooperative learning strategies in his classroom during the school year and is busy planning group activities that he can use with his students. Which of the following is an essential feature of cooperative learning?

    A. Using cooperative learning activities frees the teacher from monitoring student work.

    B. When using cooperative learning activities, students' rewards should be interdependently determined.

    C. Cooperative learning activities free the teacher from having to use strict grading policies.

    D. When using cooperative learning, group size should not be predetermined.

64. Students in a high school chemistry class are learning to prepare solutions of acids. Which of the following methods is the most appropriate way for the teacher to assess the students' understanding of this procedure?

    A. Use an observational checklist.

    B. Give a short quiz.

    C. Have students complete a worksheet.

    D. Have the students prepare a lab report.

65. A first-year middle-grades English teacher is trying to teach her students creative writing, but she is disappointed and frustrated when most of the students' papers are dull and uninteresting. She discusses her dismay with an experienced colleague and asks for advice on how to motivate the students to write better papers. The first-year teacher's decision to consult an experienced colleague illustrates which of the following principles?

    A. Teachers need to understand the importance of creating and sustaining an efficient and supportive learning environment.

    B. Teachers should work in groups to solve problems.

    C. Teachers should know collaborative strategies to support student achievement of desired learning outcomes.

    D. Teachers should show the ability to articulate their own professional judgment to colleagues.

66. A third-grade teacher wants her students to learn how a hot air balloon works. Which of the following technologies would be most appropriate for this purpose?

    A. computer simulation
    B. presentation software slide show
    C. spreadsheet
    D. video

67. In regular education classrooms, academic tasks that are assigned as independent class work or homework are typically based upon

    A. low context and low cognitive demand.
    B. low context and high cognitive demand.
    C. high context and low cognitive demand.
    D. high context and high cognitive demand.

68. In a school district that is practicing School-Based Management (SBM), authority to make decisions about how to implement the district's goals, including certain decisions about the school budget, hiring of personnel, and the curriculum

    A. is retained by the Florida Department of Education.

    B. is delegated to the superintendent.

    C. rests with the school board.

    D. is placed at the school level.

69. A third-grade teacher posts the following classroom rules:

CLASS RULES

Rule 1. Be respectful of others.

Rule 2. Work quietly.

Rule 3. Do not run indoors.

Rule 4. Complete your work.

Which rule should be restated in a more appropriate format?

A. Rule 1
B. Rule 2
C. Rule 3
D. Rule 4

70. "Given five right triangles each with the measure of one side missing, the students will be able to use the Pythagorean theorem to solve for the measure of the missing side in four out of five of the right triangles with no errors." This statement is an example of a(n)

A. affective objective.
B. cognitive objective.
C. psychomotor objective.
D. reflective objective.

71. As the regular education teacher of a student with a disability, a new teacher will be serving on the Individual Educational Plan (IEP) team for the student. The teacher is aware that the student is participating in the regular education environment because this placement meets the criterion of "least restrictive environment" for the student. With regard to students with disabilities, *least restrictive environment* means that

A. a student's classroom environment should be appropriate to his or her level of disability.
B. Exceptional Student Education (ESE) teachers should have the full responsibility for tailoring the school environment to a student's needs.
C. all children should be able to participate in regular school activities, regardless of disability.
D. disabled children should attend special schools.

72. A high school speech teacher has students conduct peer assessments of students' performances. The teacher's main purpose for using peer assessments is to

A. encourage students to explore new techniques.
B. decrease the teacher's workload and grading time.
C. allow students to deepen their understanding of the concepts.
D. provide a record of student progress over time for future reflection.

73. A student is beginning to exhibit a pattern of habitual tardiness to a high school physical education class. Which of the following should the teacher do first to address this problem?

A. Deduct points from the student's grade.
B. Give the student extra written work to complete outside of class.
C. Privately discuss the problem with the student.
D. Draw the class's attention to the student when the student arrives late.

74. Which of the following activities would be most effective in helping a teacher's English Language Learners (ELLs) develop awareness of differences in register?

A. having the students model verbal and nonverbal cues
B. having students practice interpreting idiomatic expressions
C. having the students role-play specific situations, such as discussing a community concern first with a classmate and then with the mayor of the city
D. having students role-play speaking in different dialects with a partner

75. A middle-grades language arts teacher encourages her students to write on topics they are interested in or care about. Which of the following is the teacher using to enhance motivation?

A. intrinsic motivation
B. negative reinforcement
C. positive reinforcement
D. reverse psychology

GO ON TO THE NEXT PAGE

76. A first-year middle school teacher has a class composed of students of diverse academic ability levels. Which of the following best reflects current research regarding grouping practices for teacher instruction of the students?

A. using a combination of whole-group instruction and small-group differentiated instruction

B. using small-group instruction of high achievers and mixed-ability group instruction for the other students in the class

C. using only whole-group grade-level instruction

D. using permanently identified ability-groups for instruction of all students

77. A second-grade teacher has a conference with parents whose child has been consistently off-task in the teacher's class since the beginning of the year. The teacher and parents agree that weekly updates from the teacher to the parents about the child's behavior are warranted. The most appropriate way for the teacher to keep the parents informed about their child's behavior is to update the parents by

A. sending them weekly text messages.

B. creating a notebook that the child will carry home each week and bring back the following week.

C. arranging a regular time to call each week.

D. meeting with one or both parents after school once a week.

78. A teacher responds to student work that is good or that shows improvement by writing comments such as "Good job!," "Terrific!," and "Nice work!" on the students' papers. This teacher's praise would be more effective if the teacher

A. communicated the praise orally, rather than in writing.

B. specified additional areas for improvement along with the praise.

C. specifically stated what the students have done that is praiseworthy.

D. used one particular word or phrase consistently from student to student to communicate praise.

79. For a social studies unit on government, a teacher designs lesson plans around the theme of "civic ideas and practices." The teacher's idea to use a thematic approach to the unit best demonstrates that the teacher understands the importance of

A. helping students to understand relationships within a discipline.

B. selecting developmentally appropriate instructional strategies.

C. nurturing a sense of community in the classroom.

D. enhancing students' ability to apply knowledge in various contexts.

80. A fifth-grade teacher decides to hold a class meeting to address her concerns that students in the class are disruptive and unmotivated. The teacher's decision to hold a class meeting illustrates her understanding that she

A. is a member of a learning community and knows how to work effectively with all members of that community.

B. should promote student ownership in a smoothly functioning learning community.

C. must communicate high expectations for student learning to create a climate of trust in the classroom.

D. must help students become self-motivated.

81. A first-grade teacher has a student with moderate hearing loss in the class. What is the greatest effect, if any, that this condition will have on the student's process of learning to read?

A. The student might have difficulty pronouncing the sounds of letters correctly.

B. The student might have difficulty writing the letters correctly.

C. The student might confuse written letters with each other.

D. The student's reading process will not be affected.

82. An eighth-grade science teacher, who is using innovative teaching methods, is concerned that her students might have difficulty on the Florida statewide assessment test in science because she is not "teaching to the test." The teacher could best address this concern by

A. setting aside part of the class period each day for explicit instruction in statewide assessment test-taking strategies.

B. making sure that the Next Generation Sunshine State Standards for eighth-grade science are included in her curriculum.

C. including more drill and practice lessons over the Next Generation Sunshine State Standards for eighth-grade science benchmarks.

D. making sure that the students always use their textbooks, which are correlated to the Next Generation Sunshine State Standards for eighth-grade science.

83. A middle school social studies teacher makes sure that the English Language Learners (ELLs) in his classroom have opportunities to use English not only for academic-related communication, but also for communicating with others, giving directions, expressing needs, and revealing feelings. This practice best demonstrates the teacher's understanding that

A. the structure and conventions of an ELL's native language might be different from English.

B. imagination and creativity are important components of language acquisition.

C. ELLs will feel more comfortable using English in a relaxed atmosphere.

D. using English across a wide range of language functions will improve proficiency.

84. A major motivational reason cooperative learning produces positive instructional outcomes is the

A. cooperative incentive structure.

B. model's inherent appeal to teachers.

C. competitive task structure.

D. homogeneous nature of the group.

85. Which of the following activities involving decimals would be LEAST desirable for a fourth-grade teacher to use in mathematics?

A. Working individually and with partners, students solve teacher-posed real-world problems involving decimals.

B. As a whole class, students design a project focused on decimals.

C. As the teacher models problem-solving involving decimals, students take notes and practice with the teacher.

D. Students copy decimal problems from the textbook and use calculators to obtain the answers.

86. Individual Educational Plan (IEP) team meetings to review a student's IEP, and, as appropriate, revise its provisions must be held

A. at least once every three years.

B. at least once every 12 months.

C. no less than twice a year.

D. only as needed at the discretion of the school district.

87. For most learners, an effective discipline plan is one that emphasizes

A. consistency and fairness.

B. isolation and suspension.

C. negotiation and leniency.

D. threat and fear.

88. To best maintain communication with families of students whose home language is not English, a teacher should send the families

A. the school's website address.

B. phone numbers of their student's bilingual classmates.

C. the teacher's phone number and other contact information.

D. a monthly multilingual newsletter about class events.

GO ON TO THE NEXT PAGE

89. A fourth-grade student is writing and illustrating a short story for language arts. The student plans to download graphics from the Internet to use in his story. It is important that the teacher

   A. inform the student to include the web address beneath the graphics in his story.

   B. commend the student for his clever use of technology.

   C. encourage the student to draw his own illustrations rather than use graphics from the Internet.

   D. forbid the student to download graphics from the Internet.

90. A grade K-12 English Language Learner (ELL) who is enrolled in classes specifically designed for ELLs is coded as

   A. LF.
   B. LP.
   C. LY.
   D. LZ.

91. Middle school and high school teachers who hold high expectations for their students are likely to find that teacher expectations

   A. influence student behavior and performance.

   B. are more powerful than peer pressure.

   C. create anxiety in low-ability students and cause achievement to decline.

   D. have no impact on academic achievement.

92. A teacher has selected a cooperative learning group activity to use on the first class day as a means to get acquainted with her students and to help the students get to know one another. The teacher is very excited about this idea because she is aware of the many positive benefits of cooperative learning. The teacher should

   A. follow up with written reports of the group activity.

   B. monitor the social interactions of the students while they are working in their groups.

   C. have the students evaluate each other's level of participation in the group activity.

   D. replace the group activity with a simple, enjoyable activity that involves the whole class.

93. Which of the following is a likely result of using fixed-ability groups that stay in place throughout the school year?

   A. The teacher will experience less behavior management problems.

   B. High-ability students will have an increased opportunity to become more accepting of their low-achieving classmates because they will not be held back by them.

   C. All of the students will experience achievement gains since ability grouping will allow them to experience an accelerated curriculum and advanced instruction.

   D. Students in the low-ability groups will be negatively affected.

94. A teacher ignores Carly, who blurts out answers without first raising her hand and waiting to be called on. Which technique is the teacher using with Carly?

   A. extinction
   B. negative reinforcement
   C. positive reinforcement
   D. shaping

95. If a teacher suspects a student is experiencing abuse at home, the teacher should

   A. set up a conference with the parents to see whether the teacher's suspicions are true.

   B. discuss the teacher's suspicions with some of the student's friends.

   C. notify the proper legal authorities at once and let them investigate the situation.

   D. wait a while longer and observe the student to see whether the teacher's suspicions are correct.

96. A performing arts teacher plans a recital at the auditorium of the local civic center. By doing so, the teacher is

   A. demonstrating civic responsibility.
   B. promoting cultural values.
   C. supporting private businesses.
   D. using community resources.

97. Current theories about language development share the hypothesis that formal knowledge about the rules of language are not as critical as the ability to use the language in the process of actual communication. This hypothesis is known as the

    A. acculturation hypothesis.
    B. acquisition learning hypothesis.
    C. affective filter hypothesis.
    D. assimilation hypothesis.

98. A middle grades health teacher is aware of the alarming rate of drug use among young adolescents. He decides to revise the two-week unit on drug abuse that he had planned to teach. He feels this particular unit is a very important part of the curriculum, and he wants to feel confident that it will help increase the students' understanding of the dangerous effects of drug abuse. Through the Drug Abuse Resistance Education (D.A.R.E.) organization, the teacher obtains resource materials to use in the unit that stress the hazards of minors' illegal use of drugs. He also plans to invite well-known, dynamic guest speakers to visit the class to talk with students about the social pressures that sometimes lead to drug use. Most likely, the teacher's lessons for the unit will be designed to enhance students'

    A. understanding of the society in which they live.
    B. ability to memorize and recall factual information.
    C. independent thinking and decision-making skills.
    D. ability to apply information learned.

99. According to Florida Statute 1003.32, a teacher may remove a student from class if the teacher determines that the student's behavior interferes with the ability of the student's classmates to learn. Furthermore, the principal cannot return the student to the teacher's class without the consent of the teacher unless a school placement committee determines otherwise. However, the law specifies that a teacher is required to complete professional development to improve the teacher's classroom management skills if the teacher removes what percent of his or her total class enrollment under this statute?

    A. 10 percent
    B. 25 percent
    C. 30 percent
    D. 50 percent

100. A high school mathematics teacher plans to use peer tutoring in her classes in the coming year. Research on the effect of peer tutoring on learning indicates that

    A. the results are much the same regardless of the expertise of the tutor.
    B. the tutors benefit, but usually the tutees do not.
    C. achievement of both the tutors and the tutees increases.
    D. neither tutors nor tutees benefit significantly, but achievement motivation increases for both.

GO ON TO THE NEXT PAGE

101. Marcus is an exceptionally bright student, but he seldom completes his work, makes fun of class activities, and generally behaves disruptively. Marcus's father visits the school to complain about a lower-than-expected grade Marcus received in science because he did not complete some homework assignments. Which of the following approaches would be appropriate for Marcus's teacher to use with this parent?

- **A.** She should explain to the parent that Marcus can do better work since he is obviously a bright student.
- **B.** She should explain to the parent that the other students do well under her grading policy, so she sees no reason to change Marcus's grade.
- **C.** She should explain to the parent that Marcus's problem is most likely related to his behavior problems in class.
- **D.** She should explain her grading policy to the parent and show samples of Marcus's incomplete work.

102. A first-grade teacher has been keeping track of a student's reading and writing progress by using anecdotal records and checklists. Which of the following assessment tools is another informal measure the teacher might use?

- **A.** benchmark assessment
- **B.** diagnostic assessment
- **C.** portfolio assessment
- **D.** summative assessment

103. To motivate student effort and engagement, an elementary school mathematics teacher offers points, which students can save and redeem for rewards each time they answer a problem correctly. This technique is most closely associated with a(n)

- **A.** contingency reward program.
- **B.** extrinsic reward system.
- **C.** group reward program.
- **D.** intrinsic reward system.

104. A fourth-grade teacher is selecting a computer software program for science. Which of the following features would be most critical for the program to have to be effective for use by the teacher's English Language Learners, most of whom are in the early production stage of English language acquisition?

- **A.** an introduction to keyboarding and mouse skills
- **B.** supplementary aids, such as quizzes and worksheets, that are age-appropriate
- **C.** written instructions that are easily accessible and use simple language
- **D.** extensive visual representations and other nonlinguistic graphic support

105. Most authorities agree that lecturing

- **A.** is the least effective instructional strategy for elementary school, but is very effective in middle school.
- **B.** should be used occasionally in elementary school to prepare students for its use in the upper-level grades.
- **C.** should be used in elementary school when a lot of content needs to be covered in a short time.
- **D.** should be avoided in elementary school.

106. During the first quarter of the year, a middle-grades English teacher spends most of the class period having the students complete practice exercises on punctuation and grammar. The teacher has become concerned because most of the students appear bored during the lessons, and off-task behavior has become a problem. Which of the following measures would be most effective in addressing the teacher's concerns?

- **A.** Replace the practice exercises with activities related to the students' interests and experiences.
- **B.** Use moderate punishment such as timeouts when students are not paying attention.
- **C.** Praise by name the students who are on task.
- **D.** Discuss the problem with individual students and ask for their cooperation.

107. A primary charge of the school advisory council (SAC) is to

    A. choose appropriate curricular materials for the school.

    B. select valid assessment tools for measuring student progress.

    C. monitor the professional learning of school faculty.

    D. assist in the preparation of the school's annual budget.

108. Which of the following activities would be most developmentally appropriate in promoting second-grade students' multicultural awareness and appreciation?

    A. Have students learn about geographic and environmental characteristics of the countries represented by the different cultural groups in the class.

    B. Engage students in an activity in which they are able to discover common elements in their various cultural backgrounds, as well as unique features of their own culture.

    C. Have students read about cultural traditions of several countries and discuss them in class, followed by a short quiz about the reading material.

    D. Have each student memorize a song from a different country and sing it to the class, followed by a question-and-answer period during which classmates can ask questions about the song's meaning.

109. For children in the primary grades, attitudes toward an issue tend to be most influenced by their

    A. cognitive abilities.

    B. families' attitudes toward the issue.

    C. peers' attitudes toward the issue.

    D. personal experiences related to the issue.

110. A first-year early-childhood teacher is planning for the coming year. The teacher wants to use learning centers in her classroom. Which of the following is an important feature that early-childhood learning centers should have?

    A. Learning centers should be designed for students to work in isolation, away from their peers.

    B. Learning centers should be self-contained, with all materials needed contained within the center.

    C. Learning centers should include carefully designed and easy-to-read worksheets.

    D. Learning centers should be separated from the regular classroom work area.

111. Which of the following cognitive abilities should a sixth-grade teacher expect most of the students in the class to be in the process of developing?

    A. taking another person's point of view

    B. thinking hypothetically about abstract concepts

    C. thinking in concrete terms

    D. being able to mentally reverse operations

112. Which of the following principles best applies to interdisciplinary teams?

    A. Teachers should know how to communicate effectively with colleagues to create an environment that supports innovation and risk taking.

    B. Teachers should have opportunities to learn from each other and thereby improve the educational experiences of students.

    C. Teachers should know how to apply knowledge of learning theories to classroom practices.

    D. Teachers should work with colleagues to establish strong and positive ties between the school and the community.

GO ON TO THE NEXT PAGE

113. A second-grade class includes English Language Learners who speak Haitian-Creole and Spanish. In which of the following situations would it be advantageous for the teacher to pair speakers of the same language?

   A. when students are working in cooperative learning groups

   B. when the most recently arrived student needs an orientation to classroom rules and procedures

   C. during labeling and drawing activities related to academic content

   D. during activities designed to promote social communication skills

114. A seventh-grade teacher has a student who is becoming the class clown by making distracting noises and funny faces when students are working in groups. The teacher, aware that the student has an unfortunate home life, speculates that the attention the student gets from the class makes the student feel like "one of the gang." The student's inappropriate behavior in class is probably associated with the student's fear of

   A. being rejected by peers.

   B. displeasing authority figures.

   C. failing to achieve academically.

   D. failing to learn cultural norms.

115. A first-grade teacher has planned a science unit concerning the ocean. On the first day of the unit, the children enter the classroom to see "seaweed" hanging from the ceiling, displays of seashells on tables, and pictures of ocean life on the wall. The teacher's probable purpose for transforming the classroom into a pretend ocean is to

   A. provide a concrete experience for the children.

   B. allow the children to have choices in their learning.

   C. create a safe, efficient, supportive learning environment.

   D. give students control over their learning experiences.

116. A teacher consults with an Exceptional Student Education (ESE) teacher for advice on how to implement accommodations for an ESE student in the teacher's class. The teacher's decision to consult the ESE teacher is most in accord with which of the following principles?

   A. Teachers should create a learning environment in which all students are treated equitably.

   B. Teachers should know how to plan lessons that utilize a variety of support and enrichment activities.

   C. Teachers should work cooperatively with colleagues to meet students' education needs.

   D. Teachers should communicate with and challenge all students in a positive manner.

117. Ms. Pattillo, a kindergarten teacher, overhears two of the boys in her class arguing over which one is going to marry her. She is not upset and does not reprimand the boys because she realizes their behavior is normal. The teacher's analysis of the situation best reflects her knowledge and consideration of

   A. students' developmental processes.

   B. the importance of developing students' positive self-esteem.

   C. allowing students to practice self-discipline.

   D. the need to model for students ways to resolve conflicts.

118. A fourth-grade English Language Learner (ELL) who has been determined through an aural/oral test to be fully English proficient most likely still would have difficulty comprehending which of the following sentences?

   A. The girl invited her friend to come to a party.

   B. I'm sorry that I forgot about your birthday.

   C. Your teacher will not put up with rude behavior in the classroom.

   D. My brother has been unhappy all week.

119. With regard to the Individual Educational Plan (IEP) team of a student with a disability, at least one regular education teacher of the student serves on the IEP team. As a member of the IEP team, the regular education teacher

A. assists with determining interventions and strategies for the student.

B. assists with interpreting the instructional implications of evaluation results.

C. serves as the representative of the school district.

D. serves only as an observer.

120. A science teacher believes her role is to facilitate students' pursuit of new understandings through creating an environment in which the students are constructing their own knowledge through active inquiry in light of their previous understandings. This teacher's approach to teaching is most consistent with

A. assertive discipline.

B. constructivism.

C. expository teaching.

D. teacher-centered instruction.

STOP

Answer Key for Practice Test 1

1. A	31. A	61. C	91. A
2. A	32. A	62. C	92. D
3. A	33. D	63. B	93. D
4. B	34. D	64. A	94. A
5. A	35. D	65. C	95. C
6. C	36. A	66. A	96. D
7. B	37. D	67. B	97. B
8. C	38. C	68. D	98. C
9. B	39. D	69. C	99. B
10. D	40. C	70. B	100. C
11. A	41. A	71. A	101. D
12. D	42. B	72. C	102. C
13. B	43. B	73. C	103. B
14. A	44. A	74. C	104. D
15. B	45. B	75. A	105. D
16. D	46. C	76. A	106. A
17. B	47. B	77. B	107. D
18. C	48. C	78. C	108. B
19. D	49. C	79. A	109. B
20. A	50. B	80. B	110. B
21. B	51. A	81. A	111. B
22. B	52. B	82. B	112. B
23. A	53. D	83. D	113. B
24. C	54. B	84. A	114. A
25. D	55. B	85. D	115. A
26. D	56. B	86. B	116. C
27. B	57. A	87. A	117. A
28. B	58. D	88. D	118. C
29. A	59. C	89. A	119. A
30. A	60. A	90. C	120. B

Complete Answers and Explanations for Practice Test 1

1. **A.** This question deals with study skills, which fall under **Competency 4: Assessment.** Choice **A** is the correct response. An *acronym* (**A**) is a word or phrase formed from the initial letters of a list of words that is used to help you remember the words in the list—like the example given in the question of using *HOMES* to remember the names of the Great Lakes. Eliminate **B** because *chunking* involves organizing or clustering more than one piece of information in a meaningful way in order to remember it. For example, when you remember telephone numbers, you remember them as three chunks of information—the area code, the first three digits, and the last four digits—rather than as 10 separate digits. Eliminate **C** because *rehearsal* is the process of repeating information over and over again, either aloud or silently, as a means of holding it in short-term memory and preparing it for long-term memory. Eliminate **D** because *rote* is memorization through isolated drill.

2. **A.** This question deals with a class discussion, which falls under **Competency 3: Instructional Delivery.** Closed-ended questions are used to find facts or information. Open-ended questions are used to stimulate students' thinking and generation of ideas. Eliminate **B, C,** and **D** because these purposes require an open-ended question. When a teacher wants to check for agreement among the students, it is appropriate for the teacher to ask a closed-ended question seeking that information. Thus, **A** is the correct response.

3. **A.** This question deals with using data from the learning environment as a basis for exploring and reflecting upon teaching practices, which falls under **Competency 5: Continuous Improvement.** The question asks what the teacher's decision to consult a colleague for help illustrates. Eliminate **B** because the teacher did not make her decision in a group setting. Eliminate **C** and **D** because these choices are not aligned with the question; the question does not contain ideas expressed in these answer choices. The teacher understands the importance of reflection and self-evaluation. She recognizes that she is a member of a learning community and actively seeks out other professionals as resources to enhance her professional skills and knowledge. Thus, **A** is the correct response.

4. **B.** The question falls under **Competency 3: Instructional Delivery.** Evaluation-level thinking requires students to use criteria or standards to form judgments or opinions about the value of a topic or phenomenon being considered. Eliminate **A, C,** and **D** because, for these actions, students are not required to form judgments or opinions. A class discussion in which students are asked to form an opinion about the simulation activity and give reasons for that opinion would work best for engaging students in evaluation-level thinking. Thus, **B** is the correct response.

5. **A.** This question falls under **Competency 2: Learning Environments.** The teacher in question should have realized beforehand that some, and probably most, students lack drawing talent. Therefore, the teacher should have provided a means for these students to illustrate their writing projects without having to draw. In this situation, an effective strategy for encouraging a greater sense of equity and acceptance among all students is to allow them the option of downloading free clip art from the Internet to illustrate their writing projects, making differences in student artistic ability less important and apparent. This action would contribute to a positive learning climate for all students in the class. Thus, **A** is the correct response. Eliminate **B** because this action might prompt the students with less artistic talent to compare their drawings unfavorably to those of the more artistically talented students. Eliminate **C** because this is an action that the teacher might take, but it is not the *best* response. When a discipline situation involving a "perpetrator" and a "victim" occurs, the teacher should stop the perpetrator's actions, but then focus on the victim. The teacher's best follow-up response is one that helps the students who were the targets of the rude behavior. Eliminate **D** because this action would not be under consideration had the teacher anticipated the current situation might happen and planned accordingly; further, consequences for rude behavior should have already been established.

Tip: Notice that the question asks you to select the *best* response. A word like *best* in the question stem is a marker for a priority-setting question. In these questions there may be more than one acceptable response, but you must select the <u>one</u> best response. This tip applies to other similar marker words such as *most* or *primary.*

6. **C.** This question deals with **Competency 6: Professional Conduct.** The action in **C** is a violation of the Florida Code of Ethics and Principles of Professional Conduct, which states that teachers "shall take reasonable precautions to distinguish between personal views and those of any educational institution or organization with which the individual is affiliated." Thus, **C** is the correct response. None of the actions in the other answer choices is a violation of the Florida Code of Ethics and Principles of Professional Conduct.

7. **B.** This question falls under **Competency 8: Literacy Strategies.** One requirement of the Florida legislation is that schools must use scientifically based reading instruction and/or interventions. Only **B** contains a scientifically based approach to promote struggling readers' growth as effective and competent readers of expository text. Experts agree that students should be taught comprehension strategies. Key comprehension strategies include predicting, verifying, summarizing, and thinking aloud. The approaches given in the other answer choices are not supported by research. Thus, **B** is the correct response.

8. **C.** This question deals with **Competency 4: Assessment.** Eliminate **A** and **B** because these strategies would fail to communicate to students assessment criteria and standards based on high expectations for learning. Eliminate **D** because, although having students engage in self-assessment is useful and appropriate, reliance on this strategy might fail to yield results that are reliable and accurate in terms of assessing students' actual knowledge and skills. In conducting classroom assessments to measure content area learning, teachers should strive to use a variety of assessment strategies so that students will have varied opportunities and multiple ways to show what they have learned. Thus, **C** is the correct response.

9. **B.** This question deals with **Competency 2: Learning Environments.** In her interaction with Carl, the teacher, noticing Carl's frown, responds to this nonverbal cue. Eliminate **C** and **D** because these options do not indicate that the teacher responded to a nonverbal cue. Eliminate **A** because the teacher did not paraphrase (that is, restate what Carl said in her own words). After noticing Carl's frown and going over to his desk, the teacher listens reflectively to what Carl says and responds to it. Thus, **B** is the correct response.

10. **D.** This question deals with **Competency 5: Continuous Improvement.** Eliminate **A** and **C** because the question stem provides no reason to assume that the teacher wants to be a risk-taker or innovator or to demonstrate that the teacher has clearly defined goals. (*Tip:* Don't read too much into a question.) Eliminate **B** because this response also is not supported by the question—there is no indication that the teacher will participate in collaborative decision making during the workshop. Because the teacher will be learning about a sophisticated mathematical software program, the teacher's probable purpose for attending the workshop is to enhance his or her professional skills and knowledge. The teacher demonstrates awareness that Florida educators have a professional and ethical obligation to seek out opportunities for professional growth. Thus, **D** is the correct response.

11. **A.** This question falls under **Competency 1: Instructional Design and Planning.** Eliminate **B, C,** and **D** because these tasks do not require higher-order thinking skills. Filling in the missing components of a pattern requires the higher-order thinking skills of analysis (involving the ability to examine relationships of the parts of the pattern to one another) and synthesis (involving the ability to predict what part is missing). Thus, **A** is the correct response.

12. **D.** This question deals with classroom layout, which falls under **Competency 2: Learning Environments.** Eliminate **A** and **B** because materials, resources, and technology should not be limiting factors for teachers. In other words, the teacher should decide upon a spatial arrangement based on what the teacher thinks would provide the most effective learning environment for the students, not on what materials, resources, and technology are available. Eliminate **C** because although this aspect might be a factor for the teacher to consider, it is not as important as considering the instructional approaches the teacher is planning to use with this group of diverse learners. Thus, **D** is the correct response.

13. **B.** This question deals with **Competency 6: Professional Conduct.** By discussing Jimmy's poor academic performance in front of Curtis, Ms. Kim is in violation of the principle in the Code of Ethics and Principles of Professional Conduct for the Education Profession in Florida that states that the teacher

"shall not intentionally expose a student to unnecessary embarrassment or disparagement." Thus, **B** is the correct response. Moreover, the Family Education Rights and Privacy Act (FERPA) protects the privacy of student records. FERPA requires that schools obtain written permission from minor students' parents before releasing educational records. Discussing a student's grades in front of another student might be construed as a violation of this law. Eliminate **A** because legal, ethical, and professional standards take precedence over other considerations. Eliminate **C** and **D** because Ms. Kim's behavior was inappropriate.

14. **A.** This question deals with **Competency 8: Literacy Strategies.** For most children, reading and rereading a number of stories and informational texts that are appropriate for their level of reading ability develops fluency. Thus, **A** is the correct response. Of course, instruction to increase reading fluency should begin only after a student has demonstrated strong word recognition skills. As a general rule, children should be able to read 95 percent or more of the words in a text, and do so effortlessly, when working on fluency. The strategies in the other response options would not be as effective as repeated reading.

15. **B.** This question deals with **Competency 4: Assessment.** Eliminate **A** because this response is not aligned with the question—the students are evaluating, not the teacher. Eliminate **C** because this result would not be considered a benefit. Eliminate **D** because there is no reason to expect a connection between the students' self-reflection and their leadership skills. By asking the students to reflect on their roles and participation in the cooperative learning activity, the teacher is promoting their self-reflection and self-assessment. Thus, **B** is the correct response.

16. **D.** This question falls under **Competency 3: Instructional Delivery.** Eliminate **A** because the teacher's questions should elicit divergent thinking, not factual recall. Eliminate **B** because teachers should encourage students to be independent thinkers and, thus, should not give them hints about what to think about an issue. Eliminate **C** because the teacher is not questioning what the students already know about the controversy. The teacher's questions are designed to create a climate of inquiry. The teacher does not want a particular "right answer" to the questions posed, but rather wants students to explore and develop their own ideas and opinions about the topic. The questions are meant to provide a framework for engaging students in critical thinking about the controversy. Thus, **D** is the correct response.

17. **B.** This question deals with **Competency 5: Continuous Improvement.** Eliminate **A, C,** and **D** because these answer choices are not supported by the question stem—there is no indication that the computer science teacher will be addressing the mission of the school, using community resources, or making decisions and solving problems when conducting the workshop. The computer science teacher understands that teachers have an obligation to work with each other for the advancement of mutual professional growth. The workshop will give the computer science teacher an opportunity to actively share ideas with colleagues to contribute to a successful learning community at their school. Thus, **B** is the correct response.

18. **C.** This question deals with **Competency 3: Instructional Delivery.** Notice that you must select the response that is the teacher's *main* purpose. Eliminate **B** because it is not aligned with the question—the students are debating a problem, not solving one. Although participating in a debate will provide opportunities for students to practice public speaking **(A)** and might, in some unexpected way, minimize negative effects, if any, of historical controversies on student performance **(D)**, these reasons would not be as significant as engaging students in higher-order thinking in an authentic context. Thus, **C** is the correct response.

19. **D.** This question deals with **Competency 1: Instructional Design and Planning.** Eliminate **A** because this approach has limited effectiveness in countering gender stereotyping. Eliminate **B** and **C** because these approaches might send the message that recognizing and celebrating the accomplishments of women scientists need to receive attention only for the day. Research indicates that, by age 9, students have well-established prejudices that are highly resistant to change; therefore, the teacher must go beyond brief and superficial measures to counter gender stereotyping—a long-term intervention is warranted. Bringing in, throughout the year, both male and female guests who have science-related careers will provide role models in science for all the teacher's students. Thus, **D** is the correct response.

20. A. This question deals with **Competency 6: Professional Conduct.** The Family Education Rights and Privacy Act (FERPA) protects the privacy of student records. FERPA requires that schools obtain written permission from minor students' parents before releasing educational records to others. Eliminate **B** and **D** because these answer choices conflict with FERPA. Eliminate **C** because this action works against developing effective parent-teacher partnerships. Mr. Mann should know that his legal responsibility is to deny the parents' request to see other students' grades. Thus, **A** is the correct response.

21. B. This question deals with **Competency 8: Literacy Strategies.** Vocabulary instruction is effective when students discuss new words in context. Thus, **B** is the correct response. According to *Promoting Vocabulary Development: Components of Effective Vocabulary Instruction* (resources.buildingrti.utexas.org/PDF/redbk5.pdf), "Both younger and older students appear to benefit from read-aloud activities, and older students can learn the meanings of new words as efficiently from hearing stories read to them as they can from reading the stories themselves" (p. 13). Eliminate **A** because the aspect of developing vocabulary in context is missing from this response option. Eliminate **C** because high-frequency words are associated with decoding, not vocabulary development. Eliminate **D** because rote memorization of definitions is not a meaningful strategy for vocabulary development.

22. B. This question deals with **Competency 4: Assessment.** Choice **B** is the correct response. The teacher's prompts compose an informal survey, which is being used as a type of formative assessment. Eliminate **A, C,** and **D** because these are formal types of assessment. A *criterion-referenced assessment* (**A**) uses standardized tests designed to measure mastery of specific skills. A *needs assessment* (**C**) is a systematic process to identify areas in need of improvement. A *norm-referenced assessment* (**D**) uses standardized tests that focus on a comparison of students' scores to those of a "norm" group of students. A *formative assessment* (**B**) takes place before and during the learning process; it is used to give feedback to the teacher about the instructional process and may take various forms (such as an informal survey, as shown in this question).

23. A. This question relates to **Competency 8: Literacy Strategies.** Choice **A** is the correct response. According to Florida Administrative Code Rule 6A-6.054 K-12 Student Reading Intervention Requirements, "Immediate intensive intervention must be provided daily for all [elementary] students who have been identified with a reading deficiency. This intervention must be in addition to or as an extension of the ninety (90) minute reading block in a smaller group size setting or one on one. The student must continue to be provided with intensive reading instruction until the reading deficiency is remedied." The time frames in choices **B, C,** and **D** are incorrect.

24. C. This question deals with **Competency 5: Continuous Improvement.** Eliminate **A, B,** and **D** because these answer choices are not aligned with the question. By asking for professional advice from the counselor, the teacher demonstrates that she is a reflective practitioner who knows how to work within a learning community to enhance students' academic performance. Thus, **C** is the correct response.

25. D. This question relates to both **Competency 3: Instructional Delivery** and **Competency 4: Assessment.** Eliminate **A, B,** and **C** because these questions do not challenge students to use creative thinking skills. The question in **D** prompts students to use their imaginations to create a new scenario between Jack and the giant, a cognitive activity that demonstrates creative thinking skills. Thus, **D** is the correct response.

26. D. This question relates to both **Competency 1: Instructional Design and Planning** and **Competency 7: Teaching English Language Learners (ELLs).** Notice that you must select the answer choice that would be *most* beneficial. Eliminate **B** and **C** because these actions are teacher-focused and too passive for the students. You must now decide which is the better answer choice: **A** or **D**. Eliminate **A** because although a teacher might take this action to promote diversity, it would not engage the students' interest and attention as well as taking the action given in **D** would. By inviting visitors from the different cultural backgrounds represented in the class to lead and participate in activities with the students, a teacher is creating a classroom environment that encourages active engagement of the students, while applying the teacher's understanding that teachers should use the diversity that exists within the classroom and the community to foster students' understanding and appreciation of diversity. Thus, **D** is the correct response.

27. **B.** This question deals with **Competency 6: Professional Conduct.** Teachers in Florida are expected to exhibit the highest standards of professionalism and ethical conduct. They should become knowledgeable about the Code of Ethics and Principles of Professional Conduct for the Education Profession in Florida. Eliminate **A, C,** and **D** because these answer choices contain principles in the Code of Ethics and Principles of Professional Conduct. No set of principles is specifically targeted toward parents. Thus, **B** is the correct response.

28. **B.** This question deals with **Competency 8: Literacy Strategies.** According to *Research-Based Content Area Reading Instruction* (available at resources.buildingrti.utexas.org/PDF/redbk4.pdf), teachers should "explicitly teach the meaning of key words, such as technical vocabulary, prior to introducing a topic or a selection in which the words appear" (p. 7). Thus, **B** is the correct response. The suggestions given in **A, C,** and **D** are not supported by research.

29. **A.** This question deals with **Competency 4: Assessment.** Eliminate **B, C,** and **D** because these types of assessment usually do not provide sufficient information about a student's difficulties for diagnostic purposes. Diagnostic assessments **(A)** provide teachers with specific information about an individual student's strengths and needs relative to subject matter skills and subskills. Such tests are effective tools for assessing a student's strengths and weaknesses. They provide specific information that can be used to customize instruction and/or interventions for particular students. Thus, **A** is the correct response.

30. **A.** This question deals with **Competency 3: Instructional Delivery.** Eliminate **B, C,** and **D** because these question types require only limited responses, thus, evoking only lower-level thinking. Divergent questions (for instance, "Why do you think?" or "What if … ?") allow for multiple responses, thus, evoking higher-order thinking skills. To enhance students' critical and creative thinking skills, the teacher should be mindful of Bloom's Taxonomy and ask more higher-order, divergent questions. Thus, **A** is the correct response.

31. **A.** This question deals with **Competency 5: Continuous Improvement.** Eliminate **B, C,** and **D** because these beliefs might prevent Ms. Carter from asking for assistance, but the *most* likely reason is that she is fearful that she will be perceived as ill-prepared or incompetent to teach. Like many first-year teachers, Ms. Carter is too embarrassed to ask for help because she doesn't want the other teachers to know she is having a problem. Instead of being reluctant to seek assistance from her colleagues, Ms. Carter should view them as a rich source of support and guidance. Thus, **A** is the correct response.

32. **A.** This question deals with **Competency 3: Instructional Delivery.** Eliminate **B, C,** and **D** because these are desirable strategies. When students are encouraged to take time to think before deciding on a solution strategy for a problem **(B),** they spend more time thinking about and analyzing the problem. Allowing more time for problems requiring analytical skills than for basic algebraic manipulation problems **(C)** would be more conducive to higher-order thinking and problem solving. When students rely on themselves to determine whether their work is mathematically correct **(D),** they engage in critical thinking in order to clarify their mathematical thinking. According to Van De Walle, Karp, and Bay-Williams (2009), procedural knowledge is knowledge of the rules and procedures that are used to carry out routine mathematical tasks and of the symbolism that is used to represent mathematical concepts. A highly managed classroom environment focused on procedural knowledge likely would result in less risk taking and less higher-level thinking from students. Thus, **A** is the correct response.

33. **D.** This question relates both to **Competency 2: Learning Environments** and **Competency 7: Teaching English Language Learners (ELLs).** Creating an environment that respects and confirms the dignity of students as human beings is essential in meeting the needs of diverse students. Encouraging students to share ideas relevant to their cultural backgrounds during class discussions would allow the class to celebrate and respect the diversity in the classroom and, thereby, promote harmonious relations among the students. Thus, **D** is the correct response. Eliminate **A.** As when dealing with other inappropriate behavior, teachers should respond immediately to expressions of racism. Eliminate **B** because competitive games might result in group disharmony. Eliminate **C** because although displaying artifacts is an acceptable practice, it would not be as effective as that given in **D.**

34. **D.** This question deals with **Competency 6: Professional Conduct.** Eliminate **A, B,** and **C** because these answer choices are not supported by the stimulus. Ms. Alford intentionally made false statements about Mr. Pennywell. She is in violation of the principle in the Code of Ethics and Principles of Professional Conduct for the Education Profession in Florida, which states that the teacher "shall not make malicious or intentionally false statements about a colleague." Thus, **D** is the correct response.

35. **D.** This question deals with **Competency 8: Literacy Strategies.** Eliminate **A** because the students are not skimming the passage and making predictions about the content of the passage based on what they find. Eliminate **B** because although the class discussion might result in questions arising that students would like answered, you are not given that information in the question stem. (***Remember:*** Don't read too much into a question.) Eliminate **C** because the students are not asking themselves questions; furthermore, the activity described in this option occurs during the reading of the passage, not before. The activity described in the question will help the students establish a purpose for reading the passage. They will read to gather evidence that will verify their initial positions or cause them to modify or reverse them. Thus, **D** is the correct response.

36. **A.** This question deals with **Competency 4: Assessment.** In *Helping Your Child with Homework,* the U.S. Department of Education (2005) asserted that "Homework is an opportunity for children to learn and for families to be involved in their children's education." Among recommendations for the use of homework at all grade levels are that teachers should give prompt comments and criticism when work is completed (eliminate **B**), coordinate homework assignments with other teachers to avoid homework overload (eliminate **C**), and give homework assignments that are appropriate to students' levels of achievement and individual differences in ability (eliminate **D**). Also, most experts recommend a ratio of about 10 minutes of homework per grade level, so limiting homework assignments to 15 minutes per day for middle school students is not recommended. Thus, **A** is the correct response.

37. **D.** This question deals with **Competency 3: Instructional Delivery.** Eliminate **A** and **C** because the quality of discussions will not be improved with these lower-level question types. Eliminate **B** because this action works against student participation. Choice **D** is the correct response. Asking a question first and then calling a student's name for a response is an effective method teachers can use to keep students mentally involved in the discussion. When the question comes before the student's name, all students are given the opportunity to think and process their answers because the teacher has not yet identified the student who will be asked to respond. Research shows that asking the question first increases the number of responses as well as elicits more correct and longer responses.

38. **C.** This question deals with **Competency 4: Assessment.** Good teachers are reflective practitioners who know how to use data from learning environments as a basis for reflecting on their teaching practices. Because the teacher was careful to design the assessment so that it was aligned with the instructional content that was addressed, she should be pleased with the results. The most appropriate conclusion for the teacher to draw from the assessment data from the unit test is that the students have mastered the unit content, indicating that the teacher has performed effectively in achieving the desired learning outcomes. Thus, **C** is the correct response. The students are doing well at the current pace, so there would be no reason to pick up the pace of instruction (eliminate **A**). Because the test was aligned with the instructional content, the data do not support that the test was too easy or that the teacher is targeting instruction at a level that is too low (eliminate **B** and **D**).

39. **D.** This question deals with **Competency 3: Instructional Delivery.** Eliminate **A** because *deductive reasoning* starts with basic assumptions or facts and proceeds to a logical conclusion. Eliminate **B** because *differential reasoning* would be used only to decide how items are different. Eliminate **C** because *evaluative reasoning* would involve some kind of value judgment. Choice **D** is the correct response. *Inductive reasoning* involves looking at specific examples and trying to identify a pattern or trend that fits the given examples in order to determine a general rule. Because the students are to draw a general conclusion based on a number of examples, the teacher is most likely promoting students' use of inductive reasoning.

40. C. This question deals with **Competency 1: Instructional Design and Planning.** Eliminate **A** because this approach is problematic; students might pursue interests traditionally associated with their gender roles to avoid being ridiculed by classmates. Eliminate **B** because it promotes sex-role stereotyping. Eliminate **D** because grouping boys and girls separately, generally, is not a recommended practice. Choice **C** is the correct response. Teachers should treat male and female students generally the same, unless a clear legitimate reason exists to do otherwise.

41. A. This question deals with **Competency 4: Assessment.** Eliminate **B** because the role of the reading coach is to provide support in the six major components of reading (oral language, phonological awareness, phonics, fluency, vocabulary, and comprehension). Eliminate **C** and **D** because these measures are not ways to gather data about a student's writing ability. Choice **A** is the correct response. Analyzing the writing samples in the students' writing portfolios will provide information about students' writing strengths and deficiencies from which the teacher can develop appropriate interventions.

42. B. This question deals with **Competency 8: Literacy Strategies.** *Literal comprehension* is understanding the written words of a text. Choice **B** is the correct response because the answer to the question given in **B** is explicitly stated in the paragraph, so this question will assess the student's literal comprehension. The answers to the questions in the other response options are not explicitly stated in the reading passage.

43. B. This question deals with **Competency 4: Assessment.** Teacher-made tests can provide valuable information about what students have learned. When designing tests, teachers need to be aware that guessing can compromise the validity of results. Although guessing can be a factor with any type of test item, it has the most effect on true-false items. Thus, **B** is the correct response.

44. A. This question deals with conveying high expectations, which falls under **Competency 2: Learning Environments.** At-risk students are low-performing students who are potential dropouts. Teachers should understand factors inside the classroom, such as teacher expectations, that influence these students' perceptions of their own worth and potential. Eliminate **B, C,** and **D** because these choices contain ways that represent consensus in educational research and theory about maximizing teaching and learning for all students, but especially in working with at-risk students. Teachers should encourage these students to express themselves orally **(B)** because of the need for schools to provide opportunities for development of effective oral communication skills, which are sometimes lacking in the home environments of at-risk students. Because disengagement is problematic with at-risk students, the teacher should provide a confidence-building environment, including giving them sufficient wait time **(C)** and expressing expectations clearly and directly **(D).** Praise serves to inform students of what they are doing right; therefore, it is critical that the praise be given for correct responses and appropriate behavior. Especially with at-risk students, accepting and praising all work will not be effective in facilitating learning and will send a confused message about teacher expectations. Thus, **A** is the correct response.

45. B. This question deals with **Competency 3: Instructional Delivery.** Eliminate **A** and **C** because these ways of thinking involve coming up with new ideas, which would not be expected when students are reasoning from general statements to reach a logical conclusion. Eliminate **D** because *inductive reasoning* involves looking at a number of specific examples and trying to identify a pattern or trend that fits the given examples in order to determine a general rule. Choice **B** is the correct response. *Deductive reasoning* starts with basic assumptions or facts and proceeds to a logical conclusion.

46. C. This question deals with **Competency 1: Instructional Design and Planning.** Learning style is said to be the manner in which an individual perceives and processes information in learning situations. Knowledge of learning style theory might assist teachers in designing educational conditions in which most students are likely to learn. Learning style experts generally agree that every person has an individual learning style **(C)**; that learning style is an indicator not of intelligence (eliminate **A**) but of how a person learns; that learning style strengths might change over time and with training (eliminate **B**); and that although certain learning style characteristics are biological in nature, others are developed through experience (eliminate **D**). Thus, **C** is the correct response.

47. B. This question deals with **Competency 4: Assessment.** Eliminate **A** because an *aptitude test* is a standardized test designed to predict future performance in a subject area. Eliminate **C** because *norm-referenced tests* are standardized tests that focus on comparing students' scores to those of a "norm" group of students, so this type of test would not necessarily show achievement of district academic goals. Eliminate **D** because *psychomotor tests* assess physical, not academic, skills. *Criterion-referenced tests* **(B)** are used to compare scores against a predetermined minimum standard of competency. A test of this type would be the best way to assess student progress toward the academic goals of the district. Thus, **B** is the correct response.

48. C. This question deals with **Competency 2: Learning Environments.** Eliminate **A** and **B** because by giving Sabrina sufficient wait time, the teacher is sending a positive message to Sabrina—that the teacher values her input. Eliminate **D** because it is not aligned with the question. By rephrasing the question and continuing to wait, the teacher is not giving up on Sabrina. Slavin (2008) points out that "Research has found that teachers tend to give up too rapidly on students whom they perceive to be low achievers, a practice that tells those students that the teacher expects little from them" (p. 233). The teacher's approach is effective because it communicates positive expectations to Sabrina. Thus, **C** is the correct response.

49. C. This question deals with **Competency 3: Instructional Delivery.** The teacher wants the students to take a skill previously learned in one setting and use it in a new setting. The ability to carry learning over from one setting to a different setting is called *generalization* **(C).** Therefore, the task given to the students is most likely to promote generalization. Thus, **C** is the correct response. The other answer choices do not apply as well to the task as **C.** *Creativity* **(A)** involves putting together ideas to come up with new ideas or understandings. *Discrimination* **(B)** involves recognizing differences. *Overlearning* **(D)** is practicing beyond the point of mastery to improve retention.

50. B. This question relates both to **Competency 1: Instructional Design and Planning** and **Competency 7: Teaching English Language Learners (ELLs).** Notice that you must select the *first* step that a teacher should take. Eliminate **A** because holding a campus-wide diversity week might send the message that recognizing and celebrating differences need to receive attention only during that time period. Indeed, research findings indicate that such measures might be too brief or superficial to make an impact. Choices **C** and **D** contain measures that the teacher should take to implement a more culturally diverse curriculum; however, your knowledge of effective multicultural practices should tell you that before proceeding with her plans, the teacher should *first* examine her own personal beliefs and feelings about cultural groups. Many teachers are unaware of their own biases and prejudices. Thus, **B** is the correct response.

51. A. This question deals with **Competency 4: Assessment.** Eliminate **B** and **D** because these assessment methods are not developmentally appropriate for kindergarten children. Eliminate **C** because *peer assessment* by kindergarten children is unlikely to yield reliable, authentic data. *Informal teacher observation* **(A)** allows the teacher to assess in a natural and ongoing way. This method is an authentic way to assess because the teacher collects information about what the children are learning by directly observing them. Thus, **A** is the correct response.

52. B. This question deals with **Competency 2: Learning Environments.** Eliminate **A** because quickly offering advice would be a disservice to Katlin. Eliminate **C** because interrupting Katlin to share his own personal experiences interrupts her thought processes and impedes communication. Eliminate **D** because maintaining eye contact is a way to promote communication and indicates active listening. Choice **B** is the correct response. Listening with a concerned look and limiting interruptions will send the message to Katlin that what she is saying is important to the teacher and will encourage her to continue talking with him about her problem with the bullies.

53. **D.** This question deals with **Competency 3: Instructional Delivery.** Eliminate **A** because there is no evidence in the question stem to indicate that the teacher is using multisensory approaches that might appeal to students with different learning styles and preferences. Eliminate **B** because no evidence in the question stem indicates that the assignment topic is important to the students (although it might very well be)—don't read too much into a question. Eliminate **C** because, although the assignment might encourage students to memorize key terminology, it benefits students most by engaging them in higher-order thinking such as finding connections among concepts, drawing valid conclusions, and formulating ideas. Thus, **D** is the correct response.

54. **B.** This question deals with **Competency 4: Assessment.** Eliminate **A** and **D** because these approaches are likely to have a negative impact on how the students think about themselves. Eliminate **C** because feedback is more effective and more meaningful when it occurs immediately after testing. Although in Florida public schools, the academic grade is based on academic performance only, the teacher might consider including comments related to improvement in reports to students and parents. This approach is likely to increase motivation and interest by making it possible for all students, regardless of ability, to be reinforced and recognized for effort. Thus, **B** is the correct response.

55. **B.** This question deals with **Competency 3: Instructional Delivery.** Notice that you must select the answer choice that is the *main* reason. Research regarding wait time indicates that the desire to avoid "empty silence," a cultural norm in American culture, can cause a teacher to become uncomfortable and unable to wait at least 3 seconds for students' responses, even though waiting for students to respond communicates positive expectations for them and results in more thoughtful responses, thereby enhancing achievement. Thus, **B** is the correct response. Choices **A, C,** and **D** are possible reasons teachers might find the 3-second wait time difficult to implement, but research indicates that American society's cultural norm against silence is the strongest factor working against sufficient wait time.

56. **B.** This question deals with **Competency 3: Instructional Delivery.** Eliminate **A, C,** and **D** because these approaches will enhance students' ability to think critically. The approach given in **B** is least likely to promote critical thinking because memorizing facts and formulas requires only knowledge-level thinking. Thus, **B** is the correct response.

57. **A.** This question deals with **Competency 4: Assessment.** One important method for teachers to find out what students have learned and to increase their academic achievement is through assigning homework. For students in the elementary and middle school grades, homework should be given to help them develop good study habits, develop positive attitudes toward school, and realize that learning is something to do not only at school but also at home. By the time students reach high school, the purpose of giving homework is primarily to improve their academic achievement. Thus, **A** is the correct response. The other answer choices are not primary reasons for giving homework in high school.

58. **D.** This question relates to **Competency 3: Instructional Delivery.** Eliminate **A** and **C** because the teacher is not making a point with Maria's concern or using it as an example; the teacher is merely calling attention to it. Eliminate **B** because the teacher did not modify Maria's question. The teacher uses Maria's question as a springboard for further class discussion. Thus, **D** is the correct response.

59. **C.** This question relates to **Competency 3: Instructional Delivery.** Computer simulation is a form of learning with computers in which the user may experiment with a simulated situation that strongly resembles reality. In social studies, the software programs create interactive environments that expand historical, geographical, and economic themes and opportunities while leaving the user in control. A major advantage of computer simulation is that, when using it, students are immersed in a reality-based situation that requires them to use problem solving, critical thinking skills, and decision making in a safe environment. Thus, **C** is the correct response. None of the other response options are major advantages of computer simulation—in fact, these outcomes would not be considered advantages associated with using computer simulation, although one or more might be incidental or, in some cases, designed outcomes of particular simulation activities.

60. **A.** This question deals with **Competency 2: Learning Environments.** Eliminate **B** because this answer choice is not consistent with establishing a positive social and emotional atmosphere in the classroom. Eliminate **C** because during the first days of school, effective classroom managers are involved with the whole class. Eliminate **D** because effective classroom managers respond immediately to stop any misbehavior. The first days of school are critical in establishing classroom order. During the first days of school, effective classroom managers spend much of the time teaching students specific classroom procedures. Thus, **A** is the correct response.

61. **C.** This question relates to both **Competency 2: Learning Environments** and **Competency 4: Assessment.** Eliminate **A, B,** and **D** because these responses are inconsistent with research findings that indicate, on average, that children from lower socioeconomic-class backgrounds are less likely to achieve as well in school as children from higher socioeconomic backgrounds (American Psychological Association, 2010). Regarding the difficulties for children from lower socioeconomic-class backgrounds, Slavin (2008) explained that these children (on average) are less likely to be as well prepared when entering school, and their upbringings emphasize behaviors and values different from those (such as individuality and future time orientation) expected of them in schools. Further, researchers have found that middle-class teachers often have low expectations for low-socioeconomic-class students, which is likely to influence those students' perception of their own worth and potential and, in turn, might result in low achievement for these students. Slavin (2008) made the point that teachers should be aware that in contrast to children from mainstream, middle-class backgrounds, children from lower socioeconomic-class backgrounds often are at a disadvantage in the typical school environment; and teachers should make efforts to recognize the potential of these students to achieve. Thus, **C** is the correct response.

62. **C.** This question deals with **Competency 3: Instructional Delivery.** Eliminate **A** because teachers should provide appropriate and nonthreatening opportunities for all students to be involved in the lesson, even those who sometimes are reluctant to do so. Eliminate **B** because an effective method of calling on students is to use a random process, so that all participate and are kept attentive during the teaching act. Eliminate **D** because allowing volunteers to dominate the lesson will establish a classroom climate in which some students will be likely to assume a passive role during classroom discourse; further, the teacher will not be able to adequately assess whether those not participating are learning. Choice **C** is the correct response. The teacher's strategy is limited because students who don't volunteer will miss the opportunity to actively participate in the lesson.

63. **B.** This question relates to **Competency 1: Instructional Design and Planning.** Teachers need to be able to identify activities (such as cooperative learning activities) that support the knowledge, skills, and attitudes to be learned in their subject areas. They should understand principles, procedures, advantages, and limitations associated with those activities. Teachers should closely monitor student work (eliminate **A**), adhere to strict grading policies (eliminate **C**), and determine group size (eliminate **D**) before assigning students to groups. Choice **B** is the correct response. When cooperative learning is used, rewards for students are based on group performance, so students "sink or swim" together interdependently. Research results underscore that such practices have a positive impact on student behavior and academic achievement (Slavin, 2008).

64. **A.** This question deals with **Competency 4: Assessment.** Choice **A** is the correct response. Directly observing the students preparing the solutions and using a checklist to record their implementation of the procedure is a powerful way to find out what the students know and understand about preparing acid solutions. This method is a performance assessment. It is more likely to yield valid and reliable information about the students' learning than the methods given in the other answer choices.

65. **C.** This question relates to **Competency 5: Continuous Improvement.** Eliminate **A** and **D** because these answer choices are not aligned with the question. Eliminate **B** because the teacher did not make her decision in a group setting. Choice **C** is the correct response. The teacher recognizes that she is a member of a learning community and actively seeks out other professionals as resources to support student achievement of desired learning outcomes.

66. **A.** This question relates to **Competency 1: Instructional Design and Planning.** Since this is a third-grade class, you must select the answer choice that is *most* appropriate for the topic and the learners' abilities. Eliminate **B** and **D** because, even though these technologies do provide images, they are not the *most* appropriate way for children at this age to learn how a hot air balloon works. Brain research suggests that watching a slide show or a video is a poor way for children to learn, because the children assume a passive role with these technologies. Eliminate **C** because a spreadsheet would not provide an image of a hot air balloon. The children need to see a hot air balloon to help them understand how one works. Spreadsheets are most useful when mathematical or statistical calculations are needed. Choice **A** is the correct response. In this particular instance, computer simulation software is especially useful because it affords students the opportunity to experiment with the scientific principles that explain how hot air balloons work in a safe environment without the danger from fire.

67. **B.** This question relates to **Competency 7: Teaching English Language Learners (ELLs).** Eliminate **A** and **C** because academic tasks usually have high cognitive demand, not low cognitive demand. Eliminate **D** because academic tasks assigned as independent class work or homework in a regular education classroom typically are presented in a low context. Choice **B** is the correct response. Academic tasks that are assigned as independent class work or homework are typically based upon low context and high cognitive demand.

68. **D.** This question is related to **Competency 5: Continuous Improvement.** Teachers should understand and recognize the levels of authority and important decision-making structures within the state educational system and know how to work within the system to make appropriate decisions regarding students. According to the Florida Department of Education, School-Based Management (SBM) transfers authority for making significant decisions—including decisions about the school budget, hiring of personnel, and the curriculum—from the state and district level to the school level. Eliminate **A** because the Florida Department of Education is at the state level. Eliminate **B** and **C** because the superintendent and the school board are at the district level. Thus, **D** is the correct response.

69. **C.** This question deals with **Competency 2: Learning Environments.** Classroom rules should be stated in positive terms. Choices **A, B,** and **D** are consistent with this guideline. Using negative terms often results in students exhibiting the undesirable behavior that you want them to avoid. Rule 3 should be reworded to say, perhaps, "Walk when indoors." Thus, **C** is the correct response.

70. **B.** This question deals with **Competency 1: Instructional Design and Planning.** The statement in the question is an example of an instructional objective. Instructional objectives are classified as *affective, cognitive,* or *psychomotor.* Eliminate **A** because *affective objectives* involve feelings and dispositions. Eliminate **C** because *psychomotor objectives* involve physical activity on the part of the student. Eliminate **D** because this choice is not a type of lesson objective. Choice **B** is the correct response. *Cognitive objectives* involve thinking capabilities such as solving right triangles using the Pythagorean theorem.

71. **A.** This question deals with **Competency 6: Professional Conduct.** Choice **A** is the correct response. According to the Individuals with Disabilities Education Act (IDEA; formerly PL 94-142), placement in the "least restrictive environment" means placement of the student in the regular classroom to the maximum extent appropriate. Eliminate **B** because when an Exceptional Student Education (ESE) student's placement is in the regular education classroom, the responsibility of providing an appropriate environment for the student should not be placed entirely upon the ESE team. Eliminate **C** because it is not always in the best interest of the disabled student to participate in a regular school environment. By law, the IEP team must place the student in a classroom with his or her peers, unless the student's disability is so severe that education in a regular classroom setting cannot be achieved satisfactorily. Eliminate **D** because, for students who can function in a regular classroom setting, this choice would violate the student's rights under IDEA.

72. **C.** This question deals with **Competency 4: Assessment.** Notice that you must select the teacher's *main* purpose. Eliminate **A** because it is not aligned with the question. Eliminate **B** because these outcomes of peer assessment benefit the teacher, but are not the teacher's main reason for using peer assessment.

Eliminate **D** because the point of peer assessments is to provide feedback at the moment, not for a future time. Choice **C** is the correct response. Peer assessments allow students to critically evaluate others' performances and thereby deepen their own understanding of the concepts.

73. **C.** This question deals with **Competency 2: Learning Environments.** Notice that you must decide what the teacher should do *first*. The teacher should know how to promote student membership in a smoothly functioning learning community and to facilitate a positive social and emotional atmosphere in the classroom. Eliminate **A** and **B** because these actions are punitive approaches to discipline and should be avoided. Eliminate **D** because this action is an inappropriate teacher behavior. When dealing with a discipline problem, the student's dignity must be preserved. In dealing with the student's tendency to be tardy, the teacher should keep in mind that in order to solve the problem, the teacher needs to understand the problem. The student is the most direct and accessible source of information about the problem; so, the *first* step for the teacher to take is to talk with the student to determine the student's awareness of the problem, the meaning that it holds for the student, and how the teacher and student can reach a mutual solution to the problem. Thus, **C** is the correct response.

74. **C.** This question deals with **Competency 7: Teaching English Language Learners (ELLs).** Register is the social level at which language is spoken. The context of the situation determines the socially appropriate register for the speech used. Only **C** provides an opportunity for the ELL students to consciously consider appropriate speech for two different social situations. The activities in **A, B,** and **D** do not involve register. Thus, **C** is the correct response.

75. **A.** This question deals with **Competency 3: Instructional Delivery.** The question stem does not support **B, C,** or **D.** *Negative reinforcement* is the technique of strengthening a behavior in someone by releasing that person from an undesirable situation. There is no indication in the question that the teacher is releasing the students from an undesirable situation (eliminate **B**). *Positive reinforcement* is the technique of strengthening a behavior by giving a desirable reward. There is no indication in the question that the students are receiving rewards from the teacher (eliminate **C**). In *reverse psychology,* a person (say, a teacher) tries to get another person (say, a student) to do something by asking the student to do the opposite of what the teacher really wants the student to do. Nothing in the question indicates that the teacher wants the students to do the opposite of what she is asking them to do (eliminate **D**). Choice **A** is the correct response. The teacher enhances *intrinsic motivation*—that is, self-motivation or motivation from within the student—by allowing students to have choices in their learning and by making what they are doing personally meaningful to them.

76. **A.** This question deals with **Competency 1: Instructional Design and Planning.** Eliminate **B** because, although some evidence suggests that high-ability learners might gain from ability grouping, the approach described would shortchange the other students in the class. However, this does not mean that high-ability students should have to learn and work at the same pace as struggling students; nor does it mean that they should not be given opportunities to work alone or cooperatively with other high achievers and pursue topics to a greater level of cognitive challenge. Eliminate **C** because it disagrees with research indicating that students who are academically challenged benefit from small-group instruction. Eliminate **D** because permanent ability grouping might negatively affect the attitudes, achievement, and opportunities of struggling students. Students assigned to groups should be progress-monitored to make sure their group placement is continually appropriate. Choice **A** best reflects the research-based Problem Solving/Response to Intervention initiative in Florida. Thus, **A** is the correct response.

77. **B.** This question relates to both **Competency 2: Learning Environments** and **Competency 5: Continuous Improvement.** Choice **B** is the correct response. Creating a notebook that the child will take home and bring back is the most appropriate way to update the parents. This approach allows both the teacher and the parents to review and reflect on the notebook's contents at times convenient for them. They can also note comments to each other about entries in the notebook. Eliminate **A** because, while text messages are a quick and easy way to reach parents (assuming the parents have access to texting technology), this format does

not lend itself to review and reflection. Eliminate **C** and **D** because unforeseen events too often disrupt these types of rigid arrangements.

78. **C.** This question deals with **Competency 3: Instructional Delivery.** Eliminate **A** because written praise can be as effective as oral praise. Eliminate **B** because praise does not specify what students need to work on. Eliminate **D** because using the same phrase over and over again from student to student is a type of meaningless praise. Effective praise is positive and specifies the behavior or accomplishment that is worthy of praise. Thus, **C** is the correct response.

79. **A.** This question deals with **Competency 1: Instructional Design and Planning.** Choice **A** is the correct response. By designing a unit around civic ideas and practices, the teacher will be giving students the opportunity to learn about relationships within this central theme of social studies. Eliminate **B** and **C** because these answer choices are not aligned with the question. Eliminate **D** because this answer choice is not supported by the stimulus as clearly as **A.**

80. **B.** This question relates to **Competency 2: Learning Environments.** Eliminate **A, C,** and **D** because these answer choices are not aligned with the question. The teacher knows that providing an opportunity for the students to recognize the problem and suggest solutions is likely to promote student ownership in a smoothly functioning learning community. Thus, **B** is the correct response.

81. **A.** This question deals with **Competency 8: Literacy Strategies.** Eliminate **B** and **C** because neither of these answer choices discusses options that are affected by hearing loss. Both discuss written language only. Eliminate **D** because moderate hearing loss disrupts the connection between spoken and written language, which will inevitably have an effect on the process of learning to read. Choice **A** is the correct response. Due to the hearing loss, the student might have difficulty hearing the sounds of letters and words in early reading instruction, causing him or her to mispronounce these sounds.

82. **B.** This question relates to **Competency 1: Instructional Design and Planning.** Eliminate **C** because research about best practices indicates that drill and practice should be de-emphasized in the science classroom. Eliminate **D** because reliance on the textbook can stifle the students' opportunities to co-construct their learning in a learning-centered environment. You must now choose between **A** and **B.** Use the strategy of rereading the question before making your decision. The question says you must select the "best" way for the teacher to address her concern. Eliminate **A** because although the teacher might do that, it is most important that she make sure that the grade-level benchmarks for the Next Generation Sunshine State Standards—upon which the statewide assessment in science is based—are included in her curriculum. Thus, **B** is the correct response.

83. **D.** This question deals with **Competency 7: Teaching English Language Learners (ELLs).** Eliminate **A** and **B** because these answer choices are not aligned with the question stem. You must now choose between **C** and **D.** Use the strategy of rereading the question before making your decision. The question stem tells you that the teacher is giving the English Language Learners (ELLs) opportunities to use English for a variety of purposes. Choice **D** is more aligned with this idea than **C.** According to Badía (1996), "Acquiring a language requires the opportunity to use it in meaningful context with speakers of the language in a variety of situations" (p. 3). The teacher, who understands that using English across a wide range of language functions will improve proficiency, demonstrates this principle of language acquisition. Thus, **D** is the correct response.

84. **A.** This question relates to both **Competency 1: Instructional Design and Planning** and **Competency 3: Instructional Delivery.** Eliminate **B** because it is off-topic. Whether it is appealing to teachers does not affect student motivation. Eliminate **C** because cooperative learning emphasizes group accomplishments, not competition. Eliminate **D** because effective cooperative learning groups should be heterogeneous in membership. Choice **A** is the correct response. The positive interdependence that is an essential component of cooperative learning is a strong motivational incentive for the students. Students perceive that it is to

their advantage if others students in their group learn and to their disadvantage if other students in their group do poorly. Also, a group incentive structure allows all students, even those who usually perform poorly, an opportunity to succeed, which can be highly motivating for these students.

85. **D.** This question deals with **Competency 3: Instructional Delivery.** Notice that you must select the choice that is *least* desirable. Eliminate **A, B,** and **C** because these answer choices are consistent with effective teaching practices. Choice **D** is a textbook-centered approach. Copying textbook problems and using calculators to obtain the answers would likely discourage active inquiry and result in less risk taking and less higher-level thinking from the students. Thus, **D** is the correct response.

86. **B.** This question deals with **Competency 6: Professional Conduct.** According to the Individuals with Disabilities Education Act (IDEA; formerly PL 94–142), the IEP team must meet at least once every 12 months. Thus, **B** is the correct response. Eliminate **A** and **C** because these timelines are incorrect. Eliminate **D** because the timeline for IEP team meetings is determined by federal law and is not left to the discretion of the school district.

87. **A.** This question deals with **Competency 2: Learning Environments.** Eliminate **B** and **D** because these answer choices are punitive and threatening approaches to discipline and should be avoided, if possible. Eliminate **C** because discipline problems are minimized when the classroom environment is predictable. Allowing the students to negotiate after inappropriate behavior has occurred or being lenient about infractions can send the message that students can "talk their way out of" or "get by with" unacceptable behavior. Usually, when students view a discipline management plan as fair and consistently implemented, mutual respect is the resulting behavior. Thus, **A** is the correct response.

88. **D.** This question is related to both **Competency 5: Continuous Improvement** and **Competency 7: Teaching English Language Learners (ELLs).** The newsletter is the only option that ensures communication with the families will be effective. Eliminate **A, B,** and **C** because these actions do not ensure that the families will understand information that is conveyed through these means. The teacher can contact ESOL personnel on campus for information on how to create a multilingual newsletter. Thus, **D** is the correct response.

89. **A.** This question relates to **Competency 6: Professional Conduct.** Eliminate **C** and **D** because students should be encouraged to use technology. You must now choose between **A** and **B.** Use the strategy of rereading the question before making your decision. The question says you must select the answer choice that is *important* for the teacher to do. Eliminate **B** because although this is something the teacher might do, it is not particularly important. The teacher should help the student understand the importance of citing sources from the Internet. Thus, **A** is the correct response.

90. **C.** This question deals with **Competency 7: Teaching English Language Learners (ELLs).** For purposes of data collection, the State of Florida uses a coding system for English Language Learners (ELLs) and non-ELLs (Florida Department of Education, www.fldoe.org/aala/9596data.asp). The code LY designates a K-12 ELL enrolled in classes specifically designed for ELLs. Thus, **C** is the correct response. Eliminate **A** because the code LF designates a former K-12 ELL who exited the English for Speakers of Other Languages (ESOL) program within the last 2 years. Eliminate **B** because the code LP designates a 4-12 ELL student for whom the reading/writing test is pending. Eliminate **D** because the code LZ designates a former K-12 ELL student who exited the ESOL program more than 2 years ago.

91. **A.** This question deals with the topic of teacher expectations, which falls under **Competency 2: Learning Environments.** Eliminate **B** because research indicates that for young adolescents, peer influence usually overrides adult influence. Eliminate **C** because anxiety in small doses can improve academic achievement, as long as students are not held to an unrealistic level of expectation. Eliminate **D** because teacher expectations affect student self-concept and motivation, which, in turn, affect academic achievement. Teachers need to be aware of the "self-fulfilling prophecy," which predicts that, with time, a student's behavior and achievement will conform more closely to the expectations the teacher has for that student. Thus, **A** is the correct response.

92. **D.** This question deals with **Competency 1: Instructional Design and Planning.** According to research, effective classroom managers are initially involved with the whole class; have clear, specific plans for introducing rules and procedures; use simple, enjoyable tasks; and respond immediately to stop any misbehavior. Therefore, the teacher should not break students into groups on the first day. Choices **A, B,** and **C** are incorrect because these answer choices contain measures a teacher might take when using a cooperative group activity, which this teacher should not be doing on the first day of school. Thus, **D** is the correct response.

93. **D.** This question relates to **Competency 1: Instructional Design and Planning.** Teachers should be aware that behavior management problems are a potential roadblock when within-class ability grouping is used because other students are expected to work independently while the teacher works with a particular group (eliminate **A**). Eliminate **B** because research indicates that fixed within-class ability grouping widens the gap between high-ability and low ability students. Thus, it is unlikely that the high-ability students will become more accepting of the low-ability students. Eliminate **C** because numerous experts contend that inflexible ability grouping is detrimental to low achievers because they often get locked into a low-level curriculum. Thus, **D** is the correct response.

94. **A.** This question relates to both **Competency 1: Instructional Design and Planning** and **Competency 2: Learning Environments.** Eliminate **B** because *negative reinforcement* is the technique of strengthening a behavior by release from an undesirable situation. Eliminate **C** because *positive reinforcement* is the technique of strengthening a behavior by giving a desirable reward. Eliminate **D** because *shaping* involves positive reinforcement of successful completion of steps toward a desired learning goal or behavior. Choice **A** is the correct response. *Extinction* is the technique of withdrawing reinforcers to discourage undesirable behavior in the classroom. The teacher is withdrawing recognition of the student (a reinforcer) to discourage the undesirable behavior of calling out in the classroom.

95. **C.** This question concerns **Competency 6: Professional Conduct.** Choice **C** is the correct response. According to Section 1006.061 (1), F. S., a teacher must immediately report suspected child abuse to the Department of Children and Families (DCF) central abuse hotline at 1-800-96-ABUSE. Investigation of the suspected abuse is the responsibility of the proper authorities. The teacher should not investigate on his or her own by discussing his or her suspicions with the student's parents (eliminate **A**) or the student's friends (eliminate **B**). Eliminate **D** because the teacher should not delay in making the report. Knowing failure to report is a felony of the third degree punishable as provided in Florida law (Section 39.205 (1), F. S.).

96. **D.** This question relates to **Competency 5: Continuous Improvement.** Eliminate **A** because this answer is too broad—it goes beyond the scope of the teacher's actions. Eliminate **B** and **C** because there is insufficient information to support these choices. The city civic center is a community resource available for public use. Thus, **D** is the correct response.

97. **B.** This question deals with **Competency 7: Teaching English Language Learners (ELLs).** Eliminate **A** because *acculturation* is a term describing the process of a cultural group or individual taking on traits from another culture, without loss of cultural identity. Eliminate **C** because the term *affective filter* is used to describe the emotional/psychological barriers that impede learners' language acquisition. Eliminate **D** because *assimilation* is a term describing the process of a cultural group or individual taking on traits of another culture at the expense of cultural identity. Current theories about language development are based on the work of Stephen Krashen. Krashen (in Schütz, 2005) contended that language is best learned in a natural way, through the process of actual communication, without conscious attention to formal rules. This is known as the *acquisition learning hypothesis.* Thus, **B** is the correct response.

98. **C.** This question deals with **Competency 1: Instructional Design and Planning.** Eliminate **A** because this answer choice is not supported by the question. The teacher's unit is focused on drug use, not on society in general. The teacher is aware that students will be more likely to avoid drug use if they are able to think for themselves and make informed, intelligent decisions. Eliminate **B** and **D** because although these might be additional outcomes, most likely the teacher's lessons will be designed to enhance students' independent thinking and decision-making skills. Thus, **C** is the correct response.

99. **B.** This question relates to **Competency 6: Professional Conduct.** According to Florida Statute 1003.32 (7), "Any teacher who removes 25 percent of his or her total class enrollment shall be required to complete professional development to improve classroom management skills." Thus, **B** is the correct response. The percents in the other answer choices are incorrect.

100. **C.** This question relates both to **Competency 1: Instructional Design and Planning** and **Competency 3: Instructional Delivery.** Eliminate **A, B,** and **D** because these choices disagree with research findings. Teachers who are aware of the influence of peers on students' social and intellectual development can take advantage of this factor by using peer tutoring. Research investigating the effects of peer tutoring on student achievement has shown that, in general, the achievement of both tutors and tutees increases. Thus, **C** is the correct response.

101. **D.** This question deals with working with parents, which falls under **Competency 5: Continuous Improvement.** Successful parent-teacher conferences can be the key that enhances a student's growth and promotes learning. Eliminate **A** and **C** because teachers should avoid diagnosing students to parents. Eliminate **B** because the teacher should not discuss other students' performance with Marcus's father. Choice **D** is the correct response. The teacher should explain her grading policy and show samples of Marcus's incomplete work. The teacher needs to emphasize that she expects students to be responsible and turn in work that is complete.

102. **C.** This question deals with **Competency 4: Assessment.** Of the assessment tools given in the answer choices, only portfolio assessment is an informal measure. Thus, **C** is the correct response.

103. **B.** This question deals with motivation, which falls under **Competency 3: Instructional Delivery.** The teacher is using extrinsic motivation by offering a tangible reward. Thus, **B** is the correct response. Eliminate **A** and **C** because in contingency and group reward programs, rewards for the whole class (or group) are contingent on everyone's effort and participation. Eliminate **D** because intrinsic rewards (for example, personal satisfaction) occur within an individual. It should be noted that authorities disagree about the use of rewards as a motivational strategy. Some are concerned that students' interest in gathering rewards may sabotage genuine interest in the subject area. Also, teachers find it difficult to determine rewards that are appropriate and, at the same time, desirable by students. A practice guide on Response to Intervention (RtI) for mathematics prepared by the What Works Clearinghouse suggested "As students learn and succeed more often in mathematics, interventionists can gradually fade the use of rewards because student success will become an intrinsic reward" (Gersten et al., 2009, p. 46).

104. **D.** This question deals with **Competency 7: Teaching English Language Learners (ELLs).** Eliminate **A, B,** and **C** because these features would require a level of reading ability that is probably beyond that of most students in the early production stage. Content area materials that are most effective for ELLs, especially those who are in the early production stage of English language acquisition, use nonlinguistic aids, such as charts, maps, illustrations, drawings, and pictures. It would be most critical for the software program to have extensive visual representations and other nonlinguistic graphic support to be effective for use by the teacher's ELLs. Thus, **D** is the correct response.

105. **D.** This question deals with the topic of instructional methods, which falls under **Competency 3: Instructional Delivery.** Eliminate **A** because most authorities agree that lecturing is the least effective instructional strategy for all prekindergarten through grade-12 classrooms. Further, it is an inappropriate

instructional strategy for use with elementary school students, so eliminate **B** and **C**. Lecturing should be avoided in elementary school. Thus, **D** is the correct response.

106. **A.** This question relates to both **Competency 2: Learning Environments** and **Competency 3: Instructional Delivery.** Eliminate **B** because punitive-based measures fail to preserve the dignity of the student, which is an essential component of effective classroom management. The likely reason for the students' lack of interest is the long engagement in repetitive and boring tasks. Generally, students pay closer attention and become more involved when the topics relate directly to their experiences and interests. The teacher should engage the students in activities related to their interests and experiences. Thus, **A** is the correct response. Eliminate **C** and **D** because although these answer choices are measures that the teacher might take, they would not be as effective as that given in **A.**

107. **D.** This question relates to **Competency 5: Continuous Improvement.** The SAC is an advisory group composed (by state law) of the principal, teachers, educational support staff, parents, and business and other community members. The SAC's primary duties are to assist in the preparation and evaluation of the school improvement plan (SIP) and to assist in the preparation of the school's annual budget. Thus, **D** is the correct response. None of the other answer choices accurately describes the duties of the SAC.

108. **B.** This question deals with **Competency 1: Instructional Design and Planning** and **Competency 7: English Language Learners (ELLs).** Appreciation of another's culture in a child of this age can best be approached by showing similarities and differences with the child's familiar cultural forms. Eliminate **A** because this activity would be limited to physical characteristics of countries, and besides, it focuses on differences. Eliminate **C** because the countries selected might not represent any of the cultural groups in the class. Eliminate **D** because second-graders would have difficulty with this activity. Choice **B** is the correct response. Having students participate in a class activity in which they discover cultural similarities and differences in their own classroom could readily be expanded into a discussion about the diversity of American culture. By seeing that they have things in common, the students will be less suspicious of each other's cultures, and by identifying features that are unique, they will still be able to retain their cultural identities. This activity would be the most developmentally appropriate and meaningful of all the described activities.

109. **B.** This question relates to **Competency 2: Learning Environments.** Eliminate **A** and **D,** because generally children at this age are too young to have the cognitive abilities or experiences to form strong opinions on issues. They rely more on the opinions of their family members **(B),** such as parents or older siblings, in forming their own attitudes. As they mature into young adolescents, the attitudes of their peers will begin to exert more influence, but not at this stage of their development (eliminate **C**). Thus, **B** is the correct response.

110. **B.** This question deals with **Competency 1: Instructional Design and Planning** and **Competency 3: Instructional Delivery.** Eliminate **A** because young children benefit from working in collaboration with others. Eliminate **C** because centers should involve "hands-on" activities, not worksheets (a poor practice). Eliminate **D** because learning centers should be an integral part of the early childhood classroom. When students are working in centers, they should not have to get up to go get materials. All materials needed should be contained within the center. Thus, **B** is the correct response.

111. **B.** This question deals with **Competency 1: Instructional Design and Planning.** The teacher's students are sixth-graders, so most of them are between 11 and 12 years old. Eliminate **A, C,** and **D** because these cognitive abilities are normally acquired during earlier stages of cognitive development. Choice **B** is the correct response. Most sixth-graders are in the process of developing the ability to think hypothetically about abstract concepts. They are able to handle contrary-to-fact propositions and can develop and test hypotheses.

112. B. This question relates to **Competency 5: Continuous Improvement.** Eliminate **A** and **C** because these answer choices are not aligned with the question. You must now choose between **B** and **D.** Use the strategy of rereading the question before making your decision. The question is about interdisciplinary teams. Choice **B** is more aligned with the role of interdisciplinary teams than is **D.** Teachers on an interdisciplinary team recognize that they are members of a learning community and know how to work effectively with each other to promote student learning. By implementing the use of interdisciplinary teams that meet regularly to discuss concerns and plan together, a school is affording the teachers an opportunity to learn from each other and thereby improve the educational experiences of students. Thus, **B** is the correct response.

113. B. This question deals with **Competency 7: English Language Learners (ELLs).** Eliminate **A** because cooperative groups should be "composed of students of different ethnic backgrounds and at diverse cognitive and linguistic levels, who challenge and encourage each other" (Badía, 1996, p. 4). Eliminate **C** because most ELLs, even those in the preproduction stage of English language acquisition, can do labeling and drawing activities without assistance. Eliminate **D** because ELLs should be encouraged to interact with their non–ELL classmates during activities designed to promote social communication skills. Choice **B** is the correct response. When a recently arrived student needs an orientation to classroom rules and procedures, assigning a same-language classroom "buddy" who can assist the new student with classroom orientation is a good idea.

114. A. This question relates to **Competency 2: Learning Environments.** The students are seventh-graders, so most of them are between 12 and 13 years old. Choice **A** is the correct response. A major source of anxiety for adolescents this age is fear of rejection by peers, because peer relations are so important. By comparison, displeasing authority figures **(B)**, failing to achieve academically **(C)**, and failing to learn cultural norms **(D)** are less important sources of anxiety for most adolescents.

115. A. This question deals with **Competency 1: Instructional Design and Planning.** Eliminate **B** and **D** because these answer choices are not supported by the question. The teacher did not involve the students when transforming the classroom into a pretend ocean. Eliminate **C** because this answer choice is not aligned with the question. Choice **A** is the correct response. When planning how to begin the unit, the teacher is likely to have been aware that providing the children with a concrete experience would make their study of the ocean more meaningful.

116. C. This question relates to **Competency 5: Continuous Improvement.** Eliminate **A, B,** and **D** because these answer choices are not aligned with the question. Consulting the Exceptional Student Education (ESE) teacher is most in accord with the principle that teachers should work cooperatively with colleagues to meet students' education needs. Thus, **C** is the correct response.

117. A. Essentially, this question deals with the psychosocial development of young children, which falls under **Competency 2: Learning Environments.** The teacher's response reflects her knowledge and consideration of students' developmental processes, so **A** is the correct response. The other answer choices are not aligned with the question.

118. C. This question deals with **Competency 7: Teaching English Language Learners (ELLs).** Eliminate **A, B,** and **D** because the vocabulary and grammar in these sentences would be understandable to students who have been determined through the aural/oral testing to be fully English proficient. The sentence in **C** contains an idiom "put up with," which means "tolerate." An idiom is an expression used by speakers of a language that usually doesn't make sense if taken literally. ELLs, even those who test as fully English proficient, have difficulty with idioms because the meaning cannot be determined simply by translating the words. Thus, **C** is the correct response.

119. **A.** This question relates to **Competency 6: Professional Conduct.** Choice **A** is the correct response. According to the Individuals with Disabilities Education Act (IDEA; formerly PL 94–142) and Florida law, the regular education teacher on the Individual Educational Plan (IEP) team must participate as a full member of the team (eliminate **D**), including assisting in determining interventions and strategies for the student. Eliminate **B** and **C** because the regular education teacher on the IEP team does not assume these responsibilities.

120. **B.** This question deals with **Competency 1: Instructional Design and Planning.** Eliminate **A** because this choice is a discipline management strategy, not a teaching approach. The teacher's classroom interactions reflect a learner-centered approach. Eliminate **C** and **D** because these answer choices are teacher-centered approaches. Choice **B** is the correct response. The teacher's approach to teaching is consistent with constructivism. *Constructivism* is a learner-centered approach to teaching that emphasizes teaching for understanding predicated on the concept that students construct knowledge for themselves based on what they already know and by interactions with their environment.

Practice Test 2

Answer Sheet for Practice Test 2

1 Ⓐ Ⓑ Ⓒ Ⓓ	41 Ⓐ Ⓑ Ⓒ Ⓓ	81 Ⓐ Ⓑ Ⓒ Ⓓ
2 Ⓐ Ⓑ Ⓒ Ⓓ	42 Ⓐ Ⓑ Ⓒ Ⓓ	82 Ⓐ Ⓑ Ⓒ Ⓓ
3 Ⓐ Ⓑ Ⓒ Ⓓ	43 Ⓐ Ⓑ Ⓒ Ⓓ	83 Ⓐ Ⓑ Ⓒ Ⓓ
4 Ⓐ Ⓑ Ⓒ Ⓓ	44 Ⓐ Ⓑ Ⓒ Ⓓ	84 Ⓐ Ⓑ Ⓒ Ⓓ
5 Ⓐ Ⓑ Ⓒ Ⓓ	45 Ⓐ Ⓑ Ⓒ Ⓓ	85 Ⓐ Ⓑ Ⓒ Ⓓ
6 Ⓐ Ⓑ Ⓒ Ⓓ	46 Ⓐ Ⓑ Ⓒ Ⓓ	86 Ⓐ Ⓑ Ⓒ Ⓓ
7 Ⓐ Ⓑ Ⓒ Ⓓ	47 Ⓐ Ⓑ Ⓒ Ⓓ	87 Ⓐ Ⓑ Ⓒ Ⓓ
8 Ⓐ Ⓑ Ⓒ Ⓓ	48 Ⓐ Ⓑ Ⓒ Ⓓ	88 Ⓐ Ⓑ Ⓒ Ⓓ
9 Ⓐ Ⓑ Ⓒ Ⓓ	49 Ⓐ Ⓑ Ⓒ Ⓓ	89 Ⓐ Ⓑ Ⓒ Ⓓ
10 Ⓐ Ⓑ Ⓒ Ⓓ	50 Ⓐ Ⓑ Ⓒ Ⓓ	90 Ⓐ Ⓑ Ⓒ Ⓓ
11 Ⓐ Ⓑ Ⓒ Ⓓ	51 Ⓐ Ⓑ Ⓒ Ⓓ	91 Ⓐ Ⓑ Ⓒ Ⓓ
12 Ⓐ Ⓑ Ⓒ Ⓓ	52 Ⓐ Ⓑ Ⓒ Ⓓ	92 Ⓐ Ⓑ Ⓒ Ⓓ
13 Ⓐ Ⓑ Ⓒ Ⓓ	53 Ⓐ Ⓑ Ⓒ Ⓓ	93 Ⓐ Ⓑ Ⓒ Ⓓ
14 Ⓐ Ⓑ Ⓒ Ⓓ	54 Ⓐ Ⓑ Ⓒ Ⓓ	94 Ⓐ Ⓑ Ⓒ Ⓓ
15 Ⓐ Ⓑ Ⓒ Ⓓ	55 Ⓐ Ⓑ Ⓒ Ⓓ	95 Ⓐ Ⓑ Ⓒ Ⓓ
16 Ⓐ Ⓑ Ⓒ Ⓓ	56 Ⓐ Ⓑ Ⓒ Ⓓ	96 Ⓐ Ⓑ Ⓒ Ⓓ
17 Ⓐ Ⓑ Ⓒ Ⓓ	57 Ⓐ Ⓑ Ⓒ Ⓓ	97 Ⓐ Ⓑ Ⓒ Ⓓ
18 Ⓐ Ⓑ Ⓒ Ⓓ	58 Ⓐ Ⓑ Ⓒ Ⓓ	98 Ⓐ Ⓑ Ⓒ Ⓓ
19 Ⓐ Ⓑ Ⓒ Ⓓ	59 Ⓐ Ⓑ Ⓒ Ⓓ	99 Ⓐ Ⓑ Ⓒ Ⓓ
20 Ⓐ Ⓑ Ⓒ Ⓓ	60 Ⓐ Ⓑ Ⓒ Ⓓ	100 Ⓐ Ⓑ Ⓒ Ⓓ
21 Ⓐ Ⓑ Ⓒ Ⓓ	61 Ⓐ Ⓑ Ⓒ Ⓓ	101 Ⓐ Ⓑ Ⓒ Ⓓ
22 Ⓐ Ⓑ Ⓒ Ⓓ	62 Ⓐ Ⓑ Ⓒ Ⓓ	102 Ⓐ Ⓑ Ⓒ Ⓓ
23 Ⓐ Ⓑ Ⓒ Ⓓ	63 Ⓐ Ⓑ Ⓒ Ⓓ	103 Ⓐ Ⓑ Ⓒ Ⓓ
24 Ⓐ Ⓑ Ⓒ Ⓓ	64 Ⓐ Ⓑ Ⓒ Ⓓ	104 Ⓐ Ⓑ Ⓒ Ⓓ
25 Ⓐ Ⓑ Ⓒ Ⓓ	65 Ⓐ Ⓑ Ⓒ Ⓓ	105 Ⓐ Ⓑ Ⓒ Ⓓ
26 Ⓐ Ⓑ Ⓒ Ⓓ	66 Ⓐ Ⓑ Ⓒ Ⓓ	106 Ⓐ Ⓑ Ⓒ Ⓓ
27 Ⓐ Ⓑ Ⓒ Ⓓ	67 Ⓐ Ⓑ Ⓒ Ⓓ	107 Ⓐ Ⓑ Ⓒ Ⓓ
28 Ⓐ Ⓑ Ⓒ Ⓓ	68 Ⓐ Ⓑ Ⓒ Ⓓ	108 Ⓐ Ⓑ Ⓒ Ⓓ
29 Ⓐ Ⓑ Ⓒ Ⓓ	69 Ⓐ Ⓑ Ⓒ Ⓓ	109 Ⓐ Ⓑ Ⓒ Ⓓ
30 Ⓐ Ⓑ Ⓒ Ⓓ	70 Ⓐ Ⓑ Ⓒ Ⓓ	110 Ⓐ Ⓑ Ⓒ Ⓓ
31 Ⓐ Ⓑ Ⓒ Ⓓ	71 Ⓐ Ⓑ Ⓒ Ⓓ	111 Ⓐ Ⓑ Ⓒ Ⓓ
32 Ⓐ Ⓑ Ⓒ Ⓓ	72 Ⓐ Ⓑ Ⓒ Ⓓ	112 Ⓐ Ⓑ Ⓒ Ⓓ
33 Ⓐ Ⓑ Ⓒ Ⓓ	73 Ⓐ Ⓑ Ⓒ Ⓓ	113 Ⓐ Ⓑ Ⓒ Ⓓ
34 Ⓐ Ⓑ Ⓒ Ⓓ	74 Ⓐ Ⓑ Ⓒ Ⓓ	114 Ⓐ Ⓑ Ⓒ Ⓓ
35 Ⓐ Ⓑ Ⓒ Ⓓ	75 Ⓐ Ⓑ Ⓒ Ⓓ	115 Ⓐ Ⓑ Ⓒ Ⓓ
36 Ⓐ Ⓑ Ⓒ Ⓓ	76 Ⓐ Ⓑ Ⓒ Ⓓ	116 Ⓐ Ⓑ Ⓒ Ⓓ
37 Ⓐ Ⓑ Ⓒ Ⓓ	77 Ⓐ Ⓑ Ⓒ Ⓓ	117 Ⓐ Ⓑ Ⓒ Ⓓ
38 Ⓐ Ⓑ Ⓒ Ⓓ	78 Ⓐ Ⓑ Ⓒ Ⓓ	118 Ⓐ Ⓑ Ⓒ Ⓓ
39 Ⓐ Ⓑ Ⓒ Ⓓ	79 Ⓐ Ⓑ Ⓒ Ⓓ	119 Ⓐ Ⓑ Ⓒ Ⓓ
40 Ⓐ Ⓑ Ⓒ Ⓓ	80 Ⓐ Ⓑ Ⓒ Ⓓ	120 Ⓐ Ⓑ Ⓒ Ⓓ

CUT HERE

Practice Test 2

2½ Hours
120 Questions

Directions: Read each item and select the best response.

1. Which of the following measures is a type of summative assessment?

   A. an End-of-Course assessment
   B. a homework assignment
   C. a learning styles inventory
   D. a whole-class question and answer session

2. Students in a social studies class are having a whole-class discussion about the preservation of historical landmarks in their community. What are students likely to learn from the class discussion?

   A. Historical landmarks have little economic value.
   B. Accurate information is critical for effective communication.
   C. Community problems can be solved through thoughtful discussion.
   D. Working with others can lead to better and quicker solutions to problems.

3. A new teacher is using innovative instructional methods in his English class. To best ensure a supportive attitude from the principal, the teacher should

   A. invite the principal to visit his class to observe his teaching methods and their effects.
   B. present the principal with copies of scientifically based research that supports the teacher's instructional methods.
   C. send weekly reports to the principal to keep the principal apprised of the progress of the teacher's students.
   D. organize parents to send e-mails to the principal supporting the teacher's instructional methods.

4. After a science experiment, a high school teacher asks students to respond to the following two prompts:

   > 1. Justify the results of your experiment.
   > 2. Formulate a theory based on the results of your experiment.

   The major benefit to students from this assignment is that it

   A. helps them recall facts and basic concepts.
   B. allows them to apply their learning in a new context.
   C. provides a means for the teacher to assess their learning.
   D. promotes their critical and creative thinking skills.

5. When planning learning experiences for diverse students, which of the following is an important guideline for teachers to keep in mind?

   A. Teachers should avoid incorporating the cultural backgrounds of their students into the curriculum.
   B. Teachers should recognize that, within a particular cultural group, individual variation is to be expected.
   C. Students from different cultural backgrounds will share few common educational interests and aspirations.
   D. Students' cultural backgrounds have little impact on how students construct knowledge or interact in the classroom.

GO ON TO THE NEXT PAGE

6. With regard to administration of the mandatory statewide assessments, which of the following actions by a teacher would be considered unethical?

A. to present lessons in advance that focus on the Next Generation Sunshine State Standards

B. to use a seating chart to plan and record student seat assignments in the testing room

C. to remain in the testing room when the students are taking the assessment

D. to question students on test content or test items after the days set aside for state testing have passed

7. To become successful readers, which of the following skills is most important for students to have upon entering first grade?

A. the ability to recognize letters by name

B. the ability to recite the alphabet

C. the ability to recognize short, high-frequency sight words

D. the ability to use picture clues to aid in decoding text

8. A student who scores at the 80th percentile on a standardized achievement test has

A. scored the same as or better than 80 percent of a norm group.

B. scored better than 20 percent of a norm group.

C. correctly answered 80 percent of the test questions.

D. correctly answered 20 percent of the test questions.

9. As students in a social studies class watch a video about the importance of recycling, the teacher periodically stops the video and poses questions about the ideas presented. This strategy is most probably motivated by the teacher's understanding that

A. teachers should demonstrate and model the use of higher-order thinking skills.

B. teachers' efforts to maintain and reinforce student involvement correlate with students' cognitive engagement.

C. students stay on task when they are aware that they are being monitored.

D. students need structured, well-managed environments.

10. The most appropriate way for a teacher to share an innovative instructional strategy with school colleagues is to

A. send an e-mail to all teachers describing the strategy and offering to demonstrate it in their classrooms.

B. speak with the principal about demonstrating the strategy as part of a workshop for all interested teachers.

C. speak with the superintendent about ways the strategy could be implemented throughout the school district.

D. explain the strategy at the next school board meeting.

11. Which of the following is most likely to promote the creative thinking skills of high school students?

A. in algebra, recognizing an equivalent representation of a numerical quantity

B. in economics, locating details on a graph, chart, or diagram

C. in science, predicting the logical next step

D. in English, writing an original short story

12. A student who exhibits a cognitive style that is right-brain dominant is likely to learn best through instruction based on

   A. presentation of content in small, step-by-step increments.

   B. detailed verbal explanations and instructions.

   C. visual and kinesthetic global activities.

   D. objective, short-answer questioning.

13. During a technology workshop, Mr. Black, the art teacher, tells the workshop presenter that he has been using a popular computer graphics software package in his classes and that his students thoroughly enjoy it. However, Mr. Black goes on to say that he has discovered that the school does not own any licensed copies of the software. What action, if any, should Mr. Black take?

   A. Immediately remove all copies of the software from the computers in the classroom.

   B. Continue to use the software, but contact the manufacturer about obtaining licensed copies.

   C. Continue to use the software, but contact the district technology specialist and discuss the problem.

   D. Continue to use the software and say nothing, because educators are allowed to use software without obtaining licensed copies.

14. Which of the following strategies should a fourth-grade teacher use to promote students' comprehension of expository text?

   A. giving them explicit instruction in identifying and using the various structures found in expository text

   B. routinely assigning them challenging expository text to read that requires consulting resource materials

   C. encouraging them to memorize definitions of words they encounter frequently in expository text

   D. rewarding them (for example, with free time) for reading unassigned expository text on their own

15. Which of the following types of assessment includes a variety of samples of a student's work, collected over time, that shows the student's growth and development?

   A. checklist
   B. daily quizzes
   C. portfolio
   D. running record

16. After students finish reading *Charlotte's Web,* the teacher asks, "Do you think Fern loved Wilbur?" A student replies, "Of course!" The teacher then says, "Tell us how you know that Fern loved Wilbur."

What communication technique is the teacher using in her last statement?

   A. paraphrasing
   B. probing
   C. redirecting
   D. summarizing

17. Mr. James, a new high school American history teacher, has asked Ms. Field, a mentor teacher, to observe a session of his history class because he has had difficulty motivating students to stay on task during cooperative learning activities. Mr. James can most effectively help Ms. Field prepare for the classroom observation by providing her with a

   A. seating chart that indicates the students who tend to be "ringleaders" of the off-task behavior.

   B. lesson plan for the class session that she will be observing.

   C. written detailed description of the problems he is having with students.

   D. list of all students' names along with designation of their current grades in the class.

GO ON TO THE NEXT PAGE

18. A language arts teacher attended a summer workshop on critical thinking. The teacher plans to incorporate ideas from the workshop into her lessons. Which of the following language arts tasks would best elicit students' critical thinking skills?

    A. using a dictionary to find the meaning of words

    B. identifying and summarizing the major events in a narrative

    C. evaluating the effectiveness of a written response according to audience and purpose

    D. identifying standard English grammatical structures in a written work

19. A teacher has a class composed of students from varied cultural backgrounds. DVDs, CDs, magazines, and books related to students' home cultures would be most effectively used as resources for the purpose of

    A. integrating cultural content into content area instruction.

    B. matching students according to similar cultural communication styles.

    C. determining students' personal interests related to their home cultures.

    D. improving communication with the parents of students.

20. A teacher sees another faculty member commit a violation of Florida education rules. The teacher must

    A. report the alleged misconduct to appropriate authorities.

    B. discuss the alleged misconduct with the other faculty member.

    C. wait a reasonable period to see if the other faculty member self-reports the misconduct.

    D. keep quiet about the matter because it would be unethical to tell anyone about the alleged misconduct.

21. Which of the following strategies is most effective for promoting students' content area vocabulary development?

    A. providing ongoing, corrective feedback regarding pronunciation during reading in the content area

    B. giving frequent, short quizzes over content area vocabulary

    C. having students look up the definitions of a set of assigned words related to the content area

    D. semantically grouping new vocabulary words in the content area with familiar words that have similar meaning

22. On which of the following test question types does guessing have the most effect?

    A. constructed response

    B. fill in the blank

    C. multiple choice

    D. true-false

23. When leading class discussions teachers should

    A. ask more questions of students sitting in the back of the room to make sure they are involved in the discussion.

    B. mainly use questions that elicit specific, concrete information about the topic of discussion.

    C. establish positive interactions that support students' responses.

    D. provide the correct answer if no one responds immediately.

24. A new high school English teacher joins the Florida Council of Teachers of English. Which of the following is the most significant benefit of joining a professional organization in one's content field?

    A. increased opportunities to stay abreast of current developments in the field.

    B. increased opportunities to obtain grants for school-based projects in the field.

    C. expanded access to experienced mentors in the field.

    D. expanded access to quality lesson plans and other instructional resources in the field.

25. Students in a third-grade class are working in groups doing an experiment in which they drop a ball from various heights and measure the greatest height the ball reached when it bounced. Before the experiment begins, the teacher asks the students to formulate a hypothesis about what they expect to happen. After they have collected all their data, the students create a graph that shows maximum height reached when the ball was dropped from different heights. Afterward, which of the following prompts regarding the experiment would be most effective for assessing students' higher order thinking skills?

  A. Did you always measure the bounce to either the top or the bottom of the ball?

  B. Did the ball bounce more times when it was dropped from a higher height?

  C. Write a justification for the information shown in your graph.

  D. Without referring to the instructions provided to you, write a set of step-by-step procedures that another person could follow to perform the experiment.

26. During a science unit on simple machines, a girl in the class complains to the teacher, "This is boy stuff. Why do I have to do it?" Several of the other girls in the class nod in agreement. The teacher ponders how best to deal with this incident. She should *first*

  A. check herself to make sure she is not modeling any gender stereotyping.

  B. lead a class discussion about science-related career opportunities.

  C. check classroom materials to make sure they do not reflect gender stereotyping.

  D. attend a workshop about promoting gender equity.

27. A school district permits teachers to borrow computers from their schools to take home. According to the Code of Ethics and Principles of Professional Conduct for the Education Profession in Florida, if a teacher in the district borrows a computer from the school, it would be unethical for the teacher to

  A. keep the computer for more than one business day.

  B. fail to delete his or her files before returning the computer.

  C. fail to use the computer for authorized school business only.

  D. fail to repair any damage that might occur to the computer when it is in his or her home.

28. A first-grade teacher wants to help students develop reading comprehension as they begin to read. To achieve this goal, the teacher plans to explicitly teach and model reading comprehension skills. In general, which of the following skills would be most appropriate for beginning instruction in reading comprehension skills?

  A. making inferences

  B. making predictions

  C. recalling details

  D. summarizing

29. Which of the following assessment methods is most likely to yield valid information about what students know and understand?

  A. informal observation with a checklist

  B. student self-assessment

  C. peer assessment

  D. student journaling

GO ON TO THE NEXT PAGE

30. A teacher begins a language arts class by saying, "Today, your 10-minute writing activity is on the subject of school uniforms. Please begin writing in your journals, and stop when I give the signal." Some of the students begin the writing assignment, but most of the students have puzzled expressions and are not writing. The teacher addresses the class, "Do you have a question about the assignment?" One student responds, "What do you want us to write? We don't understand."

Which of the following tenets would have been most helpful for the teacher to consider when crafting the writing assignment?

A. Effective teachers communicate instructional tasks clearly to students.

B. Effective teachers know how to shape the classroom into a community of learners engaged in active inquiry.

C. Effective teachers use a variety of modes and tools of communication.

D. Effective teachers appreciate the cultural dimensions of communication.

31. A new high school teacher wants to learn how to more effectively lead whole-group class discussions. Which of the following measures probably would most help the teacher in improving his or her practice?

A. Ask colleagues for their opinions on whether holding whole-group class discussions is a worthwhile instructional activity.

B. Search the Internet for guidelines on how to effectively lead whole-group discussions and practice the advice provided.

C. Study articles in professional journals on how to effectively lead whole-group discussions.

D. Arrange to observe a colleague who effectively uses whole-group discussions.

32. Which of the following science tasks would best elicit students' critical thinking skills?

A. solving a problem after choosing an appropriate formula

B. retrieving information from a chart, table, diagram, or graph

C. generalizing or drawing conclusions

D. recognizing examples and nonexamples of concepts

33. Middle school students who are at risk of academic failure benefit most when

A. teachers help the students understand the structure and organization of school at the middle level.

B. the students are given opportunities to experience academic success on assignments they perceive as meaningful and challenging.

C. the students are routinely grouped together to do class assignments to avoid being put in competition with their higher-achieving peers.

D. teachers minimize the use of any form of assessment to avoid causing stress due to low achievement.

34. Which of the following behaviors by a teacher most likely would be considered a violation of the Code of Ethics and Principles of Professional Conduct for the Education Profession in Florida?

A. In a private conference with a student, the teacher points out that the student is not performing as well academically as the other students in the class.

B. In front of a student's classmates, a teacher makes disparaging comments about the student's answer to a question from the teacher.

C. A teacher offers extra points for correcting tests, which tends to benefit lower-achieving students more than higher-achieving students.

D. A teacher has a disruptive student removed from the classroom and asks the principal not to return the disruptive student to the classroom.

35. Structural analysis is an especially appropriate strategy for determining the meaning of which of the following words?

A. explain

B. pressure

C. umbrella

D. unbelievable

36. A social studies teacher has planned a thematic unit called "Saving the Planet." The teacher begins the unit with the topic of natural resources. To determine students' prior knowledge about natural resources, the best graphic organizer for the teacher to use is a

    A.   decision tree.
    B.   flowchart.
    C.   story tree.
    D.   web.

37. In general, a teacher's expectations would tend to have the LEAST effect on a middle school student's

    A.   academic performance.
    B.   behavior.
    C.   peer relations.
    D.   self-concept.

38. A teacher who holds a valid Florida professional certificate wishes to add a subject coverage. The teacher most probably can obtain accurate information about adding a subject coverage to his or her professional certificate by contacting

    A.   the State Board of Education.
    B.   a member of the district school board.
    C.   the district superintendent.
    D.   his or her principal.

39. In giving students problems in which they must generalize an algebraic or geometric pattern, a mathematics teacher is most likely promoting students' use of

    A.   conditional reasoning.
    B.   deductive reasoning.
    C.   inductive reasoning.
    D.   syllogistic reasoning.

40. As a culminating activity for a unit on nutrition, a high school interdisciplinary team plans to have an informal social event at school for their classes. Which of the following is most likely to occur when the social event takes place?

    A.   Field-independent learners and field-dependent learners will be equally active during the event.
    B.   Field-independent learners will tend to be more passive than field-dependent learners during the event.
    C.   Field-dependent learners will tend to be more passive than field-independent learners during the event.
    D.   Both field-independent learners and field-dependent learners will be passive during the event.

41. It is inappropriate for a teacher to share information about a minor student without written permission from the student's parent when a

    A.   school counselor who has been seeing the student wants to examine the educational records kept by the teacher on the student.
    B.   colleague who is conducting a research project wants to use non-personally-identifiable information from the educational records kept by the teacher on the student.
    C.   colleague who has the student in another class wants to look at the educational records kept by the teacher on the student.
    D.   noncustodial parent wants to review the educational records kept by the teacher on the student.

GO ON TO THE NEXT PAGE

42. Current thinking regarding literacy instruction calls for a balanced and comprehensive approach to early reading instruction that includes

    A. intense instruction in phonics followed by literature-based, integrated language arts instruction.

    B. explicit, systematic phonics instruction in the context of meaningful connected reading of informative, engaging text.

    C. explicit, systematic phonics instruction alternated with a basal reading program that includes grade-level reading materials for students.

    D. implicit acquisition of word recognition skills in the context of literature-based, integrated language arts instruction.

43. A high school economics teacher has students work as members of an investment team in a stock market simulation activity over a period of weeks. At the end of the simulation activity, each team must summarize its activities and present a report to the entire class. After the reports have been presented, the teacher asks the students to write a journal entry in which they assess the effectiveness of their investment team's decision making during the stock market simulation. Which of the following is a primary benefit of having the students reflect on the effectiveness of their team's decision making?

    A. It will promote a healthy, competitive spirit among the students.

    B. It will allow the teacher to reward those students who exhibited leadership skills.

    C. It will provide a means for the teacher to assess the students' ability to apply decision-making skills.

    D. It will promote self-assessment on the part of the students.

44. A teacher has observed that, during whole-class discussions, English Language Learners (ELLs) in her classroom rarely volunteer comments. In leading class discussions, it is important the teacher is aware that

    A. asking the ELLs less challenging questions they can get right will make them more willing to participate in future discussions.

    B. ELLs who are more willing to speak in class are usually more proficient language users than those who are reluctant to speak.

    C. cultural factors as well as language ability affect the extent to which ELLs speak out in class.

    D. probing for further explanation or clarification when ELLs give responses should be avoided, so that they will not be embarrassed in front of their peers.

45. To encourage students to think critically and consider a variety of ideas during a class discussion, a teacher should ask

    A. affective domain questions.

    B. convergent questions.

    C. divergent questions.

    D. who, what, where, and when questions.

46. A teacher who has academically gifted students in the class can best prepare to work with these students by keeping in mind they need

    A. opportunities for independent learning that encourage them to apply creative and critical thinking.

    B. time to work independently when their peers are working in small groups.

    C. structured activities that reinforce basic skills more often than their peers.

    D. external rewards, because they often lack intrinsic motivation to learn.

47. A fifth-grade student has a grade equivalent score of 7.6 on a standardized reading test. The student's grade equivalent score indicates that the student

- **A.** is ready for seventh-grade reading material.
- **B.** is in the top 7.6 percent of students who took the test.
- **C.** did as well on the test as an average seventh-grader in the sixth month of the school year would do on a standardized seventh-grade reading test.
- **D.** did as well on the test as an average seventh-grader in the sixth month of the school year would do on the same standardized reading test that the fifth-grade student took.

48. During an informal conversation, a second-grade English Language Learner (ELL) tells his teacher, "My *madre*—I mean, my mother—she work on grocery store." Which of the following would be the most appropriate teacher feedback in response to the student's statement?

- **A.** "Oh, so the Spanish word for 'mother' is *madre?* That's good to know."
- **B.** "What should you do to the verb *work* when it comes after the word *she?*"
- **C.** "Your mother works in a grocery store? What does she do there?"
- **D.** "Should you say, 'on a grocery store' or 'in a grocery store'?"

49. Assigning students to work with a partner, a middle school language arts teacher challenges each pair with the following question: "How many uses can you think of for a book?"

In giving students this task, the teacher is most likely promoting their use of

- **A.** convergent thinking.
- **B.** creative thinking.
- **C.** deductive reasoning.
- **D.** generalization.

50. In which of the following classes is the activity LEAST consistent with a tactile/kinesthetic modality preference?

- **A.** In language arts, students put on a play and dress in costumes.
- **B.** In mathematics, students do a survey on favorite jean brands and summarize results.
- **C.** In social studies, students participate in a simulation activity acting out a historical event.
- **D.** In science, students work in small groups to compare the heat reflection properties of various fabrics.

51. The Florida Kindergarten Readiness Screener (FLKRS) is administered to all kindergarten students in Florida public schools to assess their school readiness at the beginning of the school year. This assessment practice can be expected to enhance the children's experiences in kindergarten by

- **A.** promoting the children's awareness of their own skills and needs and thereby their ability to choose personally useful learning activities.
- **B.** helping teachers to ensure instruction is developmentally appropriate for the children in their classes.
- **C.** helping teachers to determine whether teacher-directed or student-directed activities will best achieve targeted learning standards.
- **D.** encouraging children to view the classroom as a place where academic learning and progress are important.

52. During group presentations, after students have worked in cooperative learning groups to investigate the properties of magnets, a fifth-grade teacher notices that two students, Rosa and Katie, are whispering to each other instead of paying attention to the presentations. When the girls look in the teacher's direction, the teacher gives them a stern look. Immediately, the girls quit whispering and direct their attention to the presentations. The teacher's behavior is an example of

- **A.** extinction.
- **B.** negative reinforcement.
- **C.** nonverbal communication.
- **D.** modeling.

GO ON TO THE NEXT PAGE

53. A kindergarten teacher has the students sitting in a circle on the carpet while the teacher passes around a bag containing plastic letters. Each student is to reach in the bag, remove a letter, show the letter to the group, and then say the name of the letter and its sound. What concept is the teacher working on with these children?

   A. alphabetic principle
   B. decoding
   C. fluency
   D. print awareness

54. During daily mathematics activities, an English Language Learner (ELL) demonstrates an adequate proficiency in using place-value concepts. However, the student scores very poorly on items assessing understanding of place value on a standardized test. The student's mathematics teacher could best interpret this conflicting result by *first* taking which of the following steps?

   A. Calculate the deviation between the student's standardized test score and the student's average daily score to determine whether the student's overall performance is on grade level.
   B. Give the student the standardized test again, and compare the student's performance on the two tests to determine whether the test results are reliable.
   C. Analyze whether the daily mathematics activities are aligned with the way the standardized test assesses place value.
   D. Use additional multiple methods to investigate the student's actual understanding of place-value concepts.

55. Especially with young children, praise is most effective when it is

   A. global and given frequently.
   B. global and given infrequently.
   C. specific and given frequently.
   D. specific and given infrequently.

56. A middle school health teacher plans to begin a lesson on risky behaviors by having the students brainstorm about ways to respond to peer pressure. The teacher can best maximize the benefit of the brainstorming activity by asking the students to

   A. back up suggestions with personal experiences in their own lives.
   B. present any ideas that come to mind and refrain from judging the ideas of others.
   C. focus on presenting ideas that are unique instead of elaborating on the ideas of others.
   D. avoid presenting ideas that are probably unworkable and focus instead on realistic ideas.

57. Which of the following assessment tools would be best for assessing a student's ability to use contextual information to support reading comprehension?

   A. anecdotal record
   B. cloze procedure
   C. miscue analysis
   D. running record

58. Students in a sixth-grade health class are learning about interpersonal skills. One student asks, "What do we do when a bully is mean to us?" The teacher addresses the whole class, "What do you think you should do when a bully is mean to you?"

What technique is the teacher using in the last question to the whole class?

   A. paraphrasing
   B. probing
   C. redirecting
   D. summarizing

Use the following graph to answer question 59.

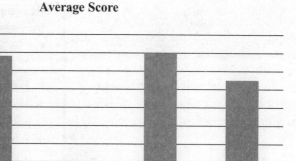

Average Score

59. At midyear, a departmental mathematics assessment of topics students should have learned is administered to eighth graders school wide. The results, shown in the graph above, of the performance of an eighth-grade math teacher's students indicate that the teacher's best response to this information is to

A. seek out and attend in-service training on teaching functions.

B. allow extra time in class for students to practice working with functions.

C. not be concerned about functions because performance of the teacher's students in all other areas is strong.

D. at the next departmental meeting, recommend that functions not be tested at midyear.

60. A second-grade teacher has set up learning centers in the classroom. In addition to work periods that make use of the learning centers, the teacher allots a block of time every day for students to have free choice to select the centers to which they want to go. To avoid overcrowding in popular centers, the teacher devises a system of organization that limits the number of students who are permitted to use a center at any one time. To accommodate as many students as possible, a bell is rung periodically during the free-choice time to signal that it is time to move to a different center. On occasion at free-choice time, some students in the class get upset when they cannot immediately go to their favorite centers. A few students even get into arguments over the centers. In general, which of the following management strategies would best promote appropriate student behavior during free-choice time?

A. modeling social skills with all students and helping them work out compromises to conflicts

B. helping students who cannot go to their favorite centers find alternative centers they are likely to enjoy

C. being flexible about the number of students who are permitted to use a center at any one time, so that students who are upset do not have to wait to go to their favorite centers

D. devising a plan for managing centers that allows all students to work in their favorite centers at least once a week

GO ON TO THE NEXT PAGE

61. Which of the following strategies would be best for increasing adolescents' motivation to learn?

   A. Provide learning opportunities that relate to their interests and experiences.

   B. Offer public recognition as an incentive for good work.

   C. Stress the importance of good grades to achievement of future success.

   D. Withdraw privileges for failure to complete work.

62. Children in a prekindergarten class complain to the teacher that the markers in the art center do not write anymore. One child says that someone dipped the markers in glue. Another child says that the caps were left off. What should the teacher do to address this situation?

   A. Ask the children to tell the teacher when they see someone misusing the markers.

   B. Hold a class meeting and guide the children to generate a set of rules for the art center.

   C. Replace the markers, but tell the children that if the markers are misused again, they will not be replaced.

   D. Speak privately to the children who are misusing the markers and warn them that they will not be able to go to the art center if they continue to misuse the markers.

63. A second-grade teacher has selected an expository text on vegetable garden plants of Florida to read to her students. The teacher can best prepare the students for the text on vegetable garden plants by

   A. helping the students make a chart in which they list what they already know and what they want to learn about vegetable garden plants.

   B. having the students memorize a list of key vocabulary words related to vegetable garden plants.

   C. drawing a diagram of a corn plant on the board and eliciting the students' help in labeling the parts.

   D. telling the students that it is important for them to learn about vegetable garden plants because humans depend on these plants for food.

Use the assessment below to answer question 64.

Directions: Write a word in the blank space so that the sentence makes sense.
1. The little girl woke up, and jumped _____ of bed.
2. The sun was very hot, so the snow _____.
3. My dad likes to _____ the newspaper every morning.
4. When the little boy let go of the _____, it floated up into the air.

64. A teacher could best use the assessment to gauge a third-grader's proficiency in which of the following reading components?

   A. comprehension
   B. fluency
   C. phonemic awareness
   D. phonics

65. Teachers in Florida are expected to maintain positive home-school relationships. Which of the following would NOT be an appropriate way to work with families?

   A. inviting parents to visit their children's classroom at all times

   B. making sure that the parents know when their children are doing better than other students

   C. providing information and ideas to families about how to help their children at home with homework

   D. recruiting parents to serve as volunteers in the school

66. The use of different language forms that depend on the setting, the relationship of the speaker to the person he or she is addressing, and the function of the interaction is known as

   A. discourse.
   B. lexicon.
   C. register.
   D. semantics.

67. A middle school teacher is meeting with a girl's parents about her low performance in social studies. As the meeting begins, the parents tell the teacher they are concerned that their child comes home upset every day and says that no one likes her. Which of the following would be the most appropriate response from the teacher?

- **A.** Paraphrase the parents' comment and ask for further information about the situation.
- **B.** Show concern and then move on to the planned agenda.
- **C.** Tell the parents they should schedule a meeting with the school counselor to discuss the situation.
- **D.** Assure the parents that most middle school students feel that way occasionally.

68. A teacher encourages family members to serve as volunteer tutors in the school. Which of the following would be the most likely purpose for such an arrangement?

- **A.** to give family members a sense of ownership in the school
- **B.** to create family awareness of problems in the school
- **C.** to allow students, while at school, the opportunity to discuss their problems with a family member
- **D.** to improve student behavior in the community at large

69. A teacher has a class of mixed-ability and diverse cultural backgrounds. When assigning students to groups for cooperative learning activities, the teacher makes sure the groups are diverse in ability level, gender, and cultural background. Grouping students this way is most likely to

- **A.** help students learn to deal with prejudice.
- **B.** promote critical thinking and problem solving in group activities.
- **C.** nurture a sense of community in the classroom.
- **D.** enhance students' ability to be thoughtful questioners.

70. "Given a paragraph, the student will identify all the nouns with 90 percent accuracy." This statement is an example of a(n)

- **A.** affective objective.
- **B.** cognitive objective.
- **C.** psychomotor objective.
- **D.** reflective objective.

71. A high school teacher has a student who seems especially unmotivated and has been performing poorly in class. Before talking with the student, which of the following should the teacher do *first* to find out additional information that would help in dealing with the student?

- **A.** Review the student's educational records.
- **B.** Discuss the problem with the school counselor.
- **C.** Talk with the student's friends.
- **D.** Hold a conference with the student's parents.

72. A kindergarten child is shown a tall, thin jar and a short, wide jar, both of which hold exactly one pint. When questioned about the two jars, the child's answers indicate that the child believes the taller container holds more liquid. Based on this evidence, the child's teacher likely would conclude that the child

- **A.** is developmentally delayed.
- **B.** has a vision problem.
- **C.** lacks the ability to conserve.
- **D.** needs to be evaluated by an Exceptional Student Education specialist.

73. A key goal of a teacher's classroom management strategy should be to

- **A.** provide an environment that eliminates unfamiliar or unexpected occurrences.
- **B.** motivate students to proceed from simple to complex in their approach to learning.
- **C.** encourage students to monitor and self-manage their own behavior.
- **D.** allow students to decide which topics will be studied and for how long.

GO ON TO THE NEXT PAGE

74. The stage of development in language acquisition wherein the second-language learner works to receive and understand the new language but produces little or no expressive language is known as

- **A.** preproduction.
- **B.** early production.
- **C.** speech emergence.
- **D.** intermediate fluency.

75. A seventh-grade science teacher's instructional methods include inquiry and discovery learning in the context of cooperative learning groups. These instructional methods will most likely

- **A.** provide structure to learning activities.
- **B.** sequence instruction.
- **C.** establish group morale.
- **D.** foster independent learning.

76. During a whole-class discussion, a student is creating a minor disruption by tapping a pencil on the desk. Which of the following interventions should the teacher use *first* with the student?

- **A.** Say the student's name and give the student a signal to stop the behavior.
- **B.** Make eye contact with the student and give a stern gaze but continue with the lesson uninterrupted.
- **C.** Ask the student to stop the pencil tapping.
- **D.** Stop the class discussion and send the student to the principal's office.

77. A running record is an oral reading assessment primarily used to

- **A.** determine a student's reading level
- **B.** assess a student's comprehension skills
- **C.** measure a student's phonemic awareness
- **D.** evaluate a student's vocabulary development

78. Which of the following situations is an example of scaffolding to promote student learning in a fifth-grade social studies classroom?

- **A.** The teacher sets up a reading center containing biographies of significant individuals in American history.
- **B.** The teacher gives students weekly geography quizzes to review important information covered during recent lessons on North American geography.
- **C.** The teacher assigns students to cooperative learning groups to create a presentation on an American invention or innovation.
- **D.** The teacher reviews and posts a timeline of key events to provide students with context for learning about factors leading up to the American Revolution.

79. Two middle school teachers agree to create an interdisciplinary science and social studies unit with coordinated learning activities between their classes. The teachers should begin their planning of the unit by *first*

- **A.** checking on the availability of materials and resources.
- **B.** deciding on student learning goals that both will emphasize in their classrooms.
- **C.** activating students' prior knowledge related to the unit theme.
- **D.** deciding on appropriate instructional strategies to address the varied needs and abilities of all the students.

80. During a whole-group activity about the characters in a book students in a third-grade class have read, most of the students are actively participating in the activity, with the exception of one student, who is rolling a small ball on the desk. Which of the following would be the *best* approach for the teacher to use with this student?

- **A.** Ignore the off-task behavior completely, so as not to lose the momentum of the class activity.
- **B.** Walk by the student's desk, unobtrusively take the ball, and then find time later to talk with the student.
- **C.** Stop the activity and reprimand the student in a calm voice.
- **D.** Stop the activity, walk to the student's desk, and quietly ask the student to put the ball away.

81. A high school economics teacher is planning a unit on the development of a market economy. Which of the following would be most effective for assessing students' prior knowledge about the unit topic?

A. using an advance organizer

B. giving students time to do some reading on the topic

C. having small-group discussions

D. inviting in a guest speaker

82. A language arts teacher's decision to use a thematic approach for teaching a unit on literature *best* demonstrates the teacher's understanding of the importance of

A. helping students to make connections between and among concepts within a discipline.

B. using multiple activities that engage and motivate students at appropriate developmental levels.

C. providing learning situations that will encourage students to practice skills and gain knowledge needed in a diverse society.

D. enhancing students' ability to apply knowledge in various contexts.

83. Which of the following practices is likely to have a negative impact on a beginning English Language Learner's acquisition of English?

A. encouraging the student to use English instead of the primary language when at home

B. creating an academically challenging environment

C. having high expectations for all learners

D. using nonverbal cues, including gestures and facial expressions

84. To help students develop decision-making skills, a middle school health teacher involves the students in role-play activities modeled on situations they are likely to encounter. The main focus of the activity is on the skills students need to resist pressure from peers to engage in unsafe activities such as drug or alcohol use. This approach demonstrates the teacher's understanding that students at this developmental stage

A. are highly responsive to suggestions from adults for modifying their behaviors.

B. cannot imagine any situation they have not personally experienced.

C. learn better when skills are practiced in a meaningful context.

D. have little concern about what others think of them.

85. A social studies teacher plans to use a simulation activity in a lesson about supply and demand. Which of the following is a major limitation of using simulation activities?

A. They focus too much on basic skills.

B. They often require a considerable amount of time.

C. Students usually do not find them interesting or fun.

D. Students find the realism too threatening.

86. Under the Individuals with Disabilities Education Act (IDEA; formerly PL 94-142), which of the following is a right of the parents of a child with disabilities who has been placed in Exceptional Student Education (ESE) in Florida?

A. the right to participate in the decision-making process regarding the educational placement of their child

B. the right to select the public school their child will attend

C. the right to interpret the instructional implications of evaluation results

D. the right to determine the most appropriate accommodations or modifications for their child

GO ON TO THE NEXT PAGE

87. A first-grade teacher is concerned about Joaquin's self-concept. He does not have many friends because he insists on being in charge at play time. Which of the following actions by the teacher would be most effective in helping Joaquin change his behavior and in improving his self-concept?

    A. Privately praise him when he plays cooperatively with others at play time.

    B. Tell him he has to let other children be in charge at play time.

    C. Send him to timeout when he starts demanding to be in charge at play time.

    D. Suggest to him that he play alone at play time.

88. A second-grade teacher is concerned about a student's performance on ongoing progress-monitoring (OPM) oral reading fluency passages. The student performed at high risk on second-grade reading passages. The teacher re-tested the student using first-grade oral reading passages, and again the student scored at high risk. After reviewing these data, the teacher should assess the student's

    A. comprehension

    B. oral language

    C. phonics skills

    D. vocabulary development

89. A teacher is considering using a tutorial software with a few at-risk students. The software presents information in small units, followed by one or two questions, and then immediate feedback to the student on his or her responses. Such software is most useful for which of the following purposes?

    A. allowing students to monitor their own progress

    B. prompting students to set higher standards of personal achievement

    C. fostering students' development of critical thinking skills

    D. encouraging students to explore creative solutions to problems

90. A former K-12 grade English Language Learner (ELL) student who exited the English for Speakers of Other Languages (ESOL) program more than 2 years ago is coded as

    A. LF.

    B. LP.

    C. LY.

    D. LZ.

91. Students in a high school sociology class are designing a questionnaire to survey students in the school about the removal of vending machines from the school building. Allowing the students to compose the questions for the questionnaire is likely to enhance their interest in the survey project by

    A. relating their learning to community issues.

    B. enabling them to pursue topics of personal interest.

    C. helping them to set their own learning goals.

    D. giving them a sense of control over their learning experiences.

92. A high school biology teacher is having students engage in a cooperative learning group activity. After the students complete the activity, each student group will make a presentation to the entire class to share the group's results. The teacher plans for the presentations to take place during the last 15 minutes of class, so the group activity must not run over into this time period. Which of the following would be the best way for the teacher to remind the students about the time, so that the group activity is completed in time for the presentations to take place?

    A. Remind them at the very beginning of the activity.

    B. Remind them every 5 minutes.

    C. Remind them every 10 minutes.

    D. Remind them 5 minutes prior to the necessary end time for the activity.

93. A fifth-grade teacher plans a unit designed to strengthen students' skills in pattern recognition and critical thinking. The teacher plans to use appropriate instructional activities in whole-group and small-group settings. As part of the initial planning process, the teacher's *first* step in defining instructional objectives for the new unit should be to

A. select appropriate instructional activities for fostering growth in pattern recognition and critical thinking.

B. analyze the benefits and limitations of various whole-group and small-group instructional strategies.

C. assess students' general areas of strengths and needs in pattern recognition and critical thinking.

D. implement procedures for promoting positive and productive group interactions.

94. With regard to a student with one or more disabilities who has been evaluated into Exceptional Student Education (ESE), *inclusion* means

A. placing the student in a separate school tailored to the student's special needs.

B. making sure that only highly qualified ESE teachers work with the student.

C. keeping the student in separate classes for all or part of the day.

D. providing instruction to the student within a regular education classroom to the maximum extent appropriate.

95. During the first week of school, a teacher observes behavior in a student that causes the teacher to suspect that the student might have a learning disability. With regard to this student, the teacher has a responsibility to

A. notify Exceptional Student Education (ESE) staff that the student needs support services in the teacher's classroom.

B. notify the student's parents that they need to contact the ESE staff about the student's difficulty.

C. initiate an evaluation for ESE as soon as possible.

D. initiate an evaluation for ESE only when it is clear that the student's needs cannot be met through the regular education program.

96. Which of the following is a necessary element of inquiry-based learning in science?

A. students writing group reports after researching a science topic together

B. a teacher showing a video presentation of a science principle related to a lesson

C. students forming hypotheses prior to a lab investigation

D. a teacher leading a question and answer session on a scientific principle

97. When an English Language Learner has developed the ability to understand a message in a second language, the student has developed

A. expressive language.

B. oral language.

C. pragmatic language.

D. receptive language.

98. Students in a social studies class are designing a learning project about ways the environment affects human systems. In assisting the students in designing their learning experiences for the project, it is most important that the teacher make certain that the tasks and activities for the project

A. address the grade-level expectations set forth in the Next Generation Sunshine State Standards for social studies.

B. be planned by the students and address only the Next Generation Sunshine State Standards for social studies that the students have identified as most relevant and consistent with the project.

C. address only the grade-level expectations of the Next Generation Sunshine State Standards for social studies that are simple enough so that even students who are academically at risk can participate in a meaningful way.

D. be preplanned by the teacher to ensure that the learning experiences are congruent with the Next Generation Sunshine State Standards for social studies.

GO ON TO THE NEXT PAGE

99. According to Florida Statutes, the number of students in core curriculum courses assigned to a teacher in grades 9 through 12 must not exceed

    A. 22 students.
    B. 25 students.
    C. 28 students.
    D. 30 students.

100. A third-grade teacher begins a mathematics lesson about polygons by reading to students the book *The Greedy Triangle,* by Marilyn Burns. This book tells a story about triangles and other multi-sided figures such as polygons. The probable purpose for this way of beginning the lesson is to

    A. gain students' attention.
    B. communicate the objective for the lesson.
    C. present the lesson content.
    D. assess student learning.

101. A teacher is concerned about Carl, a student who recently enrolled in school. Carl acts listless most of the time and appears uninterested in class activities. The teacher talks with the assistant principal about Carl and learns that Carl and his family are living in a homeless shelter. After repeated attempts, the teacher is able to talk by telephone with Carl's mother about the teacher's concerns regarding Carl. The teacher's best response to Carl's unstable home situation is to give highest priority to

    A. stressing to Carl's mother that Carl needs a more stable home environment right away.
    B. offering to put Carl's mother in touch with a church organization that provides housing for homeless families.
    C. ensuring that Carl has one or two close friends in the class with whom he can interact on a regular daily basis.
    D. providing an accepting and supportive environment for Carl in the classroom.

102. Children in a kindergarten class are going on a field trip to a fire station. The teacher asks a paraprofessional to accompany them and videotape the field trip. To ensure that the video will be a useful instructional tool, the teacher should *first*

    A. assign questions to the students to ask as they are being videotaped.
    B. write a narrative for the video.
    C. discuss with the paraprofessional the sequence of events that need to be recorded.
    D. discuss with the paraprofessional the purpose of the video.

103. Which of the following assessments is most effective in determining the extent to which students use specific problem-solving strategies in math?

    A. norm-referenced achievement test
    B. criterion-referenced skills test
    C. self-monitoring checklist
    D. holistic scoring rubric

104. To improve the effectiveness of his communication with English Language Learners (ELLs), a new fourth-grade teacher attends a workshop on Stephen Krashen's comprehensible input hypothesis. Which of the following strategies best supports comprehensible input for ELLs?

    A. incorporating gestures, visuals, and manipulatives
    B. giving noncorrective responses
    C. extending wait time
    D. using idiomatic expressions

105. Which of the following practices by a teacher would best promote a student's development of positive self-esteem?

    A. frequently praising the student for "doing a good job" when returning the student's assignments
    B. giving the student tangible rewards for finishing assignments on time
    C. pointing out the student's achievements in front of classmates
    D. routinely presenting the student with challenging tasks that, with effort, the student can accomplish successfully

106. Teachers holding class meetings to deal with problems in the classroom is most in accord with which of the following?

  A. Teachers should take opportunities to clarify consequences for inappropriate behavior.

  B. Teachers should promote student ownership in a smoothly functioning learning community.

  C. Teachers should model respect for diversity and individual differences.

  D. Teachers should use a variety of means to convey high expectations for all students.

107. A middle school English language arts teacher uses a holistic scoring rubric to assess students' weekly one-page essays. The teacher assigns an overall score of 1 to 5 based on five criteria: organization, grammar, punctuation, spelling, and clarity. Which of the following is an important limitation of using this assessment method on a regular basis?

  A. It is time-consuming for the teacher to use.

  B. It does not provide students information from which they can determine whether their writing is improving.

  C. It does not provide specific feedback on the criteria used in the rubric.

  D. It does not result in a score that can be converted to a letter grade.

108. A social studies teacher begins a unit on the similarities and differences of Native American groups in Florida by devoting time to collecting ideas from the whole class about what they already know about the topic from their own previous experiences. This approach is beneficial to students primarily because it will help them

  A. memorize detailed information quickly and efficiently.

  B. make value judgments about relevant concepts.

  C. make connections between what they already know and new learning.

  D. determine which events caused other events to happen.

109. A first-grade teacher is working with the children on a learning project about the significant aspects of the lives and accomplishments of selected men and women in the period of history before 1880 (for example, Sacajawea, George Washington, Betsy Ross, Abraham Lincoln, and Harriet Tubman). Which of the following activities related to the project would be of greatest benefit to the children?

  A. having the children play a game in which they name a historical figure when their turn comes

  B. reading aloud a children's biography of a historical figure of the relevant time period

  C. having the children color pictures of historical figures of the relevant time period to post on their classroom wall

  D. showing a video about the Revolutionary War or the Civil War

110. Which of the following is NOT one of the parts of an instructional objective?

  A. action

  B. conditions

  C. grading criteria

  D. mastery level

111. Students in a third-grade class have been gathering information about planets from websites. During an Internet session, a student in the class tells the teacher, "My mom doesn't want me doing this. She says there are bad things on the Internet." The teacher is aware that the school computers are equipped with Internet child-safety filtering software, but she has not explained what this means to the students. Nonetheless, the teacher also is probably aware that, for young children this age, attitudes toward an issue, such as whether using the Internet is a "good" or "bad" idea, tend to be most influenced by their

  A. cognitive abilities.

  B. families' attitudes.

  C. peers' attitudes.

  D. personal experiences.

GO ON TO THE NEXT PAGE

112. Teachers in a middle school set up a homework hotline that students and their families can use to obtain information about homework assignments for each class. Which of the following is the most significant benefit of this strategy?

A. It will promote students' sense of ownership of their own learning.

B. It will strengthen families' ability to be partners with the teachers in their children's education.

C. It will enhance the teachers' ability to create classroom environments that are responsive to diverse student needs.

D. It will emphasize to both students and families that the teachers have high expectations for students' achievement.

113. Thc language that is used to communicate with others in a social environment is known as

A. cognitively demanding communication.

B. cognitive academic language.

C. basic interpersonal communication.

D. context-reduced language.

114. What is an important advantage of having students assume the major responsibility for planning a class learning project?

A. It provides the teacher an opportunity to learn about and correct students' misconceptions regarding the topic of the project.

B. It makes students partners with the teacher in assessing their academic progress.

C. It facilitates the development of a project plan that best addresses individual students' strengths and weaknesses.

D. It promotes the development of autonomy, initiative, and self-reliance in students.

115. A new fifth-grade teacher is planning lessons for an upcoming science unit. The teacher uses the science grade level expectations for the Next Generation Sunshine State Standards to identify the content that should be addressed in the fifth grade. Additionally, the teacher will probably find the grade level expectations useful for obtaining information about

A. how to correlate the lesson plans with the Next Generation Sunshine State Standards.

B. useful Internet resources supporting the Next Generation Sunshine State Standards.

C. sample instructional activities addressing the unit's content.

D. the prerequisite concepts and skills that students should have acquired the previous year.

116. According to the Florida Consent Decree, each English Language Learner (ELL) is entitled to "equal access" to appropriate programming. The primary goal of all such programming is to

A. teach the student in the student's home language until the student has full English language proficiency.

B. develop the student's English language proficiency as efficiently as possible while at the same time making the basic subject matter content understandable.

C. transition the student away from dependence on the home language to speaking English exclusively.

D. develop the student's full proficiency in the home language while encouraging English language acquisition at a rate that is comfortable for the student.

117. A fourth-grade teacher has observed that Winona, who has natural artistic talent, is rushing through her class work so that she can spend time in the creative arts center. Which of the following is the best way for the teacher to deal with this situation?

    A. Have Winona bring her work to the teacher to check over before she can go to the creative arts center.

    B. Tell Winona she can go to the creative arts center if she promises to complete her class work properly at home.

    C. Provide Winona a checklist that she must complete before going to the creative arts center.

    D. Give Winona a lower grade for class work not finished properly.

118. A teacher who strives to create a climate that is positive, is supportive of intellectual risk taking, and cultivates low levels of anxiety is applying which of Krashen's theories?

    A. the Affective Filter hypothesis

    B. the Input hypothesis

    C. the Monitor hypothesis

    D. the Natural Order hypothesis

119. In working with an Exceptional Student Education (ESE) student who has a severe physical disability, the regular education teacher should place primary emphasis on

    A. fostering the student's development of emotional and social skills that will help the student cope with his or her disability.

    B. helping the student to learn specialized strategies that can enhance his or her ability to function physically.

    C. using strategies and materials that allow the student to participate as fully as possible in all class activities.

    D. identifying and using engaging alternative learning opportunities for the student whenever possible.

120. Which of the following approaches would be the most effective way for a teacher to promote dental hygiene in kindergarten students?

    A. Show a video on dental hygiene and discuss it with the kindergartners.

    B. Read simple, illustrated books about proper dental care in an interactive manner to the kindergartners.

    C. Explore with the kindergartners a website that has illustrations and animations on dental hygiene.

    D. Bring in large models of teeth and toothbrushes and have the kindergartners practice proper dental care with the models.

Answer Key for Practice Test 2

1. A	31. D	61. A	91. D
2. B	32. C	62. B	92. D
3. A	33. B	63. A	93. C
4. D	34. B	64. A	94. D
5. B	35. D	65. B	95. D
6. D	36. D	66. C	96. C
7. A	37. C	67. A	97. D
8. A	38. A	68. A	98. A
9. B	39. C	69. C	99. B
10. B	40. B	70. B	100. A
11. D	41. B	71. A	101. D
12. C	42. B	72. C	102. D
13. A	43. D	73. C	103. C
14. A	44. C	74. A	104. A
15. C	45. C	75. D	105. D
16. B	46. A	76. B	106. B
17. B	47. D	77. A	107. C
18. C	48. C	78. D	108. C
19. A	49. B	79. B	109. B
20. A	50. B	80. B	110. C
21. D	51. B	81. A	111. B
22. D	52. C	82. A	112. B
23. C	53. A	83. A	113. C
24. A	54. C	84. C	114. D
25. C	55. C	85. B	115. D
26. A	56. B	86. A	116. B
27. C	57. B	87. A	117. C
28. C	58. C	88. C	118. A
29. A	59. A	89. A	119. C
30. A	60. A	90. D	120. D

Complete Answers and Explanations for Practice Test 2

1. **A.** This question relates to **Competency 4: Assessment.** Eliminate **B** and **D** because these measures are formative assessments. Eliminate **C** because learning style inventories gather information about students to assist teachers with planning, but are not used for assessment purposes. Choice **A** is the correct response. An End-of-Course assessment is a summative measure because it occurs at the completion of a course and assesses how well students learned the course content.

2. **B.** This question deals with a class discussion, which falls under **Competency 3: Instructional Delivery.** Eliminate **A** because a discussion is unlikely to lead to an absolute conclusion, given the fact that no undisputed facts are provided. Eliminate **C** and **D** because the students are discussing a problem, not solving it. During the discussion, the teacher should monitor the effects of messages, simplifying and restating when necessary, and encourage the students to communicate effectively. The teacher should emphasize to the students that the critical elements of verbal communication are *accuracy of language, accuracy of information, standardization of language,* and *clearly defined expectations.* Thus, **B** is the correct response.

3. **A.** This question deals with developing professional relationships, which falls under **Competency 5: Continuous Improvement.** Eliminate **C** because this approach would be excessive and burdensome to the principal. Eliminate **D** because this action would be unprofessional. You must now select between **A** and **B.** Eliminate **B** because although this might be a measure the teacher could take, it would not be as effective as the approach given in **A,** which allows the principal to see firsthand what the teacher is doing and how it is impacting student learning. Thus, **A** is the correct response.

4. **D.** This question deals with both **Competency 3: Instructional Delivery** and **Competency 4: Assessment.** Notice that you must select the *major* benefit to students from the assignment. The two prompts address higher-order thinking skills. When students justify the results of their experiment, they use evaluation-level thinking. When they formulate a theory based on the results of their experiment, they use synthesis-level thinking. Thus, the prompts promote students' creative and critical thinking skills **(D).** Eliminate **A** because even though a student might recall facts and basic concepts in order to address the prompts, this type of lower-level thinking would not be the *major* benefit of responding to the prompts. Eliminate **B** because it is not supported by the question stem. Eliminate **C** because the prompts will likely be used as an assessment tool by the teacher, but the *major* benefit to students comes from engaging in higher-order thinking skills. Thus, **D** is the correct response.

5. **B.** This question relates to both **Competency 1: Instructional Design and Planning** and **Competency 7: Teaching English Language Learners (ELLs).** Eliminate **A** because incorporating students' cultural background into the curriculum contributes to an effective learning environment by validating and confirming the students' home cultures, thereby enhancing their feelings of acceptance in the classroom. Eliminate **C** because educational interests and aspirations vary widely among individual students, even within a cultural group, and often overlap with those of students of other cultures. Eliminate **D** because the way a student learns and interacts in the classroom is influenced—at least in part—by cultural norms and the norms learned as a member of a particular cultural group. Choice **B** is the correct response. Teachers should recognize that each student is a unique person and that, within a cultural group, students can be expected to exhibit a broad range of strengths, interests, and needs.

6. **D.** This question deals with **Competency 6: Professional Conduct.** Eliminate **A, B,** and **C** because these are actions that teachers are expected to do. Choice **D** is the correct response. The requirements for administration of the mandatory statewide assessments prohibit anyone from questioning students on test content or test items after testing is complete, even after the days set aside for state testing have passed. This action by a teacher would be unethical.

7. **A.** This question deals with **Competency 8: Literacy Strategies.** Choice **A** is the correct response. Children's *letter name fluency* (LNF), the ability to recognize letters by name, is a strong predictor of their success in

learning to read. LNF is included as a Dynamic Indicators of Basic Early Literacy Skills (DIBELS) measure for students in grades K and 1 as an indicator of risk. Knowing letter names helps children to remember the patterns of written language and to treat words as strings of letters. When children do not know letter names, they tend to have difficulty in learning letter sounds and in recognizing words. However, letter names should not be taught in isolation, but rather integrated into general phonics instruction. The skills in the other answer choices are not predictors of success in learning to read for first-graders.

8. **A.** This question deals with **Competency 4: Assessment.** For standardized tests, percentile scores are scores that reflect a student's standing relative to a norm group. The 80th percentile is the same as or better than 80 percent of the scores of the norm group. Thus, **A** is the correct response. The other answer choices are incorrect interpretations of a percentile score.

9. **B.** This question deals with **Competency 3: Instructional Delivery.** Eliminate **A** because it not supported by the question stem. Eliminate **C** and **D** because these answer choices relate to keeping students on task. Although the teacher's questioning strategy will likely result in better classroom behavior, this outcome probably is not the main reason for stopping the video and prompting students to consider the ideas presented. Maintaining an orderly, disciplined classroom is an important teacher function; however, the teacher's primary concern should be with promoting students' academic achievement. Choice **B** is the correct response. The teacher is most probably motivated by the understanding that the teacher's efforts to maintain and reinforce student involvement correlate with students' cognitive engagement. Giving students opportunities to think about and discuss ideas presented in the video will help them create new understandings and reflect on old ones. By posing key questions, the teacher is likely to keep the student focused, involved, and engaged in learning.

10. **B.** This question falls under **Competency 5: Continuous Improvement.** The most appropriate way for a teacher to share an innovative instructional strategy with school colleagues is to speak with the principal about demonstrating the strategy as part of a workshop for all interested teachers. Thus, **B** is the correct response. The measures given in the answer choices are not appropriate ways to share ideas with colleagues.

11. **D.** This question falls under **Competency 1: Instructional Design and Planning.** Eliminate **A, B,** and **C** because these tasks do not require creative thinking skills. Creative thinking is thinking that results in a new idea, product, or creation. Writing an original short story would promote students' creative thinking skills. Thus, **D** is the correct response.

12. **C.** This question relates to **Competency 1: Instructional Design and Planning.** Research indicates that brain hemisphericity has a strong influence on an individual's ability to process information. Right-brain-dominant learners respond best to visual and kinesthetic instruction, process information holistically, see patterns and relationships, think from whole to part, prefer to see the "big picture" before exploring small details, depend on images and pictures for meaning, and can work on several parts of a task at the same time. Hence, visual and kinesthetic global activities would work best with these learners. Thus, **C** is the correct response. The instructions described in the other answer choices would not be as compatible with the way right-brain-dominant learners process information.

13. **A.** This question deals with **Competency 6: Professional Conduct.** Teachers should be aware that using unlicensed software is illegal. Mr. Black should immediately remove all copies of the software from the computers. He should follow the principle of the Code of Ethics and Principles of Professional Conduct for the Education Profession in Florida that states teachers "shall maintain honesty in all professional dealings." Thus, **A** is the correct response. The actions given in the other answer choices would not satisfy Mr. Black's legal and ethical responsibility.

14. **A.** This question deals with **Competency 8: Literacy Strategies.** Research has established a strong relationship between students' understanding of text structure and reading comprehension. Most students benefit from explicit instruction that helps them understand and use the text structures as they encounter them in their reading materials. Thus, **A** is the correct response. The strategies offered in the other answer choices are not known to be effective measures for promoting student comprehension.

15. C. This question deals with **Competency 4: Assessment.** A *portfolio* assessment includes a variety of samples of a student's work, collected over time, that shows the student's growth and development. Thus, **C** is the correct response. Although the assessments given in the other answer choices might be included in a portfolio, none of these alone constitutes a variety of samples of a student's work.

16. B. This question falls under **Competency 3: Instructional Delivery.** Eliminate **A** because *paraphrasing* is saying what students say, but in different words. Eliminate **C** because *redirecting* is posing a question or prompt to other students for a response or to add new insights. Eliminate **D** because *summarizing* is the technique of reducing students' ideas to key points. Choice **B** is the correct response. The teacher is using the technique of *probing,* which is used to ask students to clarify or justify answers.

17. B. This question deals with **Competency 5: Continuous Improvement.** Mr. James can most effectively help Ms. Field prepare for the classroom observation by providing her with a lesson plan for the class session that she will be observing. The lesson plan will help Ms. Field know what to expect when she observes the lesson. Thus, **B** is the correct response. Eliminate **A, C,** and **D** because these measures would not be as effective in helping Ms. Field prepare for the classroom observation.

18. C. This question relates to both **Competency 1: Instructional Design and Planning** and **Competency 3: Instructional Delivery.** Eliminate **A** and **D** because these tasks are at the knowledge level of thinking. Eliminate **B** because this task is at the comprehension level of thinking. Evaluating the effectiveness of a written response according to audience and purpose requires evaluation-level thinking, which is a type of critical thinking. Thus, **C** is the correct response.

19. A. This question falls under **Competency 5: Continuous Improvement.** Choice **A** is the correct response. The teacher can most effectively make use of the DVDs, CDs, magazines, and books as resources for the purpose of integrating cultural content into content area instruction. For the purposes given in **C** and **D,** other means would be more effective. The purpose given in **B** is one that, in general, teachers should avoid.

20. A. This question deals with **Competency 6: Professional Conduct.** The Code of Ethics and Principles of Professional Conduct for the Education Profession in Florida states that educators must "report to appropriate authorities any known allegation of a violation of the Florida School Code or State Board of Education Rules" by other educators. Thus, **A** is the correct response. Eliminate **B, C,** and **D** because these actions would not comply with the Code of Ethics and Principles of Professional Conduct.

21. D. This question deals with **Competency 8: Literacy Strategies.** Eliminate **A** because it deals with pronunciation of words, not vocabulary development. Choice **D** is the correct response. Semantically grouping new vocabulary words in the content area with familiar words that have similar meanings will help students link new words to words they already know and to their background knowledge. The strategies given in **B** and **C** would not be as effective.

22. D. This question deals with **Competency 4: Assessment.** Teacher-made tests can provide valuable information about what students have learned; however, teachers should be knowledgeable of the uses and limitations of different types of test questions. When designing tests, teachers need to be aware that guessing can compromise the validity of results. Although guessing can be a factor with any type of test item, it has the most effect on true-false items. Thus, **D** is the correct response.

23. C. This question falls under **Competency 3: Instructional Delivery.** Eliminate **A** because effective teachers should attempt to ask questions of all students equally, regardless of where they are seated. Eliminate **B** because these types of questions require only lower-level thinking. Eliminate **D** because effective teachers avoid answering their own questions. Choice **C** is the correct response. When leading class discussions, effective teachers want to draw ideas from the students. To that end, they establish positive interactions that support students' responses.

24. A. This question deals with **Competency 5: Continuous Improvement.** Eliminate **B** and **C** because it is questionable whether joining a professional organization would have the results given in these answer choices. Now you must select between **A** and **D**. Although expanded access to quality lesson plans and other instructional resources in a teacher's field is a benefit of joining a professional organization in one's content field, it is not the *most* significant benefit of doing so. According to Rule 6A-10.097 (1), FAC, "Each competent educator shall … demonstrate competence in specialization by … demonstrating an awareness of current developments in the field of specialization." Therefore, **A** is the correct response.

25. **C.** This question deals with **Competency 4: Assessment.** Eliminate **A** and **B** because these questions elicit short answers that require only lower-level thinking. Eliminate **D** because although this question requires students to think about the procedures and might result in an extended answer, it does not require higher-level thinking. Choice **C** is the correct response. Writing a justification for the information shown in the graph requires students to engage in analysis, synthesis, judgment, and creative thought.

26. **A.** This question relates to both **Competency 1: Instructional Design and Planning** and **Competency 2: Learning Environments.** Notice that you must select the answer choice that the teacher should do *first.* Eliminate **B** and **D** because although these are actions that the teacher might take, they are not as important or necessary as the actions given in **A** and **C.** You must now select between **A** and **C.** Even though the teacher is a woman, she might have unconscious biases or prejudices toward girls' abilities in science. Eliminate **C** because this is something the teacher should do, but not before she examines her own personal beliefs and feelings about female students' abilities in science. Thus, **A** is the correct response.

27. **C.** This question deals with **Competency 6: Professional Conduct.** The Code of Ethics and Principles of Professional Conduct for the Education Profession in Florida states that an educator should "not use institutional privileges for personal gain or advantage." Thus, **C** is the correct response. Eliminate **A, B,** and **D** because none of these actions is a violation of the Code of Ethics and Principles of Professional Conduct.

28. **C.** This question deals with both **Competency 1: Instructional Design and Planning** and **Competency 8: Literacy Strategies.** In reading comprehension, the skills progress in level of difficulty from *literal comprehension skills* (for example, identifying stated main ideas, recalling details), to *inferential comprehension skills* (for example, inferring cause-and-effect relationships, making predictions/inferences, summarizing information), to *evaluative comprehension skills* (for example, analyzing character development and use of language, determining the author's point of view, detecting faulty reasoning). The simplest skills are taught first, and the more complex skills are taught later. Choice **C** is the correct response because recalling details is a literal comprehension skill. The skills in the other answer choices would be taught after the skill of recalling details.

29. **A.** This question deals with **Competency 4: Assessment.** Teachers should be knowledgeable of the uses and limitations of different types of assessment. Choice **A** is the correct response. Informal observation is an authentic assessment method in which teachers directly observe students performing or working on an activity. The teacher might use a checklist listing skills or performances that are critical to the task. Seeing students actually perform behaviors to demonstrate skills and knowledge is more likely to yield valid results than the methods given in the other answer choices. Eliminate **B, C,** and **D** because generally student *self-assessment, peer assessment,* and *student journaling* lack validity due to factors such as the assessor's immaturity and lack of expertise. Nevertheless, students benefit from involvement in these assessment methods because these forms of assessment give students opportunities to develop their critical thinking and evaluation-level thinking skills.

30. **A.** This question falls under **Competency 3: Instructional Delivery.** Eliminate **B** because it is not supported by the stimulus. The teacher is asking the students to write on a topic, not to engage in inquiry. Eliminate **C** because the teacher's problem is not with the teacher's means of communication, but rather with the message. Eliminate **D** because it is not supported by the stimulus because you are not told the cultural makeup of the class. Choice **A** is the correct response. The teacher should have explained the 10-minute writing assignment more precisely, so that the instructional task would have been clearer to the students. Instead of asking the students to write on the subject of school uniforms, which is rather broad and somewhat vague, the teacher might have clarified the assignment by saying, "Write why you would or would

not be in favor of our school adopting school uniforms." Effective teachers communicate instructional tasks clearly to students.

31. **D.** This question falls under **Competency 5: Continuous Improvement.** Eliminate **A** because this answer choice is not aligned with the question. This measure would not help the teacher learn how to more effectively lead whole-group class discussions. The measures given in **B, C,** and **D** are all ways the teacher can learn about appropriate techniques for leading whole-class discussions; however, the measure that probably would *most* help the teacher in improving his or her practice is to observe firsthand a colleague who effectively uses whole-group discussions. Thus, **D** is the correct response.

32. **C.** This question falls under **Competency 3: Instructional Delivery.** Eliminate **A** because this task is at the application level of thinking. Eliminate **B** because this task is at the knowledge level of thinking. Eliminate **D** because this task is at the comprehension level of thinking. Generalizing or drawing conclusions requires analysis-level thinking, which is a type of critical thinking. Thus, **C** is the correct response.

33. **B.** This question falls under **Competency 2: Learning Environments.** Eliminate **C** and **D** because these measures would shortchange the at-risk students. Now you must choose between **A** and **B.** Eliminate **A** because although this measure is one teachers might take, it would not provide as much benefit to the middle school students who are at risk as giving them opportunities to experience academic success on assignments they perceive as meaningful and challenging. This practice will help improve the self-esteem of the at-risk students, who, having confronted repeated failure in the past, might have simply quit trying. Thus, **B** is the correct response.

34. **B.** This question deals with **Competency 6: Professional Conduct.** Choice **B** is the correct response. The Code of Ethics and Principles of Professional Conduct for the Education Profession in Florida states that an educator should "not intentionally expose a student to unnecessary embarrassment or disparagement." Eliminate **A, C,** and **D** because none of these actions is a violation of the Code of Ethics and Principles of Professional Conduct.

35. **D.** This question deals with **Competency 8: Literacy Strategies.** *Structural analysis* is a strategy for determining the meaning of a word by breaking the word into its component subunits—prefixes, root words, suffixes, inflectional endings (for example, *–s, –es, –ed, –ing, –er, –est*), and derivational endings (for example, *–y, –ly, –ial, –ic*). Of the words in the response choices, only *unbelievable* (**D**) lends itself to structural analysis since the reader can break it into its component subunits: *un•believ•able.* Thus, **D** is the correct response.

36. **D.** This question falls under **Competency 1: Instructional Design and Planning** and **Competency 8: Literacy Strategies.** A *graphic organizer* is a visual depiction of abstract concepts or processes. Eliminate **A** because a *decision tree* is used to guide students in the decision-making process. Eliminate **B** because a *flowchart* is used to show a sequence or flow of events, actions, or processes. Eliminate **C** because a *story tree* is used to guide students' critical evaluation of a work of literature. Choice **D** is the correct response. To determine students' prior knowledge about natural resources, the best graphic organizer for the teacher to use is a *web.* In webbing, students list words or phrases that are connected to the central topic. This activity will reveal the students' prior knowledge and disclose their misconceptions about natural resources.

37. **C.** This question deals with teacher expectations, which falls under **Competency 2: Learning Environments.** Eliminate **A** and **B** because research studies support the self-fulfilling prophecy hypothesis that teachers get what they expect, so their expectations affect middle school students' achievement and behavior. Eliminate **D** because middle school students have a fragile self-confidence that can be impacted, either positively or negatively, by teacher expectations. Choice **C** is the correct response. With regard to middle school students, peer relations and peer influences tend to be relatively impervious to the impact of teachers. This circumstance is probably due to the great need that young adolescents have for peer acceptance.

38. A. This question relates to **Competency 5: Continuous Improvement.** Eliminate **B, C,** and **D** because although these sources might provide accurate information, it is *most* probable that accurate information would be obtained from the State Board of Education, which implements and coordinates public education in Florida—including overseeing teacher certification in the state. Thus, **A** is the correct response.

39. C. This question falls under **Competency 3: Instructional Delivery.** Eliminate **B** because *deductive reasoning* starts with basic assumptions or facts and proceeds to a logical conclusion. Eliminate **A** and **D** because *conditional* and *syllogistic* reasoning fall under deductive reasoning. Choice **C** is the correct response. *Inductive reasoning* involves looking at specific examples and trying to identify a pattern or trend that fits the given examples in order to determine a general rule. Since the students are to generalize an algebraic or geometric pattern, the teacher is most likely promoting students' use of inductive reasoning.

40. B. This question deals with **Competency 1: Instructional Design and Planning.** According to research by Witkin and Goodenough (1981), field-independent learners tend to be passive in social situations; in contrast, field-dependent learners tend to be active in social situations. Thus, **B** is the correct response. The other response options disagree with research about field dependency.

41. B. This question deals with **Competency 6: Professional Conduct.** The Family Education Rights and Privacy Act (FERPA) protects the privacy of student records. Eliminate **D** because noncustodial parents have the right to review their child's educational records. Eliminate **A** and **C** because according to FERPA, a teacher may share a minor student's educational records with a school official without written permission from the minor students' parent, provided that the school official has a "legitimate educational interest" in reviewing the records—that is, the official needs to review the educational records "in order to fulfill his or her professional responsibility." Otherwise, it is inappropriate for a teacher to share students' educational records with a colleague without written permission from parents. Thus, **B** is the correct response.

42. B. This question deals with **Competency 8: Literacy Strategies.** Choices **A** and **C** are incorrect because phonics instruction should not take place in isolation. Choice **D** is incorrect because phonics instruction should be explicit, not implicit. Choice **B** is the correct response. Current research suggests that a balanced reading program should include explicit, systematic phonics instruction in the context of meaningful connected reading of informative, engaging text.

43. D. This question deals with **Competency 4: Assessment.** Eliminate **A** and **B** because these responses contain ideas that conflict with best practices of effective teachers. Eliminate **C** because although the teacher might obtain information that relates to students' ability to apply decision-making skills by having the students reflect on the effectiveness of their team's decision making, the *primary* benefit of the activity is that it will promote self-assessment on the part of the students. When students reflect on and assess themselves, they are engaged in evaluation-level thinking, the highest level of Bloom's Taxonomy of thinking skills. Thus, **D** is the correct response.

44. C. This question deals with **Competency 7: Teaching English Language Learners (ELLs).** Eliminate **A** and **D** because these measures would shortchange the English Language Learners (ELLs) and communicate low expectations to them. Eliminate **B** because students who say little might, in fact, be just as proficient language users as more talkative students. They might have reasons other than lack of proficiency in English for not speaking up more often. The varied cultural backgrounds of students who are ELLs make assessing their grasp of spoken English difficult. Among other explanations, it might simply be that the culture in which they acquired their first language mandates silence or reticence in a wide range of social situations, including open discussions. Thus, **C** is the correct response.

45. C. This question falls under **Competency 3: Instructional Delivery.** Eliminate **A** because *affective* refers to feelings and emotions. Eliminate **B** and **D** because these types of questions elicit closed responses at lower levels of thinking. Choice **C** is the correct response. *Divergent questions* are open-ended and, thus, would elicit a variety of ideas during a class discussion.

46. A. This question falls under both **Competency 1: Instructional Design and Planning** and **Competency 6: Professional Conduct.** Eliminate **C** and **D** because these options contain ideas that are not characteristic of gifted children. Eliminate **B** because gifted students whose Educational Plan (EP) places them in the general education classroom should not be isolated when the class is involved in group activities. However, they also should be afforded opportunities for independent learning that encourage them to apply creative and critical thinking. Thus, **A** is the correct response.

47. D. This question deals with **Competency 4: Assessment.** Grade equivalent scores can easily be misinterpreted. This student's score reflects performance on the reading assessment matching the estimated performance of an "average" student in the sixth month of seventh grade on the *same* assessment. The student's score indicates his or her level of performance on fifth-grade-level reading, not seventh-grade-level reading. Thus, **D** is the correct response. The responses in the other answer choices reflect incorrect interpretations of the student's grade equivalent score.

48. C. This question deals with **Competency 7: Teaching English Language Learners (ELLs).** Eliminate **A** because although this is an appropriate response from the teacher, it is not the most appropriate feedback for the situation. The responses given in **B** and **D** would not be appropriate ways to correct the student's errors because they likely would inhibit the student's attempts at language production by raising negative affective filters. The most appropriate way for the teacher to correct the student's errors is through modeling a corrected version of what the student attempted to say. Thus, **C** is the correct response.

49. B. This question falls under **Competency 3: Instructional Delivery.** Eliminate **A** because *convergent thinking* is a type of closed-ended thinking, which would not lead to the generation of many new ideas. Eliminate **C** because *deductive reasoning* involves drawing conclusions from known facts or generalizations. The teacher wants the students to come up with many new ideas. Eliminate **D** because *generalization* is the ability to carry learning over from one setting to a different setting. Choice **B** is the correct response. The task given to the students is most likely to promote *creative thinking*.

50. B. This question deals with learning styles, which falls under **Competency 1: Instructional Design and Planning.** Notice that you must select the answer choice that is *least* consistent with a tactile/kinesthetic modality preference. Tactile/kinesthetic learners prefer to learn by touching objects, by feeling shapes and textures, and by moving things around. Eliminate **A** because the students will be acting out a play, which is tactile/kinesthetic. Eliminate **C** because the students will be participating in a simulation, which is tactile/kinesthetic. Eliminate **D** because the students will be involved in a hands-on activity, which is tactile/kinesthetic. Choice **B** is the correct response. The mathematics activity affords the least opportunity for the learners to be physically involved, so this activity is least consistent with a tactile/kinesthetic modality preference.

51. B. This question deals with **Competency 4: Assessment.** The Florida Kindergarten Readiness Screener (FLKRS) is administered to assess the readiness of each child for kindergarten. The FLKRS provides information about whether the child demonstrates age-appropriate development. Therefore, the FLKRS can be expected to enhance the children's experiences in kindergarten by helping teachers to ensure that instruction is developmentally appropriate for the children in their classes. Thus, **B** is the correct response. Eliminate **A** and **D** because these responses contain ideas that would not be characteristic of kindergarten children. Eliminate **C** because this response does not include the variety of strategies that experts recommend for early childhood instruction.

52. C. This question relates to **Competency 2: Learning Environments.** . Eliminate **A** because *extinction* is the technique of withdrawing reinforcers to discourage undesirable behavior in the classroom. Eliminate **B** because *negative reinforcement* is the technique of strengthening a behavior by release from an undesirable situation. Eliminate **D** because *modeling* is the tactic of demonstrating a skill or behavior that the teacher wants the students to mimic. Choice **C** is the correct response. The teacher uses *nonverbal communication* (that is, a stern look) to convey a message of disapproval.

53. A. This question deals with **Competency 8: Literacy Strategies.** By having the students say the letter name and the sound that corresponds to it, the teacher is providing an opportunity for the children to practice letter-sound correspondence. This skill is an important component of the *alphabetic principle* (the concept that letters and letter patterns represent the sounds of spoken language). Thus, **A** is the correct response. The activity described in the question does not specifically target the skills given in the other response options.

54. **C.** This question deals with **Competency 4: Assessment.** An important question to ask about an assessment is the following: "Does the assessment reflect the instructional methods?" In order to best interpret the conflicting results obtained with the standardized test, the teacher should *first* analyze whether the daily mathematics activities are aligned with the way the standardized test assesses place value. Thus, **C** is the correct response. The actions given in the other response choices would not be as useful in helping the teacher interpret the discrepancy that has occurred.

55. **C.** This question falls under **Competency 2: Learning Environments.** According to Slavin (2008), teachers should use praise frequently (eliminate **B** and **D**), especially with young children, and the praise should specify the particular behavior or accomplishment that warrants the praise (eliminate **A**). Thus, **C** is the correct response.

56. **B.** This question falls under **Competency 3: Instructional Delivery.** *Brainstorming* is a teaching/learning strategy in which students generate ideas, judgment of the ideas of others is forbidden, and ideas are used to create a flow of new ideas. In brainstorming, it is important that students are encouraged to think freely without risk of criticism of their ideas. Eliminate **A, C,** and **D** because these approaches would restrict students' thinking. Choice **B** is the correct response. The teacher can best maximize the benefit of the brainstorming activity by asking the students to present any ideas that come to mind and refrain from judging the ideas of others.

57. **B.** This question relates to both **Competency 4: Assessment** and **Competency 8: Literacy Strategies.** Eliminate **A** because an *anecdotal record* is a written record of a student's progress over time based on teacher observation with notes. Eliminate **C** because *miscue analysis* is a formal examination of a student's deviations (for example, reading a word incorrectly, inserting a word, skipping a word) from written text when reading. Eliminate **D** because a *running record* is an assessment tool that uses a coding system to record a student's exact oral reading performance. Choice **B** is the correct response. The *cloze procedure* is an open-ended assessment tool in which a selected word or phrase is eliminated from a sentence or paragraph, while the student is instructed to complete the missing word or words. Students use contextual information to supply the missing word or words.

58. **C.** This question deals with **Competency 3: Instructional Delivery.** Eliminate **A** because *paraphrasing* is saying what students say, but in different words. Eliminate **B** because *probing* is the technique of asking students to clarify or justify answers. Eliminate **D** because *summarizing* is the technique of reducing students' ideas to key points. Choice **C** is the correct response. The teacher is using the technique of *redirecting,* which is posing a question from a student to other students for a response or to elicit ideas.

59. **A.** This question falls under **Competency 5: Continuous Improvement.** Teachers should analyze students' data and use it to reflect upon their teaching effectiveness. The graph shows that the teacher's students did very well on number systems, equations, and geometry and fairly well on statistics and probability, but very poorly on functions. The students' performance on other topics indicates that the teacher is not generally incompetent. However, the teacher appears to need help with instructional delivery of function concepts. Choice **A** is the correct response. Seeking out and attending in-service training on teaching functions is a professional way to improve instruction and thereby improve student achievement. Eliminate **B** because if the students lack understanding, they likely will struggle with extra practice. Eliminate **C** and **D** because these are inappropriate responses to the situation.

60. **A.** This question deals with **Competency 2: Learning Environments.** Eliminate **B** and **D** because these measures are unlikely to placate the students who are acting up. Eliminate **C** because this measure would reward students for acting up, sending a wrong message to them and to the rest of the class. Teachers should use effective strategies to create positive and productive learning environments in which students are

responsible and self-disciplined. Teachers can help students learn behavioral skills needed to solve problems without adult intervention by modeling social skills with all students and helping them work out compromises to conflicts. Thus, **A** is the correct response.

61. **A.** This question falls under **Competency 3: Instructional Delivery.** Choice **A** is the correct response because providing learning opportunities that relate to adolescents' interests and experiences will help them find their own (intrinsic) motivation for learning, thereby fostering a long-term desire to learn. The strategies in the other response options are extrinsic motivational strategies, which likely would not be as effective in the long term as a strategy that promotes intrinsic motivation. Indeed, some research suggests that students who are encouraged to think about public recognition **(B)**, grades **(C)**, or privileges **(D)** become less inclined to explore ideas, think creatively, and take on challenging tasks—all undesirable outcomes from a teacher's perspective.

62. **B.** This question falls under **Competency 2: Learning Environments.** Eliminate **C** and **D** because these are measures that threaten or punish children, practices that should be avoided by teachers. Such practices are in conflict with the position given by the Florida Department of Education Bureau of School Improvement (2006) in *Strategies for Classroom Management* (available at www.astro.washington.edu/courses/astro270/ wave3.htm) that "response to student misbehavior is most effective when it maintains or enhances the student's dignity and self-esteem and encourages the student to be responsible for his or her own behavior." Eliminate **A** because this measure is a teacher-centered approach that does not allow the children to self-manage their behavior. Further, it will likely create additional conflict in the classroom. In establishing a smoothly functioning learning community in the classroom, teachers should involve students—even children as young as preschool age—in establishing rules and standards for behavior. Holding a class meeting and guiding the children to generate a set of rules for the art center will help them learn to take responsibility for their learning environment. Thus, **B** is the correct response.

63. **A.** This question relates to **Competency 8: Literacy Strategies.** Effective teachers understand how students learn and recognize instructional strategies that promote student learning. Eliminate **B** because whereas prereading activities for a lesson must provide explicit and systematic instruction in key vocabulary words that the students will encounter in the lesson, having students memorize key vocabulary before a unit begins is not recommended. Eliminate **D** because this approach involves too much teacher-telling, without giving students the opportunity to do the thinking in the classroom. Eliminate **C** because it limits students' thinking to one type of vegetable plant—corn. The teacher can best prepare the students for new learning by having them write down (1) what they already know about vegetable plants, to facilitate linking new information to prior knowledge; and (2) what they want to learn about vegetable plants, to give them ownership of their learning and make it purposeful. These actions are steps 1 and 2 in the K-W-L process that effective teachers use to promote students' active engagement in learning and construction of meaning. In step 3, students recall what they learned. K-W-L stands for what students Know, Want to know, and have Learned. Thus, **A** is the correct response.

64. **A.** This question deals with both **Competency 4: Assessment** and **Competency 8: Literacy Strategies.** To fill in the blank with an appropriate word, the student must use the surrounding text as clues to the missing word. Good readers use their background knowledge to help them comprehend what they are reading. Thus, **A** is the correct response. Eliminate **B** because fluency is assessed by students reading text that has no missing words. Eliminate **C** and **D** because these components are related to sounding out words, not producing missing words.

65. **B.** This question falls under **Competency 5: Continuous Improvement.** Eliminate **A, C,** and **D** because these actions are appropriate ways to work with parents. Choice **B** is the correct response. Informing parents about other students' progress would be unprofessional and inappropriate.

66. **C.** This question deals with **Competency 7: Teaching English Language Learners (ELLs).** Eliminate **A** because *discourse* is simply conversation or verbal expression. Eliminate **B** because *lexicon* refers to the vocabulary used in a particular profession or area of study. Eliminate **D** because *semantics* is the study of word meanings. Choice **C** is the correct response. *Register* describes the use of different language forms (for

example, formal versus informal) that depend on the setting, the relationship of the speaker to the person he or she is addressing, and the function of the interaction. A register is a situationally appropriate form of a language.

67. **A.** This question deals with parent conferences, which fall under **Competency 5: Continuous Improvement.** Parent conferences are an important way for teachers to build positive partnerships with parents. Choice **A** is the correct response. The teacher should express sympathy to the parents and then ask for further information about the situation. The parents' child might be a victim of harassment or bullying, both of which are prohibited by law in Florida schools (Section 1006.147, F. S.). The other options would be inappropriate responses from the teacher.

68. **A.** This question falls under **Competency 5: Continuous Improvement.** Eliminate **B** and **D** because although these outcomes might occur incidentally, neither would be the most likely purpose for arranging to have family members serve as volunteer tutors in the school. Eliminate **C** because it would be inappropriate for volunteer tutors to assume such a role, and teachers should guard against it by training the volunteers before they work with students. Because family members have a vested interest in the school, they are a valuable resource to teachers. Teachers should apply strategies for engaging family members in various aspects of the educational program, such as encouraging them to serve as volunteers in the school. Such an arrangement likely would cultivate strong family-school partnerships, thereby giving family members a sense of ownership in the school. Thus, **A** is the correct response.

69. **C.** This question falls under **Competency 1: Instructional Design and Planning.** Eliminate **A, B,** and **D** because these answer choices are not supported by the questions stem—don't read too much into a question! The teacher demonstrates knowing how to turn diversity in the classroom to advantage. By creating diverse learning groups that must work together, the teacher is fostering communication and collaboration among students, thereby promoting their understanding of each other. These interactions will nurture a sense of community in the classroom. Thus, **C** is the correct response.

70. **B.** This question deals with **Competency 1: Instructional Design and Planning.** The statement in the question is an example of an instructional objective. Instructional objectives are classified as *affective, cognitive,* or *psychomotor.* Eliminate **A** because *affective objectives* involve feelings and dispositions. Eliminate **C** because *psychomotor objectives* involve physical activity on the part of the student. Eliminate **D** because this choice is not a type of lesson objective. Choice **B** is the correct response. *Cognitive objectives* involve thinking capabilities such as identifying nouns in a paragraph.

71. **A.** This question deals with **Competency 2: Learning Environments.** Notice that you must select what the teacher should do *first* to find out additional information that would help in dealing with the student. This means that there might be other response options that would be appropriate for the teacher to do, but you have to pick the one the teacher should do first. Eliminate **C** because this action would be inappropriate and a violation of the student's right to privacy. Eliminate **B** and **D** because these are steps the teacher might take later, but not before the teacher talks with the student. Choice **A** is the correct response. To be well prepared for the conference with the student, the teacher should first review the student's educational records.

72. **C.** This question falls under **Competency 1: Instructional Design and Planning.** Choice **C** is the correct response. The child has not yet developed conservation, which is normal for a kindergarten student. According to Piaget, students no longer have problems with conservation when they reach the concrete operational stage, ages 7 to 11. The other answer choices are not supported by the information given in the question.

73. **C.** This question deals with **Competency 2: Learning Environments.** Eliminate **A** because this result is unrealistic and not necessarily desirable, because unfamiliar or unexpected occurrences can sometimes provide a change of pace in a classroom. Eliminate **B** because, for example, when students are engaged in discovery learning, they often proceed in a nonlinear fashion, rather than in a simple-to-complex progression. Eliminate **D** because although it is appropriate that students have input in deciding which

topics will be studied and for how long, the teacher has a responsibility—which should not be relinquished to students—to ensure that the learning activities address the state-mandated curriculum. Choice **C** is the correct response. Teachers should identify and apply effective techniques for encouraging students to monitor and manage their own behavior.

74. **A.** This question relates to **Competency 7: Teaching English Language Learners (ELLs).** In the Natural Approach to language acquisition (Nutta, 2006), the stages of second language development are *preproduction, early production, speech emergence,* and *intermediate fluency.* The stage of development wherein the second language learner works to receive and understand the new language but produces little or no expressive language is known as the preproduction or "silent period." Thus, **A** is the correct response. The stages given in the other answer choices follow the preproduction stage.

75. **D.** This question deals with the topic of instructional methods, which falls under **Competency 3: Instructional Delivery.** Eliminate **A, B,** and **C** because although these results might occur, they would not necessarily result from the use of inquiry and discovery learning or cooperative learning groups. These instructional methods are most likely to foster independent learning in the students because they give students responsibility for their own and for each other's learning. Thus, **D** is the correct response.

76. **B.** This question deals with **Competency 2: Learning Environments.** Notice that you must select the intervention that the teacher should use *first* with the student. The teacher should react quickly and calmly to the student's disruptive behavior; however, the teacher's *first* intervention should be the least intrusive. Eliminate **A, C,** and **D** because these measures interrupt the class discussion. Choice **B** is the correct response. The teacher should try nonverbal interventions, like a stern gaze, before moving to more intrusive measures. The stern gaze will likely send a clear cue to the student that continuation of the disruptive behavior will result in consequences.

77. **A.** This question deals with both **Competency 4: Assessment** and **Competency 8: Literacy Strategies.** Choice **A** is the correct response. A running record is an assessment tool in which a student reads a passage while the teacher follows along and keeps a written record that includes words read correctly, miscues (saying the wrong word), omissions, and self-corrections. This information can be used to determine a student's reading level. Running records are not used primarily for assessing the reading components in the other answer choices.

78. **D.** This question relates to both **Competency 1: Instructional Design and Planning** and **Competency 3: Instructional Delivery.** Scaffolding is the support and assistance provided for learning and problem solving, such as verbal cues or prompts, visual highlighting, diagrams, checklists, reminders, modeling, partially completed learning charts or tasks, and examples. Choice **D** is the correct response. The timeline of events posted by the teacher provides students with a tool to help record information accurately and independently while, at the same time, integrating new information into a broader historical context. The teacher actions in the other answer choices are appropriate, but none is an example of scaffolding.

79. **B.** This question deals with **Competency 1: Instructional Design and Planning.** Notice that you must select what the teachers should do *first* to begin their planning of the unit. Teachers must recognize key factors to consider in planning instruction (for example, instructional goals and objectives, students' prior knowledge, available time and other resources, and instructional strategies). The key factors the teachers should consider *first* as they plan the unit are appropriate learning goals and objectives. Thus, **B** is the correct response. This is the first step in planning because it provides a framework into which information about materials and resources **(A),** activating prior knowledge **(C),** and responsive instructional strategies **(D)** will fit.

80. **B.** This question deals with **Competency 2: Learning Environments.** Eliminate **A** because effective classroom managers respond immediately to stop or redirect inappropriate behavior. Eliminate **C** and **D** because educational research suggests that teachers should follow the principle that misbehaviors should be corrected with the simplest intervention that will work while avoiding unnecessary disruption of instructional activities. The teacher should walk by the student's desk and unobtrusively take the ball

because this action stops the misbehavior without interrupting the momentum of the lesson. Thus, **B** is the correct response.

81. **A.** This question deals with **Competency 1: Instructional Design and Planning.** Schema Theory (Badía, 1996) emphasizes the important role that prior knowledge plays in students' learning. Students construct meaning based on their background knowledge about a topic and integrate new knowledge into their existing prior knowledge. Teachers should ascertain prior knowledge and design instructional activities accordingly. Eliminate **B** because although this approach would help activate students' prior knowledge, it would not assess prior knowledge. Eliminate **D** because the students would be expected to listen to the guest speaker, not tell what they know about the topic. Eliminate **C** because the teacher could use small-group discussions to assess prior knowledge, but using an advance organizer (for example, a graphic organizer such as a concept map) would be a better strategy because it would help the students see the structure of key concepts and topics, which might not occur in the small-group discussions. Thus, **A** is the correct response.

82. **A.** This question deals with **Competency 1: Instructional Design and Planning.** Choice **A** is the correct response. By using a thematic approach for teaching literature, the teacher will give students an opportunity to see relationships between and among concepts within a central theme of the subject area. Eliminate **B** and **C** because these answer choices are not supported by the question stem. Eliminate **D** because it is not supported by the concept of a thematic approach as clearly as **A**.

83. **A.** This question deals with **Competency 7: Teaching English Language Learners (ELLs).** Eliminate **B**, **C**, and **D** because these answer choices are appropriate and positive practices to use with English Language Learners (ELLs). Choice **A** is the correct response. Encouraging the students to use English instead of the primary language when at home is likely to have a negative impact on beginning ELLs' acquisition of English because it fails to show respect and value for the students' home language. Teachers should strive to develop ELLs' pride in their home languages and cultures.

84. **C.** This question relates to **Competency 2: Learning Environments.** Current knowledge about how young adolescents learn indicates that they learn best when they are involved in active, experiential learning in a meaningful context. Role-playing provides such a context. Thus, **C** is the correct response. The other response options contain ideas that are not typical of young adolescents. Eliminate **A** because early adolescents are beginning to question adult standards. Eliminate **B** because this characteristic is typical of very young children; most adolescents are capable of imagining a situation they have not personally experienced. Eliminate **D** because young adolescents have a deep concern about what their peers think of them.

85. **B.** This question relates to both **Competency 1: Instructional Design and Planning** and **Competency 3: Instructional Delivery.** Eliminate **A** because simulations usually address higher-level concepts and skills. Eliminate **C** because students usually enjoy participating in simulation activities and find them interesting and fun. Eliminate **D** because, for a few students, the realism might be too threatening for some simulations. However, this circumstance is not a *major* limitation—given that most simulations are artificial situations with the risks encountered in real life removed. Teachers should identify activities that support the knowledge, skills, and attitudes to be learned in a subject area. In social studies, simulation activities are a good choice because they help students develop empathy and learn to see situations from different perspectives; however, a major limitation is that they often require a considerable block of time. Thus, **B** is the correct response.

86. **A.** This question falls under **Competency 6: Professional Conduct.** According to the Notice of Procedural Safeguards for Parents of Students with Disabilities (available at www.fldoe.org/ese/pdf/procedural.pdf), the Individuals with Disabilities Education Act (IDEA) gives parents the right to participate (which does *not* mean they have unilateral decision-making power) in meetings regarding the identification, evaluation, eligibility, re-evaluation, and educational placement of their child. Thus, **A** is the correct response. The "rights" in the other response options are not specified under the IDEA.

87. **A.** This question deals with **Competency 2: Learning Environments.** Choice **A** is the correct response. By privately praising Joaquin when he performs the desired behavior, the teacher will reinforce the behavior and increase its likelihood of occurring again, thereby improving his relationships with his classmates. This outcome and the teacher's praise will work toward improving Joaquin's self-concept. Eliminate **B** because this approach is too teacher-centered—it does not promote self-management. Eliminate **C** because punitive-based measures fail to preserve the dignity of the student, which is an essential component of effective classroom management. Eliminate **D** because this is an inappropriate teacher response.

88. **C.** This question relates to both **Competency 4: Assessment** and **Competency 8: Literacy Strategies.** Choice **C** is the correct response. The data indicate that the student has deficient decoding skills. The teacher should assess the student's phonics skills by administering OPM nonsense word fluency and phoneme segmentation fluency measures. Eliminate **A** and **D** because the student is not ready to be tested on these skills. Eliminate **B** because it is not aligned with the question given that oral language is spoken language.

89. **A.** This question falls under **Competency 1: Instructional Design and Planning.** By sequencing the content into small units of information and providing immediate feedback to the student on his or her grasp of the content, the software would allow students to monitor their progress as they proceed through the program. Thus, **A** is the correct response. Eliminate **B, C,** and **D** because these answer choices are not supported by the question stem.

90. **D.** This question falls under **Competency 7: Teaching English Language Learners (ELLs).** For purposes of data collection, the State of Florida uses a coding system for ELLs and non-ELLs (Florida Department of Education, www.fldoe.org/aala/9596data.asp). A former K-12 ELL who exited the program more than 2 years ago is coded as LZ. Thus, **D** is the correct response. Eliminate **A** because the code LF designates a former K-12 ELL who exited the program within the last 2 years. Eliminate **B** because the code LP designates a 4-12 ELL for whom the reading/writing test is pending. Eliminate **C** because the code LY designates a K-12 ELL enrolled in classes specifically designed for ELLs.

91. **D.** This question deals with **Competency 3: Instructional Delivery.** Teachers should apply procedures for enhancing student interest and helping students find their own motivation. Notice that the question is asking why the act of composing their own questions is motivational for the students. Eliminate **A** because this answer choice does not respond to the question—the questions in the survey might relate to community issues, but the act of composing the questions does not. Eliminate **B** and **C** because these answer choices are not supported by the question stem—the students are composing questions, not pursuing topics of personal interest or setting their own learning goals. Choice **D** is the correct response. The teacher understands that intrinsic motivation is enhanced when students are given a measure of control over their learning experiences.

92. **D.** This question falls under **Competency 3: Instructional Delivery.** Eliminate **A** because although the teacher should inform students of the time limitation for the activity, the "reminder" needs to be near the end of the activity since students are unlikely to remember the time limitation once they become involved in the activity. Eliminate **B** and **C** because these measures would be distracting to students while they are working on the activity. Choice **D** is the correct response. The best way to remind students is to give them a 5-minute warning prior to the necessary time for the activity to end.

93. **C.** This question relates to **Competency 1: Instructional Design and Planning.** Notice that you must select the answer choice that should be the teacher's *first* step in defining instructional objectives for the new unit. Eliminate **A, B,** and **D** because these measures should come after objectives have been determined. Choice **C** is the correct response. The purpose of instruction is to increase knowledge or performance on the part of the student. In order to create clearly defined objectives, the teacher needs to have a sound basis by which success can be measured—by first determining students' general areas of strengths and needs in pattern recognition and critical thinking.

94. **D.** This question deals with teachers' legal responsibilities, which fall under **Competency 6: Professional Conduct.** In Florida, the term *inclusion* means the provision of instruction to ESE students within the regular education classroom to the maximum extent appropriate—of course, along with the needed supplementary aids and support services (Section 1003.57 (1)(a), F. S.). Inclusion is not a "sink-or-swim" type of situation because it is expected that the student will be fully supported and integrated into the mainstream classroom. Thus, **D** is the correct response. Eliminate **A** because with inclusion, students must be placed in regular schools. Eliminate **B** because inclusion does not address teacher certification. Eliminate **C** because this measure is linked to outdated forms of ESE service delivery, where students were removed or "pulled out" of regular education classes all or part of the day.

95. **D.** This question deals with teachers' legal responsibilities, which fall under **Competency 6: Professional Conduct.** Eliminate **A** because the student has not yet been identified as an ESE student in need of support services. Eliminate **B** because this action would be inappropriate. At the start of the school year, the teacher in question has not had time to explore ways to help the student, so eliminate **C.** Choice **D** is the correct response. The teacher should initiate an evaluation for ESE only when classroom strategies fail to enhance student learning—that is, when it is clear that the student's needs cannot be met through the regular education program.

96. **C.** This question falls under **Competency 3: Instructional Delivery.** Notice that the question asks that you select a *necessary* element of inquiry-based learning. Choice **C** is the correct response because inquiry-based learning requires that students form hypotheses prior to investigations. Eliminate **A** because writing reports can have value, but this activity is not a necessary element of inquiry-based learning. Eliminate **B** because a video might be used to spark interest, but showing a video is not a necessary element of inquiry-based learning. Eliminate **D** because class question and answer sessions are useful, but they are not a necessary element of inquiry-based learning.

97. **D.** This question relates to **Competency 7: Teaching English Language Learners (ELLs).** Eliminate **A** because *expressive language* involves speaking or writing. Eliminate **B** because *oral language* is spoken language. Eliminate **C** because *pragmatic language* refers to social language. *Receptive language* **(D)** is the ability to receive and understand messages. Choice **D** is the only answer choice that specifically describes the ability to receive messages. Thus, **D** is the correct response.

98. **A.** This question deals with **Competency 1: Instructional Design and Planning.** Choice **A** is the correct response. In order for the standards set forth in the Next Generation Sunshine State Standards to be learned, they must be taught. Teachers may choose from a variety of instructional methods, including engaging students in in-depth studies of topics, to convey the social studies curriculum. Nevertheless, whichever method of instruction they choose, it is most important that they make certain that learning is clearly focused on the important facts, concepts, generalizations, and skills set forth in the Next Generation Sunshine State Standards. They should not relinquish this important charge to students (eliminate **B**). Eliminate **C** and **D** because these approaches shortchange students. In **C,** the learning experiences resulting from this answer choice likely will fail to address grade-level expectations of high content complexity. Choice **D** is a teacher-directed measure that would not give the students the opportunity to take initiative and responsibility for investigation of the topic. In learning projects, students take charge of their own learning—they become self-managed—but the teacher still plays a vital role and, ultimately, must ensure that learning is geared toward the state curriculum.

99. **B.** This question deals with class size, which relates to **Competency 2: Learning Environments.** Choice **B** is the correct response. According to Section 1003.03, F. S., the maximum number of students in core courses assigned to teachers in grades 9 through 12 is 25; in kindergarten through grades 3, the maximum number of students is 18; and in grades 4 through 8, the maximum number of students is 22. Thus, **B** is the correct response. The number of students in the other answer choices is incorrect for grades 9 through 12.

100. **A.** This question deals with **Competency 3: Instructional Delivery.** Eliminate **C** and **D** because these purposes occur at a later point in the lesson, after the introduction. Eliminate **B** because although a teacher should communicate the objective in the introduction of the lesson, there is no evidence to indicate that the

book *The Greedy Triangle* will communicate the objective for the lesson. Choice **A** is the correct response. The probable purpose for beginning the introduction by reading the book is to activate student interest and motivate students to engage in learning—in other words, to gain students' attention.

101. **D.** This question falls under **Competency 5: Continuous Improvement.** Eliminate **A** and **B** because it would be inappropriate for the teacher to imply that Carl's family situation is unsuitable by suggesting that it be changed or that the family seek charity. Eliminate **C** because teachers usually do not control friendship patterns in their classrooms. Although the teacher might encourage students to become friends with Carl, the teacher cannot ensure that friendships will develop, as the language in **C** implies. The teacher should be aware that Carl's unstable home environment might continue indefinitely and should understand that this situation has probably created stress that is impacting Carl's behavior at school. The teacher can best meet Carl's needs by giving highest priority to providing an accepting and supportive environment for Carl at school. Thus, **D** is the correct response.

102. **D.** This question falls under **Competency 3: Instructional Delivery.** Notice that you must select the action that the teacher should do *first* to ensure that the video will be a useful instructional tool. Eliminate **A, B,** and **C** because these actions neglect to take into consideration the age of the children and the spontaneity that is sure to occur on a field trip. To ensure that the video will be a useful instructional tool, the teacher should first discuss with the paraprofessional the purpose of the video. This measure will help the paraprofessional make good decisions about what to include in the videotape while the children are on the field trip. Thus, **D** is the correct response.

103. **C.** This question deals with the **Competency 4: Assessment.** Choice **C** is the correct response. A self-monitoring checklist can be used to cue students to use specific strategies while problem-solving. The student checks off each step (such as "I read the problem and underlined key information") as it is completed. The student turns in the checklist along with the solved problem to the teacher. Eliminate **A** and **B** because these are standardized instruments to assess skills, not strategies. Eliminate **D** because a holistic scoring rubric assigns a single score to all components considered as a whole, not individually.

104. **A.** This question relates to both **Competency 5: Continuous Improvement** and **Competency 7: Teaching English Language Learners (ELLs).** Krashen maintained that one acquires language by receiving comprehensible input (understandable messages). Eliminate **D** because this measure works against students' comprehension of input. Eliminate **B** and **C** because although these measures are appropriate to use with English Language Learners (ELLs), they do not specifically support comprehensible input. Choice **A** is the correct response. Comprehensible input can be enhanced by incorporating gestures, visuals, and manipulatives.

105. **D.** This question falls under **Competency 3: Instructional Delivery.** Experts suggest that self-esteem improves as a student grows more competent in school tasks and that, in contrast, confronted with repeated failure, a student simply will quit trying. Therefore, most of the time, teachers should give students tasks that, with effort, they can accomplish and present them with content that is accessible at their level of understanding. At the same time, teachers can challenge students with tasks just beyond their independent level (in the *zone of proximal development*), as long as they provide the *scaffolding* (assistance) necessary to help the student succeed. To facilitate this process, learning experiences should be developmentally appropriate and meaningful for the student, making it more likely that he or she will persist until achieving success. Thus, **D** is the correct response. Eliminate **A, B,** and **C** because these approaches involve reinforcing students with praise, rewards, or recognition—all of which are more closely related to motivation. Choice **A** is incorrect also because praise should be given for a specific desirable behavior or accomplishment, not for generally "doing a good job." The approaches in **B** and **C** might contribute in some indirect way to self-esteem, but these approaches are not as likely to promote a student's development of positive self-esteem as the approach given in **D**. Furthermore, the approach given in **B** should be used cautiously because some research suggests that extrinsic rewards might work against intrinsic motivation for tasks that are already intrinsically motivating.

106. B. This question deals with **Competency 2: Learning Environments.** Eliminate **A** because class meetings to solve problems that arise should focus on *solutions,* not on consequences. Eliminate **C** and **D** because there is no evidence in the question stem to support these responses. Choice **B** is the correct response. Holding class meetings illustrates a teacher's understanding that providing an opportunity for the students to recognize and clarify the problem, and then suggesting solutions, is likely to promote their ownership in a smoothly functioning learning community. Involving students in solving problems that arise is likely to lead to lasting solutions that the class embraces, because this practice allows the students to have a say in deciding how the problem should be handled.

107. C. This question relates to **Competency 4: Assessment.** Effective feedback to students should inform them of what they are doing correctly and what they need to work on. Choice **C** is the correct response because a holistic scoring method does not provide specific feedback on the criteria used in the rubric. Eliminate **A** because a holistic scoring method is designed for scoring students' work quickly. Eliminate **B** because students can get an overall sense of whether they are improving from the weekly scores. Eliminate **D** because the teacher can, for instance, convert the scores to percents (1 out of 5 equals 20 percent) and then to letter grades.

108. C. This question deals with **Competency 3: Instructional Delivery.** Notice that you must select the *primary* benefit of devoting time to collecting ideas from the whole class about what they already know about the topic from their own previous experiences. Devoting time to collecting ideas from the whole class about what they already know about the topic from their own previous experiences will activate students' prior knowledge, which will facilitate their ability to link new information and ideas to what they already know. Thus, **C** is the correct response. There is no evidence in the question stem to support the other response choices—don't read too much into a question! Eliminate **A, B,** and **D** because there is no basis to think that the students will benefit from the teacher's approach in any of these ways; even if in some incidental manner they were to do so, the primary benefit is indisputably given in **C.**

109. B. This question deals with **Competency 3: Instructional Delivery.** Eliminate **A** and **D** because these activities are not developmentally appropriate for first-graders; further, regarding **D,** brain research suggests that a video is a poor way for children to obtain information because it is too passive. Eliminate **C** because coloring pictures is not a mentally engaging experience. When teaching social studies, teachers should use a variety of rich materials such as biographies, poetry, songs, and artwork related to the time periods under study. In a read-aloud, the teacher reads a book aloud to the whole class in an interactive and animated manner. A read-aloud of a children's biography of a historical figure of the relevant time period is an appropriate and meaningful activity that will enhance the children's understanding of the historical figure as a real person. Thus, **B** is the correct response.

110. C. This question deals with **Competency 1: Instructional Design and Planning.** According to Houston and Beech (2002) in the Florida Department of Education publication *Designing Lessons for the Diverse Classroom: A Handbook for Teachers,* instructional objectives should consist of three parts: action, what the student will do (eliminate **A**); conditions, the circumstances in which the action will take place (eliminate **B**); and mastery level, the level of proficiency expected for the action (eliminate **D**). Choice **C** is the correct response. The grading criteria is not part of an instructional objective; notwithstanding, the objective should be aligned with the assessment procedure.

111. B. This question deals with the topic of psychosocial characteristics of children, which falls under **Competency 2: Learning Environments.** The teacher's students are third-graders, so most of them are between 8 and 9 years old. Eliminate **A** and **D** because in general, children of this age are too young to have the cognitive abilities or experiences to form strong opinions on issues. Eliminate **C** because although it is the case that as these children mature into young adolescents, the attitudes of their peers begin to exert considerable influence, it is not characteristic at this stage of their development. They rely more on the opinions of their family members, such as parents or older siblings, in forming their attitudes. Thus, **B** is the correct response.

112. **B.** This question falls under **Competency 5: Continuous Improvement.** Eliminate **A** because teachers promote students' sense of ownership of their own learning by, for example, allowing them to make choices about their learning opportunities, but not by setting up a way for them to obtain information about their homework assignments. Eliminate **C** and **D** because these answer choices are not supported by the question stem. Choice **B** is the correct response. Parental involvement is an integral part of a successful school program. Thus, the most significant benefit of the homework hotline is that it will strengthen families' ability to be partners with the teachers in their children's education.

113. **C.** This question relates to **Competency 7: Teaching English Language Learners (ELLs).** The language that is used to communicate with others in a social environment is known as basic interpersonal communication. Thus, **C** is the correct response. According to Reiss (2001), usually children learn basic interpersonal communication skills (BICS) with ease, taking only from 6 months to 3 years to acquire them. Eliminate **A, B,** and **D** because these options describe language typically used in the classroom.

114. **D.** This question falls under **Competency 1: Instructional Design and Planning.** Eliminate **A** because when students engage in learning projects, teachers expect that they might have misconceptions about the topic, but the teachers do not correct the students regarding the misconceptions; instead, they allow the students the opportunity to self-correct as they proceed. Eliminate **B** because assessment of academic progress occurs at a later time, not during planning. Eliminate **C** because there is no evidence in the question stem indicating that the project plan will address specific strengths or weaknesses of individual students. Choice **D** is the correct response. Allowing students to assume the major responsibility for planning their class learning project provides them an opportunity to structure and manage their own learning, thereby promoting their development of autonomy, initiative, and self-reliance.

115. **D.** This question deals with **Competency 1: Instructional Design and Planning.** The grade level expectations for the Next Generation Sunshine State Standards identify the content that should be addressed at each grade level; therefore, the teacher can obtain information about the prerequisite concepts and skills that students should have acquired the previous year. Thus, **D** is the correct response. Eliminate **A, B,** and **C** because the grade level expectations do not contain information about these topics. However, the Florida Center for Instructional Technology (FCIT; fcit.usf.edu) maintains a website to direct teachers to resources related to the Next Generation Sunshine State Standards.

116. **B.** This question falls under both **Competency 6: Professional Conduct** and **Competency 7: Teaching English Language Learners (ELLs).** According to the Florida Consent Decree, the primary goal of the mandated appropriate programming for ELLs is "to develop, as effectively and efficiently as possible, each child's English language proficiency and academic potential." This goal is achieved through "intensive English language instruction and instruction in basic subject matter areas of math, science, social studies, [and] computer literary, which is understandable to the [ELL]." Thus, **B** is the correct response. The answers in the other response options are not in accord with the Consent Decree.

117. **C.** This question falls under **Competency 2: Learning Environments.** Teachers should provide structure that will help students be self-disciplined and self-managed in the classroom. Eliminate **A** because this approach is too teacher-centered—it does not promote self-management. Eliminate **B** because Winona is at an age where she needs to prioritize her responsibilities wisely and thus, not put the creative arts center first. Eliminate **D** because although the teacher could justify giving Winona a lower grade, this approach would not be the *best* way to deal with the situation; further, it would penalize Winona for her enthusiasm about art and her need to express herself through it. Choice **C** is the correct response. The teacher can encourage Winona to be self-managed in completing her work by providing a checklist that she must complete before going to the creative arts center.

118. **A.** This question falls under both **Competency 2: Learning Environments** and **Competency 7: Teaching English Language Learners (ELLs).** Eliminate **B** because the *Input hypothesis* explains how second language acquisition takes place. Eliminate **C** because the *Monitor hypothesis* defines the role of conscious learning on language acquisition. Eliminate **D** because the *Natural Order hypothesis* deals with the order in which grammatical structures are acquired. Choice **A** is the correct response. The *Affective Filter hypothesis* explains that negative affective variables such as anxiety and fear work against second language acquisition. By striving to create a climate that is positive, supports intellectual risk taking, and cultivates low levels of anxiety, the teacher is attempting to mitigate negative affective variables so as not to impede language acquisition.

119. **C.** This question deals with teachers' legal responsibilities, which fall under **Competency 6: Professional Conduct.** Choice **C** is the correct response. ESE students with disabilities should be full participants in the regular education classroom to the greatest extent possible. Therefore, the teacher should place primary emphasis on using strategies and materials that allow the student to participate as fully as possible in all class activities. The actions in the other response options would be inappropriate.

120. **D.** This question deals with **Competency 3: Instructional Delivery.** Choice **D** is the correct response. Children at this age learn best when they have direct, hands-on experiences with concrete objects. Using nonlinguistic representations (such as the tooth models) is an evidence-based high yield instructional strategy (Marzano et al., 2000). Eliminate **A, B,** and **C** because these options do not involve concrete objects, so they would not be as effective as bringing in large models and having the children practice proper dental care with the models.

American Psychological Association. (2010). *Learner-centered psychological principles: A framework for school redesign and reform.* Washington, D.C.: American Psychological Association.

Armbruster, B., and Osborn, J. (2001). *Put reading first: The research building blocks for teaching children to read.* Retrieved from lincs.ed.gov/publications/pdf/PRFbooklet.pdf.

Badía, A. (1996). *Language arts through ESOL: A guide for ESOL teachers and administrators.* Florida Department of Education Office of Multicultural Student Language Education.

Beech, M. (2003). *Accommodations: Assisting students with disabilities,* Third Edition. Florida Department of Education. Retrieved from www.paec.org/fdlrstech/acom_edu.pdf.

Bloom, B. S. (1984). *Taxonomy of educational objectives handbook.* New York: Longman.

Borek, J. (2003). *Inclusion and the multiple intelligences: Creating a student-centered curriculum.* National Writing Project. Retrieved from www.nwp.org/cs/public/print/resource/956.

Borgmeier, C. (2006). *Classroom behavior management packet: Extending PBS into the classroom.* Retrieved from flpbs.fmhi.usf.edu/High/Classroom/Classroom%20PBS%20Mapping%20Expectations%20&%20Rules%20to%20Routines..pdf.

Brookfield, S. (1991). *Developing critical thinkers: Challenging adults to explore alternative ways of thinking and acting.* San Francisco: Jossey-Bass.

Brooks, J., and Brooks, M. (1993). *In search of understanding: The case for constructivist classrooms.* Alexandria, VA: Association for Curriculum and Development.

Brooks-Young, S. (April, 2006). "Technology in the classroom: Tap student creativity with electronic graphic organizers." *Today's Catholic Teacher.*

Brophy, J. (1983). "Classroom organization and management." *The Elementary School Journal, 83*(4), 265–285.

Bureau of Student Achievement through Language Acquisition. (2013–2014). *English Language Learners (ELLs) database and program handbook: English for Speakers of Other Languages (ESOL).* Retrieved from www.fldoe.org/aala/pdf/1314-ELL-DatabaseProgramHandbook.pdf.

Carnegie Foundation. (1988). *An imperiled generation: Saving urban schools.* Lawrenceville, NJ: Princeton University Press.

Child Welfare Information Gateway. (2007). *Recognizing child abuse and neglect: Signs and symptoms.* Retrieved from www.bvsd.org/neo/Documents/Child%20Abuse%20Signs.pdf.

Clay, M. M. (2002). *An observation survey of early literacy achievement,* Second Edition. Auckland, New Zealand: Heinemann Education.

Cotton, K. (1993). *Fostering intercultural harmony in schools.* Research findings (Issue 7 of School Improvement Research Series). Portland, OR: Northwest Regional Educational Laboratory, School, Community and Professional Development Program.

Council for Exceptional Student Education. (1990). *Giftedness and the gifted: What's it all about?* Retrieved from www.kidsource.com/kidsource/content/giftedness_and_gifted.html.

Davidson, D. (2003). *Developing creativity.* Retrieved from www.ctahr.hawaii.edu/oc/freepubs/pdf/CF-3.pdf.

Davis, K., Christodoulou, J., Seider, S., and Gardner, H. (2012). *The theory of multiple intelligences.* Retrieved from howardgardner01.files.wordpress.com/2012/06/443-davis-christodoulou-seider-mi-article.pdf.

Dean, C. B., Hubbell, E. R., Pitler, H., Stone, B. J. (2012). *Classroom instruction that works: Research-based strategies for increasing student achievement, 2nd edition.* Retrieved from www.ascd.org/publications/books/classroom-instruction-that-works.aspx.

Donnelly, M. (1987). *At-risk students.* Retrieved from www.ericdigests.org/pre-928/risk.htm.

Dunn, K., and Dunn, R. (2006). *Dunn and Dunn Model.* Retrieved from www.ilsa-learning-styles.com/Learning+Styles/The+Dunn+and+Dunn+Learning+Styles+Model.html.

Epstein, M., Atkins, M., Cullinan, D., Kutash, K., and Weaver, R. (2008). *Reducing behavior problems in the elementary school classroom: A practice guide* (NCEE #2008-012). Washington, D.C.: National Center for Education Evaluation and Regional Assistance, Institute of Education Sciences, U.S. Department of Education. Retrieved from ies.ed.gov/ncee/wwc/pdf/practice_guides/behavior_pg_092308.pdf.

Erikson, E. (1968). *Identity, youth, and crisis.* New York: Norton.

Florida Advisory Committee to the United States Commission on Civil Rights. (2011). *School discipline in Florida: Discipline practices leave many children behind.* Retrieved from www.usccr.gov/pubs/FLSchoolDisciplineReport.pdf.

Florida Consent Decree. (1990). Retrieved from www.fldoe.org/aala/lulac.asp.

Florida Department of Education. (2013). *The Florida plan for K-12 gifted education.* Retrieved from www.fldoe.org/bii/gifted_ed/pdf/StateGiftedPlan.pdf.

Florida Department of Education. (2003). *Educator accomplished practices: Preprofessional competencies for teachers of the twenty-first century.* Retrieved from www.chipola.edu/Secondary%20Education/docs/FEAPS.pdf.

Florida Department of Education. (1996). *Florida curriculum framework: Mathematics PreK–12 Sunshine State Standards and instructional practice.* Tallahassee, FL: Author.

Florida Department of Education. (1998). *Florida curriculum framework: Elementary program.* Tallahassee, FL: Author.

Florida Department of Education. (2002). *Designing lessons for the diverse classroom: A handbook for teachers.* Retrieved from www.fldoe.org/ese/pdf/4dclessn.pdf.

Florida Department of Education. (2003a). *Document 1: Florida technology literacy profile.* Retrieved from www.fldoe.org/bii/Instruct_Tech/downloads/FLTechLiteracyProfile.pdf.

Florida Department of Education. (2003b). *THE SOURCE: A curriculum guide for reading mentors.* Retrieved from www.justreadflorida.com/docs/manual.pdf.

Florida Department of Education. (2004). *Assessment for the diverse classroom: A handbook for teachers.* Retrieved from www.fldoe.org/ese/pdf/assess_diverse.pdf.

Florida Department of Education. (2005). "Emergent literacy: What it is and why it matters," presented at the Kids Incorporated 14th Annual Early Childhood Conference, Tallahassee, FL, March. Retrieved from www.fcrr.org/science/pdf/Phillips/EmergentLiteracy.pdf.

Florida Department of Education. (2005–2013). *Next Generation Sunshine State Standards.* Tallahassee, FL: State Board of Education. Retrieved from www.fldoe.org/bii/curriculum/sss.

Florida Department of Education. (2006). *Grading policies for students with disabilities,* FDOE Technical Assistance Paper Number: FY-2006-11. Retrieved from www.fldoe.org/ese/pdf/y2006-11.pdf.

Florida Department of Education. (2007a). *Professionalism through integrity: The code of ethics and principles of professional conduct.* Retrieved from www.fldoe.org/dpe/publications/coe-training.pdf.

Florida Department of Education. (2007b). "Glossary of reading terms." Retrieved from www.fcrr.org/Curriculum/glossary/glossaryOfReading.pdf.

Florida Department of Education. (2008a). *Cognitive complexity classification of FCAT test items.* Retrieved from fcat.fldoe.org/pdf/cog_complexity-fv31.pdf.

Florida Department of Education. (2008b). *Response to intervention for behavior (RtI:B): A technical assistance paper.* Retrieved from flpbs.fmhi.usf.edu/pdfs/RtIB%20Technical%20Assistance%20Paper.pdf.

Florida Department of Education. (2010a). *Florida Department of Education Professional Development System Evaluation Protocol, Third Cycle, 2010–14 (Protocol, 2010–14).* Retrieved from www.fldoe.org/profdev/pdf/pdsreviewers.pdf.

Florida Department of Education. (2010b). *Florida Statutes.* Retrieved from www.leg.state.fl.us/Statutes/.

Florida Department of Education. (2010c). *Notice of procedural safeguards for parents of students with disabilities.* Retrieved from www.fldoe.org/ese/pdf/procedural.pdf.

Florida Department of Education. (2011). *Guiding Tools for Instructional Problem Solving (GTIPS).* Retrieved from www.florida-rti.org/_docs/gtips.pdf,

Florida Department of Education. (2011–2012). *English Language Learners (ELLs) database and program handbook.* Retrieved from www.fldoe.org/aala/pdf/edph1112.pdf.

Florida Department of Education. (2013a). "CELLA interpretive guide." Retrieved from www.fldoe.org/aala/pdf/IGEnglish13.pdf.

Florida Department of Education. (2013b). *Competencies and skills required for teacher certification in Florida, 20th Edition.* Retrieved from www.fldoe.org/asp/ftce/pdf/ftce20edition.pdf.

Florida Department of Education. (2013c). *Education of gifted students in Florida.* Retrieved from www.fldoe.org/bii/gifted_ed/pdf/StateGiftedPlan.pdf.

Florida Department of Education. (2013d). *FCAT 2.0. Florida Comprehensive Assessment Test.* Retrieved from fcat.fldoe.org/mediapacket/2013/pdf/2013UFR.pdf.

Florida Department of Education. (2013e). *MTSS implementation components: Ensuring common language and understanding.* Retrieved from www.florida-rti.org/educatorResources/MTSS_Book_ImplComp_012612.pdf.

Florida Department of Education. (2013–2014). *Specifications and Instructions for Publishers 6-12 English Language Arts Instructional Materials Evaluation Form.* Retrieved from www.fldoe.org/BII/instruct_mat/pdf/EnglishLangArtsSpecifications.pdf.

Florida Department of Education Bureau of School Improvement. (2006). *Strategies for classroom management.* Retrieved from www.astro.washington.edu/courses/astro270/wave3.htm.

Florida Department of Education Bureau of School Improvement. (2006). *Strategies that enhance setting high expectations for all students.* Retrieved from www.scps.us/Portals/2/LA_Best%20Practices/Strategies%20that%20Enhance%20Setting%20High%20Expectations%20for%20All%20Students.pdf.

Florida Department of Education Bureau of School Improvement. (2006). *Learning theories and their implications to teaching and teachers.* Retrieved from www.scps.us/Portals/2/LA_Best%20Practices/Learning%20Theories%20and%20Their%20Implications%20to%20Teaching%20and%20Teachers.pdf.

Florida Department of Education Office of Professional Practices Services. (2006). *Role of professional practices services.* Retrieved from www.fldoe.org/edstandards/role_of_pps.asp.

Florida State Board of Education. (2011). Florida Administrative Code. Retrieved from www.flrules.org.

Florida's Positive Behavior Support Project. (2008). *Classroom positive behavior support: Team consultation guide.* Retrieved from flpbs.fmhi.usf.edu/revision07/secondary/Classroom%20Consultation%20Guide.pdf.

Florida's Positive Behavior Support Project. (2011). *Implementing a multi-tiered system of support for behavior: A practical guide.* Retrieved from flpbs.fmhi.usf.edu/pdfs/RTIB%20Guide%20101811_final.pdf.

Florida's Positive Behavior Support Project. (2012). *MTSS implementation components ensuring common language and understanding.* Retrieved from www.florida-rti.org/educatorResources/MTSS_Book_ImplComp_012612.pdf.

Florida Suicide Prevention Coalition. (2011–15). *Warning signs, risk & protective factors.* Retrieved from www.floridasuicideprevention.org/learn_the_signs.htm.

Gallagher, J. (1994). *Teaching the gifted child.* Boston: Allyn and Bacon.

Gersten, R., Beckmann, S., Clarke, B., Foegen, A., Marsh, L., Star, J. R., and Witzel, B. (2009). *Assisting students struggling with mathematics: Response to Intervention (RtI) for elementary and middle schools* (NCEE 2009-4060). Washington, D.C.: National Center for Education Evaluation and Regional Assistance, Institute of Education Sciences, U.S. Department of Education. Retrieved from ies.ed.gov/ncee/wwc/PracticeGuide.aspx?sid=2.

Gestwicki, C. (1999). *Developmentally appropriate practice: Curriculum and development in early education.* Albany, NY: Delmar.

Giesen, J. (2012). *Howard Gardner's Theory of multiple intelligences.* Retrieved from www.niu.edu/facdev/resources/guide/learning/howard_gardner_theory_multiple_intelligences.pdf.

Gilligan, C. (1982). *In a different voice: Psychological theory and women's development.* Cambridge, MA: Harvard University Press.

Good, T., and Brophy, J. (2002). *Looking in classrooms,* 9th Edition. New York: Harper & Row.

Gregorc, A. (2002). *Mind styles: Anthony Gregorc.* Retrieved from web.cortland.edu/andersmd/learning/gregorc.htm.

Gresham, F. M. (2003). *Responsiveness to intervention: An alternative approach to the identification of learning disabilities.* University of California-Riverside. Retrieved from www.rtimdirect.com/pdf/gresham.pdf.

Houston, D., and Beech, M. (2002). *Designing lessons for the diverse classroom: A handbook for teachers.* Tallahassee, FL: Florida Department of Education.

Jensen, E. (1998). *Teaching with the brain in mind.* Alexandria, VA: Association for Curriculum and Development.

Johnson, R., and Johnson, D. (1994). *An overview of cooperative learning.* Retrieved from clearspecs.com/joomla15/downloads/ClearSpecs69V01_Overview%20of%20Cooperative%20Learning.pdf.

Joyce, B., and Showers, B. (2003). *Student achievement through staff development.* National College for School Leadership. Retrieved from test.updc.org/assets/files/professional_development/umta/lf/randd-engaged-joyce.pdf.

Kagan, J. (1966). "Reflection-impulsivity: The generality of dynamics of conceptual tempo." *Journal of Abnormal Psychology,* 1, 17–24.

Kindsvatter, R., Wilen, W., and Ishler, M. (1996). *Dynamics of effective teaching,* 3rd Edition. White Plains, NY: Longman.

Kizlik, B. (2014). *Direct teaching information.* Retrieved from www.adprima.com/direct.htm.

Kohlberg, L. (1981). *The philosophy of moral development.* New York: Harper & Row.

Krathwohl, D., Bloom, B., and Bertram, B. (1973). "Taxonomy of educational objectives, the classification of educational goals." In *Handbook II: Affective domain.* New York: David McKay Co., Inc.

Lemlech, J. (2002). *Curriculum and instructional methods for the elementary and middle school,* 5th Edition. Upper Saddle River, NJ: Merrill.

Lonigan, C. J., Burgess, S. R., and Anthony, J. L. (2007). *Development of emergent literacy and early reading skills in preschool children: Evidence from a latent-variable longitudinal study.* Retrieved from umdrive.memphis.edu/yxu/public/Development%20of%20emergent%20literacy%20and%20early%20reading%20skills%20in%20pre-school%20children%20Chung.pdf.

Lonigan C. J., Schatschneider C., and Westberg L. (2008). *Developing early literacy: Report of the national early literacy panel.* Washington, DC: National Institute for Literacy. Identification of children's skills and abilities linked to later outcomes in reading, writing, and spelling; pp. 55–106.

MacDonald, V. (2004). *The status of English language learners in Florida: Trends and prospects.* Retrieved from nepc.colorado.edu/files/EPSL-0401-113-EPRU.pdf.

Manpreet, K. (2012). "Develop creativity among children." *Child psychology parenting guide.* Retrieved from www.4to40.com/parenting/index.asp?p=Develop_Creativity_Among_Children&c=Child_Pshychology&sc=Developing_Creativity.

Marzano, R. J., Gaddy, B. B., and Dean, C. (2000). *What works in classroom instruction.* Retrieved from www.sinc.stonybrook.edu/Class/est572td/whatworks/whatworks.pdf.

Maslow, A. (1954). *Motivation and personality.* New York: Harper & Row.

McCardle, P., and Chhabra, V. (2004). *The voice of evidence in reading research.* Baltimore, MD: Paul Brookes Publishers.

McCune, S. (2003). *TExESMaster: TExES PPR EC-4.* Port Arthur, TX: HELP, Inc.

McCune, S. (2003). *TExESMaster: TExES PPR 4-12.* Port Arthur, TX: HELP, Inc.

McCune, S., Lowe, M., and Stephens, D. (1999). *How to prepare for the ExCET Professional development tests: Examination for the certification of educators in Texas,* 2nd Edition. Hauppauge, NY: Barron's.

Mehan, H. (1979). *Learning lessons: Social organization in the classroom.* Cambridge, MA: Harvard University Press.

National Association for the Education of Young Children. (1996). *Developmentally appropriate practice in early childhood programs serving children from birth through age 8: A position statement.* Retrieved from www.naeyc.org/files/naeyc/file/positions/position%20statement%20Web.pdf.

National Association for the Education of Young Children. (2003). *Where we STAND on curriculum, assessment, and program evaluation: A position statement.* Retrieved from www.naeyc.org/files/naeyc/file/positions/StandCurrAss.pdf.

National Association for Gifted Children. (2009). *Position statement: Grouping.* Retrieved from www.nagc.org/sites/default/files/Position%20Statement/Grouping%20Position%20Statement.pdf.

National Institute for Literacy. (2008). *Developing early literacy: Report of the National Early Literacy Panel.* Retrieved from lincs.ed.gov/publications/pdf/NELPReport09.pdf.

National Institute of Child Health and Human Development. (2000). *Report of the National Reading Panel. Teaching children to read: An evidence-based assessment of the scientific research literature on reading and its implications for instruction.* Reports of the subgroup. (NIH Publication No. 00-4754). Washington, D.C.: U.S. Government Printing Office.

National Institute on Drug Abuse (2014). *Principles of Adolescent Substance Use Disorder Treatment: A Research-Based Guide.* (NIH Publication No. 14-7953). Retrieved from www.drugabuse.gov/publications/principles-adolescent-substance-use-disorder-treatment-research-based-guide.

National Reading Panel. (2000). *Teaching children to read: An evidence-based assessment of the scientific research literature on reading and its implications for reading instruction.* Retrieved from www.nichd.nih.gov/publications/pubs/nrp/documents/report.pdf.

National Research Council. (1998). *Preventing reading difficulties in young children.* Snow, C., Burns, M., and Griffin, P. (Eds). Washington, D.C.: National Academy Press.

No Child Left Behind Act of 2001, 20 U.S.C. 6301 et seq. (2002).

Nutta, J. (2006). *The natural approach: Stages of second language development.* Retrieved from tapestry.usf.edu/nutta/data/content/docs1/naturalapproachnarrative.pdf.

Palincsar, A., and Brown, A. (1984). "Reciprocal teaching of comprehension-fostering and comprehension monitoring activities." *Cognition and Instruction, 1*(2), 117–175.

Palincsar, A., and Brown, A. (1985). "Reciprocal teaching: Activities to promote reading with your mind." In T. L. Harris and E. J. Cooper (Eds.), *Reading, thinking and concept development: Strategies for the classroom.* New York: The College Board.

Paul, R., Binker, A., Jensen, K., and Kreklau, H. (1990). *Critical thinking handbook: A guide for remodeling lesson plans in language arts, social studies and science.* Rohnert Park, CA: Foundation for Critical Thinking.

Payne, R. (2006). *Understanding and working with students and adults from poverty.* Retrieved from homepages. wmich.edu/~ljohnson/Payne.pdf.

Polya, G. (1957). *How to solve it: A new aspect of mathematical method.* Princeton, NJ: Princeton University Press.

Reinhartz, J., and Beach, D. (1997). *Teaching and learning in the elementary school: Focus on curriculum.* Upper Saddle River, NJ: Merrill.

Reiss, J. (2001). *ESOL strategies for teaching content: Facilitating instruction for English language learners.* Upper Saddle River, NJ: Merrill.

Reutzel, D. R. (2008). "Learning letter names." Retrieved from earlychildhoodeducation.usu.edu/files/uploads/ 16-knowing_letter_names3.pdf.

Ritts, V., and Stein, J. (2011). *Six ways to improve your nonverbal communications.* Retrieved from www.tlsig.cba. neu.edu/?page_id=184.

Sandomierski, T., Kincaid, D., and Algozzine, B. (2007). *Response to intervention and positive behavior support: Brothers from different mothers or sisters from different misters?* Retrieved from flpbs.fmhi.usf.edu/FLPBS%20 and%20RtI%20article.pdf.

Schafersman, S. (1991). *An introduction to critical thinking.* Retrieved from smartcollegeplanning.org/wp-content/ uploads/2010/03/Critical-Thinking.pdf.

Schütz, R. (2005). *Stephen Krashen's theory of second language acquisition.* Retrieved from www.sk.com.br/ sk-krash.html.

Shoebottom, P. (1996–2014). Second language acquisition—essential information. Retrieved from esl.fis.edu/ teachers/support/cummin.htm.

Slavin, R. (2008). *Educational psychology,* 9th Edition. Boston: Allyn and Bacon.

Smith, M. (2002). "Howard Gardner and multiple intelligences." *The Encyclopedia of Informal Education.* Retrieved from infed.org/mobi/howard-gardner-multiple-intelligences-and-education/.

Snow, D. (1995–2006). *Noteworthy Perspectives: Classroom strategies for helping at-risk students.* Retrieved from teachersity.org/files/PDF/Classroom%20Strategies.pdf.

Statewide Office of Suicide Prevention. (2011–2015). *Florida suicide prevention strategy.* Retrieved from www. floridasuicideprevention.org/PDF/2011-2015%20Fl%20Suicide%20Strategy%20booklet.pdf.

Texas Education Agency. (2000). *Strategies to teach social studies SSCED toolkit.* Retrieved from www. uintahbasintah.org/papers/ssstrategies.pdf.

Texas Education Agency. (1999). *Beginning reading instruction: Components and features of a research-based reading program.* Austin, TX: Texas Education Publication Division: Author.

Thamraksa, C. (2005). *Metacognition: A key to success for EFL learners.* Retrieved from www.bu.ac.th/ knowledgecenter/epaper/jan_june2005/chutima.pdf.

Thompson, S., Morse, A., Sharpe, M., and Hall, S. (2005). *Accommodations manual: How to select, administer, and evaluate use of accommodations for instruction and assessment of students with disabilities,* 2nd Edition. Retrieved from www.ccsso.org/Documents/2005/Accommodations_Manual_How_2005.pdf.

Torgeson, J. (2005). *A principal's guide to intensive reading interventions for struggling readers in reading first schools.* Retrieved from www2.ed.gov/programs/readingfirst/support/principal.pdf.

"Types of reasoning." (2002–2011). Retrieved from changingminds.org/disciplines/argument/types_reasoning/types_reasoning.htm.

U.S. Department of Education. (1991). *What work requires of schools: A SCANS report for America 2000.* Retrieved from wdr.doleta.gov/SCANS/whatwork/whatwork.pdf.

U.S. Department of Education. (2003). *Weaving a secure web around education: A guide to technology standards and security.* Retrieved from nces.ed.gov/pubs2003/2003381.pdf.

U.S. Department of Education. (2011). Individuals with Disabilities Education Improvement Act of 2004 (Public Law 108-446, 20 U.S.C 1400). Retrieved from idea.ed.gov.

U. S. Department of Education. (2014). *Guiding principles: A resource guide for improving school climate and discipline.* Retrieved from www2.ed.gov/policy/gen/guid/school-discipline/guiding-principles.pdf.

U.S. Department of Education Office of Communications and Outreach. (2005). *Helping your child with homework.* Retrieved from www2.ed.gov/parents/academic/help/homework/index.html.

U.S. Department of Education Office of Communications and Outreach. (2005). *Helping your child with test-taking—Helping your child succeed in school.* Retrieved from www2.ed.gov/parents/academic/help/succeed/part9.html.

U.S. Department of Health and Human Services. (2005). *Bodywise handbook: Eating disorders information for middle school personnel.* Retrieved from www.womenshealth.gov/archive/bodyimage/kids/bodywise/bp/bodywise.pdf.

U.S. Department of Health and Human Services. (2006). *Substance abuse—national challenge: Prevention, treatment and research at HHS.* Retrieved from www.hhs.gov/news/factsheet/subabuse.html.

U.S. Department of Justice, Federal Bureau of Investigation, Cyber Division. (2007). *A parent's guide to Internet safety.* Retrieved from www.fbi.gov/stats-services/publications/parent-guide/parent-guide.

Van De Walle, J., Karp, K., and Bay-Williams, J. (2009). *Elementary and middle school mathematics: Teaching developmentally,* 7th Edition. Boston: Allyn and Bacon.

Vygotsky, L. (1978). *Mind and society: The development of higher mental processes.* Cambridge, MA: Harvard University Press.

Webb, N. L. (2002). *Depth-of-knowledge levels for four content areas.* Retrieved from facstaff.wcer.wisc.edu/normw/All%20content%20areas%20%20DOK%20levels%2032802.pdf.

Wilson, L. (2004). *Creativity killers: Discouraging creativity in children.* Retrieved from www4.uwsp.edu/education/lwilson/creativ/killers.htm.

Wingo, G. (1965). *The philosophy of American education.* Boston: D. C. Heath and Co.

Witkin, H., and Goodenough, D. (1981). *Cognitive styles: Essence and origins.* New York: International Universities Press, Inc.

Zemelman, S., Daniels, H., and Hyde, A. (2005). *Best practice: Today's standards for teaching & learning in America's schools* (2005). Portsmouth, NH: Heinemann.

Glossary

Note: This glossary contains general educational terms. You will find bolded terms related to the various chapter topics in the respective chapters.

This glossary used with permission of TExES Master.

ability The degree of competence present in a student to perform a given physical or mental act.

ability grouping The grouping of students for instruction by ability or achievement for the purpose of reducing heterogeneity.

abstract concepts Those concepts that can be acquired only indirectly through the senses or that cannot be perceived directly through the senses.

Academic Improvement Plan (AIP) *See* **Progress Monitoring Plan (PMP).**

academic learning time The time a student is actually on-task, or successfully engaged in learning.

academic literacy The ability to comprehend subject-area texts and literature encountered in school.

acceleration Rapid promotion through advanced studies; enables students to progress more rapidly through the standard curriculum.

accommodation The modification of an existing way of doing something to fit a new experience. Piaget used this term to describe how children change old ways of thinking to fit new information into their existing schema.

accommodations Changes in instructional methods and materials, assignments and assessments, time demands and scheduling, and the learning environment that ensure that students with disabilities have the opportunity to participate as fully as possible in the general curriculum and ultimately earn a standard diploma.

accountability A concept in which schools are held responsible for the quality of instruction and the progress of their students.

acculturation The process of a cultural group or individual taking on traits from another culture without loss of cultural identity.

achievement Level of attainment or proficiency.

achievement motivation The generalized tendency to strive for success without extrinsic reward.

achievement test A standardized test designed to measure levels of knowledge, understanding, abilities, or skills acquired in a particular subject already learned.

acronym An abbreviation formed from the first letter of each of the words in a phrase; for example, ELL is an acronym for English Language Learner.

active listening Being in tune with the words and thoughts of the speaker.

Adequate Yearly Progress (AYP) Required minimum yearly improvement for all public schools and school districts toward achievement of state learning standards, broken down by subgroups.

advance organizers Preview questions and comments that provide structure for new information to be presented to increase learners' comprehension.

affective domain The realm of feelings, emotions, and attitudes in people.

affective objectives Instructional objectives that emphasize changes in interest, attitudes, and values, or a degree of adjustment, acceptance, or rejection.

affiliation motive The intrinsic desire to be with others.

algorithm A set of rules or procedures for performing a task.

alignment Matching learning activities with desired outcomes or matching what is taught to what is tested.

allocated time The time set aside for specific school activities, such as teaching or lunch.

alternate assessment The assessment procedure used for an Exceptional Student Education (ESE) student who does not participate in the statewide assessment program, as documented on the student's Individual Educational Plan (IEP).

alternative assessment Assessment that is different from conventional test formats (for instance, *see* **authentic assessment**).

alternative education program An educational program, provided in a setting other than a student's regular classroom, that provides for disruptive students to be separated from other students.

American Sign Language (ASL) A widely used language system employed by the hearing impaired.

analysis Learning that involves the subdividing of knowledge to show how it fits together.

anecdotal record A written record of a student's progress over time based on teacher observation with notes.

anticipation guide A set of statements, some true and some false, that students discuss as a pre-reading activity.

anxiety A feeling of uneasiness associated with the fear of failure.

application Learning that requires applying knowledge to produce a result; problem solving.

aptitude test A standardized test designed to predict future performance in a subject area.

assertive discipline A classroom management approach that stresses the need for teachers to communicate classroom rules firmly, but without hostility.

assessment The process of measuring the degree to which instructional objectives have been attained.

assimilation The process of fitting a new experience into existing ways of doing things; also, in language acquisition, the process of a cultural group taking on traits from another culture at the expense of cultural identity.

assistive technology device Any item, piece of equipment, or product system that is used to increase, maintain, or improve functional capabilities of individuals with disabilities (20 U.S.C. Chapter 33, § 1401 [25])—for example, Braille writers and speech synthesizers.

at-risk student A low-performing student who, for a variety of reasons, is in jeopardy of academic failure and might drop out of school at some point.

attending behavior Use of verbal and nonverbal cues by listeners that demonstrate they are listening with attention to what is being said.

Attention Deficit Disorder (ADD) A condition characterized by an inability to concentrate.

Attention Deficit Hyperactivity Disorder (ADHD) A label applied to individuals who are extremely active, impulsive, distractible, and excitable, and who have great difficulty concentrating on what they are doing.

attitude A predisposition to act in a positive or negative way toward persons, ideas, or events.

attraction Friendship patterns in the classroom area.

authentic assessment Assessment of students' performances in real-life application tasks.

automaticity The level reached when performance of a task requires little mental effort.

barrier-free environment An environment designed to enhance accessibility for students with a disability (for example, one that has no obstructions and is equipped with nonslip surfaces and ramps).

baseline score A score calculated as a point of comparison with later test scores; a relatively stable indicator of typical performance in a content area.

basic education The general educational program in Florida's schools.

basic skills The foundational knowledge and skills students are expected to acquire in elementary and middle school, in such areas as reading and mathematics.

behavior What someone does.

behavior modification The use of learning theory to reduce or eliminate undesirable behavior or to teach new responses.

behavioral learning theory Explanations of learning that emphasize observable changes in behavior.

behaviorism A school of psychological thought that seeks to explain learning through observable changes in behavior.

benchmark A statement of expected knowledge and skills.

between-class ability grouping A system of grouping in which students are assigned to classes according to achievement and abilities.

bilingual Capable of using two languages, but usually with differing levels of skills.

bilingual education program A full-time program of dual-language instruction that provides for learning basic skills in the primary language of the students enrolled in the program and for carefully structured and sequenced mastery of English language skills.

blended learning Refers to courses consisting of both traditional classroom and online instruction.

Bloom's Taxonomy A system that describes six levels of learning: knowledge, comprehension, application, analysis, synthesis, and evaluation.

brain-based learning Using "brain-compatible" strategies for learning based on how the brain works.

brain hemisphericity Refers to a person's preference for processing information through either the left or right hemisphere of the brain.

brainstorming A teaching strategy in which students generate ideas, judgments of the ideas of others is forbidden, and ideas are used to create a flow of new ideas.

burnout The condition of losing interest and motivation in teaching.

centration Focusing attention on only one aspect of an object or situation.

character education Deliberate instruction in basic virtues or morals.

charter school A school run independently of the traditional public school system but receiving public funding.

Child Study Team A team that is assembled when a parent, teacher, or other member of the school staff raises a concern about a student that warrants study.

choral response Response to a question made by the whole class in unison; useful when there is only one correct answer.

chronological age Age in calendar years.

chunking A memory technique in which information is organized into easily memorized subparts.

classical conditioning A form of conditioning in which a neutral stimulus (such as the bell in Pavlov's experiment) comes to elicit a response (such as salivation) after it is repeatedly paired with reinforcement (such as food).

classroom climate The atmosphere or mood surrounding classroom interactions.

classroom control The process of influencing student behavior in the classroom.

classroom management The teacher's system of establishing a climate for learning, including techniques for preventing, redirecting, or stopping student misbehavior.

clique A small, exclusive group of peers.

clock hour A period of 60 minutes (with a minimum of 50 minutes) of instructional time.

closed-ended question A question that has a limited number of correct responses.

cloze procedure An open-ended comprehension assessment method in which a selected word or words are eliminated from a text selection, while the student is instructed to fill in the missing word or words.

coaching Teaching by an expert who gives feedback on performance; can be as effective as athletic coaching; results in about 83 percent retention of learning.

Code of Ethics and Principles of Professional Conduct Standards of ethical conduct for Florida teachers.

cognition The mental operations involved in thinking.

cognitive Refers to mental activity (such as thinking, reasoning, or remembering).

cognitive development Increasing complexity of thought and reasoning.

cognitive dissonance Mental confusion that occurs when new information received conflicts with existing understandings.

cognitive domain The psychological field of mental activity.

cognitive objectives Instructional objectives that require mental capabilities.

cognitive sciences The area of study that focuses on how people think and learn.

cohesiveness The collective feeling that the class members have about the classroom group; the sum of the individual members' feelings about the group.

compensatory education Federally funded education for disadvantaged students.

competency test Test of performance of certain functions, especially basic skills, usually at a level required by the state or school district.

comprehension Learning that involves making meaning of previously learned materials.

compulsory education Legally state-mandated school attendance for every child between the ages of 6 and 16.

Computer Assisted Instruction (CAI) Instruction in which a computer is used to present instructional material.

concept An abstract idea common to a set of objects, conditions, events, or processes.

concept map A procedure for organizing and graphically displaying relationships among ideas relevant to a given topic.

concrete concepts Concepts that can be perceived directly through one of the five senses.

conditioned reinforcers Reinforcers that are learned.

conflict resolution A type of intervention designed to help students resolve conflicts in a mutually agreeable way.

connectionism A model for how learning occurs that theorizes that knowledge is stored in the brain as a network of connections.

consequence A condition that follows a behavior designed to weaken or strengthen the behavior.

conservation The logical thinking ability to recognize an invariant property under different conditions.

constructivism A learner-centered approach to teaching that emphasizes teaching for understanding predicated on the concept that students construct knowledge for themselves based on what they already know and by interactions with their environment.

content validity The degree to which the content covered by a measurement device matches the instruction that preceded it.

continuous reinforcement schedule A reinforcement schedule in which every occurrence of the desired behavior is reinforced.

conventional level Kohlberg's second level of moral judgment, characterized by accepting society's rules for right and wrong and obeying authority figures.

convergent question A question that has a limited number of correct responses.

convergent thinking Thinking that occurs when the task or question is so structured that the number of possible appropriate conclusions is limited (usually to one conclusion).

cooperative learning A teaching strategy in which students work together on assigned tasks and are rewarded on the basis of the success of the group.

Coordinated Early Intervening Services (CEIS) Services provided to K-12 grade students in kindergarten (with emphasis on K-3 grade students) who are not currently identified as needing special education or related services, but who need additional academic and/or behavioral support to succeed in a general education environment.

corporal punishment The moderate use of physical force or physical contact by a teacher or principal as may be necessary to maintain discipline or to enforce school rules (Section 1003.01 (7), F. S.).

correlation The degree of relationship between two variables; usually expressed numerically as a number between -1 and $+1$. Positive correlation generally occurs when high values on one variable correspond to high values on another; negative correlation generally occurs when high values on one variable correspond to low values on another.

creative thinking The mental process of putting together information to come up with new ideas or understandings.

criterion-referenced test A standardized test that assesses the level of mastery of specific knowledge and skills that are anchored to specific standards.

critical thinking Complex thinking skills that include the ability to evaluate information, generate insights, and reach objective conclusions by logically examining the problem and the evidence.

cross-age tutoring Peer tutoring in which an older student teaches a younger student.

cues Signals.

cultural pluralism The condition in which all cultural groups are valued components of the society and the language and traditions of each group are maintained.

culturally fair test A test designed to reduce cultural bias.

dangle A lesson transition during which the teacher leaves a lesson hanging while tending to something else in the classroom.

decentralization A term that refers to decision making being done at a lower levels rather than, traditionally, at the highest level.

decision making Choosing from among several alternatives.

deductive learning Learning that proceeds from the general to the specific.

deductive reasoning Reasoning that proceeds from general principles to a logical conclusion.

deficiency needs Maslow's term for the lower-level needs in his hierarchy: survival, safety, belongingness, and self-esteem.

delayed reinforcement Reinforcement of a desired action that took place at an earlier time.

descriptive data Data that describe a population or sample but do not present a value judgment or conclusion.

development Growth, adaptation, or change over the course of a lifetime.

diagnostic procedure A procedure to determine what a pupil is capable of doing with respect to given learning tasks.

diagnostic test An assessment that provides information that can be used to identify specific areas of strength and weakness.

differential reasoning Reasoning that requires recognizing differences.

diffentiated instruction Instruction that is adapted to accommodate individual students' needs and abilities.

direct instruction An explicit instructional delivery model.

disability Any hindrance or difficulty imposed by a physical, mental, or emotional problem that substantially limits one or more major life activities.

discipline In teaching, the process of controlling student behavior in the classroom.

discourse The interactive exchanges including talking, sharing, explaining, justifying, defending, agreeing, and disagreeing among the students and the teacher in the classroom.

discovery learning An instructional strategy in which students learn through their own active explorations of concepts and principles.

disengagement Withdrawal or detachment.

disjunctive concepts Concepts that have two or more sets of alternative conditions under which the concept appears.

distance education The use of telecommunications to deliver live instruction by content experts to remote geographic settings.

distributed practice Practice repeated at intervals over time.

divergent thinking The type of thinking whereby an individual arrives at a new or unique answer that has not been completely determined by earlier information.

diversity The condition of having a variety of groups in the same setting.

drill and practice Repeated performance of a task for the purpose of reinforcing learning.

drunkenness The condition that exists when an individual publicly is under the influence of alcoholic beverages or drugs to such an extent that his or her normal faculties are impaired; conviction on the charge of drunkenness by a court of law (6A-5.056 (6), FAC).

due process Procedural safeguards afforded students, parents, and teachers that protect individual rights.

Dynamic Indicators of Basic Early Literacy Skills (DIBELS) An assessment system for measuring early literacy skills from kindergarten through sixth grade.

dyscalculia A math-related learning disability characterized by an inability to grasp and remember math concepts, rules, and formulas, despite conventional instruction, adequate intelligence, and sociocultural opportunity.

dysgraphia A deficiency in the ability to write, primarily in terms of handwriting, but sometimes in terms of coherence.

dyslexia A disorder manifested by a difficulty in learning to read, write, or spell, despite conventional instruction, adequate intelligence, and sociocultural opportunity.

early childhood The period from the end of infancy to about age 8.

eclectic Using a variety of sources.

educational goal A desired instructional outcome that is broad in scope.

educational placement The setting in which a student receives educational services.

Educational Plan (EP) A written plan developed to meet the educational needs of an Exceptional Student Education student who is gifted.

educational records Those official records, files, and data directly related to a student and maintained by the school or local education agency (Section 1000.36, F. S.).

effective school correlates A body of research identifying the characteristics of effective and ineffective schools. They are (a) safe and orderly environment, (b) climate of high expectations for success, (c) instructional leadership, (d) clear and focused mission, (e) opportunity to learn and student time on-task, (f) frequent monitoring of student progress, and (g) home/school relations.

effective schools research Educational research focused on identifying unusually effective schools, studying the underlying attributes of their programs and personnel, and designing techniques to operationalize these attributes in less effective schools.

effective teacher A teacher who is able to bring about intended learning outcomes.

egocentric Believing that everyone sees the world as you do.

egocentrism Piaget's term for the preoperational child's inability to distinguish between his or her own and another's perceptions; also, in adolescents, a preoccupation with self.

Elementary and Secondary Education Act (ESEA) A sweeping law that provides federal funding for elementary and secondary compensatory education programs.

emotional disability A disorder in which the capacity to manage individual or interactive behaviors is limited, impaired, or delayed, and is exhibited by difficulty that persists over time and in more than one setting in one or more of the following areas: the ability to understand, build, or maintain interpersonal relationships; the ability to react/respond within established norms; the ability to keep normal fears, concerns, and/or anxieties in perspective; the ability to control aggressive and/or angry impulses or behavior.

empathy The ability to understand the feelings of another person.

empirical questions Questions that require investigation in the real world to answer.

engaged time (time on-task) The actual time individual students spend as active participants in the learning process.

English for Speakers of Other Languages (ESOL) A term used to describe special programs or classes for English Language Learners.

English for Speakers of Other Languages (ESOL) program A program of intensive instruction in English from teachers trained in recognizing and dealing with language differences.

English for Speakers of Other Languages (ESOL) Pull-Out program A program of instruction in English in which students leave their English-only content classes to spend part of their day receiving ESOL instruction. Students might have different home languages.

enrichment The process of providing richer and more varied content through strategies that supplement the standard curriculum; involves assignments or activities designed to broaden or deepen the knowledge of students who master classroom lessons quickly.

epistemology The study of how knowledge is acquired.

equal opportunities for success In cooperative learning, calculations of team achievement designed to ensure that equal individual improvement results in equal individual contribution to the team score, despite differences among teammates in absolute achievement.

equilibration The process of restoring balance between what is understood and what is experienced.

essentialism Educational philosophy that holds that a common core of knowledge and ideals should be the focus of the curriculum.

ethnicity The ethnic identity (Hispanic or non-Hispanic) of an individual or group.

ethnocentrism The belief that one's culture is better than any other culture.

Eurocentrism The belief that European culture is superior to others.

evaluation The cognitive process of establishing and applying standards in judging materials and methods.

evaluation question A question that requires that a judgment be made or a value be put on something.

evaluative comprehension Forming an opinion on the effectiveness of a text selection with regard to its message or purpose.

evaluative reasoning Reasoning that requires forming an opinion or making a judgment.

Exceptional Student Education (ESE) The term used in Florida to designate special services for students with disabilities and students who are gifted.

exceptionality The special need of a student that qualifies the student for Exceptional Student Education.

explaining behavior Planned teacher talk designed to clarify any idea, procedure, or process not understood by a student.

expressive language skills Speaking and writing.

extended-school-year program A school program that provides additional instruction by extending the school year to 210 days or more (Section 1011.62 (2)(r), F. S.).

externalizing behaviors Actions directed outward toward others (such as aggression, bullying, and theft).

external locus of control Having a belief that events are caused by factors outside of one's control.

extinction The gradual disappearance of a behavior through the removal or the withholding of reinforcement.

extrinsic motivation Motivation created by events or rewards outside the individual.

facts Well-grounded, clearly established pieces of information.

factual questions Questions that require the recall of information through recognition or rote memory.

Family Educational Rights and Privacy Act (FERPA) The federal law that protects the privacy of student education records (20 U.S.C. § 1232g; 34 CFR Part 99).

fidelity of implementation The degree to which instructional strategies and delivery follow the intent and design of a curriculum or program.

feedback Information from the teacher to the student, or vice versa, that provides disclosure about the reception of an intended message; also, information from the teacher to the student that informs the student of what he or she is doing correctly and what he or she still needs to work on.

field-dependent Learning style in which patterns are perceived as wholes.

field-independent Learning style in which separate parts of a pattern are apparent.

fine-tuning Making small adjustments in the planned procedures for a lesson during its teaching.

fixed-interval reinforcement schedule A pattern in which reinforcement is given after a desired observable behavior has occurred only at certain periodic times; often results in a great deal of work (cramming) at the last minute, just before the reinforcement is given. *Example:* Final exams are fixed-interval reinforcements.

fixed-ratio reinforcement schedule A pattern in which reinforcement is given after a desired observable behavior has occurred a fixed number (1, 5, 10, or so on) of times; effective in motivating students to do a great deal of work, but runs the risk of losing its value if the reinforcing is done too frequently. *Example:* Giving students stars after they read 10 books is fixed-ratio reinforcement.

flip-flop A lesson transition in which the teacher changes back and forth from one subject or activity to another.

Florida Administrative Code (FAC) The official compilation of all rules adopted by each Florida agency, citing the specific rule-making authority pursuant to which each rule was adopted (Section 120.55, F. S.).

Florida Commissioner of Education The head of the Florida Department of Education.

Florida Comprehensive Assessment Test 2.0 (FCAT 2.0) The Florida state-mandated test that assessed students' knowledge and skills in reading, math, writing, and science.

Florida Continuous Improvement Model (FCIM) The continuous process of data-driven instruction in Florida schools with a focus on student achievement with the Next Generation Sunshine State Standards.

Florida Department of Education (FLDOE) The state agency that oversees public education in Florida in accordance with the Florida K-20 Education Code (Title XLVIII, F. S.).

Florida Statutes (F. S.) The collection of Florida state laws.

Florida Virtual School An accredited, online Florida public school serving students in grades K-12.

focus Component in a lesson in which the teacher secures the attention of the students and communicates the lesson objectives.

focusing question A question used to focus students' attention on a lesson or on the content of a lesson.

formative assessment Assessment that takes place both before and during the learning process; used to guide the content and pace of lessons.

Free Appropriate Public Education (FAPE) Provision of IDEA (formerly PL 94–142) that guarantees special education and related services to children with disabilities, at public cost.

frequency measurement A measure of the number of times specified, observable behaviors are exhibited in a constant time interval.

gender bias Conscious or unconscious favorable treatment of females or males based on their sex.

general curriculum The curriculum that is taught in regular education classes in Florida's public schools.

generalization The carryover of learning from one setting to a different setting.

gifted student A student who has superior intellectual development and is capable of high performance (6A-6.03019, FAC).

goals Extremely broad statements of school or instructional purposes.

Goals 2000 A federal program that codifies national educational goals. (See Goals 2000: Educate America Act, available at www2.ed.gov/legislation/GOALS2000/TheAct/index.html.)

goal structure The degree to which students have to cooperate or compete for classroom rewards.

grade-level team A group of teachers who share responsibility for planning, instructing, and evaluating a common group of students.

graphic organizers Visual, hierarchical overviews designed to show relationships among abstract concepts or to illustrate processes. Types include concept or semantic maps, webs, decision trees, Venn diagrams, flowcharts, cause-effect charts, story trees, and K-W-L charts.

gross insubordination Constant or continuing intentional refusal to obey a direct order, reasonable in nature, and given by and with proper authority; also called **willful neglect of duty** (6A-5.056 (4), FAC).

group contingencies Strategies in which the entire class is rewarded on the basis of everyone's behavior; removes peer support for misbehavior.

group discussion Verbal interaction with other learners.

group-focus behaviors Behaviors teachers use to maintain a focus on the group, rather than on an individual student, during individual recitations.

group investigation A cooperative learning strategy in which students brainstorm a set of questions on a subject, form learning teams to find answers to questions, and make presentations to the whole class.

growth needs The term for the following three higher-level needs in some versions of Maslow's hierarchy of needs: intellectual achievement, aesthetic appreciation, and self-actualization.

guided practice Refers to practice by students under the direct guidance of the teacher.

halting time A teacher's pause in talking, used to give students time to think about presented materials or directions.

handicap Any hindrance or difficulty imposed by a physical, mental, or emotional problem.

hands-on Describes work by students with tools, manipulatives, models, physical representations, and so forth.

Head Start A federal program that provides economically deprived preschoolers with education, nutrition, health, and social services.

heritage language A non-English language to which a student has had exposure outside the formal education system, such as the language of immigrants (for example, Spanish) and indigenous peoples (for example, Navajo).

heterogeneous grouping A method of grouping in which students with mixed abilities, interests, achievement levels, and/or backgrounds are grouped together.

hidden curriculum The unintended and nonacademic learning that occurs in schools.

holistic evaluation Determination of the overall quality of a piece of work or an endeavor.

home language The language spoken by the parents of a student.

home schooling The practice of parents teaching their children at home rather than sending them to public school.

homogeneous grouping A method of grouping in which students with similar abilities, interests, achievement levels, and/or backgrounds are grouped together.

humanistic education Educational system designed to achieve affective outcomes or psychological growth; oriented toward improving self-awareness and mutual understanding among people.

hypermedia A nonlinear presentation of information that allows users to access related materials or images from a single computer screen.

hypothesize To make an educated guess to explain a phenomenon.

idealism The educational philosophy that embraces a belief in unchanging principles and eternal truths.

identity diffusion The inability of an adolescent to develop a clear sense of self.

identity foreclosure An adolescent's premature choice of a role.

IEP team Under IDEA, a committee formed by the school to identify a student as requiring special education or related services and to develop, review, or revise a student's Individual Educational Plan (IEP).

illiterate The condition of being unable to read or write or perform everyday tasks (for example, understanding a bus schedule).

imagery Details and descriptions that authors use to create a sensory experience for the reader and to improve the reader's comprehension and retention.

imaginary audience An aspect of adolescent egocentrism that follows the belief that the adolescent is the focus of attention of others around them.

I messages Clear teacher messages that tell students how the teacher feels about problem situations and implicitly ask for corrected behaviors.

imitation Carrying out the basic rudiments of a skill when given directions and supervision.

immorality Conduct that is inconsistent with the standards of public conscience and good morals. It is conduct sufficiently notorious to bring the individual concerned or the education profession into public disgrace or disrespect and to impair the individual's service in the community (6A-5.056 (1), FAC).

improvement scores Scores calculated by comparing the entering achievement levels with the performance after instruction.

impulsivity The tendency to respond quickly, but often without regard for accuracy or consequences.

incapacity Lack of emotional stability, lack of adequate physical ability, lack of general educational background, or lack of adequate command of one's area of specialization (6A-5.056 (3)(b), FAC).

inclusion Means that a student is receiving education in a general education regular class setting with appropriate services provided (Section 1003.57 (1), F. S.).

incompetency The inability or lack of fitness to perform duties required by law as a result of inefficiency or incapacity (6-5.056 (3), FAC).

independent practice Refers to practice by students on their own without teacher supervision. *Example:* Homework is independent practice.

independent study An instructional strategy in which students are allowed to pursue a topic in depth on their own over an extended period.

indirect teaching Learner-centered teaching using such strategies as discovery and inquiry-based learning.

individual accountability In cooperative learning, making sure that all individuals are responsible for their own learning.

Individual Educational Plan (IEP) A written plan developed to meet the educational needs of an Exceptional Student Education student with disabilities.

individualized instruction An instructional strategy characterized by a shift in responsibility for learning from the teacher to the student.

Individuals with Disabilities Education Act (IDEA) Far-reaching legislation that provides special education and services for children with disabilities.

inductive reasoning The process of drawing a general conclusion based on several examples.

inefficiency Repeated failure to perform duties required by law; repeated failure on the part of a teacher to communicate with and relate to children, to such an extent that pupils are deprived of minimum educational experience (6A-5.056 (3)(b), FAC).

inference A conclusion derived from, and bearing some relation to, assumed premises.

inferential comprehension Grasping the implied message in a text selection.

informal observation An assessment method in which teachers directly observe students performing or working on an activity.

information processing model A model for how learning occurs based on theories about how the brain processes information.

informational objectives Abbreviated instructional objectives in which only the student performance and the product are specified.

inquiry Obtaining information by asking.

inquiry learning A learner-centered instructional strategy in which the learners design the processes to be used in resolving a problem.

in-service training The professional learning workshops, demonstrations, and so forth provided by districts to keep teachers current (Section 1012.98 (4), F. S.).

instructional event Any activity or set of activities in which students are engaged (with or without the teacher) for the purpose of learning.

instructional grouping Dividing a class into small subunits for purposes of teaching.

instructional objective A clearly written statement of what students are expected to know and be able to do as the result of an instructional learning experience.

instructional strategy A strategy for delivering instruction.

instructional time Blocks of class time used for productive learning activities.

integrated language arts Teaching reading, writing, and spelling, not as separate subjects, but as an unsegregated whole.

intelligence General ability to learn and understand.

Intelligence Quotient (IQ) A measure of intelligence for which 100 is the score assigned to those of average intelligence.

interdisciplinary instruction Teaching by themes or activities that cross subject area boundaries; most frequently, involves bringing ideas, concepts, and/or facts from one subject area to bear on issues or problems raised in another (also called multidisciplinary approach).

interference A process that occurs when information to be recalled gets mixed up with other information.

intermediate grades Usually, grades 3 through 5.

intermittent reinforcement schedule A pattern in which correct responses are reinforced often, but not following each occurrence of the desirable behavior.

internalization The extent to which an attitude or value becomes a part of the learner.

internalizing behaviors Actions directed toward one's self (such as being shy, nonresponsive, and nonparticipating).

interval reinforcement schedule A pattern in which reinforcement is dispensed after desired observable behavior has occurred for a specified length of time.

intonation The rise and fall of the voice when speaking or reading aloud.

intrinsic motivation An internal source of motivation associated with activities that are rewarding in themselves.

intuition Knowing without conscious reasoning.

invented spelling Spelling based on how a word sounds; used when the writer does not know the conventional spelling of the word.

inventory questions Questions asking individuals to describe their thoughts, feelings, and manifested actions.

invincibility fable An aspect of adolescent egocentrism that follows the belief that bad things happen to other people, not to them.

jigsaw A cooperative learning strategy in which students become "experts" and teach other students.

judgment Estimate of present conditions or prediction of future conditions; involves comparing information to some referent.

knowledge learning Cognitive learning that entails the simple recall of learned materials.

knowledge questions Questions requiring the student to recognize or recall information.

labeling Assigning a category (especially a special education category) to an individual.

laboratory learning model An instructional model focusing on hands-on manipulation and firsthand experience.

language experience approach An approach to teaching, reading, and language arts that uses words and stories from the student's own language and experiences.

large muscle activity Physical movement involving the limbs and large muscles.

leadership Those behaviors that help the group move toward the accomplishment of its objectives.

learned helplessness The learned belief, based on experience, that one is doomed to failure.

learning A relatively permanent change in an individual's capacity for performance as a result of experience.

learning center A defined space in the classroom where materials are organized in such a way that children learn without the teacher's constant presence and direction.

learning cycle model An instructional approach such as the 5E model that includes the following components: engage, explore, explain, extend/elaborate, and evaluate.

learning disability In general, a discrepancy between a child's intelligence and his or her academic ability.

learning environment The surrounding conditions in which instruction takes place.

learning style Orientation for approaching learning tasks and processing information.

Least Restrictive Environment (LRE) The placement mandated under IDEA that requires that students with disabilities be educated in a regular classroom to the maximum extent appropriate.

lecture Planned teacher talk designed to convey important information in an effective and efficient manner.

lesson cycle model An instructional approach that includes the following components: focus, explanation, check for understanding, re-teach, guided practice, check for mastery, independent practice, enrichment, and closure. The components of the lesson cycle do not necessarily all occur in a single lesson, nor must a particular sequential order be followed.

lesson plan The teacher's plan for delivering instruction.

Likert scale Usually, a five-point attitude scale with linked options: strongly agree, agree, undecided, disagree, and strongly disagree.

Limited English Proficient (LEP) Used to describe a student whose home language is other than English and whose English language skills are such that the student has difficulty performing ordinary class work.

literal comprehension Understanding the explicit message in a text selection.

local education agency (LEA) A public authority that acts an administrative agency to provide control of, and direction for, kindergarten through grade 12 public educational institutions (Section 1000.36, F. S.).

long-term memory Component of the memory system that can hold a large amount of information for a long time.

magnet school A school that focuses on special themes (science, mathematics, language arts, and so on).

mainstreaming Including students with special needs in regular education classrooms for part or all of the school day.

maintenance The continuation of a behavior.

mandated time The set amount of time, established by the state, during which school is in session.

massed practice Repeated practice over and over in a concentrated period.

mastery learning A teaching strategy designed to permit as many students as possible to achieve objectives to a specified level, with the assignment of grades based on achievement of objectives at specified levels.

mastery learning model An instructional approach that emphasizes the mastery of stated objectives by all students by presenting the material in a logical progression and allowing learning time to be flexible.

measurement The assignment of numerical values to objects, events, performances, or products to indicate how much of a characteristic being measured they possess.

melting pot theory The belief that other cultures should assimilate and blend into the dominant culture.

mental age An age estimate of an individual's level of mental development, derived from a comparison of the individual's IQ score and chronological age.

mental set A student's attitude toward beginning the lesson.

mentors Experienced teachers who support, guide, and advise the development of less experienced teachers.

metacognition The process of thinking about and monitoring one's own thinking.

methodology The patterned behaviors that form the definite steps by which the teacher influences learning.

misconduct in office Violation of the Code of Ethics and Principles of Professional Conduct for the Education Profession in Florida that is so serious as to impair the individual's effectiveness in the school system (6A-5.056 (2), FAC).

miscue analysis A formal examination of a student's deviations (reading a word incorrectly, inserting a word, skipping a word, and so on) from written text when reading.

middle school School that has been planned for students ranging in age from 9 through 14 and generally has grades 5 through 8, with grades 6 through 8 being the most popular organization.

minority group An ethnic or racial group that is a minority within a larger society.

mission statement A broad statement of the unique purpose for which an organization exists and the specific function it performs.

mnemonic A method to assist memory, such as using acronyms, rehearsal, or chunking.

modality *See* **sensory modality strength.**

modeling The teacher tactic of demonstrating a skill or behavior that the teacher wants the students to mimic.

modifications Changes that are made in the curriculum for students who cannot meet the Next Generation Sunshine State Standards for their grade level.

monitor To oversee a situation, activity, or process.

moral turpitude Crime that is evidenced by an act of baseness, vileness, or depravity in the private and social duties, which, according to the accepted standards of the time, a person owes to society in general. The doing of the act itself, and not its prohibition by statute, fixes the moral turpitude (6B-4.009 (6), FAC).

morphology The study and description of word patterns.

motivation The willingness or drive to exhibit a behavior, such as to engage productively in a learning experience.

movement management behaviors Those behaviors that the teacher uses to initiate, sustain, or terminate a class-room activity.

multicultural education A structured process designed to foster understanding, acceptance, and constructive relations among people of various cultures.

multimedia Software that combines text, sound, video, animation, and graphics into a single presentation.

multiple intelligences A theory that proposes several different intelligences as opposed to just one general intelligence; other intelligences that have been described are verbal-linguistic, musical-rhythmic, logical-mathematical, visual-spatial, body-kinesthetic, interpersonal, intrapersonal, and naturalistic.

National Education Association (NEA) The largest professional employees organization in the United States, the purpose of which includes working for improved education and enhancing the status of teachers.

negative reinforcement Strengthening a behavior by release from an undesirable situation.

negligence Lack of ordinary care in one's actions; failure to exercise due care.

Next Generation Sunshine State Standards (NGSSS) State-mandated public K-12 curricular standards, by grade and subject area.

no-lose tactic A problem-resolution tactic whereby a teacher and one or more students negotiate a solution such that no one comes out the loser.

nondiscriminatory testing Assessment that properly takes into account a child's cultural and linguistic background.

noninstructional responsibility Duties assumed by or assigned to teachers that are outside of their regular teaching responsibilities.

nonverbal cues Eye contact, facial expressions, gestures, movement toward someone, placing a hand on someone's shoulder, or another physical act that communicates a message without the use of speech or writing.

nonverbal reinforcement Using some form of physical action as a positive consequence to strengthen a behavior.

normal curve A bell-shaped curve that describes the distribution of scores or measurements; approximately 95 percent of the data fall within two standard deviations of the mean.

norming group A large national sample of people who are similar to those for whom a particular standardized test is designed and who take the test to establish the group standards; serves as a comparison group for scoring the test.

norm-referenced test A standardized test that focuses on a comparison of a student's score to the average of a norm group.

norms Rules or practices that apply generally to all members of a group.

novice A person who is inexperienced in performing a particular activity.

object permanence The ability to recognize that objects continue to exist even when they can no longer be seen or touched.

objective A clear and unambiguous description of instructional intent.

observable behavior An overt act by an individual.

observation The process of looking and listening, noticing the important elements of a performance or a product.

on-task behavior Student behavior that is appropriate to the task.

open-ended question A question that has an unlimited number of correct responses.

orthography The practice or study of correct spelling.

outcome-based education (OBE) An effort designed to focus and organize all of the school's programs and instructional efforts around clearly defined outcomes that students are able to demonstrate.

overlapping Attending to and supervising more than one thing at a time.

overlapping behaviors Those behaviors by which the teacher indicates that he or she is attending to more than one thing when several things are going on at a particular time.

overlearning Practicing beyond the point of mastery to improve retention.

pacing Determining the speed of performance of a learning task.

paired-associate learning A task involving the linkage of two items in a pair so that when one is presented, the other can be recalled.

paradigm A pattern or model; sets of rules that establish boundaries.

paraphrasing Restating in one's own words.

parent Either or both parents of a student, any guardian of a student, any person standing in parental relationship to a student, or any person exercising supervisory authority over a student in place of a parent (Florida K-20 Education Code).

parenting styles The different ways parents interact with their children, including (a) authoritarian (parents are restrictive, place limits and controls on the child, and offer very little give-and-take); (b) authoritative (parents are warm and nurturing and encourage the child to be independent, but still place limits, demands, and controls on the child's actions); (c) permissive/indulgent (parents allow great freedom to the child and are undemanding, but are responsive and involved in the child's life); and (d) permissive/indifferent (parents are neglectful, unresponsive, and highly uninvolved in the child's life).

pedagogy The art and science of teaching.

percentile A score at or below where a given percentage of the scores fall. *Example:* The 75th percentile is the score at or below where 75 percent of the scores fall.

peer assessment Assessment by students of their classmates' products or performances.

peer teaching A procedure that provides teachers with an opportunity to practice new instructional techniques in a simplified setting, teaching lessons to small groups of their peers (other prospective or experienced teachers).

peer tutoring An instruction practice in which students assist with the instruction of other students needing supplemental instruction; the main types are same-age tutoring, where the tutor is the same age as the tutee, and cross-age tutoring, where the tutor is older than the tutee.

peers Individuals equal in age and/or status.

performance assessment Assessment that measures a student's ability to perform a specific cognitive or physical task correctly.

performance-based instruction Instruction designed around evaluating student achievement against specified and predetermined behavioral objectives.

personal fable An aspect of adolescent egocentrism that follows the belief that their personal situation is unique and that no one else understands them.

perspective taking Assuming another person's viewpoint.

phonics approach A literacy instructional strategy that emphasizes sounding out words based on letter-sound relationships.

pitch The highness or lowness of sound.

planning Decision-making process in which the teacher decides what, why, when, and how to teach; composed of three elements: task analysis, planning for student behaviors/outcomes, and planning for teacher behaviors/ strategies.

portfolio A collection of a student's work and achievements that is used to assess past accomplishments and future potential.

positive reinforcement Strengthening a behavior by giving a desirable reward.

postconventional level Kohlberg's first level of moral judgment, characterized by making decisions based on one's own needs and desires.

PQ4R A study strategy where students preview the reading, create questions, read to answer questions, reflect, recite, and review the original material.

pragmatics The study of what words mean in context.

precision Psychomotor ability to perform an act accurately, efficiently, and harmoniously.

primacy effect The tendency to be able to recall the first things in a list.

primary motives Forces and drives, such as hunger, thirst, and the need for security, that are basic and inborn.

principal The instructional leader of the school.

principal autonomy A system wherein the principal is authoritarian and makes all the decisions.

principle A rule that explains the relationship between or among factors.

private speech Children's self-talk.

probing The communication technique of eliciting additional information from a student, often for the purpose of obtaining clarification of or justification for the student's contribution to a discussion or response to a question.

probing questions Questions following a response that require the respondent to provide more support, be clearer or more accurate, or offer greater specificity or originality.

problem solving A strategy that involves the application of knowledge and skills to produce a result or solution.

procedural safeguards The rights of gifted students and students with disabilities and their parents.

procedure A sequence of steps and activities that have been designed to lead to the acquisition of learning objectives.

productive questions Broad, open-ended questions, with many correct responses, that require students to use their imagination, think creatively, and produce something unique.

professional autonomy Freedom of professionals or groups of professionals to function independently.

professional learning The process of engaging in activities that promote growth in one's profession.

programmed instruction A program in which students work through specially constructed print or electronic self-instructional materials at their own pace.

progressivism A learner-centered educational philosophy, popularized by John Dewey, based on the belief that the interaction of the student with the environment creates experience that encourages the student to learn by doing.

progress monitoring The use of assessments to keep track of a student's progress toward meeting learning goals during the school year.

Progress Monitoring and Reporting Network (PMRN) A web-based data management system used in Florida.

Progress Monitoring Plan (PMP) A plan that is written when a student does not meet specific levels of performance in reading, math, writing, or science (provided the student does not already have a written educational plan in place); formerly, the **Academic Improvement Plan (AIP).**

promotion Moving up to the next grade.

prompting The communication technique of giving hints and clues to aid students in answering questions or in correcting an initial response.

puberty Developmental stage at which a person becomes capable of reproduction.

Public Law 94-142 Federal law requiring that all schools receiving federal funds must provide for every child with a disability a free, appropriate public education in the least restrictive environment.

pull-out programs Programs in which students with special needs are taken out of regular classes for instruction.

punishment Using unpleasant consequences to weaken or extinguish an undesirable behavior.

Pygmalion effect The tendency of individuals who are treated as capable or incapable to act accordingly.

qualified reinforcement Reinforcement of only the acceptable parts of an individual's response or action or of the attempt itself.

questionnaire A list of written statements regarding attitudes, feelings, and opinions that are to be read and responded to.

rating scale A scale of values arranged in order of quality, describing someone or something being evaluated.

ratio reinforcement schedule A pattern in which reinforcement is dispensed after a desired observable behavior has occurred a certain number of times.

reality therapy Therapy in which individuals are helped to become responsible and able to satisfy their needs in the real world.

receiving Affective learning that involves being aware of and willing to freely attend to a stimulus.

receiving skills Skills used when listening to someone.

recency effect The tendency to be able to recall the last things in a list.

receptive language skills Listening and reading.

reciprocal teaching An instructional approach in which the teacher helps students learn to ask teacher-type questions; designed to increase comprehension.

redirecting The technique of directing a student away from the student's current activity; also, in communication, the technique of asking several individuals to respond to a question in light of or to add new insight to the previous responses.

referent That to which you compare the information you have about an individual to form a judgment.

referral A request for an individual evaluation of a student who is suspected to be in need of Exceptional Student Education (ESE) services (after strategies in the regular education classroom have failed to meet the needs of the student).

reflection Giving direct feedback to individuals about the way their verbal and nonverbal messages are being received; also, quiet thought or contemplation that includes analysis of past experience.

reflective listening The act of listening with feeling as well as with cognition.

reflective practitioner A teacher who systematically reflects on his or her own performance in the classroom and development as a teacher.

reflectivity Examining and analyzing oneself and one's thoughts before taking action.

regular class A typical classroom designed to serve students without disabilities.

rehearsal Repetition (often done mentally) of information to aid retention.

reinforcement Using consequences to strengthen the likelihood of a behavior or event.

reinforcement schedule The frequency with which reinforcers are given. Common schedules are fixed-ratio, which includes continuous reinforcement; variable-ratio; fixed-interval; and variable-interval.

relational concepts Concepts that describe relationships between items.

reliability The consistency of test scores obtained in repeated administrations to the same individuals on different occasions or with different sets of equivalent items.

remediation Additional instruction given to struggling students that supplements regular instruction.

repertoire A set of alternative routines or procedures, all of which serve some common purpose and each of which serves some additional, unique purpose.

reproduced data Data that have been recorded in video, audio, or verbatim transcript form and can be reproduced when desired.

resiliency The ability to cope with difficult and challenging situations and to "bounce back" from them.

responding Affective learning that involves freely attending to a stimulus as well as voluntarily reacting to it in some way.

Response to Intervention (RtI) A process that studies the response of students to different types of instructional interventions at differing levels of intensity.

restructuring A radically altering reform of schools as organizations and the way schooling is delivered.

reteach Instruction in the original objective that is substantially different from the initial instruction; differences may be reflected in an adjustment or modification of time allocation, practice depth, length, or instructional modality.

retrieval strategy Strategy used by a learner to remember something.

reversibility The ability to change direction in thinking and go back to a starting point.

ripple effect The spreading of behaviors from one individual to others through imitation.

role playing An activity in which students act out roles.

rote learning Memorization of facts or associations.

routine An established pattern of behavior.

rubric A set of criterion-referenced guidelines for scoring a student's work.

running record An assessment tool that uses a coding system to record a student's exact oral reading performance.

salad-bowl theory The belief that various cultures should mix, but still retain their unique characteristics.

same-age tutoring Peer tutoring in which one student teaches another student (usually a classmate) of the same age.

scaffolding Providing temporary support for learning and problem solving, such as giving clues, reminders, encouragement, and examples.

SCANS Report A report issued in 1992 by the Secretary's (of Education) Commission on Achieving Necessary Skills that recommended changes in the school curricula and teaching methods in order to better prepare students for the workplace.

schema Mental diagrams that guide behavior.

schizophrenia Abnormal behavior patterns and personality disorganization accompanied by less-than-adequate contact with reality.

School Advisory Council (SAC) A state-mandated advisory group composed of the principal, teachers, education support employees, students, parents, and other business and community citizens whose primary purpose is to assist in the preparation, evaluation, and implementation of the School Improvement Plan (Section 1001.452, F. S.).

School-Based Management (SBM) The decentralization of decision-making authority from state and district level to the school level.

School Improvement Plan (SIP) A plan developed each school year by the principal of the school campus, with the assistance of the School Advisory Council, that sets forth the school's plan for improving student performance.

secondary motives Forces and drives, such as the desire for money or grades, that are learned through association with primary motives.

Section 504 Plan A written education plan for students who are not qualified for Exceptional Student Education (ESE), but who might need special accommodations.

self-actualization Reaching one's fullest potential.

self-concept How a person thinks of himself or herself.

self-directed learning Learning by designing and directing one's own learning activities.

self-efficacy The confidence a person has that he or she has the power within himself or herself to be successful.

self-esteem The value a person places on what he or she is; self-worth.

self-fulfilling prophecy A phenomenon that occurs when one's biased beliefs about what should occur influences the results to conform to one's expectations.

semantics The study of the meanings created by words, phrases, sentences, and such.

sending skills Skills used when speaking to someone.

sensory modality strength The predominant way an individual takes in information through the five senses (see, hear, smell, taste, touch).

seriation The ability to sequentially order objects from smallest to largest, shortest to tallest, and so forth.

set induction Teacher actions and statements at the outset of a lesson to get student attention, trigger interest, and establish a conceptual framework.

sexual harassment Unwelcome written or verbal comments or physical gestures or actions of a sexual nature.

shaping The behavior modification technique of achieving a desired learning goal or behavior by using positive reinforcement at incremental steps along the way.

short-term memory Component of the memory system that can hold a limited amount of information for a short period.

silent time The time the teacher waits following a student response before replying or continuing with the discussion.

simulation An enactment of an artificial situation or event that represents real life as much as possible, but with most of the risk and complicating factors removed; works best when students are assigned roles and the teacher acts as a facilitator but does not become actively involved in the make-believe situation.

small muscle activity Physical movement involving the fine muscles of the hand.

social cognition The ability to understand other people's feelings and actions.

social objective A requirement of the cooperative learning model dealing with the social skills, roles and relationships, and group processes that students need to accomplish the learning task.

sociodrama A form of role playing that focuses on a group solving a problem.

socioeconomic status (SES) The relationship of an individual's economic status to social factors, including education, occupation, and place of residence.

special education Programs designed to serve children with mental and/or physical disabilities under the Individuals with Disabilities Education Act (IDEA).

standard diploma The diploma that is awarded for meeting the general requirements for high school graduation.

standardized test A commercially developed test that samples behavior under uniform procedures; used to provide accurate and meaningful information on students' levels of performance.

stimulation approach Emphasis on the viewpoint that factors outside the individual account for behaviors.

story tree A graphic organizer that is used to guide students' critical evaluation of a work of literature.

structural analysis A strategy for determining the meaning of a word by breaking the word into its component subunits (for example, *un-success-ful*).

structuring the task Specifying the processes and procedures students are to follow to be successful with a learning experience.

success Attainment, achievement, or accomplishment.

summarizing Stating key points of a speaker's message.

summative assessment Assessment that follows instruction and evaluates at the end of a unit, semester, and so on; used to guide programs, curricula, and the like.

symbolic medium A representational medium for acquiring concepts through symbols such as language.

synthesis Thinking that involves putting together ideas or elements to form a whole.

synthesis question A question that requires the student to put together elements and parts to form a whole.

target mistake The error that occurs when a teacher stops the wrong student or desists the wrong misbehavior.

task analysis Analyzing a task to determine its underlying and prerequisite subskills.

taxonomy A classification system; used here in reference to a classification system of educational objectives or skills.

teachable moment A peak learning moment that usually occurs unexpectedly.

teacher certification or licensure A process through which individuals are recognized by the state as having acquired the necessary skills and knowledge to teach in that state.

teacher empowerment The concept of putting decision making in the hands of teachers, the school personnel closest to students.

teacher expectations A teacher's opinion of the likelihood that students will be successful.

teacher-made test An assessment instrument developed and scored by a teacher to meet particular classroom needs.

teaching style The way a teacher teaches; that teacher's distinctive mannerisms complemented by his or her choices of teaching behaviors and strategies.

Teams Games Tournaments (TGT) A cooperative learning strategy in which teacher presentation is followed by team practice and individual mastery is tested in tournaments, with two or three students of matched achievement, rather than tests.

terminal behavior That which has been learned as a direct result of instruction.

terminal goals Goals one can expect to reach at the end of a given learning experience.

test A device used to determine whether learning objectives have been met.

Test of English as a Foreign Language (TOEFL) A standardized test used to assess English language skills; frequently required of foreign students applying for admission to colleges and universities in the United States.

thematic teaching The organization of teaching and learning around a specific theme or topic. Although themes may be used in a single subject area, such as English, sociology, or literature, two or more subject areas may be integrated using a single thematic approach.

theoretical knowledge Concepts, facts, and propositions that make up much of the content of the disciplines.

think-pair-share A cooperative strategy in which students work individually, next with a partner, and then share with the rest of the class.

timeout A form of punishment in which the student is removed for a short while from the rest of the class (to sit in the corner, stand out in the hall, and so on); used when the teacher believes the student misbehaves because he or she wants attention.

token reinforcement system A system in which students perform actions or behaviors desired by the teacher in order to earn neutral tokens that can be exchanged periodically for rewards.

tracks Classes or curricula targeted for students of a specified achievement or ability level.

trust A value relationship between and among individuals; includes such subordinate terms as confidence, reliance, stability, and absence of deception.

unit plan A plan for a sequence of several lessons dealing with the same general topic.

usability In regard to a test, practical considerations, such as cost, time to administer, difficulty, and scoring procedure.

validity The ability of a test to measure what it purports to measure.

value data Data that involve a value judgment on the part of an observer.

values clarification A teaching program that focuses on students' understanding and expressing their own values.

valuing Affective learning that involves voluntarily giving worth to an object, phenomenon, or stimulus.

variable A characteristic that varies from entity to entity.

variable-interval reinforcement schedule A pattern for giving reinforcements in which the time at which reinforcement will occur is unpredictable; effective for maintaining a high rate of behavior and highly resistant to extinction. *Example:* A teacher checking students' work at random intervals is variable-interval reinforcement.

variable-ratio reinforcement schedule A pattern for giving reinforcements in which the number of desired responses before reinforcement is given is unpredictable; effective in motivating individuals to work a long time, even after reinforcement has stopped, and highly resistant to extinction. *Example:* A teacher checking random samples of students' work is variable-ratio reinforcement.

verbal component The actual words and meaning of a spoken message.

verbal reinforcement Using positive comments as consequences to strengthen a behavior or event.

vocal component The meaning attached to a spoken message, resulting from such variables as voice firmness, modulation, tone, tempo, pitch, and loudness.

wait time The amount of time a teacher waits for a student to respond to a question; also, a term used to describe the time a teacher waits before calling on a student to answer after posing a question to the whole class.

whole-class discussion A discussion among the whole class with the teacher as facilitator; seating arrangements should be U-shaped or in a circle.

willful neglect of duty *See* **gross insubordination.**

within-class ability grouping A system for accommodating differences between students by dividing a class into groups for instructional purposes (such as reading groups).

withitness A teacher's awareness of what is going on in all parts of the classroom.

year-round school program A school program whose calendar provides for instruction for the entire year, with short vacation periods throughout the year.

you messages Teacher messages that attack students.

zero-tolerance policy A state-mandated district policy that requires that students found to have committed certain offenses (for example, bringing a firearm or weapon to school) be expelled from the student's regular school for a period of not less than one full year and be referred to the criminal justice or juvenile justice system (Section 1006.13, F. S.).

zone of proximal development The level of development one step above the current level; learning in this zone requires assistance of a peer or adult.